Also available from Hungry Minds, Inc.:

the Unofficial Guide® to New England and New York with Kids

1st Edition

Laurie Bain Wilson

Dedication: For my son Alexander, my mentor, who has given me a true appreciation for the meaning behind Robert Frost's "The Road Not Taken."

Please note that price fluctuate in the course of time, and travel information changes under the impact of many factors that influence the travel industry. We therefore suggest that you write or call ahead for confirmation when making your travel plans. Every effort has been made to ensure the accuracy of information throughout this book and the contents of this publication are believed correct at the time of printing. Nevertheless, the publishers cannot accept responsibility for errors or omissions or for changes in details given in this guide or for the consequences of any reliance on the information provided by the same. Assessments of attractions and so forth are based upon the author's own experience and therefore, descriptions given in this guide necessarily contain an element of subjective opinion, which may not reflect the publisher's opinion or dictate a reader's own experience on another occasion. Readers are invited to write to the publisher with ideas, comments, and suggestions for future editions

Your safety is important to us, so we encourage you to stay alert and be aware of your surroundings. Keep a close eye on cameras, purses, and wallets, all favorite targets of thieves and pickpockets.

Published by Hungry Minds, Inc.
909 Third Avenue
New York, New York 10022

Produced by Menasha Ridge Press

ISBN 0-7645-6216-9

ISSN 1532-9925

Manufactured in the United States of America

10 9 8 7 6 5 4 3 2 1

First edition

Contents

List of Maps

Acknowledgments

Wow, so many people to thank. First, thanks to my son, Alexander, who is everything to me. To my mother, Jackie, whose New England roots are as deep as her love. To my dad, Donald, who bangs out book after book after book—I don't know how he does it. To my sister, Pam, whose idea of a great trip is to her backyard—and I love her for that. To my nephews, Zachary, Jacob, and Lucas, who think Aunt Laurie is a real trip, I'm sure. Special gratitude to editor Molly Merkle at Menasha Ridge Press—if you look up "patience" in the dictionary you'll find her name. And to editor Molly Harrison, whose name appears next to "patience" in the thesaurus. To Glenn and Bill, who not only contributed to these pages in writing, but also helped pave the way with itineraries and inspiration. To Stephen Gronda and his daughter Kelsey, thanks for friendship and for Stephen's poetic take on New England in these pages. Thanks to dear New England friends Jamie Stone and Phil Maffa, for their great tips and most of all for their friendship. To much-missed Donna, a packing expert, thanks not to vacations but to moving so much. Thanks to June Douglas White, for wonderful Cape Cod Thanksgiving memories. Thanks to the Boston State Teachers College gang for their recommendations for New England family fun. Many thanks to Carmine Calzonetti for his office support and friendship. Thanks to Debbi Karpowicz Kickham and Stephen Jermanok for their guidance. Thanks to Sea Cliff and Glen Head kids—Anna and Lily Fagin, Amanda and Joshua Epstein, Kyle Essex, Kaitlin, Sean, Liam Traube, Robbie, Samantha and Danny Grabher—for recommendations from their travels to New England. Thanks to Laurie Petroske for her kindness. Thanks to Cheryl Coutts for turning me on to travel writing and, more importantly, for her friendship, which I adore.

—*Laurie Bain Wilson*

About the Author
and the Contributor

Laurie Bain Wilson lives in Sea Cliff, New York, with her ten-year-old son, Alexander. She has spent many family vacations in New England, and studied English at Boston University and dance at Harvard University. She is a travel editor at a national magazine.

Mitch Kaplan, who wrote the New York chapter, has been covering adventure and family travel for more than ten years, with a special interest in skiing. The author of *52 New Jersey Weekends, 535 Wonderful Things to Do This Weekend,* and *The Unofficial Guide to the Mid-Atlantic with Kids,* he has contributed to numerous national publications. Kaplan, a father of two, lives in suburban New Jersey.

Introduction

My Family and Travels

Recently, I told my ten-year-old son, Alexander, "Home is where the heart is." He replied, "No, Mom, a hotel is where my heart is."

Alex inherited the love for travel from me. I could be on the road 364 days a year—the exception being Christmas because there is no place like home for the holidays. We live in Long Island, New York, but it's to New England that we most frequently head—to visit his grandmother, born and raised in South Boston, to explore the leaves that explode into color each autumn, to the shores of Cape Cod, Nantucket, and Martha's Vineyard to spy a whale or comb the beach for beach glass, to Vermont to schuss the slopes and slurp hot cocoa kept warm by the thick blanket of marshmallows, to New Hampshire to mountain bike the velvety hills, stopping along the way to pick the wildflowers, and to Maine to hike glorious Acadia Park.

We've traveled to other corners of the world, snorkeling the incredibly stunning beaches of Turks and Caicos, trekking through the desert in Arizona, kayaking the calm waters off Prince Edward Island, and tracking down Mickey Mouse at Walt Disney World in Florida. But it's New England that has stolen our hearts and where we return repeatedly. It doesn't matter the season; in fact, that's one of the beauties of the area, where the seasons are as distinct as night and day, and where the great outdoors invites families to play. Summer sun means splashing in the sea and butter-dripping lobster and clambakes, while winter means white-carpeted mountains and time spent on the slopes and in front of crackling fireplaces. Autumn in the Northeast is leaf-peeping time—we share memories of picking pumpkins and drinking apple cider in the Berkshires and of jumping in leaf piles that are, sadly, no longer bigger than Alex, now that he's grown so tall.

As a little girl I traveled to Cape Cod each summer with my Mom and Dad and sister—long, non-air-conditioned journeys in a packed-to-the-brim station wagon (two dogs and bird, included). As a young adult, I studied at Boston University and fell absolutely head over heels in love with that city. I am not alone; Boston's population swells by a quarter-million people each fall as students from the world over begin the school year at one of the prestigious universities in and around the city. Boston is the hub of New England—a great base from which to explore this bounteous region rich with possibilities for fabulous family vacations.

The time I spend traveling with my small family—it's just Alexander and me—are the times I know I can catch up on what's going on in his life. Long car rides through New England have set the stage for talks about sports, who Kaitlin likes, sports, who Erik likes, sports, and, if I'm lucky, who Alex likes. Some families buy those new video cassette recorders for the car, but I don't think I ever will for fear that I'd miss out another window of opportunity to enjoy my son, to teach my son, and, most importantly, to listen to my son. About halfway home on a recent trip to Boston, as I was silently growing weary from the rainy drive and wishing I could click my heels and be home, Alexander chimed in from the backseat, "Isn't this cozy, Mom?" I looked in the rear-view mirror and saw Alex snug as a bug, stuffing another piece of bubble gum in his mouth, gazing out the window. Suddenly, the road was no longer so long.

The Dynamics of Family Travel

Don't even think about planning a family trip until you answer this question: What does each member of the family want to get out of the vacation?

It seems like a simple question, but it'll take more time and thought to answer than you might realize. It means assessing your current relationship with your kids and spouse. It means taking stock of your children's passions and fears, as well as your own. It means attaching a budget to everyone's wishes. And it invariably means compromise.

Start by asking yourself some questions. Is this vacation a time for togetherness, for time alone for you while the children are entertained, or for a little of each? Are you a single dad who doesn't get to see the kids much? Are you an at-home mom who never gets a break? Are you looking for exhilarating adventures or a laid-back getaway? Do you want intellectual stimulation for you and the kids? How well do your kids handle spontaneity?

Because your family's dynamics change with every birthday, the answers may surprise you. One child may be more ready for adventure than you've realized; another might be more ready for peace and quiet than you think.

THE PLEASURES OF PLANNING

It's best to decide what you want to do and come up with some options to start the ball rolling. Then call a family meeting and include your kids in the planning process. Let everyone ask questions. Show them brochures or books about the potential vacation spots. Pull out maps and a globe. Jump on the Internet. Teenagers in particular appreciate it when they can influence the planning process. The getaway is much more enjoyable when everyone wants to be there.

This shared planning time can be a great routine to continue as the trip itself gets under way. Remember, your kids may not be able to easily visualize your destination or the plane ride. And if you're traveling from place to place during your vacation, each day dawns on the unknown, so keep the brochures and guidebooks handy. Offer an advance agenda every now and then, referring again to your original planning sessions ("Remember we thought that the Bubbling Brook motel sounded like a good one?") and letting the kids develop anticipation rather than anxiety.

It's essential to be realistic when you plan a family vacation. Parents of young children may have to concede that the days of romantic sunsets are over for a while if there's a toddler tugging at their shorts. With infants and toddlers, the best vacations are the simple ones. The idea is to be somewhere comfortable and intriguing for the adults, with a pleasant environment in which to relax and enjoy your children. In the Northeast, destinations like Cape Cod are ideal for parents of the youngest group of kids. School-age kids revel in attractions created for their enjoyment—miniature golf, arcades, and bonfires at the National Seashore. The metropolitan regions, like Boston, can also be a blast with elementary-age kids. Teens may seem reluctant, but if a pilgrimage to a special point of interest for them (a certain kayak shop, a cool junior ranger program) is included, the whole trip becomes "worthwhile." And they thrive in safe, explore-it-on-your-own situations like The Cape Cod Bike Trail.

LESS IS MORE THAN ENOUGH

As you plan, I urge you to leave plenty of down time in the schedule. Some of our most memorable moments are simple breakfasts on the beach or early evening walks to nowhere, when the conversation naturally flows. Kids treasure moments, not places or days. Give your children plenty of room to run and play; a morning collecting seashells or an afternoon at the hotel pool can be more satisfying than standing in line at a crowded attraction.

A good rule of thumb may sound stringent: no more than two activities in a day. For instance, in Boston, if you spend the morning at a museum and plan to go to dinner at Faneuil Hall, go back to the hotel in the afternoon to rest and swim. If you're driving from Boston to Vermont, plan to hit the slopes the next day. Then you can stop on the way at an outlet mall or an off-the-beaten-path restaurant for blueberry pancakes and maple syrup (the real stuff). Remember that travel itself is an activity.

Also, plan some activities that allow you to take a break from each other. The quarters get a little close after a week together in a hotel room, particularly if children are of significantly different ages. Schedule an afternoon where mom and dad split duties, giving each other a break; take advantage of child and teen programs offered in many resorts to make sure there's at least one evening alone with your spouse. Everyone benefits from a little elbowroom.

Reconnections

Family vacations are a necessary indulgence in today's hurried-up world, a time for togetherness without the day-to-day distractions. Whether it's a car trip on a budget or a transcontinental flight, it's a time to reconnect with your family, especially teenagers. And the best times are the serendipitous moments—a heart-to-heart conversation on an evening hike or silly "knock-knock" jokes while enjoying a lobster roll at a roadside lobster shack. Roles are relaxed when schedules are flexible, and kids can have the opportunity to see their parents as interesting companions, not just bossy grown-ups. We all can learn from one another when there's time to listen and when we take the time to see the world through a loved one's eyes.

A seasoned traveler friend once scoffed at the notion of traveling with young children, "since they don't remember anything." I couldn't disagree more. My son's memories of some of his journeys when he was three or four astound me. He recalls with passion the sandy hours he spent at the Castle in the Clouds playground on Cape Cod and the various playmates he latched on to while playing there. He tells stories of our first ski lesson together at Okemo Resort in Vermont where we were instructed to make our skis like pizza. He was five years old. Given the open hearts and all the innocence of childhood, new impressions may sink in even more deeply with kids than with adults.

Children develop a greater understanding of the rest of the world as a result of traveling to new places and experiencing new ideas. Siblings form a special bond from traveling together, a bond less likely to be formed at home, where they have separate classrooms, separate friends, separate rooms. As parents, it's up to us to be sure there's some fun in a trip for each member of the family. And as a family, we all need to remember to indulge our traveling companions from time to time. Remember, your responses to challenges on the road—delayed flights, long lines, unsatisfactory accommodations—will influence the way your children will deal with frustrations. Be patient, be calm, and teach your children these important lifelong skills.

Vacations are times for adventure, relaxation, shared experiences, time alone—whatever your family decides. Our goal with this book is to evaluate each destination with that in mind—recognizing that your family has needs, based on ages, backgrounds, and interests, that are quite different from any other family's. We want to provide you with some structure to analyze your family's needs and create a vacation that works.

I've traveled extensively with Alexander from the British Virgin Islands to Arizona to Mackinac Island to Florida. Yet some of our most wondrous trips have been close to home. We've admired the paintings at the Norman Rockwell Museum in Stockbridge, Massachusetts, we've skied (and fallen on) the slopes in Vermont, oohed and aahed at exploding fireworks over a reflecting lake in the New Hampshire's White Mountains, and sampled buttery, milky clam chow*dah* on Martha's Vineyard. I can't imagine ever tiring of exploring the Northeast, whether we're stalking the newest miniature golf course, building sand castles on a newly-discovered beach, or braving a more challenging ski run.

This book is not meant to be a compendium of every family-priced hotel or every advertised attraction, though we have strived to cover a variety of interests for a variety of ages. Instead of compiling a family-travel yellow pages, we've edited out the less worthy places to better draw attention to the destinations that will make your trip a hit.

Dozens of families have contributed their opinions to this book; it is evaluative and opinionated, and it offers our best advice for families traveling together.

Survival Guide for Little Kids

Think Small. Little ones love little pleasures: splashing in the hotel pool, playing hide-and-seek in the lobby, stacking up rocks on the beach. Don't overload them.

Seek Creative Transportation. For really young children, getting there is often more fun than being there. When Alexander was a toddler, we took the 24-plus-hours Amtrak ride to Florida's Disney World. He's always been enthralled by trains, and the train trip practically upstaged his Disney experience (although I can't say the same for myself). Seek out the ferries, trolleys, shuttles, trains, surreys, and double-decker buses, and you'll be rewarded with a cheap thrill that's great fun for little ones.

Limit the Shopping. Our rule at attractions is a firm one: No shopping, not even looking, until we are leaving the place. Young children can get consumed by and panicky about choosing a souvenir, and they'll enjoy the museum or beach more if they can focus on the activity, not the trinkets.

Give Them a Voice. Even a four-year-old will benefit from feeling like he has some control over his vacation. When possible, let him make simple choices for the family—like "Should we walk to the beach or ride the trolley?"

Allow for Lots of Down Time. Remember, their ability to tackle the big world is much more limited than yours. Bring books or quiet hobbies to amuse yourself during nap times or play times.

Accept Some Slowness.   It's stressful enough to get a kindergartner out the door to school each morning, so don't keep up the stress on vacation. They need a break from being rushed, too. If they're happy playing in their pajamas for an extra half-hour, the museum can wait. Conversely, accept that the times you like to be more leisurely—like dinnertime—lead to impatience in children.

Survival Guide for School-Age Kids

Give Them Their Own Space. Whether it's a backpack, a carry-on train case, or one of those shoebag-like hanging pockets that fit over the car seat in front of them, each kid needs a portable room of his or her own in which to stow gum, cards, books, disposable cameras, and souvenirs.

Make a New Routine. At least until middle-school years, most kids do best with a certain amount of predictability, so it's a kindness to create little travel routines and rituals. Knowing that his parents will always stop sightseeing by 3 p.m. to swim (or will never check out without one last hour in the pool) is a comforting thought to many a fourth-grader. Knowing that you will have $5 spending money each day can do away with shopping anxiety. Having set turns as map-reader can add some fun to a hundred-mile drive.

Avoid Eating Breakfast Out. Many savvy traveling parents don't eat breakfast in restaurants. School-age kids are at their brightest and best in the morning, and waiting for table service at a ho-hum restaurant can start the day on the wrong foot. We carry fruit, cereal, milk, and juice in coolers or spring for room service—it's the least expensive and most wonderfully indulgent time to do so.

Beware Befuddled Expectations. School-age kids are old enough to have some reference points, and young enough to have great gaping holes in their mental pictures of the world. Alexander feared that the waffles he was served for breakfast at one of the authentic taverns at historic Colonial Williamsburg were also "old;" he imagined that our car would tumble off one of Cape Breton's especially curvaceous roads in Nova Scotia; and he expected to be able to pet the whales during a whale watch in Cape Cod. Ask what's going on in their minds. Listen. Don't overpromise.

Watch the Diet. It's fun to let vacation time be a time of special treats, but overindulgence in junk food, sweets, and caffeinated drinks may contribute to behavior changes in kids who aren't sleeping in their own beds and are full of adrenaline as it is.

Remember that Kids Hate Scenery. Drive them through it if you must, but don't make them actually look at too much of it.

Give Them a Ship's Log. A roll of tape and a blank book are all that's needed to turn ticket stubs, menus, brochures, and postcards from a clutter of trash into a wonderful scrapbook that's always ready to be shared and enjoyed.

Hotels and Motels Are Not Just for Sleeping. Allow time for getting ice, playing in the pool, reviewing all items and prices in the minibar, packing and unpacking, using the hairdryer, putting laundry into the laundry bags, trying out the vending machines, etc.

Hit the Playgrounds. Check your maps and ask ahead about public playgrounds with climbing and sliding equipment, and on days when you'll be sight-seeing, driving, or absorbing culture, allow for an hour's lunch or rest stop at the playground. Even on city vacations, try to set aside at least one day for pure physical fun at a beach or water park or ski slope.

Just Say Yes to Ranger Tours. These tours are often designed with school kids in mind. We'd never have understood the ecosystem of Cape Cod's marshlands if we hadn't signed on to take the ranger-led hike.

Survival Guide for Teenagers

Don't Try to Fool Them. Don't tell them they'll have more fun with you than with their friends. They won't. But if you offer them the possibility of doing things they might want to tell their friends about later, they'll be interested.

Respect Their Culture. Let your teenager play an active role in planning the vacation. Ask his or her opinion of your arrangements. Sometimes a teenager will offer a great suggestion or an alternative that we may not have considered. And look for pop culture landmarks—movie locations, palaces of fashion or music or sport. Add a ball game to the itinerary.

Night Moves. A vacation is a great time to go with your teenager to a music club or a midnight movie or on a moonlight hike. Go to the theater or the ballet; check out a jazz club. If you have other kids needing earlier bedtimes, let the parents switch-hit on going out at night with the older kids.

Give Them Options. You don't need to go everywhere with everyone. If your younger child wants to go see the dolphins at the Mystic Seaport Aquarium, this is the time for a split plan: mom and son see the dolphins while dad and daughter take in a movie or explore one of the ships at the seaport. If you have teenagers who appreciate their sleep time, let them snooze late at least one morning. Slip out with younger siblings and take a walk or read a book. Also, set wake-up time before everyone says good night so that there are no grouchy morning risers (at least not because they've been awakened unexpectedly).

Give Them Freedom. Before age 12, kids are bound to parents, preferring to stay in your orbit; when adolescence hits, they're programmed to push away from you. Choose a vacation spot that is safe and controlled enough to allow them to wander or spend time with other teenagers. If you can't do that, look for an afternoon or evening at a controlled hangout place like the park where a band concert is held. Give them the day to themselves sunbathing at the beach. Send them off to the ranger campfire by themselves at the Cape. Sign them up for an afternoon's private snowboarding lesson in Vermont.

Compromise on the Headphone Thing. Headphones can allow teens to create their own space even when they're with others, and that can be a safety valve. But try to agree before the trip on some non-headphone parameters so you don't begin to feel as if they're being used to keep other family members and the trip itself at a distance. If you're traveling by car, take turns choosing the radio station or CD for the trip.

Don't Make Your Teenager the Built-in Baby-Sitter. It's a family vacation—a time for reconnecting, not for avoiding the kids. A special night out for parents also should be special for the children; let them order videos and room service, for example, or participate in age-appropriate hotel programs.

Make Peace with Shopping. Look for street markets and vintage stores; spend some time in surf shops and record stores. If you go with your teenager, you may find that the conversation in such an environment flows easily. Or hit the outlets—many a summer vacation has included a day of back-to-school shopping.

Just Say Yes to at Least One Big-Ticket Excursion. Teenagers will get a lot out of a half-day adventure. What looks at first like expensive tours (often available through the hotel sports desk or concierge) can be memorable and important experiences for your kids that you, as parents, are simply not able to offer by yourselves. A whale watch, a kayak trip, a mountain bike trail, a snorkeling trip—each will take you far into the country you're exploring, and each is worth every cent. Or let the teenager sign up for a lesson: sailing, rock-climbing, swimming, windsurfing, and skiing.

A Word on Homework

Alexander's third-grade teacher sent home a notice requesting that if children will be traveling during non-designated vacation times, they should keep a journal of their journey in lieu of completing assignments. However, if this is not the policy in your school, and if a surprise major assignment comes up and plans can't be changed, there will be an unavoidable strain on the trip. Parents should consider strategies such as bringing along a laptop computer, scheduling vacation fun in half-day chunks so that the home-worked kid gets some work and some play, and/or a marathon session at a library at the vacation spot. You can also shamelessly beg the teacher for a reprieve, but make that a last resort.

The Secret to Visiting Art Museums

Room after room of paintings and sculptures are numbing to children. They need a focal point and a sense of adventure. Before your visit, find out what some of the major works on display are, and locate pictures of them (perhaps the museum will mail you a brochure with pictures, or you can look online or get an art book from the library). Let each child pick one or two works to sleuth out. They can learn a little about the artist and the work in question, and then when you visit the museum, they can go on a hunt for "their" artwork.

A Few Words for Single Parents

Because single parents generally are working parents, planning a special getaway with your children can be the best way to spend some quality time together. But remember, the vacation is not just for your child—it's for you, too. You might invite along a grandparent or a favorite aunt or uncle; the other adult provides nice company for you, and your child will benefit from the time with family members. As a single parent, I find it especially crucial that the resort or hotel where we'll be staying has a reputable children's program. Or, I scope out local programs for children in the town or city we're visiting. For instance, while on the Cape this summer, I signed Alex up for a one-week baseball camp sponsored by the Cape Cod League Baseball organization held each morning from 9 a.m. to noon. It was inexpensive and gave him a chance to play ball and to meet other children his age. It also bought me some time to enjoy myself.

Don't try to spend every moment with your children on vacation. Instead, plan some activities for your children with other children. Look for hotels with supervised activities, or research the community you'll be visiting for school-vacation offerings at libraries, recreation centers, or temple or church day camps. Then take advantage of your free time to do what you want to do: read a book, have a massage, take a long walk or a catnap.

Tips for Grandparents

A vacation that involves several generations can be the most enriching experience for everyone, but it is important to consider the needs of each family member, from the youngest to the oldest. Here are some things to consider.

- If you're planning to travel alone with your grandchildren, spend a little time getting to know them before the vacation. Be sure they're comfortable with the idea of traveling with you if their parents are not coming along.

- It's best to take one grandchild at a time, two at the most. Cousins can be better than siblings, because they don't fight as much.

- Let your grandchildren help plan the vacation and keep the first one short. Be flexible, and don't overplan.

- Discuss mealtimes and bedtime. Fortunately, many grandparents are on an early dinner schedule, which works nicely with younger children. Also, if you want to plan a special evening out, be sure to make the reservation ahead of time. Stash some crayons and paper in your bag to keep kids occupied.

- Gear plans to your grandchildren's age levels, because if they're not happy, you're not happy.

- Choose a vacation that offers some supervised activities for children in case you need a rest.

- If you're traveling by car, this is the one time we highly recommend headphones. Teenagers' musical tastes are vastly different from most grandparents', and it's simply more enjoyable when everyone can listen to their own style of music.

- Take along a nightlight.

- Carry a notarized statement from parents for permission for medical care in case of an emergency. Also, be sure you have insurance information.

- Tell your grandchildren about any medical problems you may have so that they can be prepared if there's an emergency.

- Many attractions and hotels offer discounts for seniors, so be sure you check ahead of time for bargains.

- A cruise may be the perfect compromise—plenty of daily activities for everyone, but shared mealtimes.

- If planning a child-friendly trip seems overwhelming, try Grand-travel (800) 247-7651, a tour operator/travel agent aimed at kids and their grandparents.

FOR TRAVELERS WITH DISABILITIES

Facilities for the physically challenged are plentiful in the Northeast. All public buildings have some form of access for those who use wheelchairs.

In addition, many public buses are equipped with wheelchair lifts. Most of the states' attractions offer facilities and services for those with physical challenges, and many hotels have specially equipped rooms. However, there are exceptions to the rule, and you should call ahead to ensure that the hotel or inn where you'll be staying has accommodations for travelers with disabilities. For specific information about traveling with disabilities in Massachusetts, contact The Very Special Arts Massachusetts, (617) 350-7713; www.vsamass.org or e-mail vsamass@aol.com for access information about more than 200 arts and entertainment facilities in Massachusetts.

How the Unofficial Guide Works

ORGANIZATION

Our informal polling shows that most families tend to choose a vacation spot based on geography—a place that's new and different, or familiar and comfortable. This book features family-related travel information for seven states: the six states of New England (Connecticut, Maine, Massachusetts, New Hampshire, Rhode Island, and Vermont) and the state of New York. The New England states are organized alphabetically, with New York following at the end. Each state is broken down into regions. For great places to stay within those regions, see the Family Lodging section within each chapter; kid- and parent-pleasing restaurants are recommended in the Family-Friendly Restaurants sections found in each chapter.

The states break down as follows:

- **Connecticut** We'll begin on the Gold Coast (some consider it more New York than New England because of its southern location), move on to Central Connecticut and Hartford, then move down to the busy Southeast Coast, including Mystic Seaport and Stonington.

- **Maine** We first cover the beaches of the Southern Coast and the city of Portland. Then we move up the coast to the Mid-Coast region, including Freeport and Monhegan Island. Finally, it's up to the stunningly beautiful Downeast area, with Mt. Desert Island, Acadia National Park, and Bar Harbor.

- **Massachusetts** In this diverse state, we first cover Cape Cod and the islands of Martha's Vineyard and Nantucket. Then it's over to New England's hub—Boston, including Cambridge and side trips to nearby Salem, Rockport, and Plymouth. Finally, we take you to the rolling interior of the state to visit the beautiful Berkshire Mountains.

- **New Hampshire**   We begin on the state's small Seacoast and then move up to recreation-filled Lake Winnipesaukee area. Then it's up to the Great Outdoorsæthe White Mountains and the remote North Country.

- **Rhode Island**   We'll visit historic Providence and then head down to South County, with the lesser-known beach towns of Watch Hill and Narragansett. We also take a step back in time to Block Island and visit the tony mansions in Newport.

- **Vermont**   We start in southern Vermont with the city of Manchester, then move into the Woodstock region with the picture-perfect town of Woodstock and the ski resort of Killington. We then cover Lake Champlain, the Green Mountains, and the Northeast Kingdom, including the lakeside city of Burlington and the ski resort of Stowe.

- **New York**   We start with the northwestern section, including Buffalo, Niagara Falls, and the state's far western corner. We continue our explorations in the central region—Rochester and Syracuse—and move on to the Finger Lakes, including Cooperstown. From there it's into the outdoorsy Adirondacks and the Saratoga Springs area, then down through the Hudson Valley and Catskills. We then take you into New York City and, finally, move east onto Long Island.

WHAT'S THERE TO DO?

For each state, we recommend the best beaches, parks, and family outdoor adventures. For each region in the state, we cover attractions ranging from theme parks to science museums. We've also included serendipitous sidebars on offbeat places that you'll want to know about, from picnic spots in the Berkshires to baseball camps on Cape Cod. If you're looking for some healthy family bonding, stretch beyond the man-made attractions. Have a sense of adventure and plan some activities that are new and exciting—not necessarily strenuous, but memorable. Each state has specific spots for the following activities:

Biking. Cycling is one of the best ways to experience an area firsthand and can be enjoyed seasonally in much of the Northeast. For beginners, we have recommended miles of paved—and unpaved—bicycle trails; older kids will like the mountain-biking spots we've found. You don't even have to bring your own bike; you can rent one at many resorts and bike shops, and many shops have trailers to rent for small children (age 5 and under) to travel safely behind you—they're much safer than bicycle seats. Know that helmets are the law for children, and it is strongly advised that all cyclists wear helmets.

Camping. We've selected a few choice family-friendly campgrounds throughout New England and New York. If it's your family's first camping experience, ask about the possibility of renting a cabin.

Hiking. New England is a hiker's paradise; we've concentrated on the easiest spots suitable for kids, from urban nature hikes to more challenging treks.

Kayaking and White-Water Rafting. From sea-kayaking the coves of the rocky Maine to white-water rafting the tamer rivers of New Hampshire, these are wonderful bonding adventures for families with kids over five years of age (although some excursions are only suitable for older kids).

Surfing. While not as popular, or challenging as say California or Hawaii, New England—particularly Cape Cod—has its share of hang-ten beaches ideal for surfing. We've recommended the best beaches for wave riders of all kinds, including body boarders.

Whale-Watching. Summertime visitors won't want to miss a whale-watching trip, offered up and down the northern seaboard. Even if you don't spot one of the great humpback whales, you'll surely enjoy dolphins, seals, and sea birds, and an exhilarating ride on the Atlantic Ocean.

WHAT'S "UNOFFICIAL" ABOUT THIS BOOK?

The material in this guide originated with the author, contributor, and researchers and has not been reviewed, edited, or in any way approved by attractions, restaurants, and hotels we describe. Our goal is to help families plan a vacation that's right for them by providing important details and honest opinions. If we've found a family-oriented destination to be dreary or a rip-off, we simply don't include it.

Readers care about the author's opinion. The author, after all, is supposed to know what he or she is talking about. This, coupled with the fact that the traveler wants quick answers (as opposed to endless alternatives), dictates that authors should be explicit, prescriptive, and, above all, direct. The *Unofficial Guide* tries to do just that—it spells out alternatives and recommends specific courses of action. It simplifies complicated destinations and attractions and allows the traveler to feel in control in the most unfamiliar environments. The objective of the *Unofficial Guide* is not to have the most information or all of the information, but to have the most accessible, useful information, unbiased by affiliation with any organization or industry.

This guide is directed at value-conscious, consumer-oriented families who seek a cost-effective, though not spartan, travel style.

The *Unofficial Guide* Rating System for Attractions

Our system includes an Appeal by Age Group category, indicating a range of appeal from one star ★: Don't bother, up to five stars ★★★★★: Not to be missed.

Letters and Comments from Readers

We expect to learn from our mistakes, as well as from the input of our readers, and to improve with each book and edition. Many of those who use the *Unofficial Guides* write to us asking questions, making comments, or sharing their own discoveries and lessons learned. We appreciate all of the input, both positive and critical, and encourage our readers to continue writing. Readers' comments and observations are frequently incorporated into revised editions of the *Unofficial Guide* and will contribute immeasurably to its improvement.

How to Write the Author

Laurie Bain Wilson
The Unofficial Guide to New England and New York with Kids
P.O. Box 43673
Birmingham, AL 35243

When you write, be sure to put your return address on your letter as well as on the envelope—sometimes envelopes and letters get separated. And remember, our work takes us out of the office for long periods of time, so forgive us if our response is delayed.

Getting Ready to Go

WEATHER AND WHEN TO GO

There's a saying in New England that applies to whatever season you choose to visit here: "If you don't like the weather, wait a minute." The weather tends to change dramatically and quickly in most of New York and New England, no matter the time of year and, of course, it also varies tremendously from season to season. There are, generally speaking, three seasons preferable for visiting New England: summer, fall, and winter. Come summer, every one of the six states is bounteous with warm sunshine during the day and mild, sometimes even cool evenings come night, especially the farther north you travel in Maine—great sleeping weather.

The fall is glorious in every state in New England—it's peak foliage peeping and, because the window of opportunity for optimum viewing is short lived, hotels fill up quickly. Tip: Fall foliage generally peaks right around Columbus Day in much of New England, exceptions being way up north where it peaks a couple of weeks earlier. For up-to-date information about peak foliage periods throughout the region, see wwwvisitnewengland.com.

Northeast winters are prescription-strength and long. While Southern Connecticut is often spared the harshest of snowstorms, the rest of the states are accustomed to snow—lots of it. Spring is mud season throughout most of New England and not recommended for vacationers—albeit hotel rates are lower in most destinations. New York City, Long Island, and The Hamptons are fabulous in the spring, however. Also keep in mind that many of the states and regions in New England are seasonal—that is, many of the inns, resorts, restaurants, and activities shut down for the winter. They include: Cape Cod and the Islands, Block Island, and many vacation spots in Maine, especially northern Maine. While New England never encounters brutally hot summers, there can be stretches of time when a heat wave will blanket the region and things get particularly sticky and humid, especially mid-summer. Of course, way up north in the Maine woods, even in the thick of summer, the temperatures can cool off considerably after the sun sets. Bringing a wooly sweater to Maine is always a good idea. New York City summers are renowned for their stifling heat and humidity.

We're fondest of visiting the Northeast in the late summer and early fall for lazy days at the beach and lobster-stuffed nights, when there's still plenty of warm sun and the Atlantic has had time to heat up. We also love moody days in New England when a misty fog encapsulates the region. If you'll be staying at the beach, know that May and June are often iffy; you may spend more time strolling the strands than sunning on them, and swimming is for the well-insulated, hearty soul. New York beaches are always warmed up by June. We like Boston best in winter, especially around the holidays, when the city is festive and the air is brisk, or in September and October, when the city is abuzz with back-to-school activity and Indian Summer days are the rule rather than the exception. The mountains are ideal for wintertime play and skiing, from Jiminy Peak in southern Massachusetts to Sunday River in northern Maine.

In general, popular tourist sights are busier on weekends than weekdays, and Saturdays are busier than Sundays. Of course, much depends on the weather. In beach destinations, rainy days mean few beach goers. Many of the mountains make their own snow so even if ol' man winter doesn't produce much of the white stuff, you'll find the slopes primped for skiing wherever you travel in the Northeast.

Of course, family travel schedules often center around school holidays, which tend to be the busiest times to travel. But consider taking your children out of school for special family trips—a well-planned week of family travel is just as enriching as five days in a classroom. Make it clear that traveling is a privilege, and agree that all missed work must be made up upon return. Talk with teachers ahead of time.

Pack Light

We limit ourselves to one carry-on bag each and a backpack, no matter what the duration of the trip or how we are traveling. (The exception is a ski or snow trip, which demands bulky clothes.) If you have small children, stashing an extra T-shirt and pair of shorts in your backpack comes in handy in emergencies. An upstate New York or New England trip generally is casual, though you may want to pack one nice outfit for a special evening out in Boston or New York City.

Make a list of necessities and let the kids pack their own bags (subject to your inspection). T-shirts, shorts, and bathing suits are perfect in the warmer regions, but never travel without a jacket or sturdy sweatshirt. Northeast weather is fickle, and you may be surprised with cold. Take along a small bottle of detergent for hand washing. The vacation is much more enjoyable if you don't have a bunch of bags to haul around busy airports or hotel lobbies.

Let your children pack their own backpack, then ask them to wear it around the house to test how comfortable it will be on a long trip. With practice, children will become savvy packers, aware that each piece counts. Of course, you should check their bags before departing, just to be sure the essentials are all there.

Finally, you may want to take along a "surprise bag" for young travelers. Sticker books, a card game, or a new book are perfect, lightweight diversions to bring out when everyone's patience is wearing thin.

What to Take with You: A Checklist

No matter what your means of transportation, be sure you take along (and have handy at all times):

- Sunglasses and hats to protect you from the sun.
- Sunscreen, at least 15 SPF.
- Emergency information—who to contact at home in case of an accident or emergency, medical insurance cards, and your pediatrician's telephone number (they can often diagnose and call in a prescription by phone).

- A travel-size bottle of antibacterial gel (the kind that doesn't require water).

- Basic first-aid kit—children's aspirin and aspirin substitute, allergy medication, Dramamine for motion sickness, insect repellent, bandages, gauze pads, thermometer, cough syrup, decongestant, medication for diarrhea, antibiotic cream, tweezers, and fingernail scissors.

- Prescription medications.

- Unscented baby wipes that can be used for any clean up.

- A small sewing kit with scissors.

- A small nightlight to ease fear of darkness.

- A couple of extra paperback books, especially for teenagers. Although, many New England towns have exceptionally well-stocked libraries, and you can usually get visitor borrowing cards.

- A folding cooler. Perfect for carrying fruit, drinks, even sandwiches to theme parks, on walks, or in the car.

- Lightweight windbreakers for cool evenings at the beach.

- Inexpensive rain ponchos for surprise rainstorms.

- Comfortable walking shoes for nature trails, botanical gardens, and beachside strolls.

- Each child should bring along some cash of her own, even just a few dollars. Tell them it is theirs to spend on souvenirs or whatever they choose. When it's their money, they're much more judicious shoppers.

- A sense of humor. Traveling with children can be trying at times.

REMEMBERING YOUR TRIP

When you choose a destination, write or call for information (listed at the end of each chapter). The travel brochures can later be used as part of a scrapbook commemorating your trip.

Purchase a notebook for each child and spend time each evening recording the events of the day. If your children have trouble getting motivated or don't know what to write about, start a discussion; otherwise, let them write, or draw, whatever they want to remember the day's events.

Collect mementos along the way and create a treasure box in a small tin or cigar box. Months or years later, it's fun to look at postcards, seashells, or ticket stubs to jump-start a memory.

Add inexpensive postcards to your photographs to create an album, then write a few words on each page to accompany the images.

Give each child a disposable camera to record his or her version of the trip. When Alexander was four years old he snapped practically an entire roll of film of the seagulls that escorted our ferry crossing from Cape Cod to Martha's Vineyard.

Nowadays, many families travel with a camcorder, though we don't recommend using one—parents end up viewing the trip through the lens rather than enjoying the sights. If you must, take it along, but only record a few moments of major sights (too much is boring anyway). Let the kids tape and narrate.

Even better, because it's more compact, carry a palm-sized tape recorder and let everyone describe their experiences. Hearing a small child's voice years later is so endearing, and those recorded descriptions will trigger an album's worth of memories, far more focused than what most novices capture with a camcorder.

Family Lodging

HOTELS, MOTELS, AND RESORTS

In each regional chapter you'll find our favorite family-friendly hotels, motels, and resorts. Note that I said favorite family-friendly hotels, not favorite hotels—many wonderful retreats were excluded because they're aimed at romantics or businesspeople, and they'd make parents of an energetic four-year-old feel like lepers. These reviews cover only places that particularly caught my fancy or seem suitable for families, and I've strived to find places with character. If you don't see an accommodation in the region you wish to visit, call the 800 number of your favorite chain to find out what they can offer.

Tips on Hotels, Motels, and Resorts with Kids

One room or two? Large or small? Upscale hotel or basic motel? Old or new? There are pros and cons with each of these overnight options, and we've found that on different days on the same vacation, we might make different choices.

Overall, one of the hardest things for some of us parents to adjust to is being awake when the kids are asleep but not wanting to leave them alone in the room. Although adjoining rooms are a good option in some hotels, they're not offered everywhere, and the choice between one or more rooms for a family always seems to come up.

If you're on an extended family vacation during which you're moving from place to place, book yourselves into several different kinds of facilities. In a hub city where you're not necessarily expecting to be in a picturesque setting, look for a business-suite chain, especially on the weekends, when discounts are often offered (but check to see that all amenities, like breakfasts, continue). The price for a spacious suite may be the same as for a cramped room at the motel down the street, and it's great to be able to watch the late show while the little ones snooze.

Big landmark hotels or luxury hotels with character are worth the splurge if the location is workable, and they might come at the end of a road trip, when the only choices in small-town stops on the way have been inexpensive roadside motels. Alex loves the excitement of big hotels, the bigger the better. And room service is God's gift to traveling parents. Kids love it too! I'll never forget overhearing four-year-old Alexander say to a friend over for a playdate, "Okay, now when I knock on the door, you ask 'Who is it?' and I'll say, 'Room service.'" I also always ask about the executive, concierge, or butler floor because the lounge areas often offer breakfast, coffee, snacks, and wine at various hours. For one thing, it's convenient for grabbing a muffin for a kid in the room; for another, it's a place for parents to escape to, like a living room, without being far away.

The all-American motel is, of course, a favorite with families. No need to find a bellman—you park in front of your room and unload only what you need. Kids love roaming the corridors for ice, soda from the machines, and the spotting of other children. Lack of towel service poolside may be compensated for by the existence of a coin laundry. At this kind of hostelry, you might opt for one room, but you should request a room near the pool with a patio or veranda. Proximity to the pool allows kids of a certain age to come and go; the patio extends the living space nicely.

CAMPING

Included is a small but choice collection of Northeast campgrounds— ones that are easily accessible, fun for children, and not too demanding of parents (we consider bathrooms and running water, for instance, to be essential). Camping can be a wonderful family experience, slowing down the pace so you can all take pleasure in the small things, from fishing in a stream to chasing butterflies. And, of course, camping takes you to the most beautiful places for very little money.

Nearly all of these campgrounds are state properties, and all are popular; for those that take reservations, make them early.

Tips on Camping with Children

Basically, if you are regular campers and your children are used to it from birth, you'll be happy at any of the campgrounds we recommend. If you are not regular campers, we'd recommend the motel option while your children are between infancy and the age of at least three, maybe four.

Camping is a superb opportunity to teach children independence and self-reliance. If they're all expected to pitch in, and the adventure aspect is played up, they'll help prepare food, pitch tents, and do all the camp chores.

Remember, though, that camping is tiring, and after a few days of sleeping on the ground, tempers of both children and adults can get frayed. After two or three nights of roughing it, nothing cheers a family up like clean hotel sheets, a swimming pool, and a restaurant hamburger.

WHAT TO LOOK FOR IN A HOTEL

Some families want every moment planned; others just want advice on interesting hotels that other families recommend. Many of our recommendations are suites, since the best vacations give everyone a space of their own. Four in a hotel room may be economical, but adjoining rooms or an apartment or condominium may save your sanity and be worth the extra dollars.

Here are some important questions you might want to ask before booking a reservation:

- Do kids stay free?
- Is there a discount for adjoining rooms? How much?
- Can you rent cribs and rollaway beds?
- Does the room have a refrigerator? A microwave?
- Is the room on the ground floor? (Particularly important if you have small children.)
- How many beds in the room?
- Is there a swimming pool? Is there a lifeguard? Is it fenced?
- How close is the room to the pool?
- Are there laundry facilities on the premises?
- Is there a kid-friendly restaurant? A breakfast buffet? Other kid-friendly restaurants nearby?
- Is there a supervised children's program? What are the qualifications of the staff? How much does it cost? How do you make a reservation?
- Is there in-room baby-sitting? What are the qualifications of the caregivers? How much does it cost per hour? How do you make a reservation?
- Are the rooms childproofed? Can patio or balcony doors be securely locked and bolted?
- Is there an on-site doctor or a clinic nearby that the hotel recommends?

WHAT'S IN A ROOM?

Here are a few of the things we check:

Room Size. A large and uncluttered room is generally preferable for families, especially if you are taking advantage of the "kids stay free with parents" offered at many hotels. Ask if the hotel has suites, or if they will offer you a discount for an adjoining room for children.

Temperature Control and Ventilation. The guest should be able to control the temperature of the room. The best system, because it's so quiet, is central heating and air-conditioning, controlled by the room's own thermostat.

The vast majority of hotel rooms have windows or balcony doors that have been permanently secured shut. Though there are some legitimate safety and liability issues involved, we prefer windows and balcony doors that can be opened to admit fresh air.

Safety. Every room should have a fire or smoke alarm, clear fire instructions, and preferably a sprinkler system. Bathtubs should have a nonskid surface, and shower stalls should have doors that either open outward or slide side to side. Bathroom electrical outlets should be high on the wall and not too close to the sink. Balconies should have sturdy, high rails.

Noise. Most travelers have been kept awake by the television, partying, or amorous activities of people in the next room, or by traffic on the street outside. Better hotels are designed with noise control in mind. Wall and ceiling construction are substantial, effectively screening routine noise. Carpets and drapes, in addition to being decorative, also absorb and muffle sounds. Mattresses mounted on stable platforms or sturdy bed frames do not squeak, even when challenged. Televisions enclosed in cabinets, and with volume governors, rarely disturb guests in adjacent rooms.

Lighting. Poor lighting is an extremely common problem in American hotel rooms. The lighting is usually adequate for dressing, relaxing, or watching television, but not for reading or working. Lighting should be bright over tables and desks and alongside couches or easy chairs. If you're sharing a room with children, ask for a room with separate lights over the bed, so you can stay up reading after the kids have lights-out.

Furnishings. At bare minimum, the beds must be firm. Pillows should be made with hypoallergenic fillers, and, in addition to the sheets and spread, a blanket should be provided. With a family of four or more sharing a hotel room, you may not have enough dresser space to give everyone more than a drawer. You can request extra luggage racks if there is wall space to accommodate. Many well-designed hotel rooms have a sleeper sofa, which is

Childproof Your Room
When you arrive at the hotel, some childproofing may be in order. Be sure that both the front door and any patio or balcony doors and windows can be securely locked and bolted. Some hotels offer electrical outlet coverings if you have toddlers, and protective covers for sharp furniture corners. They will also remove glass objects or other knick-knacks that might be easy for a toddler to break. And if the minibar is stocked with junk food and alcoholic beverages, it should be locked.

invaluable for families. Other family-friendly amenities to look for include a small refrigerator, a microwave, a digital alarm clock, and a coffeemaker.

Bathrooms. Two sinks are better than one, and you cannot have too much counter space. A sink outside the bath is a great convenience when families are bathing and dressing at the same time.

Overall Appearance. We recommend that you ask to be sent a photo of a hotel's standard guest room before you book, check it out at the hotel's website, or at least get a copy of the hotel's promotional brochure. Be forewarned, however, that some hotel chains use the same guest room photo in their promotional literature for all hotels in the chain and that the guest room in a specific property may not resemble the photo in the brochure. When you or your travel agent call, ask how old the property is and when the guestroom you are being assigned was last renovated. If you arrive and are assigned a room inferior to that which you had been led to expect, demand to be moved to another room.

CHILDREN'S PROGRAMS

Many large hotels and resorts offer supervised programs for children, some complimentary, some with fees. If you decide to take advantage of the kids' programs, call ahead for specific children's events that are scheduled during your vacation. Ask about cost and the ages that can participate; the best programs divide children into age groups. Make reservations for activities your child might enjoy (you can always cancel after arrival).

After check-in, stop by and visit with the kid's program staff. Ask about counselor-child ratio and whether the counselors are trained in first aid and CPR. Briefly introduce your children to the staff and setting, which typically will leave them wanting more, thereby easing the separation anxiety when they return to stay.

Some hotels offer in-room baby-sitting, but if your hotel does not, there is a national, nonprofit referral program called Child Care Aware that will help you locate a good, high-quality sitter. You can call (800) 424-2246, Monday to Friday, 8:30 a.m. to 4:30 p.m.

Be sure to ask if the sitter is licensed, bonded, and insured. To ease your children's anxiety, tell them how long you plan to be away, and be sure they feel good about the person who will be caring for them. Finally, trust your own instincts.

CHAIN HOTEL TOLL-FREE NUMBERS

This guidebook gives details on some of the family-friendly hotels in the Northeast. However, for your convenience we've listed toll-free numbers for the following hotel and motel chains' reservation lines:

Best Western	(800) 528-1234
Comfort Inn	(800) 228-5150
Courtyard by Marriott	(800) 321-2211
Days Inn	(800) 325-2525
Doubletree	(800) 424-2900
Choice Hotels	(800) 424-4777
Embassy Suites	(800) 362-2779
Fairfield Inn by Marriott	(800) 228-2800
Four Seasons Hotels and Resorts	(800) 332-3442
Hampton Inn	(800) 426-7866
Hilton	(800) 445-8667
Holiday Inn	(800) 465-4329
Howard Johnson	(800) 654-2000
Hyatt	(800) 233-1234
Marriott	(800) 228-9290
Quality Inn	(800) 228-5151
Radisson	(800) 333-3333
Ramada Inn	(800) 228-3838
Residence Inn by Marriott	(800) 331-3131
Ritz-Carlton	(800) 241-3333
Sheraton	(800) 325-3535
Swissotel	(800) 621-9200
Renaissance Hotels	(800) 468-3571
Wyndham	(800) 822-4200
Westin	(800) 228-3000

Family-Friendly Restaurants

I love food and adore eating out, and Alexander loves to eat out, too, but rarely do we agree on what constitutes a good restaurant. I prefer comfort, good service, creative cooking, and a nice glass of wine. Alex digs action and noise and could care less what is on the menu. Hence the challenge: to put together a roster of restaurants throughout New York and New England that make both parents and children happy.

You'll note that most major chain restaurants and all the chain fast-food restaurants are not found in the listings of this book. We encourage you to skip McDonald's whenever possible and make the effort to patronize local places — not only is it better for your health, but you're more likely to get a feel for an area when you sit with the locals and eat a burrito or dim sum or pancakes. As for the big chain restaurants, we find most of them to be soulless and dull. There are exceptions, especially in such smaller, regional chains as Hearth 'n Kettle on Cape Cod and Friendly's, that are good family restaurants that have New England flair.

Tips on Dining Out with Children

Be Realistic about Age Limits   I ate at elegant restaurants when Alex was a sleeping infant in his car seat. By the time toddlerhood hit, I restricted our eating out to quality fast food, child-friendly ethnic restaurants (Chinese, Cuban, Mexican), and takeout food enjoyed in park picnic areas. I began restaurant-training in earnest at about age four, the dawn of a years-long process of gentle reminding about napkins on laps, feet off chairs, and proper butter-knife etiquette. I expect to achieve success around the junior year of college.

Don't Battle a Picky Eater.   You'll never win this one. If everything looks yucky, order them some plain rice and plain bread. Enjoy your food with gusto, and if the kids get hungry enough, they'll break down and ask to try some.

Look Beyond the Children's Menu.   The vast majority are monotonous and unhealthy, consisting mostly of burgers, deep-fried chicken, and french fries. Encourage experimentation in the grown-up menu, and ask if it's possible to order smaller portions of the "adult" food.

Remember the Picnic.   We love to picnic. Grocery stores, delis, upscale gourmet shops, and mini-marts are all stocked with foods that seem almost too decadent to buy at home — but if you're picnicking, you have to go for the convenience foods. So I'd get takeout salads and chicken, made-to-order sandwiches, fresh baguettes, imported cheeses, and exotic fruits. The price is still less than a bad meal at a roadside coffee shop.

Watch the In-Betweeners. When they feel too old for (or don't like) the children's menu but can't really eat a big meal, some parental diplomacy is in order, or the in-betweener will be taking one bite from a huge order of whatever and then stopping, overwhelmed. Some kids will agree to splitting or sharing a meal, but let them choose most of it. Sometimes it's just a matter of ordering three meals for four people, so you avoid huge quantities of leftovers (which you can't take home when traveling) and yet allow for some tasting of different things.

Soup, Soup, Soup. Not only is it comforting and homey, but soup is often a tasty, nutritious, affordable basis for a kid's meal that needs only an appetizer to complete it.

Let Them Be Weird. Alex loves backward dinners—dessert is eaten before the main course. As much as possible, let your kids enjoy the get-what-you-want pleasure of restaurant eating as part of their vacation. Remember, they're also missing home, routine, and the certainty of their daily meal rituals.

Special Challenges to a New England or New York Vacation

Most families with children visit the Northeast states during the summer months, when school is out. So before starting off on a day of touring or a visit to the beach, parents should keep some things in mind.

Overheating, Sunburn, and Dehydration. While New England doesn't cook in the summer months like other destinations, it can get warm during July and August, especially during the one or two heat waves that usually hit for short duration. New York is stifling in July and August, though. The most common problems of smaller children are overheating, sunburn, and dehydration. A small bottle of sunscreen carried in a pocket or fanny pack will help you take precautions against overexposure to the powerful sun. Be sure to put some on children in strollers, even if the stroller has a canopy. Some of the worst cases of sunburn we have seen were on the exposed foreheads and feet of toddlers and infants in strollers. To avoid overheating, rest at regular intervals in the shade or in an air-conditioned museum, hotel lobby, restaurant, or public building.

Don't count on keeping small children properly hydrated with soft drinks and water fountain stops. Long lines at popular attractions often make buying refreshments problematic, and water fountains are not always handy. The same goes for the beach. What's more, excited children may not inform you or even realize that they're thirsty or overheated. We recommend renting a stroller for children six years old and under, and carrying plastic water bottles.

Blisters. Blisters and sore feet are common for visitors of all ages, so wear comfortable, well-broken-in shoes or sandals. If you or your children are usually susceptible to blisters, carry some precut "moleskin" bandages; they offer the best possible protection, stick great, and won't sweat off. When you feel a hot spot, stop, air out your foot, and place a moleskin over the area before a blister forms. Moleskin is available by name at all drugstores. Sometimes small children won't tell their parents about a developing blister until it's too late. We recommend inspecting the feet of preschoolers two or more times a day.

Sunglasses. If you want your smaller children to wear sunglasses, it's a good idea to affix a strap or string to the frames so the glasses won't get lost and can hang from the child's neck while she's indoors.

Beach Safety. To avoid a severe sunburn that can ruin a child's—and your—vacation, dress your kids in light-colored clothing (although not too light or they'll burn through the cloth), gob the sunscreen on exposed skin (don't forget behind the ears), and give 'em little hats.

More advice: Never let your children swim unattended. While many Northeast beaches have lifeguards, many do not, and the beaches tend to get crowded during peak summer months.

Lyme Disease. The first case of this tick-borne disease was diagnosed in Lyme, Connecticut, in 1975. The disease is transmitted by tiny deer ticks that burrow into the skin. The initial symptom is a bulls-eye-like rash (three-to-eight inches in diameter). Later, fever, muscle and joint pain, and fatigue set in. It's important to get treatment early, as heart damage is possible if left untreated. Antibiotics are usually prescribed. To prevent Lyme disease, you should wear socks, long pants, and long-sleeved shirts when hiking or traveling in forest-like areas where deer congregate. And, you can use insect repellant to ward off ticks.

Poison Ivy. This shiny, three-leaf plant grows rampant in New England. If you come into contact with it you could break out into an extremely itchy and ugly rash, although for some reason the extent to which the rash spreads varies from person to person. Still, it is never a pleasant experience. Most parks and hiking trails identify the pesky plant with signage. Take heed and don't touch.

SAFETY

- Discuss safety with your family before you leave home.

- Discuss what to do if someone gets lost. If you are going to a crowded theme park or anywhere that there's a possibility you and your child could get separated, write your child's name on adhesive tape and tape it inside their shirt. Be sure that young children know their full name, address, and phone number (with area code).

- Carry photos of your kids for quick ID.

- Travelers' checks are the easiest way to protect your money.

- In emergencies, call 911 for assistance in reaching paramedics, law enforcement, or the fire department.

- Teach your children to find the proper authorities if they are lost. Tell them to approach a security guard, a store clerk, or "a grown-up who is working where you're lost."

- Before heading out for a stroll, if you are unsure about the safety of an area, ask the front desk manager or concierge in your hotel.

- Always lock your car when it is parked.

- Always try to keep your gas tank full.

- At night, try to park your car under a street light or in a hotel parking garage. Never leave wallets, checkbooks, purses, or luggage in the car. It's best to lock your luggage out of sight in the trunk.

- Keep your wallet, purse, and camera safe from pickpockets. A fanny pack, worn around the waist, is the most convenient way to stash small items safely.

- Leave your valuables at home, and if you must bring them along, check with your hotel to see if there is a safe.

- Be sure you lock sliding doors that lead to your hotel balcony or porch while you are in your room and always when you leave. Never open the hotel room door if you are unsure about who is at the door.

- Keep medicine out of reach of small children; it's easy to forget and leave it out in hotel rooms.

- Check with the front desk, hotel security, or guest services at attractions for lost property. Report lost or stolen travelers' checks and credit cards to the issuing companies and to the police.

- Crime can happen anywhere, so use common sense and take necessary precautions.

FREE NEW ENGLAND AND NEW YORK PUBLICATIONS FOR VISITORS

For information about traveling to New York, contact the New York State Department of Economic Development at (800) 225-5697, www.ilove ny.state.ny.us. For information about traveling to Connecticut, contact the Connecticut Vacation Center at (800) 282-6863, www.ctbound.org. For information about traveling to Rhode Island, contact the Rhode Island Tourism Divisions Travel Center at (800) 556-2484, www.visitrhodeisland.com. For information about traveling to Massachusetts contact the Massachusetts Office of Travel and Tourism at (800) 447-6277, www.massvacation.com. For information about traveling to New Hampshire, contact the New Hampshire Office of Travel and Tourism at (800) 258-3608, www.visitnh.gov. For information about traveling to Vermont, contact Vermont Travel and Tourism at (800) 837-6668, www.travel-vermont.com For information about traveling to Maine, contact the Maine Office of Tourism at (888) 624-6345, www.visitmaine.com.

Part One

Connecticut

This compact state, the smallest in the nation, is full of surprises—the first one being that some parts of the state are considered to be New England in the first place. This is especially true of southern Connecticut, which is a closer sibling to New York than New England. This is so because many of the folks who live in southern Connecticut's stretch of wealthy communities work in The Big Apple, nearby. As you move farther up the coast and into the interior of the state, you'll see more and more evidence of New England's Puritan past. It shows up in the cuisine (lobster and chowder prevail), in the accommodations (bed-and-breakfasts and quintessential New England inns), and in the lay of the land (sprawling town greens and a sprinkling of fishing villages).

Connecticut's most popular family attraction is **Mystic Seaport,** a step-back-in-time, nineteenth-century village where kids can board a historic ship, the *Amistad,* and dress up in period clothing at the Children's Museum. Older kids can hoist a sail on the *Charles W. Morgan.* Then there's the Mystic Aquarium and Institute for Exploration—don't miss the Penguin Pavilion and the dolphin and whale demonstrations. A couple of miles away is the nation's impressive Mashantucket Pequot Museum and Research Center, which traces heritage and history of the Pequot tribe in southeastern Connecticut.

Connecticut's beauty is in the eye of the beholder—whether it's the stunning sandy beaches along the Long Island Sound or the rolling pastoral hills of Litchfield. The Nutmeg State is home to some of the wealthiest communities in the nation and an Ivy League School, Yale University.

Connecticut is often considered a welcome mat to New England. If it's an authentic taste of New England that you're craving, we recommend that you marry your visit to Connecticut with a visit to one of the other five states that make up New England. If you'll be driving through Connecticut to

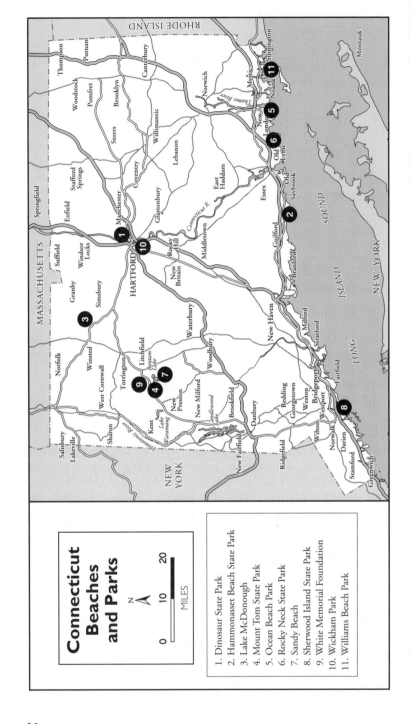

Connecticut Beaches and Parks

1. Dinosaur State Park
2. Hammonasset Beach State Park
3. Lake McDonough
4. Mount Tom State Park
5. Ocean Beach Park
6. Rocky Neck State Park
7. Sandy Beach
8. Sherwood Island State Park
9. White Memorial Foundation
10. Wickham Park
11. Williams Beach Park

reach points north, do plan a stop at Mystic Seaport and the Mystic Aquarium. It's so easy to do—you'll spy both of these tremendously popular attractions from I-95, the main route through Connecticut. Plan to spend at least a couple of hours here. It's also a great stomping ground for lunch at (where else?) Mystic Pizza, just up the road in the quaint town of Mystic. (You'll be tempted by Friendly's restaurant early on, but resist the temptation—it's well worth the extra mileage to reach Mystic Pizza.) You'll most likely whiz by Hartford while traveling to northern New England, and if you have older kids (10 and up), you might want to plan a pit stop to see Mark Twain's house.

If, on the other hand, Connecticut is your chosen destination, you will probably want to base yourselves in Mystic or not too far away because this is the state's best family-friendly attraction and region.

GETTING THERE

By Car. Interstate 95 runs along Connecticut's Long Island Sound shoreline, providing a direct link to all points in the state, whether you come from New York City, Boston, or Providence, Rhode Island. To reach southern Connecticut, if traveling from the south, the popular route is I-95. However, you'll have lots of company—especially tractor-trailers. If you don't like sharing your drive with these rule-the-road vehicles, opt for the Hutchinson and Merritt Parkways, where trucks are banned. Caveat: Watch carefully for deer (there are lots of them in the area and unfortunately they tend to leap across these roadways) and keep in mind that there aren't many highway eateries and rest stops.

If you're traveling to southern Connecticut from eastern Massachusetts and northern Connecticut, take I-84 south to Danbury and hook up with Route 7 south into Fairfield County. Interstate 84 enters Connecticut at Danbury (I-684 interchange) and runs northeast through Hartford to its link with I-90 at Sturbridge, Massachusetts. It also interchanges with I-91 at Hartford.

Interstate 91 heads north from New Haven (I-95 interchange) through Hartford, connecting with I-90 (the Massachusetts Turnpike) north of Springfield, Massachusetts. It continues north through New England to Canada.

Interstate 395 enters the northeast corner of Connecticut at Thompson and continues south along the eastern border, and through Norwich until it connects with I-95 in Waterford.

The Merritt Parkway (Connecticut 15) links with New York State's Hutchinson River Parkway at Greenwich; it becomes the Wilbur Cross Parkway near Bridgeport and links with I-91 at Meriden.

By Plane. Bradley International Airport at Windsor Locks is served daily by several airlines. Call (888) 624-1533.

By Train. Metro North (the New Haven Line) runs between New York City's Grand Central Terminal and New Haven, with connecting service from Stamford to New Canaan, South Norwalk to Danbury, and Bridgeport to Waterbury. Call (800) 638-7646. Note: Metro North offers special excursion packages with round-trip rail service from New York City. The packages are sold by Metro North ticket agents on the day of travel at Grand Central Terminal. Call (800) 638-7646.

Amtrak's main line runs between New York City's Penn Station and Boston, with stops along the shore. It also links at New Haven, with service to Hartford and Springfield, Massachusetts. Call (800) USA-RAIL. Note: A new high-speed train, the Acela, has begun service with 10 daily round trips from New York to Boston, making stops in Stamford, New Haven, and New London. However, at press time, the high-speed train was not yet operating.

By Ferry. From Bridgeport to Port Jefferson, New York, a year-round auto ferry operates daily. It departs and arrives at the Water Street Dock in Bridgeport. Call (888) 443-3799 or (516) 473-0286.

The Chester/Hadlyme Ferry crosses the Connecticut River, carrying eight to nine cars per trip. April through November, it departs from 54 Ferry Road (Rte. 148), Cheshire. Call (860) 443-3856.

The New London to Block Island (Rhode Island) Auto Ferry operates mid-June to mid-September. It departs from Ferry Street, New London. Call (860) 442-9553.

The New London to Fishers Island (New York) Ferry is a year-round auto ferry. It Departs from New London Pier in New London. (860) 443-6851, (860) 442-0165, (516) 788-7463.

The New London to Montauk (New York) Ferry carries foot passengers and bicycles on Friday and Sunday from Memorial Day to Labor Day. It departs from State Pier in New London. Call (516) 668-5700.

The New London to Orient Point (New York) Ferry is a year-round vehicle and passenger ferry with a crossing time of approximately 1 hour and 20 minutes. High-speed passenger service has a 40-minute crossing time. It departs from Ferry Street in New London. Call (860) 443-5281.

The New London to Glen Cove (New York) Ferry is a year-round passenger ferry from Long Island's North Shore. Call Fox Navigation, (888) SAIL-FOX.

How to Get Information before You Go

The Mystic & More Convention and Visitors Bureau, P.O. Box 89, 470 Bank St., New London, CT 06320; (860) 444-2206.

The Housatonic Valley Tourism District, P.O. Box 406, Danbury, CT 06813; (800) 841-4488.

The Coastal Fairfield County Convention and Visitors Bureau, 383 Main Avenue, Norwalk, CT 06851; (800) 473-4868.

Connecticut Campground Owner's Assocation, 14 Rumford Street, Dept. VG, W. Hartford, CT 06107; (860) 521-4704.

The Litchfield Hills Visitor Bureau, P.O. Box 968, Litchfield, CT 06759; (860) 567-4506.

The Greater New Haven Convention & Visitors Bureau, 59 Elm Street, New Haven, CT 06510; (800) 332-STAY.

The Best Beaches and Parks

Hammonasset Beach State Park, Madison. The state's largest shoreline park has a two-mile beach, camping, scuba diving, a nature center with programs for kids and the whole family, and concession stands. It's accessible for disabled people, and is open year-round from 8 a.m. to sunset. Admission: Memorial Day through Labor Day, weekdays $5 in-state vehicles, $8 out-of-state; weekends and holidays $7 in-state vehicles, $12 out-of-state; mid-April through Memorial Day, Labor Day through October, weekdays are free, weekends $5 in-state vehicles, $8 out-of-state. It's free in the off-season. Route 1 (I-95, Exit 62). Call (203) 245-2785.

Lake McDonough, Barkhamsted (Litchfield Hills). A pretty setting for swimming, boating, fishing, and hiking. Rowboats and paddleboats are available to rent beginning the third Saturday in April through November. Fishing from shore is allowed beginning Labor Day through November. The park is open Monday through Friday from 10 a.m. to 8 p.m. and Saturday, Sunday, and holidays from 8 a.m. to 8 p.m. Call for parking, boating and rental fees. Route 219 (off Route 44). Call (860) 379-3036.

Ocean Beach Park, New London. This park has ocean swimming and a freshwater pool, a water slide, a penny arcade, picnic areas, miniature golf, bathhouses, a restaurant, and a gift shop. It's accessible for disabled people. It's open Memorial Day through Labor Day 9 a.m. to 11 p.m. Call for admission rates, (800) 510-SAND 1225 Ocean Avenue (1-95, Exit 75 N./83 S.).

Rocky Neck State Park, East Lyme. This park offers a half-mile crescent beach with bathhouses, a boardwalk, camping, hiking, and fishing. Lifeguards, toilets, and disabled access are onsite. It's open daily 8 a.m. to sunset. Parking: Memorial Day through Labor Day, weekdays $5 in-state vehicles and $8 out-of-state vehicles; weekends and holidays, $9 in-state vehicles and $12 out-of-state vehicles. Mid-April through Memorial Day and Labor Day through September, admission is free on weekdays; on weekends it's $5 in-state vehicles, $8 out-of-state vehicles. Admission is free in the off-season. Route 156 (I-95, Exit 72). Call (860) 739-5471.

Sandy Beach, Morris (Litchfield Hills) A secluded (relatively speaking) cove on Bantam Lake with a bathhouse, raft, slide, canoe launch, lifeguards, and a snack bar. It's open on weekends from Memorial Day through June and daily from 9 a.m. to 7 p.m. from July through Labor Day. Admission is $5 for vehicles and boats, $1 for walkers and bicycles. (Note: The park is at least a three-mile walk/bike ride along country roads from the center of Litchfield.) Bantam Lake, E. Shore Road (Route 109). Call (860) 567-7550.

Sherwood Island State Park. This state park offers a one-and-a-half-mile beach, two picnic areas, scuba diving and fishing, and concession stands. It's open daily, 8 a.m. to sunset. Admission is charged from Memorial Day through September: weekdays $5 for Connecticut vehicles and $8 for out-of-state vehicles; weekends and holidays $7 for in-state vehicles and $12 for out-of-state vehicles. It's free to visit in the off-season. The park is in Green Farms (near Westport). Exit 18 off I-95 or U.S. 1. Call (203) 226-6983.

Family Outdoor Adventures

Biking. Farmington Canal Heritage Trail has abandoned railbeds that are paved for family-friendly recreational use. They vary in length from two miles to almost three miles, making an easy outing for kids and adults. It's located in Farmington, Avon, and Simsbury.

Boating. A river runs through Hartford—and around it, too. The best way to explore is in an inner tube or canoe. To get on the water, call Farmington River Tubing, open Memorial Day through Labor Day from 10 a.m. to 5 p.m. Bonus: Sign on for the canoe tour of Hartford's underground tunnels. Satan's Kingdom Recreation Area, Route 44 New Hartford. Call (860) 739-0791.

Mystic Whaler Cruises, Inc. offers cruises aboard *Mystic Whaler,* a recreation of a New England schooner. It makes one-, two-, three-, and five-day sailing journeys, as well as evening dinner cruises. Kids are encouraged to lend a hand in the sailing of this 110-foot vessel. Children must be 10 years of age and older for the overnight trips. Kids age 5 and older are welcome aboard the day sail from 9:30 a.m. to 3:30 p.m. (but kids under age 5 are not allowed aboard the ship). Bonus: A lobster dinner cruise from 4:30 to 7:30 p.m. is especially fun and half-price for kids ages 5–10. There are also theme cruises offered throughout the season, such as a pirate cruise and lighthouse cruise. Rates vary considerably depending on the length and type

Connecticut Firsts

The following firsts occurred in Connecticut

- First public library, New Haven (1656)
- First submarine (1775)
- First trimmed and illuminated Christmas tree, Windsor Locks (1777)
- First cotton gin, by New Haven's Eli Whitney (1794)
- First American cookbook, by Amelia Simmons (1796, published in Hartford)
- First U.S. statehouse, Hartford (1796)
- First dictionary, by West Hartford's Noah Webster (1806)
- First U.S. amusement park, Lake Compounce Theme Park, Bristol (1846, and still operating)
- First football game, played at Yale (1873)
- First three-ring circus, staged by Bethel's P.T. Barnum (1881)
- First nuclear submarine, *The Nautilus,* Groton (1954)
- First woman elected governor, Ella Grasso (1975)

of cruise. Departure is from 15 Holmes Street from Memorial Day through October. Call (800) 697-8420 for rates and more information.

Cross-Country Skiing. Cross-country skiing can be done in so many places throughout the state, it's impossible to list them all here. A couple of the best spots are White Memorial Foundation in Litchfield (phone (860) 567-0857) and Winding Trails Cross Country Ski Center in Farmington (near Hartford) with 13 miles of cross-country trails (phone (860) 678-9582).

Downhill Skiing. With 23 downhill trails (20 percent beginner, 60 percent intermediate, 20 percent expert) and five miles of cross-country trails, Mohawk Mountain Ski Area is Connecticut's most ambitious ski resort. Still, don't expect a mega ski resort like you'd find in Vermont. Night skiing and snowboarding are allowed, and there is a kids' ski program called Ski-wee for ages 5–12 on weekends and holidays. The full-day program begins at 10 a.m. and ends at 3 p.m. and is $74 per child, including rental equipment and lunch. A half-day program from 10 a.m. to noon or 1 to 3 p.m.

Fun Connecticut Facts

The following things were invented in Connecticut. Who knew?

- Portable typewriter (1843)
- Sewing machine (1846)
- Ice-making machine (1853)
- Can opener (1858)
- Tape measure (1868)
- Pay phone (1877)
- Collapsible toothpaste tube (1892)
- Hamburgers (1895)
- Electric light socket with pull chain (1896)
- Erector set (1911)
- Frisbee (1920)
- Vacuum cleaner (1933)
- Polaroid camera (1934)
- Helicopter (1939)
- Color television (1948)

is $47 per child, including rental equipment. Mohawk Mountain Ski Area, 46 Great Meadow Road, Cornwall (off Route 4); call (800) 895-5222.

Hiking. Almost 90 percent of Connecticut is countryside—suffice it to say, hiking opportunities are plentiful.

In the Mystic region, The Denison Pequotsepos Nature Center is great for hiking, with more than seven miles of trails amidst this 200-acre wildlife sanctuary. There's also a natural history museum and gift shop. It's open Monday through Saturday from 9 a.m. to 5 p.m. and Sunday from noon to 5 p.m. *Admission:* adults $4, children $2, kids ages 5 and younger get in free. 109 Pequotsepos Road, Mystic (I-95, Exit 90). Call (860) 536-1216.

Dinosaur State Park in Rocky Hill (in the Greater Hartford region) is especially popular with kids and adults who want to hike. It offers two miles of nature trails and a trail map. After or before the hike, kids will dig the Jurassic-period dinosaur tracks housed under a geodesic dome and an 80-foot diorama. The park and hiking trails are open year-round from

State Symbols

- State nickname: Nutmeg State
- State insect: Praying mantis
- State bird: American robin
- State tree: Charter oak
- State gem: Garnet

- State flower: Mountain laurel
- State shellfish: Eastern oyster
- State hero: Nathan Hale
- State ship: USS *Nautilus*
- State song: "Yankee Doodle"

9 a.m. to 4:30 p.m. The exhibit center is open Tuesday through Sunday from 9 a.m. to 4:30 p.m. Admission to the park and center are free. 400 West Street, Exit 23 off I-91, (860) 529-8423.

Hammonasset Beach State Park, a spawling state park and beach (see Best Beaches and Parks), has marked trails through a salt marsh. It's open year-round from 8 a.m. to sunset. It's accessible for the disabled. *Admission:* Memorial Day through Labor Day, weekdays $5 in-state vehicles, $8 out-of-state vehicles; weekends and holidays $7 in-state vehicles, $12 out-of-state vehicles; mid-April through Memorial Day and Labor Day through October, weekdays are free; weekends $5 in-state vehicles, $8 out-of-state vehicles. Admission is free in the off-season. Route 1 (I-95, Exit 62). Call (203) 245-2785.

In Coastal Fairfield County, The Nature Conservancy is idyllic for hikes. Called Devil's Den, it offers more than 20 miles of hiking trails on 1,746 acres. Adjacent to the conservancy is the 62-acre Katharine Ordway Preserve, with three miles of hiking trails and an arboretum. 33 Pent Road (Route 15, Exit 42) in Weston. Admission is free. It's open from dawn to dusk year-round. Call (203) 226-4991.

White Memorial Foundation is the Nutmeg State's largest nature center and wildlife sanctuary with 4,000 acres and 35 miles of trails for hiking. You can take a guided tour or hike at your own pace. One of the best hikes for kids is The Natural Wonders of the Wetlands. Begin at the museum and take a right out of the Nature Museum. Follow the blue-blazed trail to the white and black square trail, to a loop around the boardwalk and then retrace your steps back to the museum. It's a three-hour walk (just over 3 miles) but considered an easy level. Bicycles, horses, and cars are not allowed, making it very kid friendly. You can get a trail map in the museum gift shop. It's open daily. Admission is free. Route 202 in Litchfield (Route 8, Exit 42). Call (860) 567-0857.

Cool Websites for Connecticut-Bound Kids

Connecticut Impressionist Art Trail: www.arttrail.org

The Beardsley Zoological Gardens: www.beardsleyzoo.org

Central Connecticut: www.centralct.org

Coastal Fairfield Connecticut: www.coastalCT.com

Connecticut Tourism: www.ctbound.org

Essex: www.essexCT.com

Foxwoods Casino and Resort: www.foxwoods.com

Housatonic Valley Tourism: www.housatonic.org

Lake Compounce Theme Park: www.lakecompounce.com

Litchfield Hills: www.litchfieldhills.com

Madison: www.madisonCT.com

Maritime Aquarium, Norwalk: www.maritimeaquarium.org

Mark Twain House: www.marktwainhouse.org

Mashantucket Pequot Museum and Research Center:
www.mashantucket.com

Mystic and More: www.mysticmore.com

Mystic Seaport: www.mysticseaport.org

New Haven: www.newhavencvb.org

Stamford Museum: www.stamfordmuseum.org

Stepping Stones Museum: www.steppingstonesmuseum.org

United Wrecking Company: www.United-Antiques.com

Connecticut's Quiet Corner: www.webtravels.com/quietcorner

Waterbury Region: www.wrcvb.org

Wickham Park, the former estate of the gentleman who invented windowed envelopes, is a great spot to hike along walking trails. Stop along the way for a picnic (there is a snack bar open on weekends). Bonus: A playground for the kids. It's open April through October daily from 9:30 a.m. to dusk. Parking fee: Monday through Thursday $1; Friday through Sunday $2; holidays $3. 1329 W. Middle Turnpike, Manchester (I-84, Exit 60). Call (860) 528-0856.

With a summit at 1,325 feet above sea level and a stone tower on top, on a clear day you can see forever (or so it seems) at Mt. Tom State Park.

You'll find a hiking trail, a lake for swimming, picnic areas, even scuba diving, and ice-skating. It's open daily 8 a.m. to sunset. Parking: weekdays $4 in-state vehicles, $5 out-of-state; weekends $4 in-state vehicles, $5 out-of-state. Admission is free in the off-season. Route 202, Litchfield. Call (860) 868-2592.

Calendar of Festivals and Events

May

Annual Lobsterfest, Mystic Seaport. Old-fashioned lobster bake on the banks of the pretty Mystic river. Music and activities. 75 Greenmanville Avenue; (888) 9-SEAPORT.

June

Annual International Festival of Arts & Ideas, New Haven, Hartford, Stamford, New London. A two-week festival that showcases the world's finest performing and visual arts, including art-related discussions; (203) 498-1212.

Annual Subfest, Groton. This is a family festival with a boat show, a carnival, food, and a fireworks show; Naval Submarine Base, Athletic Field Complex, Groton; (860) 694-3238.

July

Annual Riverfest, Hartford, East Hartford. This dual-community festival along the river celebrates the country's independence and the Connecticut River. Lots of entertainment, kids' activities, and food. Grand finale: Fireworks shot from a river barge; (860) 713-3131.

Annual Litchfield Open House Tour, Litchfield. A fun, full-day, self-guided tour of the prettiest gardens and historic homes in Litchfield; (860) 567-9423.

Annual Mashantucket Pequot Thames River Fireworks. A huge fireworks event (one of the country's grandest), complemented by audio. The location is between Groton and New London; (860) 443-1980.

August

Annual Mystic Outdoor Art Festival, Mystic. A huge sidewalk art show with 300 artists displaying and selling their masterpieces. There's also plenty of food and entertainment, all in historic downtown Mystic; (860) 572-5098.

Annual Country Fair, Bridgewater. This is a major agricultural fair with animal competitions, a lumberjack competition, an antique tractor pull, and

Connecticut's Not-to-Be-Missed Attractions

Gold Coast

- The Maritime Aquarium at Norwalk
- Stepping Stones Museum for Children, Norwalk
- A day trip to Lake Compounce Theme Park, Litchfield

Central Connecticut/Hartford

- Mark Twain's House, Hartford (especially at Christmas)
- Jonathan's Dream Playground, West Hartford
- A day trip to New Haven

Southeast Connecticut

- Mystic Seaport, Mystic
- Mystic Aquarium & Institute for Exploration, Mystic
- Fried belly clams at The Cove, Mystic
- Mashantucket Pequot Museum and Research Center, Mashantucket
- Abbott's Lobster in the Rough, Noank

lots of entertainment. The fair takes place at the Bridgewater Fairgrounds; (860) 354-4730.

September

Annual Norwalk Oyster Festival, Norwalk. A huge, festive, waterfront celebration of the Long Island Sound's seafaring past, with lots of entertainment, arts and crafts, vintage vessels, and fireworks. Bonus: special kids' entertainment and activities. Events take place at Veteran's Memorial Park; (203) 838-9444.

Annual Durham Fair, Durham. This is Connecticut's largest agricultural fair, with well-known country music stars, thousands of exhibits, and competitions for prizes; Routes 17 and 18, Durham; (860) 349-9495.

October

Annual Walking Weekend, throughout the Connecticut River Valley. More than 50 guided walks that highlight the historic, natural, and scenic heritage of the region, specifically the Quinebaug and Shetucket Rivers Valley National Heritage Corner; (860) 928-1228.

November

Stamford Parade Spectacular, Stamford. A two-hour balloon parade with more than 30 helium-filled character balloons, marching bands, Santa, and more. The parade takes place in downtown Stamford; (203) 348-5282.

Annual Manchester Road Race, Manchester. A four-and-three-quarter-mile race that attracts more than 12,000 runners, this is the second-oldest road race in the East. Some runners dress in colorful costumes, and kids love to cheer those people on. The races takes place on Main Street at 10 a.m.; (860) 649-6456.

Annual Festival of Light, Hartford. White lights—200,000 of them—are formed into angels, bells, and other whimsical things. Santa arrives by helicopter to turn on the lights at the beginning of the festival; Constitution Plaza, Hartford; (860) 728-3089.

December

Annual Lantern Light Tours, Mystic Seaport. Ride a horse-drawn omnibus and take in the holiday festivities at Mystic Seaport. Tours run on selected evenings throughout the week; 75 Greenmanville Avenue; (888) 9-SEAPORT.

First Night Hartford. An annual New Year's Eve celebration of the arts, plus an evening fireworks display. Events take place at over 20 locations throughout the downtown area. The fun begins at 2 p.m. and goes on through midnight; (860) 728-3089.

The Gold Coast: Stamford, Westport, and Norwalk

For the most part, this region of Southwestern Connecticut is a bedroom community for New York City commuters (visit any Metro North railroad platform here during rush hour on weekday mornings and evenings and you'll see what we mean). There's really no compelling reason to spend more than a half-day in these parts—for a true taste of New England you'll want to travel north. In fact, if you order a cup of chowder off a menu on Connecticut's Gold Coast, you're much more likely to get a cup of Manhattan clam chowder (tomato based) rather than New England clam chowder (milk based). And you won't be able to access most of the beaches because they are private.

Still, this area has a couple of good attractions that you should consider visiting on your way to points north (if traveling from New York and points farther south).

Family Lodging

The Inn at National Hall

As long as you're staying on the rich Gold Coast, you might as well live in the lap of luxury. This very lovely Relais & Chateux property, built in 1873, has 15 rooms, including seven themed suites. Continental breakfast is included in the rate. It's located in the heart of very upscale Westport, a hop, skip and jump from area attractions in neighboring Norwalk and Stamford. Double room rates begin at $150 per night. 2 Post Road W., Westport; (800) NAT-HALL.

Stamford Marriott

This large (over 500 rooms), business hotel also attracts families thanks to its game room, indoor and outdoor pools, and sports court. Double room rates begin at $100 per night. 2 Stamford Forum, Stamford; (203) 357-9555.

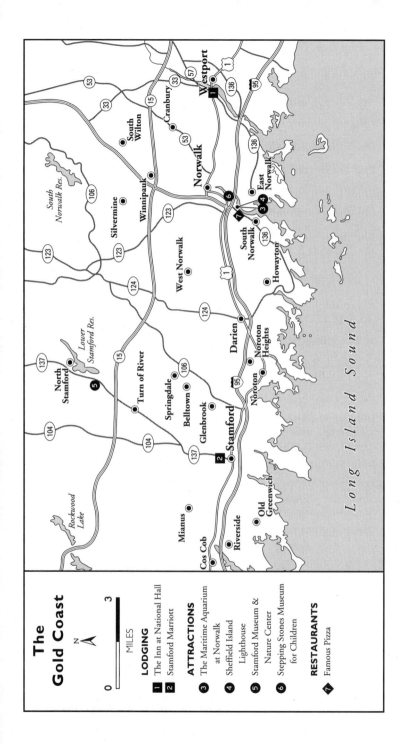

The
Gold Coast

N

MILES

0   3

LODGING
1 The Inn at National Hall
2 Stamford Marriott

ATTRACTIONS
3 The Maritime Aquarium at Norwalk
4 Sheffield Island Lighthouse
5 Stamford Museum & Nature Center
6 Stepping Stones Museum for Children

RESTAURANTS
7 Famous Pizza

Long Island Sound

Take Me Out to the Ballgame

There are several minor-league baseball teams throughout Connecticut. They are:

The Bridgeport Bluefish, Harbor Yards, Bridgeport, (203) 334-TIXX

The New Britain Rock Cats, New Britain Stadium, New Britain, (860) 224-8383

The New Haven Ravens, Yale Field, New Haven, (800) RAVENS-1, (203) 782-1666

The Norwich Navigators, Dodd Stadium, Norwich, (800) 64-GATOR

Attractions

The Maritime Aquarium at Norwalk

10 N. Water Street (off I-95, Exit 14 N/15 S); (203) 852-0700

Hours: July–Labor Day, daily 10 a.m.–6 p.m.; day after Labor Day–June, daily 10 a.m.–5 p.m.

Admission: $8.25 adults, $7.50 seniors, $6.75 children ages 2–12, free for children under age 2. IMAX tickets: $6.75 adults, $5.75 seniors, $5 children, free for children under age 2. Combination tickets: $12.50 adults, $11 seniors, $9.75 children ages 2–12

Appeal by Age Groups:

Pre- school	Grade School	Teens	Young Adults	Over 30	Seniors
★★	★★★	★★	★★	★★	★★

Touring Time: Average 2 hours; minimum 1 hour

Rainy-Day Touring: Yes

Services and Facilities:

Restaurants Yes	Lockers No
Alcoholic beverages No	Pet kennels No
Disabled access No	Rain check No
Wheelchair rental No	Private tours Yes
Baby stroller rental No	

Description and Comments   This aquarium showcases the marine life of Long Island Sound. The IMAX movie theater is a big hit with grade school kids and teens and a must if you are going to visit the aquarium. There's also an environmental education center to enhance this attraction as an edu-

---

Send in the Clowns

If the kids starting clowning around, stop at **The Barnum Museum,** 820 Main Street in Bridgeport (about ten miles up I-95 from West-port). Built in 1893, this museum houses a collection of circus-related finds that belonged to P.T. Barnum, including a five-ring, hand-carved miniature circus, clown props, and sideshow attractions from the days when Barnum was the ringmaster. Admission is $5 for adults, $4 for seniors, $3 for children ages 4–18, and free for ages 3 and under. Hours are Tuesday through Saturday from 10 a.m. to 4:30 p.m. and Sunday from 12 to 4:30 p.m. Call (203) 331-9881 for information.

---

cational one. If you're going to be traveling farther north in Connecticut (and if you are on a budget), you might opt to skip this aquarium and instead go for the larger one at Mystic.

Sheffield Island Lighthouse

Cruises depart at Hope Dock, corner of Washington Street and N. Water Street; (203) 838-9444

Hours: Memorial Day–September; call for daily ferry schedule

Admission: $12 adults, $10 seniors, $8 children under age 12

Appeal by Age Groups:

Pre-school	Grade School	Teens	Young Adults	Over 30	Seniors
★★	★★★	★★★	★★★	★★★	★★★

Touring Time: Average a half day; minimum 2 hours

Rainy-Day Touring: Yes

Services and Facilities:

Restaurants No	Lockers No
Alcoholic beverages No	Pet kennels No
Disabled access No	Rain check No
Wheelchair rental No	Private tours No
Baby stroller rental No	

Description and Comments   You must take a ferry to the lighthouse, and most kids love the ride over as much as they do the destination. Once there, you'll find a three-acre island park where the kids can cut loose and a four-level, 10-room lighthouse for exploring. Pack a picnic. Bonus: On Thursday evenings there are clambakes.

What a Wreck!

If antiques are your bag and you'll be staying in or driving through Stamford on your way to points north, absolutely make a pit stop at United House Wrecking (Exit 9 off I-95). My mother would make day trips from our Long Island, New York, home just to visit this unique spot with over 35,000 square feet of antiques, furniture, outdoor garden and patio finds . . . you name it, it's here. Older kids will enjoy shopping here; you'll need to bribe younger ones with a promise to visit the super-kid-friendly Stepping Stones Museum up the road in Norwalk. Hours are Monday through Saturday 9:30 a.m.–5:30 p.m. and Sunday noon-5 p.m. 535 Hope Street, Stamford; (203) 348-5371; www.United-Antiques.com.

Stamford Museum & Nature Center

39 Scofieldtown Road, Exit 35 off Route 15; (203) 322-1646; www.stamfordmuseum.org

Hours: Monday–Saturday 9 a.m.–5 p.m., Sunday 1–5 p.m.

Admission: Adults $5, seniors and children ages 5–13 $4

Appeal by Age Groups:

Pre-school	Grade School	Teens	Young Adults	Over 30	Seniors
★★	★★★	★★★	★★	★★	★★

Touring Time: Average 3 hours; minimum 1 hour

Rainy-Day Touring: Yes

Services and Facilities:

Restaurants No	Lockers No
Alcoholic beverages No	Pet kennels No
Disabled access No	Rain check No
Wheelchair rental No	Private tours No
Baby stroller rental No	

Description and Comments   This sprawling center has 118 acres with a New England farm, wooded trails for hiking, a picnic area, and Nature's Playground with a live pond-life exhibit. On Sunday, there are planetarium shows. For rainy days, there's a different experience: seven indoor galleries with exhibitions such as Native American art and Americana.

Stepping Stones Museum for Children

Mathews Park, 303 West Avenue, Norwalk (I-95, Exit 14 N/15 S); (203) 899-0606

Beep, beep! An Old-Fashioned Drive-In

Not technically on the Gold Coast but only a bit farther north off Route 84 near Danbury, the Sycamore Drive-In is a one-of-a-kind dining experience. You order from your car and eat in your car—if that's your pleasure (and what kid wouldn't eat this up?). Or, you can sit inside. This gem is open seven days a week for breakfast, lunch, and dinner. While it doesn't have a kids' menu, it does have kid-friendly fare such as grilled cheese sandwiches, hot dogs, and steak burgers (thin hamburgers). It's worth the detour, whether you're in the Gold Coast area or traveling through Connecticut to Boston (it's minutes off Route 84 at 282 Greenwood Avenue in Bethel.) No credit cards. Call (203) 748-2716.

Hours: Memorial Day–Labor Day, Monday–Saturday 10 a.m.–5 p.m., Sunday noon–5 p.m.; after Labor Day–late May, Tuesday–Saturday 10 a.m.–5 p.m., Sunday noon–5 p.m.

Admission: $6, children under age 1 get in free

Appeal by Age Groups:

Pre-school	Grade School	Teens	Young Adults	Over 30	Seniors
★★★	★★★				

Touring Time: Average 2 hours; minimum 1 hour

Rainy-Day Touring: Yes

Services and Facilities:

Restaurants No; snack machines	Lockers No
Alcoholic beverages No	Pet kennels No
Disabled access Yes	Rain check No
Wheelchair rental No	Private tours Yes
Baby stroller rental No	

Description and Comments   This new interactive learning center/museum is designed for kids age 1–10. Kids love exploring the ongoing exhibits as well as participating in arts, sciences, technology, and culture programs.

Family-Friendly Restaurants

FAMOUS PIZZA

23 N. Main Street, Norwalk; (203) 838-6100

Meals served: Lunch and dinner

Cuisine: Italian/American
Entree range: $3.95 and up
Children's menu: No
Reservations: No
Payment: Major credit cards accepted

This is a great spot to hit before or after a visit to the nearby Norwalk Aquarium. While there is no children's menu, the offerings at this casual spot are stuff kids love anyway—pizza, burgers, pasta, and grinders (hero sandwiches).

Side Trip: Litchfield Hills, New Milford, Washington, Litchfield, Bristol

This is the new "in" spot for Manhattan celebs yearning for more privacy than the tall, manicured hedges the Hamptons provide. Yes, there are *hills,* which are dotted by a sprinkling of New England inns frequented by Manhattanites. And a river runs through it—The Housatonic—providing venues for picnics and cruises.

The intellectual town of **Litchfield** is a magnet for families who appreciate a true New England town when they see one. Its white, steepled church surely has been a photo opportunity for generations of families— and will be for many more.

There is always an exception to the rule—and in Litchfield Hills, a region known more for what it lacks, the only real attraction is the **Lake Compounce Theme Park** in Bristol, one of the oldest theme parks in the country with a 1911 carousel and 1927 roller coaster.

FAMILY LODGING

The Litchfield Inn

We love this large inn, especially its close location to the town of Litchfield and its large rooms. While there are eight theme rooms (such as the lavender-hued Lady Agnew room with brass bed), it's best to book those when you're on a romantic holiday without the kids (as if!). With kids, your best bet is a deluxe room with two queen beds and a sleeper sofa and small refrigerator or a standard room with two queen beds. Double-room rates begin at $120 per night, including a continental breakfast each morning. Children of all ages are accepted. On the premises, you'll find a lovely, comfy restaurant and a pub with kid-friendly fare. Bonus: The 4,000-acre White Memorial Foundation Park is within walking distance, just a few feet up the road, and it's ideal for a hike or for cross-country skiing. You can also drive through most of this sprawling park. Route 202, Litchfield; (860) 567-4503.

Mayflower Inn

If you'll be traveling with kids older than age 12 and have money to spare, this 100-year-old inn is a treat. The Mayflower is renowned as the place to escape in Connecticut, and romance is what most guests expect from this inn. There are only 25 rooms (so book *waaaaay* ahead, especially during fall foliage season), including eight suites. There's also a restaurant (pricey) and a health club with a sauna, an outdoor pool, and tennis. 118 Woodbury Road (Route 47), Washington; (860) 868-9466.

ATTRACTIONS

Lake Compounce Theme Park

822 Lake Avenue, Bristol (Exit 31 off I-84); (860) 538-3300

Hours: Memorial Day–late September, daily; October, Friday–Sunday nights

Admission: $7.95 general admission; $29.95 Ride All Day (RAD); $17.95 RAD under 5'2" or seniors; free for kids age 3 and under

Appeal by Age Groups:

Pre-school	Grade School	Teens	Young Adults	Over 30	Seniors
★★★	★★★★	★★★★	★★★	★★	★

Touring Time: Average a full day; minimum a half day

Rainy-Day Touring: No

Services and Facilities:

Restaurants Yes	Lockers No
Alcoholic beverages No	Pet kennels No
Disabled access Yes	Rain check No
Wheelchair rental No	Private tours No
Baby stroller rental No	

Description and Comments   Cowabunga! A wooden roller coaster, a 1911 carousel, and dozens of wet and dry attractions will keep everyone happy for hours. Bonus: The new Splash Harbor Water Park, a water-themed attraction that kids love.

FAMILY-FRIENDLY RESTAURANTS

THE COUNTY SEAT

3 West Street, Litchfield; (860) 567-8069

Meals served: Breakfast, lunch, and dinner
Cuisine: You name it—salads, sandwiches, soup, pasta

Good Advice

If you'll be visiting the Lake Compounce Theme Park (and you really should if you're visiting the Litchfield area, as the amusement park is the best kid attraction in the region), your best bet for eating is to travel a couple of miles away to Route 10. Here, you'll discover the usual kid-friendly restaurants, including Ruby Tuesday's and Chili's.

Entree range: $3.95 and up
Children's menu: No
Reservations: No
Payment: All types accepted

This is *the* gathering spot in Litchfield, a pinecone's throw from the village green. It's a very comfortable spot to eat a meal, enjoy an ice cream cone or sip a cappuccino. A sophisticated yet casual ambiance makes this a great spot for a hearty lunch or dinner after a hike or cross country ski run at nearby White Memorial Foundation and Conservation. Not that hungry? Plop yourselves down in one of the easy chairs, settle in to read the paper and nurse a coffee or hot cocoa. If you've got older teens, come after dinner to take in the folk music.

WOOD'S PIT BBQ & MEXICAN CAFÉ

123 Bantam Lake Road (Route 209), Litchfield; (860) 567-9869

Meals served: Lunch and dinner
Cuisine: Mexican and barbecue
Entree range: $6.95 and up
Children's menu: Yes
Reservations: No
Payment: All types

Near Litchfield Center, this lively family restaurant has good Mexican food, as well as popular barbecue items such as ribs, beef brisket, and pulled pork. The children's menu has tacos, cheeseburgers, and chicken.

Central Connecticut: Hartford, West Hartford, Simsbury

There are two obviously compelling reasons to visit Connecticut's capital city of Hartford—**The Mark Twain House** and its neighbor, the **Harriet Beecher Stowe House.** If you're traveling from the south, you will want to stop in Hartford to visit these two homes of Americana—especially if you'll be driving through in mid-August when three Mark Twain Days take center stage. Boston is a mere one and a half hours away—and a preferred spot to stay.

Family Lodging

Centennial Inn Suites

If you opt not to stay in the concrete jungle of Hartford, plant yourselves instead at this pretty country-type inn in the nearby suburb of Farmington, 15 minutes from downtown Hartford. Suites feature fireplaces and one or two bedrooms, there's an outdoor pool, and continental breakfast is included in the rate. There is no restaurant on property, but there is a T.G.I. Friday's about a 10-minute-drive away. Double room rates begin at $149 per night. 5 Spring Lane, Farmington; (800) 852-2052.

Attractions

Bushnell Park Carousel

Jewell Street, Hartford (I-91 or I-84 Capital Area exit); (860) 522-6400
Hours: May 1–mid-October, Tuesday–Sunday 11 a.m.–5 p.m.
Admission: 50¢ a ride

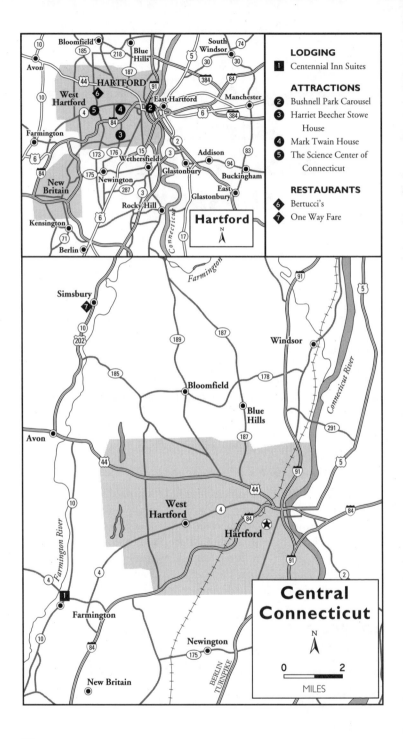

LODGING

1 Centennial Inn Suites

ATTRACTIONS

2 Bushnell Park Carousel

3 Harriet Beecher Stowe House

4 Mark Twain House

5 The Science Center of Connecticut

RESTAURANTS

6 Bertucci's

7 One Way Fare

Hartford

N

Central Connecticut

N

0   2

MILES

Appeal by Age Groups:

Pre-school	Grade School	Teens	Young Adults	Over 30	Seniors
★★★★	★★★★	★★★	★★	★	★

Touring Time: Average 15 minutes; minimum 15 minutes

Rainy-Day Touring: Yes

Services and Facilities:

Restaurants No	Lockers No
Alcoholic beverages No	Pet kennels No
Disabled access No	Rain check No
Wheelchair rental No	Private tours No
Baby stroller rental No	

Description and Comments   This 1914 Stein & Goldstein hand-carved merry-go-round with 48 horses and a Wurlitzer band organ excites kids of all ages. It's located in Bushnell Park across from the Capitol. Tip: Because this is a business region, you'll find plenty of hot dog vendors and the like, so plan an easy, inexpensive lunch after your carousel ride.

Harriet Beecher Stowe House

73 Forest Street, Hartford (I-84, Exit 46); (860) 525-9317

Hours: June 1–Columbus Day and December, Monday–Saturday 9:30 a.m.–4:30 p.m., Sunday noon–4:30 p.m. The rest of the year, same hours but closed on Monday. Visits by guided tour only

Admission: $6.50 adults and seniors, $2.75 children ages 6–16

Appeal by Age Groups:

Pre-school	Grade School	Teens	Young Adults	Over 30	Seniors
None	★★★	★★★	★★★	★★★	★★★

Touring Time: Average 1 hour; minimum 1 hour

Rainy-Day Touring: Yes

Services and Facilities:

Restaurants No	Lockers No
Alcoholic beverages No	Pet kennels No
Disabled access No	Rain check No
Wheelchair rental No	Private tours Yes
Baby stroller rental No	

Description and Comments   Adjacent to Mark Twain's house (see following listing), the Harriet Beecher Stowe House allows you to cram in two lessons about American literature in one fell swoop. Harriet Beecher

Stowe, of course, wrote *Uncle Tom's Cabin*. If you don't already own a copy, it's not a bad idea to borrow one from the library and at least read a couple of passages before visiting this Victorian cottage because it will make it that much more interesting to visit.

The Mark Twain House

351 Farmington Avenue, Hartford; (860) 247-0998

Admission: $9 adults, $8 seniors, $7 students ages 13–18, $5 children ages 6–12, free for ages 5 and under

Hours: May 1–October 31 and December, Monday–Saturday 9:30 a.m.–5 p.m. and Sunday noon–5 p.m.; January 2–April 30 and November, Monday and Wednesday–Saturday 9:30 a.m.–5 p.m. and Sunday noon–5 p.m.; last tour is at 4 p.m.

Appeal by Age Groups:

Pre-school	Grade School	Teens	Young Adults	Over 30	Seniors
None	★★★	★★★	★★★	★★★	★★★

Touring Time: Average 1 hour; minimum 1 hour

Rainy-Day Touring: Yes

Services and Facilities:

Restaurants No	Lockers No
Alcoholic beverages No	Pet kennels No
Disabled access No	Rain check No
Wheelchair rental No	Private tours Yes
Baby stroller rental No	

Description and Comments Mark Twain, the curmudgeon America loves, lived in this Victorian mansion from 1874 to 1891, giving life to some of his most important and memorable characters within these walls. Both Tom Sawyer and Huck Finn became inventions of Mark Twain's imagination here. Twain's vivid imagination and sly wit were extended in equal parts to the design of his home, which he often described as "part house, part steamboat."

Though Twain is often noted for his use of the vernacular, the design of his home could be considered bombastic by contrast. It is a striking landmark on Farmington Avenue. Three stories of red brick with red and black Chinese stripes and numerous porches and gables, the home stands proudly on a site known as Nook Farm, once a teeming artist community in the heart of Hartford.

The Twain family had the home redecorated by Louis Comfort Tiffany in 1881, and it has been meticulously researched and restored to reflect its appearance at that time. Most of the home's 19 rooms are on display and are furnished with almost half of the family's original furnishings, including paintings and photographs. As you tour the home with a well-versed guide, you may hear about the carved fireplace by which Twain devised stories for his daughters at night. Or you hear famous Twain quotes, such as, "I would rather decline three whiskeys than a German verb!" In the basement of the home you can also see the printing press, a new invention at that time (which Twain lost a fortune on), as well as purchase souvenirs and Twain memorabilia.

The home is decked colorfully and festively for the holidays. This is a must-see for travelers to the Hartford area, and it is especially interesting for kids who have read at least one of his books. In fact, if you do plan to visit, it's a good idea to have the children familiarize themselves with his works to enhance their visit. To get there, take Exit 46 off I-84, turn right onto Sisson Avenue, then right onto Farmington Avenue; the house is a half-mile down the road on the right.

The Science Center of Connecticut

950 Trout Brook Drive, West Hartford (I-84, Exit 43); (860) 231-2824

Hours: Tuesday and Wednesday, Friday and Saturday 10 a.m.–5 p.m., Thursday 10 a.m.–8 p.m., Sunday noon–5 p.m. Open Mondays in July and August and holidays

Admission: $6 adults, $5 seniors and children (ages 3–15), free for ages 2 and under; additional charge for the planetarium and laser shows

Appeal by Age Groups:

Pre-school	Grade School	Teens	Young Adults	Over 30	Seniors
★★	★★★	★★	★	★	★

Touring Time: Average 2 hours; minimum 1 hour

Rainy-Day Touring: Yes

Services and Facilities:

Restaurants Yes	Lockers No
Alcoholic beverages No	Pet kennels No
Disabled access No	Rain check No
Wheelchair rental No	Private tours Yes
Baby stroller rental No	

Description and Comments The Science Center offers hands-on fun for all ages and a laser light show. If you are heading up to Boston and are tight for time and/or on a budget, you can skip this museum and opt instead to take in Boston's Science Museum, Planetarium and Omni Theater.

Playin' Around

Jonathan's Dream is the name of one awesome playground in West Hartford, the kind where kids can play for hours on end. The playground was inspired by a little boy in the area who died and whose parents wanted to keep his memory alive. We have dear friends who spend hours here. It's located behind the jewsih Community Center on Bloomfield Avenue in West Hartford.

Family-Friendly Restaurants

BERTUCCI'S

330 N. Main Street, West Hartford; (860) 231-9571

Meals served: Lunch and dinner
Cuisine: Italian
Entree range: $5.95 and up
Children's menu: Yes
Reservations: Yes
Payment: All types

Convenient to the Science Center of Connecticut (just a mile away), this chain restaurant (which has a strong presence throughout New England) is a good bet for families. Expect salads, pizzas with some with creative toppings, and pasta dishes.

ONE WAY FARE

4 Railroad Street, Simsbury; (860) 658-4477

Meals served: Lunch and dinner (open all day from 11:30 a.m. until about 11 p.m.)
Cuisine: Burgers, steak, sandwiches
Entree range: $7.95 and up
Children's menu: Yes
Reservations: Parties of eight or more
Payment: All types accepted

This restaurant is right on track for kids. It's housed in an old train station and is said to be an underground railway. There's reputed to be a ghost downstairs—that'll keep them intrigued. The food is not as mysterious as

> ### Hamburger History
>
> When in New Haven, you must visit Louis' Lunch. After all, this is where the hamburger was born in 1895. Apparently, owner Louis Lassen made patties out of ground-up steak scraps, broiled them and served them on white toast. In fact, if you like your hamburger on a bun you can forget it here—buns are banned (strict bun-control laws). It's open Tuesday through Saturday, but it's closed for the month of August. They'll make a small burger for the kiddies at only $1.65 each. No credit cards accepted. 263 Crown Street, New Haven; (203) 562-5507.

the ghost legend—hamburgers, Reuben sandwiches, steak. The kids' menu has grilled cheese, hot dogs, chicken tenders, and macaroni and cheese.

Side Trip: Greater New Haven

Make no mistake about it—New Haven is a college town, thanks to **Yale University,** which has a tremendous presence here. There are several museums at Yale, but the most family-friendly is the **Peabody Museum of Natural History**—don't miss it! If you'll be traveling from the south (New York and points south), you can detour a bit and plan to visit this museum and have lunch at one of New Haven's famous lunch spots before moving on to your final destination.

FAMILY LODGING

Colony Inn

Right next to Yale University, this is a good spot to stay if you're looking for a moderately sized hotel/motel (86 units, six suites). There's a restaurant and lounge, but no pool. Double room rates begin at $150 per night. 1157 Chapel Street, New Haven (I-91, Exit 1; I-95, Exit 47); (800) 458-8810.

Residence Inn by Marriott

If you plan to visit New Haven in the muggy summer months, a pool is a requisite for kids. Your search has ended. There's an outdoor pool at this 112-suite property—and because of the suite configuration of the rooms, families can spread out a bit. Bonus: Some of the suites even have fireplaces and kitchens. Extra bonus: Complimentary breakfast is included in the room rate. Double room rates begin at $195 per night. 3 Long Wharf Drive, New Haven (I-95, Exit 46); (800) 331-3131.

ATTRACTIONS

Peabody Museum of Natural History

Yale University, 170 Whitney Avenue, New Haven (I-91, Exit 3); (203) 432-5050

Hours: Monday–Saturday 10 a.m.–5 pm., Sunday noon–5 p.m.

Admission: $5 adults, $3 seniors and children ages 3–15

Appeal by Age Groups:

Pre-school	Grade School	Teens	Young Adults	Over 30	Seniors
★★★	★★★★	★★★	★★★	★★★	★★★

Touring Time: Average 2 hours; minimum 1 hour

Rainy-Day Touring: Yes

Services and Facilities:

Restaurants No	Lockers No
Alcoholic beverages No	Pet kennels No
Disabled access No	Rain check No
Wheelchair rental No	Private tours Yes
Baby stroller rental No	

Description and Comments   Reputed to be one of the best museums in the country, the Peabody will wow kids and adults with the dinosaur fossil exhibits, wildlife dioramas, and cultural exhibits, including ancient Egypt and Native North American cultures. This museum is the *raison d'etre* for visiting New Haven. Calling all paleontologists . . .

FAMILY-FRIENDLY RESTAURANTS

FRANK PEPE PIZZERIA

157 Wooster Street, New Haven; (203) 865-5762

Meals served: Lunch, dinner, and late night
Cuisine: Pizza
Entree range: Pies begin at $6.10 plus tax (slices are not served)
Children's menu: No
Reservations: Not accepted
Payment: No credit cards

This is where the original American pizza was reputedly born in 1925. Today there are many gourmet variations to the original tomato pies, including white pizza. Note: There is an annex location right behind the one called Frank Pepe The Spot. Same food, same prices, just smaller size

Southeast Coast: Mystic, Stonington, and Shoreline

You'll first view Mystic from the turnout on the I-95 E overpass over the Mystic River, or from the sporadic panoramic glimpses of the river along Route 27, the main artery to downtown. You'll know you've arrived because you'll spy white-on-white captains' homes dotting the river's edge to the west and the masts of the whaling ship *Charles W. Morgan* that stretches into the sky to the east. Home to **Mystic Seaport Museum** and the world-class **Mystic Aquarium,** this is the most visited location in Connecticut. What was once a proud whaling and shipbuilding center is now a fabulously exciting educational experience embodied by the seaport and aquarium. In fact, Mystic is to family vacations in Connecticut what Disney World is to family vacations in Florida—*everything*.

The downtown Mystic area bustles with foot traffic, the comings and goings of tourists and locals to the many shops, boutiques, restaurants, and galleries. You can cruise down the river on the steamship *Sabino,* dine al fresco on some of the best seafood the area has to offer, or simply while away the time watching the river flow from the counter-balance drawbridge in the heart of Mystic. While there are beaches in the region, the best of the best of them will have you making the short 20-minute trip to Rhode Island—Watch Hill, in particular, has great beaches and an old-fashioned carousel, too.

After spending time in Mystic, be sure to travel a few miles east on Route 1 to Stonington Village. The village occupies a one-mile-long spit of land that protrudes into the Atlantic Ocean at the mouth of Long Island Sound. As you cross the causeway into the village, you are suddenly aware that you are in a very special place. The square and stately architecture reminds one of sea captains, salt air, and wealth from abroad. During warm months, the air is filled with the sweet scent of flowering shrubs, sunlight dapples the seaside homes, flags wave in the breeze . . . life is good! Stonington Village is a wonderful place to stroll, especially along Water Street.

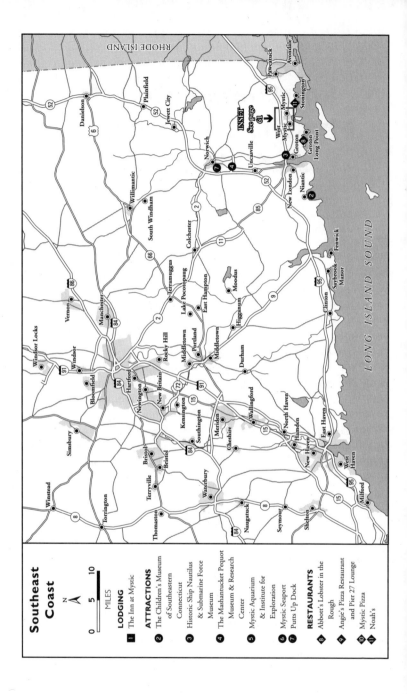

Southeast Coast

N

0   5   10
MILES

LODGING
1. The Inn at Mystic

ATTRACTIONS
2. The Children's Museum of Southeastern Connecticut
3. Historic Ship Nautilus & Submarine Force Museum
4. The Mashantucket Pequot Museum & Research Center
5. Mystic Aquarium & Institute for Exploration
6. Mystic Seaport
7. Putts Up Dock

RESTAURANTS
8. Abbott's Lobster in the Rough
9. Angie's Pizza Restaurant and Pier 27 Lounge
10. Mystic Pizza
11. Noah's

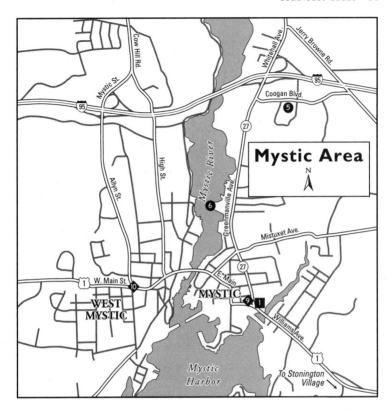

One of Stonington's traditions, the Blessing of the Fleet, always held during the last weekend of July, is particularly noteworthy. Thousands of spectators come each year to the town dock to watch the parade of fishing vessels in colorful regalia be blessed with the hopes of bountiful catches and safe fishing. The festivities include an official blessing, a parade of fishing vessels, a traditional New England lobster bake (including chowder, steamers, and corn-on-the-cob), and a variety of traditional Portuguese fare. Music is provided for dancing and merriment. The traditional Saturday/Sunday celebration, or any part thereof, is always worthwhile.

Family Lodging

The Inn at Mystic

Overlooking busy Mystic Harbor and Long Island Sound, this 1904 mansion is a great spot to stay if you plan on exploring Mystic Seaport; it's only about a mile away. The rooms in the older section of the hotel are modest and family-friendly, and other rooms come with more jazzed-up touches such as balconies (which you might want to steer away from if you have preschoolers and young grade-school kids.) Double room rates begin at $65 per night; Junction of Route 1 and Route 27; (800) 237-2415.

Attractions

The Children's Museum of Southeastern Connecticut

409 Main Street, Niantic (I-95, Exit 72 N/74 S); (860) 691-1111

Hours: Tuesday–Saturday 9:30 a.m.– 4:30 p.m., Friday 9:30 a.m.–8 p.m., Sunday noon– 5 p.m.; Memorial Day through Labor Day and school vacations, also Monday 9:30 a.m.– 4:30 p.m.

Admission: $3.50, free for children under age 2

Appeal by Age Groups:

Pre-school	Grade School	Teens	Young Adults	Over 30	Seniors
★★★	★★★★				

Touring Time: Average 2 hours; minimum 1 hour

Rainy-Day Touring: Yes

Services and Facilities:

Restaurants No	Lockers No
Alcoholic beverages No	Pet kennels No
Disabled access No	Rain check No
Wheelchair rental No	Private tours No
Baby stroller rental No	

Description and Comments This museum has interactive exhibits and programs for kids ages 1 to 12 on topics of science, arts, culture, history, health, and safety. It's very hands-on. This is an especially good museum for the littlest of kids—Nursery Rhyme Land is one good reason to visit.

Historic Ship Nautilus & Submarine Force Museum

Off Route 12, Groton (Exit 86 off I-95); (800) 343-0079

Hours: May 15–October 31, Wednesday–Monday 9 a.m.– 5 p.m., Tuesday 1– 5 p.m.; November 1–May 14, Wednesday–Monday 9 a.m.– 4 p.m.

Admission: Free

Appeal by Age Groups:

Pre-school	Grade School	Teens	Young Adults	Over 30	Seniors
★	★★★	★★★	★★★	★★★	★★★

Touring Time: Average 1 hour; minimum 1 hour

Rainy-Day Touring: Yes

Services and Facilities:

Restaurants No (but there is a picnic area)	Baby stroller rental No
	Lockers No
Alcoholic beverages No	Pet kennels No
Disabled access Yes	Rain check No
Wheelchair rental No	Private tours Yes

Description and Comments Kids love exploring this cool submarine, the world's first nuclear-powered sub. Older kids enjoy the exhibits on the history of the U.S. Submarine Force. Kids especially love to peer through the periscopes. Try to tour at non-peak times because the wait can get long and little ones grow antsy.

The Mashantucket Pequot Museum & Research Center

11 Pequot Trail, Mashantucket; (800) 411-9671

Hours: Labor Day–Memorial Day, Wednesday–Monday 10 a.m.–6 p.m. (last admission at 5 p.m.); Memorial Day–Labor Day, daily 10 a.m.–7 p.m. (last admission at 6 p.m.); closed Thanksgiving, Christmas, and New Year's days

Admission: $10 adults, $8 seniors age 55 and older, $6 kids ages 6–15, free for kids age 6 and under

Appeal by Age Groups:

Pre-school	Grade School	Teens	Young Adults	Over 30	Seniors
★★★	★★★★	★★★	★★★	★★★	★★★

Touring Time: Average 4–5 hours; minimum 2–3 hours

Rainy-Day Touring: Yes

Services and Facilities:

Restaurants Yes	Lockers No
Alcoholic beverages Yes	Pet kennels No
Disabled access Yes	Rain check No
Wheelchair rental Yes	Private tours Yes
Baby stroller rental Yes	

Description and Comments Where once there was nothing but the bucolic countryside and gently rolling hills of Connecticut, you will now find the trappings of unbridled success at the Foxwoods Casino and Resort Complex in southeastern Connecticut, built by the Mashantucket Pequot Nation. One of the many positive things that the Mashantucket Pequot Nation has done for families is to design and build an expansive (308,000-square-foot) museum and research center housed in a completely separate building from any gaming activities at the casino. The multilevel museum has been designed to allow the visitor to explore this region of Connecticut, its metamorphosis through the glacial retreat 12,000 years ago, and its inhabitants and their lives. There is an entire village, built in striking diorama, with life-like mannequin representations of the Mashantucket people. You are permitted to walk among the numerous stations with an infrared radio into which you key each station number; descriptive information is then played into your earphones. There are 37 such stations within the village, which, together with the diorama, describe the daily life and societal structure of the Pequot villagers in striking detail. The system is ingenious, and small children won't have much trouble with it after an initial explanation. The museum is well designed and informative, an the interactive diorama adds an educational dimension to the experience.

When you're finished viewing the exhibits at the museum, be sure to visit the on-site restaurant, just above the main entrance. You will find a few interesting Native-American items on the menu as well as typical family fare, all reasonably priced.

Mystic Aquarium & Institute For Exploration

Exit 90 off I-95, Mystic; (860) 572-5955

Hours: Daily 9 a.m.–5 p.m., summer hours (July 1–Labor Day) extend to 6 p.m.

Admission: $15 adults, $14 seniors, $10 children ages 3–12, free for ages 2 and under

Appeal by Age Groups:

Pre-school	Grade School	Teens	Young Adults	Over 30	Seniors
★★★	★★★	★★★	★★	★★	★★

Touring Time: Average 3 hours; minimum 2 hours

Rainy-Day Touring: Yes

Services and Facilities:

Restaurants	Yes	Lockers	No
Alcoholic beverages	No	Pet kennels	No
Disabled access	No	Rain check	No
Wheelchair rental	No	Private tours	Yes
Baby stroller rental	No		

Description and Comments Some of the new exhibits at this ambitious aquarium, which recently underwent an enormous renovation project, are noteworthy, including the 800,000-gallon, outdoor beluga whale pool and the Roger Tory Peterson Penguin Exhibit. Perhaps one of the most notable

---

Two if by Sea

For New Yorkers and Long Islanders, getting to Connecticut really is half the fun. You have two options. You can drive to Orient Point on Long Island's North Fork and take the car ferry that whisks you over to New London. Retrieve your car and you can drive to Mystic in no time. Or, opt to leave your wheels behind and board the new fast, trimaran ferry out of Glen Cove, Long Island, and Liberty State Park (on Jersey's shore but it can be reached via car or water taxi from the World Financial Center in Manhattan.) Call Fox Navigation, (888) 724-5369.

---

changes is the presence of the *Discovery,* tender for U.S. Navy Submersible *Turtle,* which sits on the *Discovery's* stern in its own pool adjacent to the entrance pavilion. The *Discovery* signals the Aquarium's association with the Institute for Exploration, headed by Dr. Robert D. Ballard, who discovered of the *Titanic* on the ocean floor.

The new Institute for Exploration wing, "Challenge of the Deep," could keep you busy for days. The Institute's primary mission is stated as "Documenting human history in the deep sea." As you wind your way through this fascinating exhibit, you'll be amazed as you look inside the inner workings of remotely operated vehicles (ROV) for deep-sea exploration, view artifacts collected from the sea floor, and check out some of the alien-like creatures found in the deep. This grand, interactive, high-tech museum addition is not to be missed. You and your children will find this experience extraordinary, from the eight-minute film that briefly chronicles the other-worldly nature of the deep sea to the submersible that you can climb into, to the interactive grasping claws that you are invited to operate.

The main building has been separated into four areas, each of which flows into the other. Moving from one area to the next is effortless since they are all housed in the same building. Separate tanks display thousands of marine specimens in the Sunlit Seas, Coral Reef, and Upwelling Zones ecosystems and in Conserving Our Oceans. The shark tank is a natural focal point in the main building. This 30,000-gallon tank, in which ocean predators swim effortlessly, hide within the coral reef, and dart in and out, was that much more exciting when staff members in scuba gear entered the tank during our morning visit. You can view specimens that you'd never have the chance to see in a natural habitat.

Sleeping in Stonington

Looking for a quintessential New England inn experience while visiting the Mystic Seaport and Aquarium? Opt to stay in nearby Stonington (a two-and-a-mile, five-minute drive away), one of Connecticut's loveliest towns. There are a handful of places to stay in this charming village, but one of the best is Antiques and Accommodations, a bed-and-breakfast inn with seven units. Breakfast is taken very seriously here; expect four courses and candlelight. Antiques lovers will be tempted to buy the many goodies throughout the inn—go right ahead, everything's for sale. And yes, they do accept children "who appreciate antiques." Translation: Kids who can behave. Double room rates begin at $99 per night, including breakfast. Call (800) 554-7829.

The 800,000-gallon beluga whale pool is a wonderful addition. The one-acre pool and surrounding environment were designed to replicate the Alaskan coast, which is home to the beluga whale. You can see the belugas' torpedo-like bodies thunder through the water from above at various viewing stations, or from below the waterline at one of three 20-foot windows built into the pool. These playful mammals will swim past the windows regularly, and one child I visited with swore that they had winked at her.

The outdoor Roger Tory Peterson Penguin Exhibit captivates children's hearts. Here, you can also view from above or below the waterline as the penguins eat, dive, huddle, or swim through the pool. The adjacent Pribilof Islands Exhibit, designed to replicate Alaska's Bering Sea ecosystem, displays northern fur seals and endangered Stellar sea lions. These adorable mammals have plenty of room to display their uniquely adapted bodies in the pool, or you might find them lolling about on the rocks.

Don't miss the dolphin show in the Marine Theater. Watch as the dolphins display many of their unique adaptations and remarkable survival skills during a half-hour show in a theater-like setting. The dolphins jump through hoops, swim on their tails, and jump 20 feet into the air. Children will be thrilled with the awesome display of nautical prowess and intelligence these mammals present.

Mystic Seaport

Exit 90 off I-95, Mystic; (888) 9-SEAPORT

Hours: Summer, daily 9 a.m.–5 p.m.; winter months, daily 10 a.m.–
   4 p.m.

Kids Stay Free

These hotels each have kids-stay-free promotions and are centrally located for exploring Mystic Seaport, Mystic Aquarium and other kid-friendly attractions. They are: the 125-room **Days Inn** with an outdoor pool (phone (860) 572-0574); the 120-room **Comfort Inn** with complimentary continental breakfast (phone (860) 572-8531); the 36-room **Holiday Inn** with an outdoor pool (phone (860) 442-0631); the 120-room **Courtyard Marriott** with an indoor pool and Jacuzzi (phone (860) 886-2600); the all-suite **Spring Hill Suites** by Marriott with an indoor pool and whirlpool spa (phone (860) 439-0151); and in mid-2001 the **Mystic Marriott Hotel & Spa** will open with 285 guest rooms, a spa, and a fitness center (phone (860) 446-2600). For more information about the above properties, call the Waterford Hotel Group, Inc. at (800) 572-3993 or visit www.whghotels.com. Be sure to inquire about special packages and promotions.

Admission: $16 adults, $8 children ages 6–12, free for ages 5 and under

Appeal by Age Groups:

Pre-school	Grade School	Teens	Young Adults	Over 30	Seniors
★★★	★★★★	★★★	★★	★★	★★

Touring Time: Average 2 hours; minimum 1 hour

Rainy-Day Touring: Yes

Services and Facilities:

Restaurants Yes	Lockers No
Alcoholic beverages Yes	Pet kennels No
Disabled access Yes	Rain check No
Wheelchair rental No	Private tours Yes
Baby stroller rental No	

Description and Comments This 17-acre, recreated nineteenth-century seaport village has provided many hours of fun and excitement for our family. Among the many attractions: horse and carriage rides, boat rides and rentals, participatory plays, story-telling, sail-handling demonstrations, hands-on activities for children throughout the day, and an eyes-open-wide gift shop (high-quality items with a nautical theme—books, tapes, and souvenirs abound). Immediately adjacent to the gift shop you'll find the Seaport Gallery (some of the paintings will take your breath away) and an incredible maritime gallery.

While here, grab a light bite to eat at The Galley, sit down for lunch at the Spouter Tavern, or stop into Seamen's Inne Restaurant & Pub, a favorite of the locals too. All are located on the grounds of the Seaport.

Putts Up Dock

Norwich; (860) 886-PUTTS

Hours: June–October 7 a.m.–9 p.m.

Admission: $5 and up

Appeal by Age Groups:

Pre-school	Grade School	Teens	Young Adults	Over 30	Seniors
★★★★	★★★★	★★★	★★★	★★	★

Touring Time: Average 1½ hours; minimum 1 hour

Rainy-Day Touring: No

Services and Facilities:

Restaurants Yes	Lockers No
Alcoholic beverages Yes	Pet kennels No
Disabled access Yes	Rain check No
Wheelchair rental No	Private tours No
Baby stroller rental No	

Description and Comments An erupting volcano makes this miniature golf course a hole-in-one kids delight.

Family-Friendly Restaurants

ABBOTT'S LOBSTER IN THE ROUGH

117 Pearl Streeet, Noank; (860) 536-7719

Meals served: Lunch and dinner
Cuisine: Seafood
Entree range: $8 and up
Children's menu: Yes
Reservations: Not accepted
Payment: All types accepted

What fun we had here, sitting at a picnic table by the water indulging in masses of food—chowder, steamers, boiled shrimp, corn-on-the-cob, and lobster. It's a short (two-and-a-half-mile) jaunt from Mystic, but off-the-beaten path (via Route 215). Sit indoors or outdoors (outdoors gets our vote) at picnic tables with three-state views. The salty sea air complements the fresh, just-plucked seafood here. A great find! It's open in early May on

---

Cinetropolis at Foxwoods

While we certainly don't advocate exposing children to a gambling environment, and yes, Foxwoods is a mega casino complex (the largest in the world), there are quality family diversions here worth discovering—especially on rainy days. Kids will enjoy the 1,500-seat Fox Theatre and three Turbo Rides. The Turbo Rides have movement in six directions that work in sync with film action on an oversized screen. There are also state-of-the-art video games at this complex. Exit 92 off I-95, Ledyard; (800) PLAY-BIG.

---

weekends then daily through Labor Day and then back to weekends only through Columbus Day.

ANGIE'S PIZZA RESTAURANT & PIER 27

Routes 1 and 27, Mystic; (860) 536-7300 or (860) 572-9276

Meals served: Lunch and dinner
Cuisine: Italian (pizza, calzones, pasta), Greek (gyro and souvlaki), seafood, steak
Entree range: $5 and up
Children's menu: Yes
Reservations: No
Payment: All types accepted

Angie's is a locals' favorite. You can order pizza with almost any combination of toppings, grinders hot or cold (in Connecticut when you order a "hero," or a "sub," it is called a "grinder"). Now, it may seem that a restaurant that can't be well defined by food of one ilk or another is spreading itself too thinly. Wrong! All of the food at Angie's is well worth your consideration. Of course, pizza rules here. It's open year round.

MYSTIC PIZZA

W. Main Street, Mystic; (860) 536-3700

Meals served: Lunch and dinner
Entree range: $5.95 and up
Cuisine: Pizza/American
Children's menu: Yes

Feeling Clammy

In a clamshell, these are the best spots in the Mystic region to indulge in fried clams, according to long-term, one-time resident and clam expert Stephen Gronda.

Among the "clams-with-bellies" (as opposed to clam strips, sans bellies) cognoscenti, **Sea Swirl,** at the junction of Route 1 and Route 27 in Mystic, is always noted as the premier location to satisfy the peculiar and oft-maligned desire to eat whole fried bivalves. Some have been moved to wax poetic about Sea Swirl's allure, based solely on the gustatory delights of a plate mounded with fried, whole clams, french fries, some tartar sauce, and a bit of fresh cole slaw eaten on a picnic table with the Route 1 traffic a mere 30 feet away. Sea Swirl also offers a full line of fried food from the sea, including fish and chips, scallops, shrimp, and, for the conservative, clam strips, burgers, and hot dogs. As an added treat, Sea Swirl serves soft ice cream, frozen yogurt, and all-natural hard ice cream. Open March through October; (860) 536-3452.

Not to take anything away from the pleasure that the true aficionado of whole clams will experience at Sea Swirl, but a personal favorite is the **Cove Fish Market & Take Out** for whole clams. The Cove is just a short ride east from the center of Mystic on Route 1 (take Route 27 S., then left on Route 1, go one mile to take a left on Old Stonington Road; the address is 20 Old Stonington Road)). One of the things that sets this venue apart, in our opinion, is the copse of trees separating it from Route 1 that allows the diner a slightly more enjoyable sense of privacy. Here, you can also sate your appetite with a mountain of fried whole clams, a wonderful, clear-broth clam chowder, scallops, shrimp, or fish and chips. Instead of ice cream, the Cove serves slushies, finely ground ice in numerous eclectic flavors and suspect colors that children love to slurp; (860) 536-0061.

Reservations: No
Payment: All types

This pizza joint is where Julia Roberts played her breakout role in the movie by the same name. Although it served up pizza before the movie was ever conceived, Julia put Mystic Pizza on the map and it could be argued vice versa. It has since become one of the most popular eateries in downtown Mystic. It's easy to find—it's the place with all the tourists smiling into a camera. The pie is worthy of your attention too. You'll also find spaghetti, hamburgers, and grinders. Seating is limited so expect to wait. There is another Mystic Pizza in North Stonington (call (860) 599-3111) with the same menu but more seating in two dining rooms.

NOAH'S

113 Water Street, Stonington; (860) 535-3925

Meals served: Breakfast, lunch, and dinner
Cuisine: Sandwiches, fish, pasta, salads
Entree range: $6 and up
Children's menu: No but can get half-orders of pasta and sandwiches
Reservations: Yes, for dinner
Payment: All types

My friend Stephen Gronda, who grew up in Stonington, recommends this spot on Stonington's charming main drag as a great spot for a fabulous home-cooked meal and great service. While you can get the standard fried-flounder sandwich and hamburgers, there is also a trained chef who dishes out incredible stuff such as salmon with a pineapple salsa and breaded flounder with almonds.

Side Trip: Connecticut River Valley, Old Lyme, Essex

This pocket of Connecticut is all about the Connecticut River and darling New England villages such as **Essex,** whose accolades include being named the No. 1 small village in America by the book, *The 100 Best Small Towns in America*. Expect a visit to the Connecticut River Valley to include a river cruise, a picnic by the river, and a requisite visit to the **Connecticut River Museum.** You can do this area in a day before moving on, hitting just the best of what the Connecticut River Valley has to offer—unless time is on your side and you can afford to linger longer.

FAMILY LODGING

Griswold Inn

Smack in the center of America's best small village, this lovely inn does Essex's reputation justice. It has with 30 rooms and suites, and continental breakfast is served each morning in the library (included in rate). If you're visiting in winter, request a room with a fireplace. Double room rates begin at $140 per night. 36 Main Street, Essex; (860) 767-1776.

ATTRACTIONS

Connecticut River Museum

67 Main Street, Essex (Steamboat Dock); (860) 767-8269

Hours: Tuesday–Sunday, 10 a.m.–5 p.m.

Admission: $4 adults, $2 children ages 6–12, free for kids under age 6

Appeal by Age Groups:

Pre-school	Grade School	Teens	Young Adults	Over 30	Seniors
★	★★★	★★	★★	★★	★★★

Touring Time: Average 2 hours (longer if you take in weekend afternoon workshops); minimum 1 hour

Rainy-Day Touring: Yes

Services and Facilities:

Restaurants No	Lockers No
Alcoholic beverages No	Pet kennels No
Disabled access Yes	Rain check No
Wheelchair rental No	Private tours Yes
Baby stroller rental No	

Description and Comments   A restored nineteenth-century dockhouse is home to scale models of the river's maritime past, including steamboats and warships. Ongoing, changing workshops (knot tying, celestial navigation) and concerts entertain kids in the summer months and are free with museum admission. Other family-themed events occur on Columbus Day weekend.

Essex Steam Train and Riverboat

Valley Railroad, 1 Railroad Avenue (Route 9, Exit 3), Essex; (800) ESSEX-TRAIN

Hours: May–end of October and the day after Thanksgiving–December (call for schedule)

Admission: $10.50 adults, $5.50 children; train and boat: $16.50 adults, $8.50 children ages 3–11

Appeal by Age Groups:

Pre-school	Grade School	Teens	Young Adults	Over 30	Seniors
★★	★★★	★★★	★★★	★★★	★★

Touring Time: Average 2 hours; minimum 1 hour, if you take the train only

Rainy-Day Touring: Yes

Services and Facilities:

Restaurants Yes	Lockers No
Alcoholic beverages Yes	Pet kennels No
Disabled access No	Rain check No
Wheelchair rental No	Private tours Yes
Baby stroller rental No	

Description and Comments   Most kids love trains, especially this kind, in which they ride in 1920s coaches pulled by an authentic steam locomotive. There's a gift shop and a grill car. All aboard! In November, Thomas the Tank Engine makes an appearance. Other theme trains include he Easter Eggspress and the North Pole Express. After the train ride, you can opt to board a riverboat and cruise along the Connecticut River.

Part Two

Maine

The Pine Tree State is all about rolling hills, pristine lakes, blueberry pancakes laced with maple syrup, cool summer nights under woolly blankets, and silent, snow-frosted mountaintops. But Maine's soul is the Atlantic Ocean. Visualize 5,500 miles of rocky coastline and just as many reclusive islands, a perfume of salty air, and a setting sun with a lone lighthouse in the foreground. Maine is big—in fact, it's as big as the other five New England states combined. It's home to the second-most visited national park in the United States and also to the northern end of the Appalachian Trail.

While this enormous state is typically divided into eight regions, for the purposes of this book, we've divided it into three, encompassing the most family-friendly and popular regions in the state.

The South Coast is a region of contrasts with **Portland,** Maine's largest city, contrasted by intimate **Cape Elizabeth** and **Cape Porpoise.** Elegant **Kennebunk** and super family-friendly **Ogunquit** are just a few miles from the busy boardwalk of **Old Orchard Beach. Kittery's** mile-long outlet center stands in contrast to miles and miles of sandy beaches and offshore islands.

The Mid-Coast region is defined by coastal Route 1, which skirts an irregular rocky shoreline with peninsulas that jut out from several spots. There are numerous fishing villages where you can go out on the pier and watch the lobster and fish brought in daily. The Mid-Coast region also includes shop-til-you-plop **Freeport,** chock full of outlet stores, and **Monhegan Island,** an island artist's haven accessible only by boat. Monhegan has the sunsets to die for plus **Cathedral Woods,** a cool hiking trail through natural evergreen forest.

The Downeast/Acadia region takes in the 22-square-mile **Acadia National Park,** the second-most visited national park in the country. **Bar Harbor** is a bike ride away from Acadia National Park and home to lots

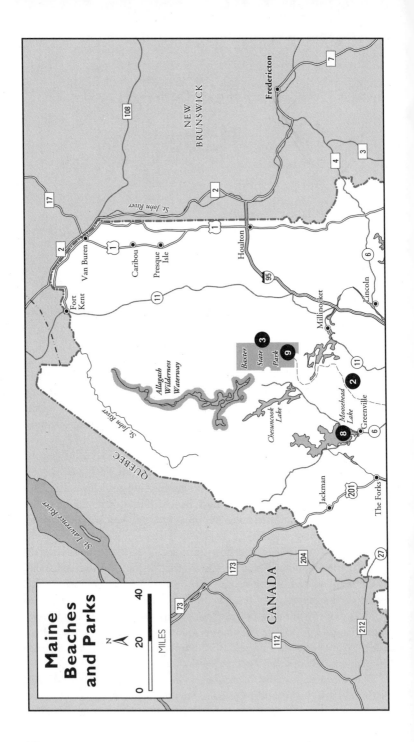

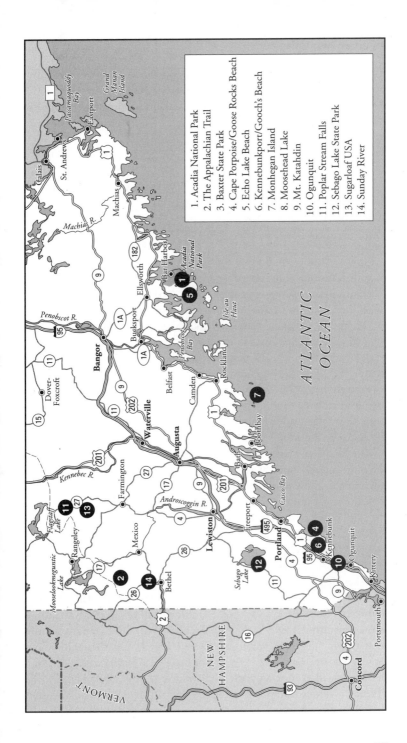

1. Acadia National Park
2. The Appalachian Trail
3. Baxter State Park
4. Cape Porpoise/Goose Rocks Beach
5. Echo Lake Beach
6. Kennebunkport/Gooch's Beach
7. Monhegan Island
8. Moosehead Lake
9. Mt. Karahdin
10. Ogunquit
11. Poplar Stream Falls
12. Sebago Lake State Park
13. Sugarloaf USA
14. Sunday River

State Symbols	
■ State capital: Augusta	■ State fish: Landlocked Salmon
■ State nickname: The Pine Tree State	■ State insect: Honeybee
■ State motto: Dirigo (I lead)	■ State tree: White Pine
■ State bird: Chickadee	■ State fossil: *Pertica quadrifaria*
■ State animal: Moose	■ State gemstone: Tourmaline

of galleries, restaurants, shops, and hotels; it's a great base for exploring Acadia (unless camping is your preferred accommodation, in which case Acadia will oblige—in designated areas). You can take it all in atop **Cadillac Mountain** in Acadia National Park, the highest point in the park and reputed to be the first place in the United States to be touched by the sun most of the year. The Downeast region also has a couple of offshore islands, including **Isle au Haut,** an idyllic spot to camp.

Foodies love Maine for its fresh fruit (it has the largest wild blueberry crop in the nation) and its shellfish (90 percent of all American lobster is trapped in Maine). For some reason, lobster tastes better here than anywhere else in the world.

The Pine Tree State is a super family destination for several reasons. It's the most sparsely populated state east of the Mississippi—so crowds are not as big a problem as in some New England states. Maine woos families with healthy, natural diversions—hiking, biking, and sailing in the summer, and skiing in the winter. Maine is a festival-lovers destination—from lobster, maple syrup, and music festivals to sled-dog races, arts fairs and moose safaris, there's always a cause for celebration. The folks in this gorgeous slice of wilderness love a good excuse to celebrate the great outdoors.

When it comes to parks, Maine is no slouch. It's home to Acadia National Park, (the second-most visited national park in the United States) and **Baxter State Park,** which is the location of towering **Mt. Katahdin** as well as the northern end of the **Appalachian Trail.** Mt. Katahdin, approximately one mile high (5,268 feet above sea level), offers stunning views. Acadia National Park is *raison d'etre* for many to visit rugged Maine. You'll need to spend at least a couple of days here to reap all its benefits. **Bar Harbor,** a stone's throw from the park, offers many choices in accommodations and restaurants.

Fun Maine Facts

- Acadia National Park is the second-most visited national park in the United States
- Maine has the largest wild blueberry crop in the United States
- Almost 90 percent of all American lobster is trapped in Maine
- Maine is the most sparsely populated state east of the Mississippi
- Maine is the only state in the continental United States to be bordered by only one other state (New Hampshire)
- Maine contains 32,000 miles of rivers and streams equal to more than the combined length of the Mississippi, Amazon, Yangtze, and Nile rivers
- Maine entered the Union on March 15, 1820, as the 23rd state

Shopping is a revered pastime in parts of Maine, whether along the renovated oceanfront shopping district in Portland or the outlets in Freeport, where L.L. Bean has its headquarters store, open 24 hours a day, 7 days a week, 365 days a year. But, we can't emphasize enough—Maine's biggest attractions are the kind that nature provides.

Maine winters are looooooong. Just how frigid and how long, you ask? Get this. While staying at the Harraseeket Inn in Freeport, I called housekeeping for two extra blankets and also lit and stoked a fire in our in-room fireplace—in mid-August! (Of course, the heat wasn't on in the room, but still . . .) There's nothing cozier and more heart-warming than a family game of Scrabble or cards in front of a fireplace in Maine. It's something about knowing it's freezing outside and so warm and toasty indoors that melts hearts and nurtures family bonding.

To explore the southern coast and mid-coast of Maine, opt to stay in the Freeport area. It's a great middle base from which to explore Portland and points south as well as points north that you might decide to skip because of the distance if you were anchored down Route 1 in Portland. If you intend to just explore Portland and points south, stay in Ogunquit, an especially gracious, family-friendly spot.

GETTING THERE

By Car. Much of southern Maine is accessible via I-95 (the Maine Turnpike) or Route 1; the two roads run parallel before I-95 turns inland.

Maine's Best Bets

Southern Coast
- Strolling Marginal Way, Ogunquit
- Splurging on a meal at the White Barn Inn, Kennebunkport
- Goose Rocks Beach, Kennebunkport
- Portland Head Light, Portland
- Shopping at Portland Public Market
- A Portland Sea Dogs baseball game
- Old Orchard Beach

Mid-Coast
- Shopping at L.L. Bean, Freeport
- Lobster stew and an overnight stay at Harraseeket Inn, Freeport
- Taking the mailboat or ferry to Monhegan Island
- Skiing Sunday River

Downeast Region
- Spending as much time outdoors as possible
- Hiking, mountain biking, or driving Park Loop Road at Acadia National Park
- Eating popovers at Jordan's Pond House Restaurant in Acadia National Park
- Staying at The Balance Rock Inn, Bar Harbor
- Camping at Isle au Haut

Route 1 is the more scenic road, affording travelers with coastal views at times. However, it is the slower of the two roads, and much of it is a monotonous journey through nondescript towns and tourist traps. Route 1 runs right through Freeport, and if you plan to travel to Portland from Freeport, you can just as easily take Route 1 all the way down as you can get over to I-95 and take that (there is an exit for downtown Portland).

Cool Websites for Maine-Bound Kids

Acadia National Park: www.nps.gov/acad

Bethel: www.bethelmaine.com

Destination Maine: www.destinationmaine.com

Freeport: www.freeportusa.com

L.L. Bean: www.llbean.com/about/retail

Maine arts: www.mainearts.org

Maine Resource Guide: www.maineguide.com

Midcoast: www.midcoast.com

Moosehead Lake region: www.moosehead.net/moose/chamber

Old Orchard Beach: www.oldorchardbeachmaine.com

Portland Vacation Planning: www.visitportland.com/vaca.html

Portland: www.portlandmaine.com; www.visitmaine.com

By Plane. The Portland International Jetport (call (207) 774-7301) is served by several major airlines. The airport is located right across the Fore River from downtown Portland and is about a $12 cab fare to and from downtown (or you can rent a car). For those interested in Acadia National Park and Bar Harbor, there is a small airport in Trenton, which is served year-round by Colgan Air (call (800) 523-3273). There is also an airport in Bangor (call (207) 774-7301), which is served by several major U.S. carriers.

HOW TO GET INFORMATION BEFORE YOU GO

Acadia National Park Hulls Cove Visitor's Center, P.O. Box 177, Bar Harbor, ME 04609; (207) 288-3338; www.nps.gov.acad

Bar Harbor Chamber of Commerce, P.O. Box 158, Bar Harbor, ME 04609; (207) 288-5103; www.acadia.net/bhcc

Bethel Area Chamber of Commerce, 30 Cross Street, Bethel, ME 04217; (800) 442-5826

Kennebunk-Kennebunkport Chamber of Commerce, P.O. Box 740, Kennebunk; (800) 982-4421, (207) 967-0857; kkcc.maine.org

---

How to Eat a Lobster

One of life's greatest pleasures is eating a lobster in Maine. Here, according to the Maine Lobster Promotion Council, is the easiest way to do it. For more lobster-related info you can check out their website at www.mainelobsterpromo.com.

Twist off the large claws.

Crack each claw and knuckle with a nutcracker, pliers, knife, or rock.

Separate the tail from the body and break off the tail flippers. There's a morsel of meat in each flipper, too.

Insert a fork and push the tail meat out in one piece. Remove and discard the black vein that runs the entire length of the tail meat.

Separate the shell of the body from the underside by pulling them apart and remove and discard the green substance, called the tomalley.

Open the underside of the body by cracking it apart in the middle, with the small walking legs on either side. Lobster meat lies in the four pockets, or joints, where the small walking legs are attached. The walking legs also contain excellent meat that can be removed by biting down on the leg and squeezing the meat out between your teeth.

Maine Office of Tourism, 33 Stone Street, Augusta, ME 04333; (207) 287-5711; www.visit.maine.com

Maine Tourism Association, P.O. Box 2300, Hallowell, ME 04347; (800) 533-9595, 207-623-0363; www.visitmaine.com

Ogunquit Welcome Center, P.O. Box 2289, Ogunquit, ME 03907; (207) 646-5533; www.ogunquit.org

The Best Beaches and Parks

While Maine hugs the coast of the Atlantic, its beaches aren't necessarily what draw families to its shores. Why? For one, the water tends to be quite chilly, except for a few days in late August. Of course, this doesn't preclude visitors from swimming. There are 32,000 miles of rivers and streams throughout the state and also more than a handful of lakes (Moosehead Lake is one of the biggest and most popular) that titillate swimmers with warmer waters. Baxter State Park and Acadia National Park are fabulous for hiking (see the Hiking section in Family Outdoor Adventures).

Southern Coast. Beaches on the southern coast of Maine, mainly Ogunquit, tend to be slightly warmer—but remember, it's all relative to what you're used to. There are two beaches in Acadia National Park, but the water temperature at Sand Beach (one of two lifeguarded beaches in the park) rarely makes it to 55°. At the west side of the island, freshwater Echo Lake Beach tends to be warmer.

Kennebunk/Kennebunkport. The Kennebunk/Kennebunkport area has many beaches. Gooch's Beach on Beach Avenue is a popular strand for families, but there are no lifeguards. To avoid traffic and parking jams, take the Intown Trolley, which stops across the street from Gooch's Beach. A quieter beach, Goose Rocks Beach, can be found on Cape Porpoise, about four miles from Kennebunkport's Dock Square. There is more to Cape Porpoise than beach—there are restaurants and a small dock where you can take in all the action when the fishermen bring home their catch. The beach is great for your youngest ones—the surf is practically nonexistent and the sand is gentle.

Family Outdoor Adventures

Bicycling. Maine's back roads provide easy-does-it bike outings for families. But for serious mountain-biking adventures, you'll want to head for the curvaceous trails of Sugarloaf USA and the Sunday River ski region. When they're not frosted in white during the winter months, the velvety slopes are perfect for family adventures.

If heading to Acadia National Park, a unique way to see the park is by quadracycle—four-wheel bicycles for one or two with gears for each rider and a steering wheel. Kind Cycle will deliver a quadracycle to the Carriage Road (a bicycle path throughout the park with no cars). Four-hour rentals cost $50, and full-day rentals cost $80. Call (207) 288-0444. You can also rent bicycles from Acadia Bike, 48 Cottage Street, Bar Harbor; (800) 526-8615 or (207) 288-9605.

For an overview of the best biking opportunities in the state, call the Maine Bicycle Coalition, (207) 288-3028.

Cruises. Atlantic Seal Cruises, South Freeport, (207) 865-6112. A great way to while away a morning is to visit Eagle Island via a cruise on one of this line's boats. Take the 9:30 a.m. cruise and be sure to bring a picnic along for a late breakfast or early lunch. The three-hour tour will whisk you to the island, where you'll be left to explore and picnic for an hour-and-a-half. The island was once home to Admiral Robert Peary, the first man to reach the North Pole. His house stands as a museum and is worth a brief visit before you set out to hike the trails. Tip: The two-mile Sunset Trail hugs the coast and is pretty at any time of day. Warning: The sea gulls can be fiercely territorial here and have been known to protect their young by harassing visitors. My son can attest to this! Treat: On your way back to the wharf, your captain will stop along the way to haul in some lobster traps. A nice touch, as is the snack of brownies and soda that is served. We didn't spy any seals on our trip, but that's the luck of the draw. Apparently, the cruises that venture out early evening usually have better luck. We did, however, see some osprey.

Cathedral Woods, Monhegan Island, (207) 372-8848. Grab the ferry out of Port Clyde (a 70-minute ride) and be prepared for a slice of heaven on earth. This inland, forest-rich trail is lots of fun for kids and adults—pack a picnic!

Downhill Skiing, Cross-Country Skiing, and Snowboarding. Maine skiing is in a league of its own. You can forget about encountering long lines, and you'll experience the only tree-line-and-up skiing in the East.

Many of New England's biggest ski resorts have been gushed over by the American Skiing Company, a conglomerate that scooped up the resorts several years back and gussied them up. Maine's biggest ski resorts, Sugarloaf/USA and Sunday River, are part of this team. ASC also opened Grand Summit Resort Hotels at five of the six resorts in New England and standardized the ski school programs, so that the programs are similar in scope and philosophy.

Sugarloaf/USA, Carrabassett Valley; (800) THE-LOAF; www.sugarloaf.com. Families love this ski resort, surrounded by Maine's Western Mountains with Maine's second-highest peak at 4,237 feet. Accolades include the only lift-serviced, above-tree line skiing in the East, 45 miles of developed trails, 62 miles of cross-country trails, two SuperQuad lifts, and two high-capacity lifts. Diehard skiers know this mountain—shaped like an ice-cream sundae—for its famous double-black diamond Snowfields.

Families flock to this resort for its kids' programs and self-contained village, including more than 20 restaurants and bars, grocery stores, ski and snowboard shops, a Laundromat, two health clubs, a hair salon, and an art gallery. There are several lodging options, including on-mountain lodging at The Grand Summit Resort Hotel and Conference Center, Sugarloaf Inn, and Sugarloaf/USA condos. There are many bed-and-breakfast inns, motels, and hotels in the surrounding area (for more info, call (800) THE-AREA). The Child Care Center takes babies as young as six weeks (really!), while Sugarloafers age 3 and up can learn to ski with Amos the Moose, Pierre the

Lumberjack, Blueberry the Bigelow Bear, and their buddies in the Perfect Kids clinic. Teens also dig Sugarloaf, especially The Avalanche, the teen hangout at night. Younger kids can also "party" in the Mountain Magic Room. Other hits: turbo tubing under the stars and moonlight and a weekly Family Adventure Supper, where families join other families for dinner.

And then, of course, there's the skiing. There are several levels of ski school—Mountain Magic for kids ages 3–6, where the philosophy is to coach the kids in the same skills as the older children, using games and activities to enhance the learning process. Cost is $59 full day and $44 half day or, without lunch, $56 full day and $41 half day. Kids ages 7–12 participate in Mountain Adventure, where they'll learn skiing and snowboarding for different levels. Kids are grouped according to ability and age. Cost is $47 full day and $35 half day or, without lunch, $44 full day and $32 half day. Mountain Teen is for kids ages 13–18, and the emphasis is on improving their skiing and snowboarding skills and making new friends. This group meets on weekends all season and every day during holiday times. The resort also has a unique program for adults called The Guaranteed Learning Method, a method that uses graduated ski and snowboard lengths and graduated slopes with what they term a Perfect Turn coaching system.

Family Fun Packages are available throughout the season and include things such as lift tickets, equipment rentals, Perfect Kids learning programs, Perfect Turn adult clinic, access to the Sugarloaf/USA Sports & Fitness Club, family music shows, and fireworks.

Sunday River, P.O. Box 450, Bethel, ME 04217; (800) 543-2SKI; www.sundayriver.com. Note: While its address reads Bethel, Sunday River is actually located in the little town of Newry, about six miles north of Bethel. About 60 miles southeast of Sugarloaf, Sunday River is closer for skiers traveling from the south. The resort features 126 trails and glades stretching three miles across a mountain chain in the Mahoosuc Range. Sunday River ski resort is very proud of its trail layout, having won awards for its design and philosophy, which is that advanced skiers can ski right along with less advanced, keeping the family together. Each of Sunday River's eight interconnected mountain peaks has differing trails (according to ability) that skiers can choose from. Another thing this resort has going for it is its slope-side lodging.

Like its main competitor in Maine, Sugarloaf/USA, Sunday River uses a Perfect Turn philosophy in its approach to teaching skiing and snowboarding. And it also employs the Guaranteed Learning Method. And not unlike Sugarloaf, the resort woos families with its tremendous kids' ski programs.

Up for Sail

The ultimate sailing adventure in Maine can be enjoyed on one of The Maine Windjammer Association's fleet of ten traditional sailing ships. Choose from three- to six-day sailing adventures. Each trip guarantees sightings of lighthouses, sea birds, seals, and porpoises. Two of the schooners cater to families with younger children. The *Timberwind* offers family cruises and accepts kids from the ages of 5 and older, while the *Isaac H. Evans* accepts kids from the ages of 8 and up. For more information, call (800) 807-WIND.

Its location, 75 miles north of Portland, makes it easy for families to couple a stay in Portland, Freeport, or other points south.

Hello teens! The Nite Cap Fun Center here features a lighted tubing park, a lighted halfpipe, an ice-skating rink, guided snowshoe tours, and an arcade.

Cross-country skiers will love The Sunday River Inn and Cross Country Center (call (207) 824-2410), located less than a mile from the main entrance to Sunday River; it's got an extensive network of cross-country trails for all skill levels.

There is plenty of slopeside lodging. The Jordan Grand Resort Hotel and Conference Center and the Grand Summit Resort Hotel and Conference Center are full-service hotels. There are also slope-side condos and several inns. For more information about Sunday River, call (800) 543-2SKI or visit www.sundayriver.com.

For the latest ski condition updates at Maine's ski resorts, call (207) 773-SNOW.

Hiking. Let's get serious. Hiking is to Maine what race-car driving is to Daytona Beach, what surfing is to California, and what theatre is to New York. There are a gazillion scenic places to hike in Maine—way too many to include in these pages. Here, though, are some of the best for families.

Acadia National Park has well-marked trails, several of them easygoing. They include: The Jordan Pond Nature Trail, a one-mile (about 30 minutes) self-guided nature walk alongside Jordan Pond, with views of The Bubbles (a pair of rounded mountain peaks). The level of expertise is considered very easy. The trailhead is at the Jordan Pond parking area off Park Loop Road. The Ocean Trail, a rolling footpath with splashy views of the rocky coast, is considered another very easy hike but is three and a half miles and takes about two hours. The trailhead is at the Sand Beach parking area. Bird lovers will want to flock to the Ship Harbor Nature Trail in the Park. This just-over one-mile (approximately 40-minute) self-guided walk takes hikers through spruce forests and Ship Harbor's salt marsh shore. Its level is considered to be easy. The trailhead is at the Ship Harbor parking area off Route 102A. Note: There are also ranger-led hikes throughout Acadia National Park. For more information about hiking in Acadia National Park, call (207) 288-3338.

In the North Woods, Baxter State Park and Mt. Katahdin are also hiker-friendly and great for bird-watching; call (207) 723-5140.

If a waterfall does it for you (and what kid doesn't love a waterfall?), the Poplar Stream Falls just outside the town of Carrabassett has a lovely hike with twin waterfalls. Leave your car at Valley Crossing and take a quick dip in the swimming hole just off the road.

Of course, the Appalachian Trail runs through parts of Maine but is usually traversed by hearty souls with sculpted bodies.

For a selection of hiking maps for state parks, call The Maine Bureau of Parks and Lands at (207) 287-3821.

Rafting. Three of Maine's rivers provide the ultimate setting for whitewater rafting. Unlike most other rivers in the East where water volume peaks only during the spring run-off, Maine's rivers are dam-controlled, providing high-water rafting from late April through mid-October. Two of the rivers—the Kennebec and the Dead—converge at the Forks, a wilderness village about five hours north of Boston. Here is where you'll find most of Maine's rafting companies. The Penobscot River is the largest of the three rivers and flows in the shadow of Mt. Katahdin, the state's highest mountain. Note: Whitewater rafting trips are not for the very young or the faint of heart. For more information about whitewater rafting in Maine call (800) RAFT-MEE.

Calendar of Festivals and Events

May

Maine Maple Sunday An annual springtime celebration of Maine's many sugarhouses, which are open to the public statewide. Call the Maine Department of Agriculture, (207) 287-3291; www.state.me.us/agriculture/marketprod/maple.html.

MooseMania, Moosehead Lake Region A month-long celebration featuring moose safaris, educational exhibits, mountain-bike races, a rowing regatta, a family fun day, and more; (207) 695-2702; www.moosehead.net/moose/chamber.html.

Moose Mania

"Will we see a moose? Will we, will we?" No doubt your kids are aware that Maine is Mooseville and one of the main joys of visiting is to spy one of these Maine mascots. What are the chances of seeing a moose?

Consider this: There are about 3,000 moose in Maine, more than in any other New England state. While moose live throughout the state, the majority of them live in northern and western Maine forests. The best time to see them is from mid-May through July. The best place to see them is along the road. Why? They lick salt from the surface. You might also spy them by a pond where they eat aquatic plants. What is the best time of day to see a moose? You have a chance of a moose sighting at any time of day, but dawn and dusk are the mo st probable times.

June

Windjammer Days Festival An annual (in its 37th year) Down East tradition that celebrates the Boothbay Harbor Region's shipbuilding heritage. Visitors can view windjammers as they sail, fully rigged, into the harbor. Take tours of Navy and Coast Guard vessels, watch waterfront concerts, and more. Boothbay Chamber of Commerce; (207) 633-2353; www. boothbayharbor.com.

July

Yamouth Clam Festival, Yarmouth Annual parade, food booths, entertainment, crafts vendors; 207-846-3984; www.yarmouthmaine.org.

August

Annual Lobster Festival, Harbor Bay, Rockland Celebrate the region's heritage with thousands of pounds of Maine lobster and more than 60,000 lobster lovers. Exhibits, crafts, boat rides, children's activities, and more; (207) 596-0376; www.midcoast.com/~rtacc/.

Annual Maine Festival, Portland Storytellers, comedians, musicians, exhibitors, and lots of food at Thomas Point Beach: (800) 639-4212; www.mainearts.org.

Illumination Night-Ocean Park, Old Orchard Beach The residents of Ocean Park community at Old Orchard Beach light their homes during this annual festival of lights. Strawberry shortcake and band concert are also offered; (207) 934-2500; www.oldorchardbeachmaine.com.

Annual Beach Olympics, Old Orchard Beach Three days of competition, music, and displays to benefit the Maine Special Olympics. On the beach in the square and surrounding areas, Old Orchard Beach; (207) 934-5714; www.oldorchardbeachmaine.com.

Capriccio in Ogunquit Annual ten-day event celebrating the arts with performances in theater, music, story telling, poetry reading, and a performance by the Portland Ballet; (207) 646-6170.

September

Annual Fall Festival, Harbor Park, Camden Eighty-five artists and crafts people show their stuff each October; (207) 236-4404; www.camdenme.org.

Annual "Chowdah" Challenge, Freeport Local chefs compete to win the best chowder award—you're the judge; (800) 865-1994; www.freeportusa.com.

December

Victorian Holiday Horse and Carriage Parade, Portland More than 25 horse-drawn carriages parade throughout downtown as part of holiday festivities; (207) 772-6828; www.portlandmaine.com.

Country Christmas, Bethel Weekend events include wagon rides church fairs, open houses, caroling, Christmas tree lighting, music, children's events, a live nativity scene, and shopping specials; (800) 442-5826; www.bethelmaine.com.

Christmas by the Sea, Camden, Rockport, and Lincolnville Weekend celebration of the holidays with Santa's arrival by a lobster boat, horse-drawn wagon rides, and a holiday house tour; (207) 236-4404; www.camdenme.org.

Annual Freeport's Sparkle Weekend, Freeport A holiday parade, Santa, carolers, horse-drawn carriage rides, a fun run to benefit the Maine Special Olympics, and more; (800) 865-1994; www.freeportusa.com.

Annual Christmas Parade, Kennebunk Events, entertainment, shopping, crafts fairs, and Santa's arrival in a lobster boat; (207) 967-0857.

Annual Harbor Lights Festival, Boothbay Harbor Local artisans display their wares at an all-day Christmas fair. Santa and his elves arrive by boat, the Christmas tree is lit, and a lighted boat parade takes place in Boothbay Harbor; (207) 633-2353; www.boothbayharbor.com.

Annual Christmas-by-the-Sea Festival, Ogunquit Sing-alongs, inn tours, puppet shows, a public supper, live theater, caroling, and the town's legendary chowder-tasting contest; (207) 646-2939; www.ogunquit.org.

New Year's Portland A day-long festival celebrating the new year with live entertainment and midnight fireworks; (800) 639-4214; www.mainearts.org.

The Southern Coast: Kittery to Portland

This is a region of contrasts. You've got **Portland,** Maine's biggest city, with quaint island communities to the west. Upon first visiting Portland, we were surprised to discover that Portland is *really* a city with office buildings and hustle bustle (albeit Maine tempo). It's got a children's museum and art museum, both worth visiting, but we think you're best off staying outside of Portland unless it is a city environment you seek. The sophisticated charm of the **Kennebunks** and **Ogunquit** are mere miles from the frenetic boardwalk of **Old Orchard Beach** (kid and teen heaven) and **Saco,** also known as the Children's Miracle Mile with an outdoor amusement park and waterslides. Shopaholics flock to this region for the boutiques and shops in the six-block historic Old Port Shopping District in Portland—and most definitely to **Kittery** for the mile-long outlet center. This well-rounded region also has more than a handful of beaches, salt marshes, and wilderness preserves—it's all about the Great Outdoors in Maine, no matter where in the state you travel. And you wouldn't want it any other way—Mother Nature pulled out all the stops here. All of the towns we mention are within a 60-mile stretch.

The Kennebunks comprise the adjoining communities of **Kennebunkport, Kennebunk,** and **Kennebunk Beach.** Former President George Bush put this region on the map (he has a home in the pretty harbor town of Kennebunkport), but this curvaceous coastline region doesn't need a presidential endorsement. It's got everything you'd want from a family vacation—quaint villages with outdoor evening band concerts, budget-friendly lobster restaurants, family-friendly accommodations, and beaches. Visitors hoping to get a glimpse of the former president should join the throngs of tourists and park their cars across the inlet from his 11-acre compound, Walker's Point, that juts into the ocean. All the other action here is at Dock Square, Kennebunkport's centerpiece, with shops and art galleries. Dock Square can get quite congested, especially for vehicular traffic, so it's wise to

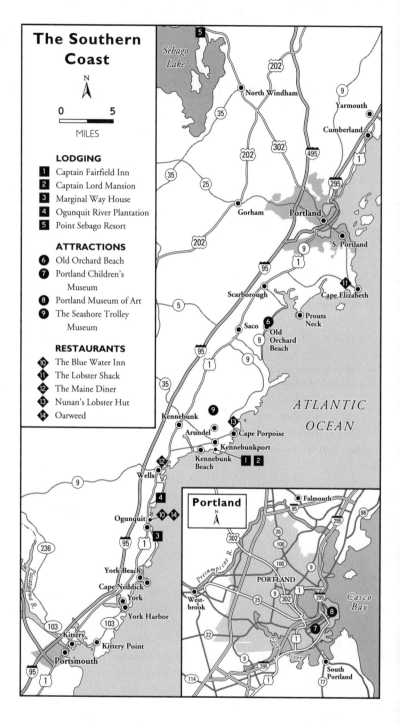

The Southern Coast

N

0   5
MILES

LODGING

1 Captain Fairfield Inn
2 Captain Lord Mansion
3 Marginal Way House
4 Ogunquit River Plantation
5 Point Sebago Resort

ATTRACTIONS

6 Old Orchard Beach
7 Portland Children's
   Museum
8 Portland Museum of Art
9 The Seashore Trolley
   Museum

RESTAURANTS

10 The Blue Water Inn
11 The Lobster Shack
12 The Maine Diner
13 Nunan's Lobster Hut
14 Oarweed

Sebago Lake

North Windham

Yarmouth

Cumberland

202

9

35

302

495

295

25

Gorham

Portland

202

S. Portland

9

1

Scarborough

Cape Elizabeth

5

Prouts Neck

Saco

Old Orchard Beach

9

95

1

9

35

ATLANTIC OCEAN

Kennebunk

9

Arundel

Cape Porpoise

Kennebunkport

Kennebunk Beach

1 2

12

Wells

9

4

Ogunquit

10 14

3

95

1

York Beach

Cape Neddick

York

York Harbor

236

Piscataqua R.

103

103

Kittery

Kittery Point

Portsmouth

95

1

Portland

N

Falmouth

95

295

88

26

302

100

100

9

Presumpscot R.

PORTLAND

1

295

Casco Bay

West-brook

25

302

9

8

7

22

1

Fore River

9

295

South Portland

114

1

77

Inn Style
In Kennebunkport, there are two charming New England inns across the street from one anotheræthe stately **Captain Lord Mansion,** which takes kids age 12 and older, and the lovely **Captain Fairfield Inn,** which takes children age 6 and older. The Captain Fairfield is the smaller of the two and more unassuming; the Captain Lord Mansion is replete with pricey antiques and Chippendale furniture. Both are equally gracious and located within walking distance of the ocean, restaurants, shops and galleries in Kennebunkport. Breakfast is included in the rate in both properties. Double-room rates at both properties begin at about $100 per night in the off-season. Captain Lord Mansion, 6 Pleasant Street; (207) 967-3141. Captain Fairfield Inn, 8 Pleasant Street; (207) 967-4454.

park elsewhere and stroll into and about this very pedestrian-friendly village. One of the most photographed structures in this region is Kennebunk's Wedding Cake House, a whimsically designed yellow-and-white building with Gothic filigree woodwork adorning its façade.

Drive along Ocean Avenue and you'll see the clichéd rocky coast of Maine. You'll spy Goat Island Light, a once-manned lighthouse, and **Cape Porpoise,** one of the Maine's last fishing villages.

Ogunquit has the fabulous three-mile strand known as Ogunquit Beach, where families can while away the entire day enjoying sun, sea, and sand. Marginal Way is a great mile-and-a-quarter-long footpath along rocky cliffs; it spans from the beach's main entrance and **Perkins Cove,** a darling fishing village where you can still watch the fishing and lobstering boats come and go. This has been through the years a magnet for artists, and today there are also several galleries and restaurants.

For a good sidetrip, head inland to **Sebago Lake State Park,** on Maine's second-largest lake. This park is all about swimming, sailing, and boating. Only about 32 miles from downtown Portland, it's got one of the few public beaches on the lake—and there's a lifeguard and plenty of sand to go around. You can camp here and rent boats nearby. It's open from early May through mid-October. Day-use cost is $2.50 adults, 50¢ cents for ages 5–11 years old. It's off US 302 between Naples and South Casco; call (207) 693-6231.

Family Lodging

Marginal Way House

This is an excellent, downscale, old-fashioned inn. There are no phones in the rooms, the beach is an eight-minute walk away, and the lawn and gardens overlook the confluence of ocean and Ogunquit River. You can choose from motel units, guest rooms, or efficiency apartments. Double room rates begin at $100 per night, and it's open from April to October; Wharf Lane, Ogunquit; (207) 363-6566 (winter months), (207) 646-8801 (in-season).

Ogunquit River Plantation

Nature lovers will love the location of this budget-friendly, 80-room hotel overlooking the ocean and river lagoon—it borders the Rachel Carson Wildlife Refuge. Kids love the outdoor heated pool and Jacuzzi. Complimentary breakfast and shuttle to the beach are included in the room rate. Double room rates begin at $125 per night; US 1, Ogunquit; (800) 422-9611.

Point Sebago Resort

The best place to stay while enjoying the Sebago Lake is the Point Sebago Resort, smack on the lake. While the lake is the centerpiece of this sprawling family resort, there are also plenty of other diversions, including miniature golf, volleyball, shuffleboard, cruise boat tours on the *Princess,* fishing, ten tennis courts, water-skiing, canoeing, kayaking, power boat rentals, sailboat rentals . . . phew! This resort plays up its family theme with evening entertainment, including family campfire sing-alongs. Not only is there a supervised kids program, but also there are organized tournaments and activities for adults. Something unique is The Outer Limits Teen Program for kids ages 16–20. Think basketball, dart contests, sailing classes, canoe trips, and a teen dance cruise aboard the *Princess.* Opt to stay in a travel trailer, park home, or a resort cottage. During the summer season, rentals are on a week-to-week basis. Rates for a family of four begin at $665 for a travel trailer and $1,365 for a resort cottage. Rates include all amenities, kids' programs, use of the golf course, tennis, family and adult activities, happy hours, and fishing. Note: There are many packages and rates offered at other times during the year; call for rates and information. RR 1, Box 712, Casco; (207) 655-3821.

Old Orchard Beach

Just 20 minutes from Portland, Old Orchard Beach has more than the name implies. True, there are four miles of sandy beach. But there's also the busy, carnival-like pier, exciting Pirate's Cove Adventure miniature golf course, Palace Playland Amusement park, Funtown Splashtown U.S.A., and festivals galore, including the annual Beach Olympics and the annual Car Show. During the summer, there are free concerts on Monday and Tuesday nights and fireworks every Thursday evening. Just three miles away is Scarborough Marsh, the largest saltwater marsh in Maine; guided canoe trips on the Scarborough River are great family fun.

There are more than 40 restaurants in the Old Orchard Beach region and just as many places to stay. The Clambake at Pine Point is a great family-friendly restaurant with a children's menu and a prime sea gull-feeding location smack on the Scarborough Salt Marsh. This restaurant gets packed, though it has a seating capacity of over 700. The specialty of the house? Lobster! (207) 883-4871.

Campers will especially love Old Orchard Beach. More than 3,065 sites are within one mile of the celebrated seven-mile beach spread out over the campgrounds. Most of Old Orchard Beach's campgrounds are full-service resorts with pools, Jacuzzis, recreation and entertainment centers, miniature golf courses, horseback riding, ballfields, movies, and tennis courts. Many offer shuttle-bus service to the beach. Many of the camping sites are available for overnights, as well as weekly and seasonal rentals. For more information about camping in Old Orchard Beach, call (207) 934-2500.

Attractions

Portland Children's Museum

142 Free Street, Portland; (207) 828-1234

Hours: Labor Day–Memorial Day, Wednesday–Saturday 10 a.m.–5 p.m., Sunday noon–5 p.m.; Memorial Day–Labor Day, Monday–Saturday 10 a.m.–5 p.m., Sunday noon–5 p.m.

Admission: $5; first Friday of each month is free

Shop 'Til You Plop

Calling all shopaholics! If you'll be driving from the south (and most of us do considering Maine is as north as you can get on the East Coast), the first town you'll come to is Kittery (a pine cone's throw from Portsmouth, New Hampshire). This historic shipbuilding city is better known today for its more than 120 outlet stores spread out in 13 malls (call (888) KITTERY; or visit www.thekitteryoutlets.com.) However, if you're going to hit just one shopping destination while visiting Maine, skip the Kittery outlets and head farther north to the Cadillac of shopping outlets in downtown Freeport (just about an hour away). Thrifty shoppers will want to head to New Hampshire, where there is no sales tax; there is five percent sales tax in Maine.

Appeal by Age Groups:

Pre-school	Grade School	Teens	Young Adults	Over 30	Seniors
★★★	★★★★				

Touring Time: Average 2 hours; minimum 1 hour

Rainy-Day Touring: Yes

Services and Facilities:

Restaurants Concessions	Lockers No
Alcoholic beverages No	Pet kennels No
Disabled access Yes	Rain check No
Wheelchair rental No	Private tours No
Baby stroller rental No	

Descriptions and Comments   The Portland Children's Museum has more than 25 exhibits that give kids the opportunity to be kids in a safe, fun environment. Let them loose, and they'll dress up as firefighters, explore an underwater submarine, and shop in a pseudo supermarket. The Explore Floor is super for older kids—it's like a science lab where kids can check out the ocean bottom, the treetops in a Maine forest, find constellations in the night sky, even listen to the heartbeat of a life-sized black bear slumbering in his den. This is also a very toddler-friendly museum with opportunities for them to tumble in a soft play area.

Sweet Diversions

When it rains or when you're just tired of the beach, head to The Shell Emporium at York Beach near Ogunquit for great souvenir shopping, then stop for ice cream at Shain's of Maine. In Ogunquit, slip into The Harbor Candy Shop on Main Street for some of the best fudge and candy around.

Portland Museum of Art

7 Congress Square, Portland; (207) 775-6148

Hours: Summer, Saturday–Wednesday 10 a.m.–5 p.m., Thursday and Friday 10 a.m.–9 p.m.; off–season Tuesday–Sunday 10 a.m.–5 p.m.

Admission: $6, $5 seniors and students (with ID), $1 children ages 6–12, free for kids ages 6 and under

Appeal by Age Groups:

Pre-school	Grade School	Teens	Young Adults	Over 30	Seniors
★	★★★	★★★★	★★★★	★★★★	★★★★

Touring Time: Average 2 hours; minimum 1 hour

Rainy-Day Touring: Yes

Services and Facilities:

Restaurants	Yes	Lockers	No
Alcoholic beverages	No	Pet kennels	No
Disabled access	Yes	Rain check	No
Wheelchair rental	Yes	Private tours	No
Baby stroller rental	Yes		

Description and Comments   Maine's largest museum is home to works by Winslow Homer and Andrew Wyeth. This museum will bore the young ones but is a great spot to visit for teens and adults. It's located right next door to the Portland Children's Museum, so if you really want to visit this art museum might we suggest you tell the kids that if they behave in the art museum they'll be rewarded with a fun visit to the Children's Museum. Bribery isn't always bad!

White Barn Inn

I held my breath when we first sat down to eat in this rustic yet sophisticated barn. This is the kind of place where that big question is often popped! I wondered if my son (seven at the time) would behave in such a romantic setting? Bring a stash of goodies—a new book, a book of puzzles and mazes—to keep school-age kids busy, and you'll be glad you opted to eat here. Still, it's not the place to dine with babies, toddlers, and preschoolers. This is a celebratory kind of place, not a place to dine if you're on a budget. Just a short drive from the Kennebunkport's main drag, you can also stay at the inn, but keep the kids away from the honeymoon cottage out back—better yet, why not revisit sans children to celebrate an anniversary? Beach Avenue, about a quarter-mile down the road from the junction of Routes 9 and 35; (207) 967-2321. This is the spot to go for a really special birthday. It's not your typical family-friendly restaurant, but it can be and should be, especially if you've got teens—they'll feel grown up.

The Seashore Trolley Museum

195 Log Cabin Road, Kennebunkport; (207) 967-2800

Hours: May and last week of October, weekends 10 a.m.–5 p.m.; June–mid-October, daily 10 a.m.–5 p.m. (closes at 6 p.m. in July and August); ice cream and sunset rides offered in July and August; call for schedule

Admission: $7 adults, $4.50 children ages 6–16; free for ages 5 and under; $2.50 for ice cream and sunset rides; senior rates available

Appeal by Age Groups:

Pre-school	Grade School	Teens	Young Adults	Over 30	Seniors
★★★	★★★★	★★	★★	★★	★★

Touring Time: Average 1½ hours; minimum ½ hour (depends on whether you take trolley ride)

Rainy-Day Touring: Yes

Services and Facilities:

Restaurants Yes	Wheelchair rental No
Alcoholic beverages No	Baby stroller rental No
Disabled access Limited on rides	

Portland Public Market

The market has something for everyone—literally. This is the place for families with diverse tastes. Stroll this indoor market and choose from Maine cheeses, fresh lobster and crab, crusty breads, and even such delicacies as elk sausage and buffalo meat. Skip the small restaurant in the back (although if it's a nice day there are tables outside; pass on the sludgy lobster bisque, though). After you've made your selections, head upstairs for seating. This is a particularly great spot for rainy-day dining and shopping. There are several vendors selling unique-to-Maine items such as blueberry jams. If it's a nice day, why not stop here to create the ultimate picnic and then head to Cape Elizabeth (about 20 minutes over the bridge) for a picnic by the sea. Market hours are Monday through Saturday 9 a.m. to 7 p.m. and Sunday 10 a.m. to 5 p.m. The Portland Public Market is located at 25 Preble Street; (207) 228-2000. There's free indoor parking in the Public Market Garage.

Lockers No

Pet kennels No

Rain check No

Private tours No

Description and Comments   With 250 streetcars, this museum has the oldest and largest antique streetcar collection in the world. The best part of a visit to this museum is the ride on one of the old-fashioned streetcars.

Family-Friendly Restaurants

THE BLUE WATER INN

On the Main Beach, Ogunquit; (207) 646-5559

Meals served: Breakfast, lunch, and dinner

Cuisine: Seafood

Entree range: $10 and up

Children's menu: Yes

Reservations: No

Payment: All types accepted

A nice surprise for lunch right off the beach, with a dining deck (and heated patio) that overlooks the Ogunquit River. The seafood is great, but fresh salads and wraps provide a nice respite from seafood or hamburgers and fries.

THE LOBSTER SHACK

225 Two Lights Road, Cape Elizabeth; (207) 799-1677

Meals served: Lunch and dinner
Cuisine: Seafood
Entree range: $10 and up
Children's menu: No
Reservations: No
Payment: Credit cards not accepted

For one of the most family-friendly restaurants in the Portland area (with a killer location), take the 20-minute drive over the bridge to Two Lights at Cape Elizabeth. Make time to first visit the very photogenic Portland Head Light, Maine's oldest lighthouse, (just off Cape Elizabeth's Shore Road) before heading the short distance to The Lobster Shack. With an ocean setting (not many great restaurants can claim they are right on a beach), this small, unpretentious "shack" packs 'em in. You can eat in or take out.

THE MAINE DINER

US 1 N., Wells (just before Route 9 on the way to Kennebunkport);
    (207) 646-4441

Meals served: Breakfast, lunch, and dinner
Cuisine: Seafood
Entree range: $4.95 and up
Children's menu: No
Reservations: No
Payment: All types accepted
Open: Daily 7 a.m. to 9:30 p.m.

This homespun diner has the best fried belly clams around, swears my New York neighbor who visits Ogunquit and the region every summer. The diner also has great seafood chowder, lobster pie, and blueberry pancakes. Check out the gift shop, Remember the Maine, next door.

NUNAN'S LOBSTER HUT

50 Mills Road, Route 9, Cape Porpoise; (207) 967-4362

Meals served: Seafood
Entree range: $7.95 and up
Children's menu: Yes
Reservations: No
Payment: All types accepted

A hut it is, but it's got some of the best seafood around—and it won't cramp your budget. If lobster and steamers don't get the kids excited, the homemade pies will.

OARWEED

Perkins Cove, Ogunquit; (207) 646-4022

Meals served: Lunch and dinner
Cuisine: Seafood
Entree range: $8.95 and up
Children's menu: Yes
Reservations: No
Payment: All types accepted

If you crave an ocean view while dining on lobster, clams, and chowder, this is a great spot. You'll get high-quality seafood—no fried foods—at reasonable prices. Order the scallops—they're succulent. Caveat: The wait can be long, but it's worth it.

The Mid-Coast: Freeport to the Pemaquid Peninsula

Families visiting this region of Maine are compelled to visit **Freeport,** thanks to its shopping possibilities. **L.L. Bean's** Freeport headquarters is a destination in itself. The store is open around the clock, every day of the year. The kids' store is a separate building replete with a waterfall, a rock-climbing wall, and stationary mountain bikes. But you shouldn't consider Freeport a place only to shop while passing on through to other destinations. In fact, we recommend you base yourselves in the Freeport region and use this centrally located town as a springboard to explore northern and southern points, such as Portland and Old Orchard Beach to the south (within an hour's drive tops) and Camden, Boothbay and Rockport to the north (about an hour drive). And you can explore some of the small islands off Freeport, including **Eagle Island,** where Admiral Robert E. Peary, the first man to reach the North Pole, summered. You can also raft the Kennebee River. Note: As we mentioned in the introduction to Maine, there are few attractions in the state—it's best to enjoy the Great Outdoors.

Family Lodging

The Harrasekeet Inn

Just a credit-card's throw away from the outlets in downtown Freeport, this family-hospitable inn has been in the same family for generations. Chip Grey, current owner, is master of his domain. Many families end up spending their days exploring parts of Freeport and its environs with Chip as their fearless leader. His enthusiasm for Maine is contagious, his admiration for it a joy to behold. A father himself, he knows what makes kids tick, and he is a great source of insider Maine information. Double-room rates begin at $100 per night in the off-season and $175 during peak times, including a bountiful buffet breakfast. 162 Main Street, Freeport; (800) 342-6423.

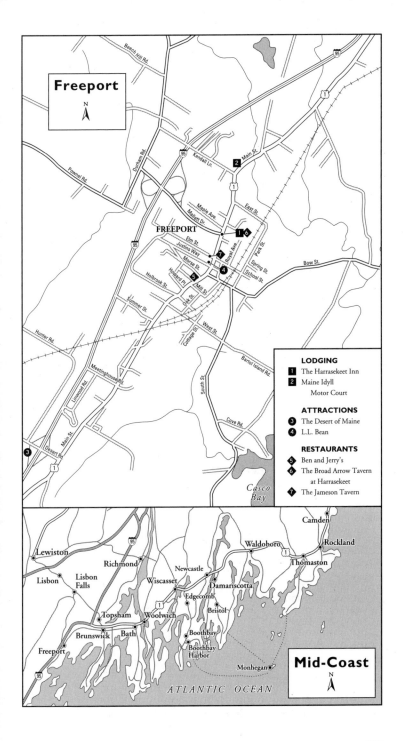

Freeport

N

FREEPORT

LODGING
1 The Harrasekeet Inn
2 Maine Idyll
   Motor Court

ATTRACTIONS
3 The Desert of Maine
4 L.L. Bean

RESTAURANTS
5 Ben and Jerry's
6 The Broad Arrow Tavern
   at Harrasekeet
7 The Jameson Tavern

Mid-Coast

N

Monhegan Island

This is the island of artists. For more than a century, painters, including Edward Hopper, Rockwell Kent, and Andrew Wyeth, have been attracted to this sliver of civility for the way the sun shines upon it, as well as its moody cliffs, tumultuous ocean, and fields of lupine. Kids are also drawn to it for its miles and miles of trails, especially the evergreen-rich Cathedral Woods trail. Kids are naturally drawn to the rocky cliffs on the backside of the island (which will make nervous parents appreciate the inland trails at Cathedral Woods).

Monhegan is picnic heaven. If you'll be visiting the island for a day trip only, you can pick up some yummy sandwiches at the Port Clyde General Store before you board the ferry over to the island. The Port Clyde dock is the preferred ferry departure spot, but you can also ferry over from Boothbay Harbor and New Harbor. There is one general store on the island that makes sandwiches. Other kid-friendly diversions include a perfect lighthouse and great bird-watching. For budding Wyeths, some of the working artists' studios encourage visitors to stumble in.

To get to the island you can take the *Laura B* mail boat (with parcels and letters) or the more passenger-friendly ferry (albeit not as adventurous) *Elizabeth Ann*. No cars are allowed on the island (you can park near the dock for less than $5 a day). You'll need to make ferry reservations during busy summer months (call (207) 372-8848 or log onto www.monheganboat.com). The ferry ride is one hour. Note: While there are two nice places to stay on the island, you should know that you might need to share bathrooms with other guests (think: dormitory). This arrangement is not for everyone, but others love it. If you fall into the latter category, the resorts are The Monhegan House (call (800) 599-7983) and the Island Inn (call (800) 533-9595). At the Island Inn, some of the guest rooms have private bathrooms. Both are open from mid-May to mid-October. There is very little electricity on the island. The hotels run on generators, and you must have a flashlight to get around at night.

Maine Idyll Motor Court

You get a lot of bang for your buck at this attractively priced year-round cottage motel. There aren't a lot of frills, unless you consider a television set a frill. No phones, no credit cards accepted—this is a real back-to-basics prop-

---

Full Moon Sundae

What is the perfect way to end a perfect day? We decided it would be to take the ten-minute stroll from our room at The Harraseeket to the nearest Ben & Jerry's store (a cherry's throw from the L.L. Bean store) for triple-scoop hot fudge sundaes. Hey, this is New England, home of Ben & Jerry's. Bonus: The moon was full and gorgeous—a memorable sight we never would have seen had we not had a hankering for Ben & Jerry's.

---

erty for families on a tight budget. Unfortunately, I-95 is within honking distance. If, when you think of Maine, you think of a small cottage, a woodburning fireplace, and a porch, this is the place for you. Double-room rates begin at $44 per night. 325 Route 1, Freeport; (207) 865-4201.

Attractions

The Desert of Maine

95 Desert Road, Freeport; (207) 865-6962

Hours: Early May to mid-October, daily 9 a.m.–dusk.

Admission: $6.50 adults, $4.50 ages 14–16, $3.50 ages 6–12

Appeal by Age Groups:

Pre-school	Grade School	Teens	Young Adults	Over 30	Seniors
★★	★★★	★	★	★	★

Touring Time: Average 1 hour; minimum 1 hour

Rainy-Day Touring: Yes

Services and Facilities:

Restaurants No	Lockers No
Alcoholic beverages No	Pet kennels No
Disabled access No	Rain check No
Wheelchair rental No	Private tours Yes
Baby stroller rental No	

Description and Comments There's a lot of hype surrounding this attraction—much of it undeserved. Still, visitors to the Freeport region feel compelled to visit—just to make sense of the concept of a desert in Maine. You'll take a guided tram ride during which there is way too much information offered—but can spend time exploring nature trails on your own if the mood strikes you. Your best bet is gemstone hunting—kids run through a couple of "dunes" hunting for gems. My son loved this.

Family-Friendly Restaurants

THE BROAD ARROW TAVERN AT HARRASEEKET

162 Main Street, Freeport; (800) 342-6423

Meals served: Pizza, pasta, seafood
Entree range: $10 and up
Children's menu: Yes
Reservations: Yes
Payment: All types accepted

Order a cup of milky, buttery, chunky lobster stew, and you'll consider your vacation to Maine complete. It is perfection, as are most of the items on the menu here. The children's menu features the usual kid-friendly items such as chicken fingers. An open kitchen shows off the chef's culinary skills. The ambiance is family-friendly—we sat beneath a stuffed moose's head and the Red Sox game was playing on the bar TV in the distance. Don't miss a meal here.

THE JAMESON TAVERN

115 Main Street, Freeport; (207) 865-4195

Meals served: Lunch and dinner
Entree range: $10 and up
Children's menu: Yes
Reservations: Yes
Payment: All types accepted

Definitely try to get a table on the patio, and you'll enjoy a delicious lunch as well as be in the thick of all the L.L. Bean shopping frenzy (the store is right across the street). You'll know many of your fellow diners by name, as they'll be wearing nametags. Why? This spot is a favorite of the many tour bus groups that descend on L.L. Bean and the other outlet shops. But don't let that be a turnoff—the friendly service and pretty patio make for a relaxing lunch. Croissant sandwiches and burgers are served in the Tap Room and outside on the lovely patio. In the dining room, things are turned up a notch with such entrees as filet mignon. For families, your best bet is the Tap Room, or better yet, the patio in nice weather.

The Downeast Region: Mount Desert Island, Acadia National Park, and Bar Harbor

Many visitors come to Maine for just one thing—glorious **Acadia National Park.** One of Mother Nature's best efforts, Acadia comprises 41,000 acres of rocky coast on **Mount Desert Island,** a portion of the **Schoodic Peninsula** on the mainland, and darling offshore islands, including the **Porcupine Islands** and **Isle au Haut.** Meadows, marshes, deep valleys, expansive lakes, and the chilly Atlantic Ocean make Acadia an outdoor paradise. Thanks to glaciers that carved through an east-west ridge of granite, leaving mountains separated by vast valleys, Acadia is also home to the only fjord located on the eastern seaboard of the United States—Somes Sound.

You could easily spend a week exploring and enjoying all this glorious park has to offer. Think hiking, biking, swimming, camping, junior ranger programs, and more. The busy but pretty town of **Bar Harbor** is located on the eastern part of Mount Desert Island. It's the populated, commercial area, with many restaurants and shops for the tourists who frequent the area. This coastal town is a perfect base for families visiting Acadia National Park. The park's entrance is about a mile from Bar Harbor. Isle au Haut, accessible by ferry, is a superb place to camp.

Family Lodging

Acadia Hotel

This budget-friendly, ten-room hotel is in downtown Bar Harbor. The rooms and ambience are more reminiscent of an inn than a hotel. You can hang out on the pretty porch and balcony that overlooks the Village Green. Double-room rates begin at $45 per night; you can also get a breakfast plan (call for details). 20 Mt. Desert Street, Bar Harbor; (207) 288-5721.

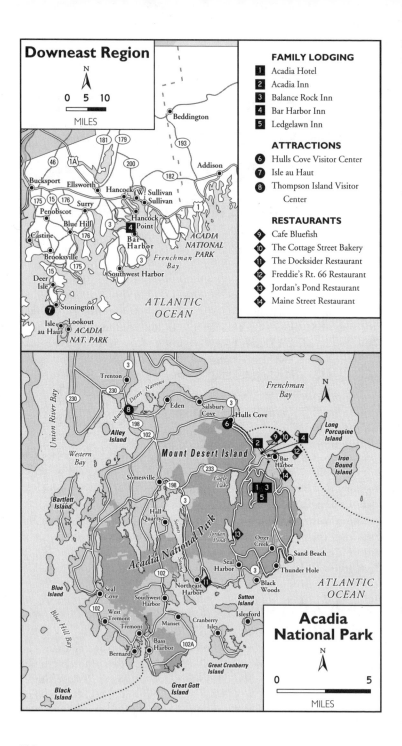

Downeast Region

N

0   5   10
MILES

FAMILY LODGING

1 Acadia Hotel
2 Acadia Inn
3 Balance Rock Inn
4 Bar Harbor Inn
5 Ledgelawn Inn

ATTRACTIONS

6 Hulls Cove Visitor Center
7 Isle au Haut
8 Thompson Island Visitor Center

RESTAURANTS

9 Cafe Bluefish
10 The Cottage Street Bakery
11 The Docksider Restaurant
12 Freddie's Rt. 66 Restaurant
13 Jordan's Pond Restaurant
14 Maine Street Restaurant

Acadia National Park

N

0   5
MILES

Camping at Isle au Haut

Located in Acadia National Park, this darling island is the place to camp because you'll get the Maine coast and the Maine woods at the same time. Cost is $25 per site for up to six people. It's open May 15 (bring your woolliest blankets) to October 15 (ditto). Reservations are taken by mail beginning the first of April. Write to Acadia National Park, Attn: Isle au Haut Reservations, P.O. Box 177, Bar Harbor, ME 04609. For more info call (207) 288-3338. Bonus: Getting there really is half the fun—take the mail boat from Stonington, a fishing village. Call Isle au Haut Ferry Service, (207) 367-5193. Cost is $24 round trip.

Acadia Inn

This 95-room hotel is family friendly and budget friendly with such amenities as complimentary continental breakfast, a heated outdoor pool and Jacuzzi, and a guest laundry room. It is one mile from downtown and one and a half miles from Acadia National Park. There are value packages that include meals and activities (harbor cruises and national park tours); call for more information. Double-room rates begin at $53 per night. 98 Eden Street, Route 3, Bar Harbor; (800) 638-3636.

Balance Rock Inn

A sister property to Ledgelawn (see subsequent entry), the Balance Rock is a notch up on the romance and amenity scale, but it's also family-friendly with a beautiful pool. Its off-the-beaten-path location on the bay can't be beat, and it's a mere two-minute walk into town. Aptly named for a rock that seems to balance on one point in the sea, this inn has accommodations with kitchens that are perfect for families. The generous, complimentary, buffet breakfast can be enjoyed outside on the patio or in the small dining room. This is one of those rare properties that parents will love just as much as the children. Double-room rates begin at $100 per night. Call (800) 753-0494.

Bar Harbor Inn

If you want action, a full-service resort, and a central location right in the center of town, this is the spot. But take note: This is not a quiet place to stay, as Bar Harbor can get quite crowded during peak season. Breakfast is included, and many of the rooms have ocean views and balconies. The outdoor heated pool and Jacuzzi are a hit with the kids. It's open April

---

Boxed In

Grab a boxed lunch to go and head for the ultimate picnic in Acadia National Park. The Cottage Street Bakery in Bar Harbor has yummy sandwiches and wraps such as pastrami, turkey, liverwurst, and lobster rolls. 59 Cottage Street, Bar Harbor; (207) 288-3010.

---

through December. Double-room rates begin at $139 per night. Newport Drive, Bar Harbor; (800) 248-3351.

Ledgelawn Inn

The Ledgelawn is a grand summer mansion that's very family-gracious with a pool and Jacuzzi and affordable fall and summer packages. It's only a short, five-minute walk from the center of town. Stay here for New England hospitality instead of a motel-type experience. A lounge and wine bar will make adults happy. Double-room rates begin at $55 per night. 66 Mount Desert Street, Bar Harbor; (800) 274-5334.

Attractions

Diversions and activities in this neck of the Maine woods are not the manmade kind. Instead, you'll spend your days exploring Acadia (see Biking and Hiking in Family Outdoor Adventures on page 83).

Thunder Hole is one of Acadia National Park's most popular attractions. When the wind blows hard (as it often does), the water surges into the chasm, compressing and trapping the air and causing a resounding boom. When the wind barely blows, the boom is barely audible. Note: Thunder Hole isn't always open. The day we visited, Thunder Hole was closed because of a hurricane brewing in the Atlantic. It was considered dangerous, even though the storm was way to the south off the coast of Florida. There are two visitor centers in Acadia: Hulls Cove Visitor Center (call (207) 288-3338) and the Thompson Island Visitor Center (call (207) 288-3411). Both are on Route 3, about seven and a half miles apart.

If you're in Bar Harbor on a rainy day, The Criterion Theater on Cottage Street (call (207) 288-5829) is where you'll want to hang your umbrella. It's a true art-deco find. Come early and get a seat in the Loge section, with velvet curtains. Kids' movies are shown often.

Family-Friendly Restaurants

CAFE BLUEFISH

122 Cottage Street, Bar Harbor; (207) 288-3696

Meals served: Dinner
Cuisine: Seafood and vegetarian
Entree range: $8.95 and up
Children's menu: No
Reservations: Yes
Payment: All types accepted

With an eclectic decor and fabulous, award-winning vegetarian dishes—and just as tremendous fish dishes—this is a popular Bar Harbor eatery. While there is not a bona fide children's menu, the chef will prepare children's portions or cook pasta for the children if the restaurant isn't too busy. Don't count on special treatment in the summer, though, when this place gets really crowded.

THE DOCKSIDER RESTAURANT

14 Sea Street, Northeast Harbor; (207) 276-3965

Meals served: Lunch and dinner
Cuisine: Seafood
Entree range: $6.95 and up
Children's menu: Yes
Reservations: Yes
Payment: All types accepted

A short-drive from Bar Harbor (ten minutes), the Docksider is well worth the effort. The food is consistently good, and the harbor location is lovely. Early bird specials (ten percent off menu prices) are from 4:30 to 6 p.m.

FREDDIE'S RT. 66 RESTAURANT

21 Cottage Street, Bar Harbor; (207) 288-3708

Meals served: Lunch and dinner
Cuisine: Mexican, seafood, vegetarian, Italian
Entree range: $6.95 and up

Children's menu: Yes
Reservations: No
Payment: All types accepted

Picky eaters rejoice! You can get anything here—clam chowder, nachos, vegetarian lasagna, a hot turkey dinner, and, yes, lobster. Freddie's is reasonably priced and smack in the middle of town.

JORDAN'S POND RESTAURANT

Acadia National Park; (207) 276-3316

Meals served: Lunch, dinner, and afternoon tea
Cuisine: Sandwiches, chowder, popovers
Entree range: $11 and up
Children's menu: No
Reservations: Yes
Payment: All types accepted

Nestled in Acadia National Park on Park Loop Road, this is the place to park your bikes (a carriage road runs right behind this restaurant) and enjoy a lobster roll. Or, visit later in the afternoon for the restaurant's signature item—popovers. Served piping hot with fresh jam, a couple of these will tide the little ones over until dinner and fuel them for some more biking. Opt to sit outside, if you can, at one of the picnic tables that overlook Jordan Pond and "the bubbles," but note that many tables are not in the shade. If there's a wait for a table, and there very well may be, visit the shop located next to the restaurant and pick up a couple of bags of the popover mix. They make great gifts for the folks back home.

MAINE STREET RESTAURANT

297 Main Street, Bar Harbor; (207) 288-3040

Meals served: Lunch and dinner
Cuisine: Seafood, American fare
Entree range: $6.95 and up
Children's menu: Yes
Reservations: No
Payment: All types accepted

Sit inside or better yet park yourselves on the outdoor self-service deck for fried seafood and sandwiches. Locals and tourists alike love this place for its consistently good lobster, clam chowder, pot roast, chicken, and sandwiches. Early bird specials are offered from 1 to 6 p.m.

Part Three

Massachusetts

The most popular of the New England states, Massachusetts woos families with its bounty of beaches, mountains, lakes, and, of course, **Boston,** the heart of the state—and of New England. All this is crammed into one of the smallest states in the country.

You can easily combine a visit to Boston with day or overnight trips to the worth-visiting spots north of town **(Salem, Rockport, Gloucester),** south of town **(Plymouth),** or west **(Lexington** and **Concord).** In fact, part of the beauty of this Brahmin town is that it's compact enough to enjoy over the span of a few days. But you could also spend much more time in this city, if you have that luxury.

Take note: Massachusetts, known as the Bay State, is perhaps the most seasonal of the New England states, especially when considering **Cape Cod, Nantucket,** and **Martha's Vineyard.** These havens for summer fun practically hibernate for winter. Beach towns like Gloucester and Rockport also come alive in the summer. Boston is not a seasonal destination, unless you consider the student season, September through May, when the population swells by a quarter of a million, thanks to the wealth of academic institutions, including Harvard, MIT, Boston University, and Boston College. Plymouth enjoys its biggest burst of tourism at Thanksgiving, when families travel here to make their children's textbooks come alive. **Salem,** home of the Salem Witch Museum and the Witch Dungeon Museum, certainly enjoys its biggest rush of visitors in October, with events such as Haunted Happenings that take place all month and peak at Halloween. The **Berkshires** are uniquely a summer, fall, and winter destination, with challenging skiing when the mountains are frosted with snow, incredible leaf-peeping when the trees explode with color in the fall, and a brilliant summer-long outdoor musical event called Tanglewood. **Sturbridge Village** is another appealing day-trip destination.

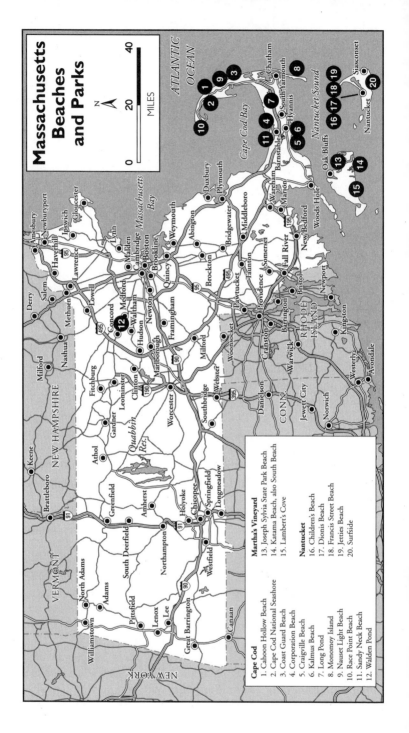

Massachusetts Beaches and Parks

Cape Cod
1. Cahoon Hollow Beach
2. Cape Cod National Seashore
3. Coast Guard Beach
4. Corporation Beach
5. Craigville Beach
6. Kalmus Beach
7. Long Pond
8. Monomoy Island
9. Nauset Light Beach
10. Race Point Beach
11. Sandy Neck Beach
12. Walden Pond

Martha's Vineyard
13. Joseph Sylvia State Park Beach
14. Katama Beach, also South Beach
15. Lambert's Cove

Nantucket
16. Children's Beach
17. Dionis Beach
18. Francis Street Beach
19. Jetties Beach
20. Surfside

GETTING THERE

By Car. To get to Boston from the south, take I-95 to I-90 (also known as the Mass Pike). Interstate 93 will take you from Boston north to New Hampshire. Caveat: The Big Dig is underway, an ambitious, messy project to turn the part of I-93 that runs through the city into an underground highway. This project is expected to take many years, so expect delays.

To get to Cape Cod from Boston (about an hour drive), take I-93 south to Route 3 south and cross the Sagamore Bridge, which turns into Route 6. To get to the Cape from northeastern New York, western Massachusetts, and northern Connecticut, take I-84 east to I-90 (the Mass Pike) to I-495 south and east to the Bourne Bridge. Traveling from the south (New York City), take I-95 north to Providence, Rhode Island, to I-195 east (the small sign reads "Cape Cod and the Islands") to the Bourne Bridge.

Massachusetts is fully accessible by car, but be forewarned that traffic can be tough going in some spots, notably on summer weekends. Don't even think of driving in Boston; pahk your cah and plan to foot it. Bostonians love to escape to the Cape on summer weekends—all the better reason why you shouldn't. Plan to arrive on the Cape any time other than late Friday afternoon and evening.

By Plane. Logan International Airport, (800) 23-LOGAN, three miles from downtown Boston, is accessible by public transportation, taxi, water shuttle, and limousine services. A free MASSPORT shuttle bus stops at each airline terminal, the rapid-transit station (T), and the water shuttle dock. Albany County Airport services the Berkshires; (518) 242-2200. Barnstable Airport in Hyannis services Cape Cod, (508) 775-2020, as does Provincetown Municipal Airport in Provincetown; (508) 487-0241. Bradley International Airport in Windsor Locks, Connecticut, serves Greater Springfield, Franklin County, and the Berkshires; (888) 623-1533. T.F. Green Airport in Warwick, Rhode Island, serves southeastern Massachusetts; (401) 737-8222. Martha's Vineyard Airport in West Tisbury serves the island of Martha's Vineyard; (508) 693-7022. Nantucket Memorial Airport serves Nantucket Island; (508) 325-5300. Other airports include New Bedford Regional Airport in New Bedford, (508) 991-6160, and Worcester Regional Airport in Worcester, (508) 799-1741.

Tip. One of the fastest, easiest and more interesting ways to get into town from the airport is to take the airport water shuttle that makes the trip from the airport across Boston Harbor into Boston's Rowes Harbor in seven minutes. You can grab a free shuttle bus between the ferry dock at the airport and the terminals. Fares are $10 for adults, $5 for seniors, and free for ages 12 and under. You can buy tickets on the boat; (800) 23-LOGAN.

State Symbols

- State nicknames: Bay State, the Puritan State, the Baked Bean State

- State folk hero: Johnny Appleseed (real name: John Chapman)

- State dog: Boston Terrier, a cross between an English bulldog and an English terrier; the first purebred dog developed in America in 1869

- State cat: Tabby cat, in response to the wishes of Massachusetts schoolchildren in 1988

- State bird: Black-capped chickadee, a.k.a. the titmouse

- State game bird: Wild turkey, eaten at the first Thanksgiving

- State fish: Cod

- State insect: Ladybug

- State fossil: Dinosaur tracks, which were made over 200 million years ago in this area

- State flower: Mayflower, a.k.a. ground laurel

- State tree: American elm, to commemorate the fact that General George Washington took command of the Continental Army beneath one on Cambridge Common in 1775

- State drink: Cranberry juice (the Massachusetts cranberry industry grows the largest crop in the world)

- State muffin: Corn muffin

- State dessert: Boston cream pie

- State cookie: Chocolate chip cookie, invented in 1930 at the Toll House Restaurant in Whitman

By Train. Amtrak's Northeast Corridor trains provides service to Boston (South Station and Back Bay Station), Worcester, Amherst, Springfield, and Pittsfield; (800) USA-RAIL.

By Ferry. (Note: Only the Steamship Authority transports vehicles). To get to Cape Cod: from Boston to Provincetown, Bay State Cruise Company, (617) 457-1428; from Gloucester to Provincetown, Gloucester to Provincetown Boat Express, (800) 877-5110; from Plymouth to Provincetown, Cape Cod Cruises, (800) 242-2469.

To Martha's Vineyard: from Woods Hole, Cape Cod to Vineyard Haven (year-round), Steamship Authority, (508) 477-8600; from Woods Hole to Oak Bluffs, Steamship Authority, (508) 477-8600; from Hyannis, Cape Cod to Oak Bluffs, Hy-Line, (508) 778-2600; from Falmouth, Cape Cod to Edgartown, Falmouth-Edgartown Ferry, (508) 548-9400; from Falmouth to Oak Bluffs, Island Queen, (508) 548-4800; from Onset, Cape Cod to Vineyard Haven, Sea Comm Transport, (888) 335-1448; from Nantucket to Oak Bluffs, Hy-Line, (508) 778-2600; from New Bedford to Vineyard Haven, Cape Island Express, (508) 997-1688; from New London, Connecticut, to Vineyard Haven, Fox Navigation, (888) SAIL-FOX.

To Nantucket Island (all ferries arrive and depart from Nantucket Harbor): from Hyannis, Cape Cod, Steamship Authority, (508) 477-8717 (year-round); from Hyannis, (high-speed catamaran, year-round), Hy-Line, (508) 778-0404; from Hyannis (high-speed catamaran), Steamship Authority (passengers only), (508) 495-FAST; from Hyannis, Hy-Line, (508) 778-2600; from Oak Bluffs, Martha's Vineyard, Hy-Line, (508) 778-2600; from Harwich Port, Cape Cod, Freedom Cruise Line, (508) 432-8999; from Gloucester, The Yankee Fleet, (800) WHALING.

A super way to reach Martha's Vineyard from New York environs (namely Long Island) is via Fox Navigation's ferry from Glen Cove (on Long Island's North Shore about 25 miles from New York City) with a stop in New London and then onward to Martha's Vineyard's Vineyard Haven. This is a passenger ferry only, but you do not need a car to get around the Vineyard and this is a quick (four hours) trip. Kids will see that getting there really is half the fun. Call (888) SAIL-FOX.

HOW TO GET INFORMATION BEFORE YOU GO

Bristol County Convention and Visitors Bureau, 70 N. Second Street, P.O. Box 976, New Bedford, MA 02741; (800) 288-6263; www.bristol-county.org.

Cape Ann Chamber of Commerce, 33 Commercial Street, Gloucester, MA 01930; (800) 321-0133. www.capeannvacations.com.

Cape Cod Chamber of Commerce, Hyannis, MA 02601, (888) CAPECOD; www.capecodchamber.org.

Central Massachusetts Tourist Council, 33 Waldo Street, Worcester, MA 01608; (800) 231-7557; www.worcester.org.

Franklin County Chamber of Commerce, 395 Main Street, P.O. Box 790, Greenfield, MA 01302; (413) 773-5463; www.co.franklin.ma.us.

Greater Boston Convention and Visitors Bureau, 2 Copley Place, Suite 105, Boston MA 02116; (888) SEE-BOSTON, www.visitus@bostonusa.com.

Greater Merrimack Valley Convention and Visitors Bureau, 22 Shattuck Street, Lowell, MA 01824, (800) 443-3332; www.lowell.org.

Greater Springfield Convention and Visitors Bureau, P.O. Box 15589, Springfield, MA 01115-5589; (800) 723-1548; valleyvisitor.com.

Martha's Vineyard Chamber of Commerce, P.O. Box 1698, Vineyard Haven, MA 02568-1698; (508) 693-0085; www.mvy.com.

Massachusetts Office of Travel and Tourism, State Transportation Building, 10 Park Plaza, Suite 4510, Boston, MA 02116; (800) 447-6277; www.mass-vacation.com.

Mohawk Trail Association, P.O. Box 2031, Charlemont, MA 01339; (413) 664-6256; www.mohawktrail.com.

Berkshire Hills Visitors Bureau, Berkshire Common Plaza Level, Pittsfield, MA 01201; (800) 237-5747; www.berkshires.org.

Nantucket Island Chamber of Commerce, 48 Main Street, Nantucket, MA 02554; (508) 228-1700; www.nantucketchamber.org.

Nantucket Visitors Services & Information Bureau, 25 Federal Street, Nantucket, MA 02554; (508) 228-0925.

North of Boston Convention and Visitors Bureau, 17 Peabody Square, Peabody, MA 01960, (800) 742-5306; www.northofboston.org.

Plymouth County Convention and Visitors Bureau, 345 Washington Street, P.O. Box 1620, Pembroke, MA 02359; (800) 231-1620; www.plymouth-1620.com.

The Best Beaches and Parks

Life is a beach on the peninsula of Cape Cod, as well as on the islands of Martha's Vineyard and Nantucket, mere dots in the blue Atlantic about seven miles and 30 miles respectively from the Cape. There are ponds throughout the state (Thoreau's Walden Pond is in Concord), but for the most part it is the coastal beaches that visitors adore.

CAPE COD

Cape Cod National Seashore. Cape Cod's most popular beach region is the Cape Cod National Seashore—over 40 miles of stunning beaches run by the National Park Service. Six towns encompass the National Seashore: Chatham, Orleans, Eastham, Wellfleet, Truro, and Provincetown. The Cape Cod National Seashore has an ambitious program of family eco-adventures, hiking and biking trails, ranger-guided activities, and self-guided tours that extend over six beaches.

Cool Websites for Massachusetts-Bound Kids

Berkshires: www.berkshireweb.com

Boston: www.Boston.com; www.theinsider.com/boston;
www.bostonsidewalk.com; www.bostonbyfoot.com;
www.bostonusa.com; www.boston-online.com/wicked.html;
www.bostonphoenix.com

Cape Cod: www.capecodchamber.org; www.capecod.com;
www.allcapecod.com

The Computer Museum: www.tcm.com

Concord: www.concordmuseum.org

Lighthouses: http://zuma.lib.utk.edu/lights/newengl.html

Martha's Vineyard: www.mvy.com

Massachusetts: www.mass-vacation.com

Nantucket: www.nantucketchamber.org

New England: www.visitnewengland.com/;
www.newenglandusa.com/; www.newenglandtravel.com/

Plymouth: www.Plimoth.org.htm; www.Plimoth.org/mayflower.htm

Salem: www.salemwitchmuseum.com

For an overview of the National Seashore, there are two terrific visitors centers stocked with schedules and maps. The centers also offer exhibits and audiovisual programs. Nature films are shown on summer evenings in the amphitheaters. The Salt Pond Road Visitor Center is off Route 6 in Eastham; (508) 255-3421. The Province Lands Visitor Center is on Race Point Road off Route 6 in Provincetown; (508) 487-1256. In the summer, these centers are open daily from 9 a.m. to 6 p.m.; spring and fall hours are daily from 9 a.m. to 4:30 p.m. The Salt Pond Visitor Center is also open January through mid-February on weekends only.

The Cape Cod National Seashore beaches include *Cahoon Hollow, Nauset Light,* and *Race Point,* all of which are family friendly and post lifeguards. You can surf at Cahoon Hollow and Nauset Light–teens love both–but Cahoon is only accessible by hiking over a dune, so be sure kids are old enough to make the trek and help tote beach gear.

Corporation Beach, Dennis. The name isn't very enticing, but this is a super family beach with lifeguards, a snack bar, rest rooms, and even a children's playground. This strand is disabled accessible thanks to a boardwalk that runs through it.

Massachusetts's Not-to-Be-Missed Attractions

Cape Cod, Martha's Vineyard, Nantucket

- Cape Cod National Seashore
- The Chatham Bars Inn, Chatham
- Biking the Cape Cod Bike Trail and stopping in at Arnold's Lobster and Clam Bar for incredible fried clams
- Cape Cod Potato Chip Company, Hyannis
- The Flying Horses Carousel, Oak Bluffs, Martha's Vineyard
- Maria Mitchell Aquarium and Maria Mitchell Observatory, Nantucket
- Nantucket's Lighthouses

Boston/Cambridge

- A Red Sox game at Fenway Park
- Ice-skating at Frog Pond, Boston (and then afternoon tea at the Four Seasons across the street)
- The Museum of Science, Boston
- Enjoying an ice cream cone while strolling Newbury Street
- The Boston Duck Tours
- The Freedom Trail, Boston
- Grazing at Faneuil Hall
- Eating seafood at Legal Seafoods
- Strolling Cambridge and Harvard Square
- A day trip to Plimoth Plantation in Plymouth or to Salem

Interior Massachusetts

- Skiing Brodie Mountain or Jiminy Peak
- Sturbridge Village, Sturbridge
- Tanglewood, Lenox
- Norman Rockwell Museum, Stockbridge
- Thoreau's Walden Pond, Concord
- Sterling and Francine Clark Art Institute, Williamstown

Craigville Beach. On the warm, calm Nantucket Bay, this is the teen scene on Cape Cod. Located between Centerville and Hyannisport. It has lifeguards, rest rooms, and snack bars.

Kalmus Beach, Hyannisport. Combine a visit to the John F. Kennedy Hyannis Museum with a couple hours at this small stretch of sand that juts into the harbor. There's a lot of action at this strand—ferries bustle back and forth—but there is little surf. There are lifeguards, rest rooms, and a snack bar.

Long Pond. When my son was in the baby and toddler stages, we'd plop our blankets and chairs here. The water is always calmer and warmer than the ocean. Plus, there is ample shade, and the sunsets from the banks of this enormous pond are life-changing (make sure to sit on the Harwich side). The pond is so big that half of it is in Harwich and half in Brewster.

Monomoy Island. Make like Gilligan and spend the day on Monomoy Island, a 2,750-acre islet with a bird sanctuary (285 species of birds) that's accessible only by boat from Chatham. There are no facilities out here (translation: no rest rooms). To spend the day on the island, call the Outermost Harbor Marine at (508) 945-2030. Don't forget to pack a picnic and bring lots of water.

Sandy Neck Beach. This elongated stretch of sand off Route 6A in Barnstable is considered one of the Cape's best beaches for families. There are lifeguards, rest rooms, and a snack bar. There are tide pools that are good for hours of safe amusement. Tip: The sand is somewhat rocky so bring beach chairs for sunning. Lifeguards staff the strand.

Walden Pond, Concord. There's a little swimming beach here with lifeguards, a snack bar, and rest rooms. Combine wading and splashing with a short stroll to visit a replica of Thoreau's cabin (free admission). For older kids, bring along a copy of Thoreau's *Walden Pond* to enrich the experience. Open daily from 5 a.m. to a half hour before sunset. Walden Pond State Reservation, Route 126, Concord; (978) 369-3254.

MARTHA'S VINEYARD

With 124 miles of beaches, Martha's Vineyard has plenty of sand to go around, and even the most discriminating beachcomber can find a beach with a compatible personality. Some are notable for their isolation and paucity of sunbathers, some for their fabulous sunsets, some for their flora. The northern and eastern beaches tend to be shallow and relatively calm, while those on the south-facing side of the island have fairly active surfs. Parking and/or beach permits are required at some of the beaches; others are open to the public without restriction. Tip: If you intend to rent a cottage for a week in a town with a beach that you want to visit, be sure to get the appropriate permit from the home's owner. Otherwise, permits can be obtained by contacting the town hall in the appropriate community. Another tip: If you plan to spend a day on the beach (and why not?) be sure to pack a lunch. While there are some food trucks that move among the beaches and a few food/lemonade stands, they are scarce.

Joseph Sylvia State Park Beach. Immediately adjacent to Beach Road and Sengekontacket Pond, on the northeast shore, this is one of the most accessible beaches. It is approximately two miles long and because of its location is fairly calm with mild surf. With Sengekontacket Pond across the road for crab catching, the infamous canal bridge, and the fine sand, this could become a favorite beach destination. Caveat: There is no lifeguard on duty. There is also a paved, off-road bicycle path that parallels the beach and doubles as a jogging path and stretches the entire route between Edgartown and Oak Bluffs. This may be some of the most scenic exercising you will ever do.

Katama Beach, also South Beach. This three-mile-long barrier beach is along the southern shore of the island; it is reached by driving directly south from Edgartown on Katama Road. Parking is first come, first serve along the local uninhabited beach roads; the earlier you go, the closer you will be to the beach. Caution: The Atlantic Ocean kisses the Vineyard here, so the surf can be fairly strong. Lifeguards are on duty.

Lambert's Cove. If you are staying in West Tisbury, you must get a pass for this beach. It is considered by many to have the finest sand and clearest water on the north shore. Unless you know exactly where it is, you won't find it; unlike many of the beaches on the island, the parking location yields little evidence that the ocean is a shell's throw away. The small, wooded lot is on Lambert's Cove Road, which forms one very large loop off State/Vineyard Haven Road between Tisbury and West Tisbury. Once you do find the lot and provide the parking attendant with proof that you belong there, you approach the beach along a long, wooded path that still gives no hint of the secret you are about to discover. As the path approaches the cove, you will find that sand has spilled onto it and it seems out of place where the trees are still towering over you. Thirty more feet and suddenly you stumble upon a long stretch of disembodied shoes lining the sanded portion of the path. You are almost there! Continue walking through a noisome expanse of sea rose bushes, and suddenly the path opens up to an apron of sand and then the beach beyond. The walk is a quarter- to a half-mile. The water is clean, and we can see the surf-rounded pebbles on the bottom in every photograph we've ever taken here. Caveat: No lifeguards.

NANTUCKET

With more than 80 miles of beaches, Nantucket is a child's paradise. Yet, not all of Nantucket's spectacular beaches are ideal for families with children. Children can collect shells, beach glass, and stones as well as make sandcastles and romp in the surf. But some of the island's beaches have strong surf and/or undertows, which make bathing, swimming, and body surfing dangerous for all but the strongest, most expert swimmers. The following beaches have gentle surf and are ideal for children. Naturally, parents should remain alert and must always be aware of their children's whereabouts at the beach, regardless of the gentle surf.

Children's Beach. It's all in the name. Located on Nantucket Harbor on the North Shore, the Beach is an easy walk from town. It's great for long shoreline walks, and it has a park, a playground, games tables, and a bandstand. Lifeguards, rest rooms, showers, a restaurant, take-out food service, and picnic tables are available.

Dionis Beach. Dionis Beach is an easy three-mile bicycle ride from town. This wide, expansive spot is great for picnics and cookouts (don't forget your charcoal fire permit from the fire department) and for surf-casting and swimming. It also has the largest dunes on the island (don't walk or drive on the vegetation!).

Francis Street Beach. Just a five-minute walk from Main Street, this North Shore harbor beach features extremely calm harbor water and is great for swimming. Although there is no lifeguard, there is a jungle gym, and kayak rentals are available.

Jetties Beach. On the North Shore, this is the closest family-recommended beach to town. It is an easy bike ride from town, and the shuttle stops here. The beach provides lifeguards, changing rooms, showers, public telephones, a restaurant, a playground, public tennis courts, volleyball nets, windsurfing, and sailboat and kayak rentals. The Park & Recreation Commission offers swimming lessons for children ages 6 and older from July Fourth to Labor Day from 9:30 a.m. until noon.

Family Outdoor Adventures

Biking. The Cape Cod Rail Trail has more than 25 miles of biking paths from South Dennis to Wellfleet to amuse all levels of cyclists. Kettle ponds, salt marshes, and cranberry bogs dot the landscape (bring your camera), and road crossings are well marked. However, there are *many* road crossings—and many traverse very busy roads, so while the scenery is gorgeous, you must use caution, especially with young bikers. You can access the bike path from a number of junctures: the Salt Pond Visitors Center in the

Beach Permits

Many Cape Cod and island beaches require beach permits for nonresidents. You can usually get a beach permit for a week or month for most beaches. Costs vary considerably depending on the town. Some beaches also offer day passes, but these are the exception rather than the rule. Costs range from $4 to $10 a day. For more information, call the Cape Cod Chamber of Commerce at (888) 332-2732 or visit their website at www.capecodchamber.org.

Cape Cod National Seashore is an especially popular starting point, as is Nickerson State Park in Brewster, with eight miles of trails within that park alone. Make sure to plan your biking excursion around a stop at Arnold's (just off the bike path in Eastham) for some of the best fried clams, lobster, and chowder anywhere.

While the inner Cape also has biking paths, it is not as ambitious as those found in the mid and upper Cape. Still, the three-and-a-half mile Shining Sea Bikeway runs from Falmouth to Woods Hole and the two Cape Cod Canal service roads. For a copy of the Cape Cod Rail Trail brochure, call (800) 831-0569 in Massachusetts or (617) 727-3180, or write Massachusetts Division of Forests and Parks, 100 Cambridge Street, Boston, MA 02202.

Nantucket has five bicycle paths ranging in length from two-and-a-half miles to 8 miles. These paved paths provide scenic byways along Cliff, Madaket, Milestone, Surfside, and Polpis roads. Because of the island's wonderful geography and scenic beauty, this is an ideal way to experience Nantucket in its natural splendor. Families can plan picnics and bring along their swimsuits to take a cooling dip. Keep your eyes peeled for wild blueberries, blackberries, and beach plums, which grow near the paths in many locations. For safety's sake, all cyclists should wear helmets and keep to paved portions of the path. There are several bicycle rentals shops in town that rent by the half-day, day, and week. Try: Young's Bicycle Shop, Broad Street, Steamboat Wharf, (508) 228-1151, www.youngsbicycleshop.com; or Island Bike, Old South Road, (508) 228-4070, www.bikenantucket.com.

Boating. Boating opportunities are endless throughout Massachusetts, thanks to the state's coastal position and countless inland ponds. You can rent sailboats, canoes, and kayaks just about anywhere you visit in Massachusetts. For kayaking and canoeing in Boston, try the Charles River Canoe and Kayak Center, near Routes 128 and 30 in Newton and Soldier's

Field Road in Allston, (617) 965-5110. On the Cape, you can rent kayaks at Jack's Boat Rentals with two locations: Route 6, Wellfleet, (508) 349-9808, and Nickerson State Park, Brewster, (508) 896-8556. For guided kayaking and canoeing tours in the Berkshires, try Rick Moon's Outdoors in Great Barrington on Route 7, (413) 528-4666.

Hiking. The Appalachian Trail, which runs from Maine to Georgia, includes Massachusetts at Mount Greylock. At 3,491 feet, this mountain in the Berkshires is the highest peak in the state and accessible only by foot or car. There's a lodge here, the Bascom Lodge, run by the Appalachian Mountain Club. Work up an appetite by hiking one of the many trails before stopping for a bite to eat (you must make reservations). Also at the top is the War Memorial Tower that was built in 1933 to honor the dead who fought in the war. It also serves as an airplane tower—make time to stand on its observation deck to see views of five states (on a clear day): New Hampshire, Connecticut, Massachusetts, New York, and Vermont. Visit Mount Greylock in the fall and you're in for a treat—the mountain explodes with color. Call (413) 743-1591.

Nickerson State Park in Brewster on Cape Cod has more than 1,900 acres of woodlands, eight freshwater kettle ponds (swimming holes), and meandering trails. You can camp in the park. There's a series of crafts programs offered at the Nature Center for kids age 12 and under and a terrific junior ranger program for kids ages 8 to 15. Call (508) 896-3491.

The Wellfleet Bay Wildlife Sanctuary, a 1,000-acre bird sanctuary, has the easy-does-it, mile-long Goose Pond Trail. This trail is a winner for families seeking a beginner stroll in the woods on a salt marsh boardwalk. The Audubon Society leads naturalist wildlife tours for families in the summer months; reservations are required. It's located off West Road in South Wellfleet; (508) 349-2615.

In Cape Cod National Seashore, you will find absolutely stunning seashore hikes. There are self-guided trails (11 in all), most of which are less than a mile long. We especially love the sensory Buttonbush Trail. It's an effortless (a quarter-mile long) boardwalk trail with a guide rope and Braille text. The best things for families are the ranger programs that include hour-long beach hikes at Nauset Light Beach, Marconi Beach, and the Province Lands (all within the Cape Cod National Seashore). Older kids dig the night walks, which begin around 8 p.m. and end after dark. The best night walk is the Race Point Beach hike, in which the rangers re-create a night-watch by old shipwreck patrols. Call (508) 255-3421 or (508) 487-1256 for more information about the hiking in the Cape Cod National Seashore.

We love the self-guided hike behind the Cape Cod Museum of Natural History, leading through the salt marshes to the bay. It's easy, lovely, and a perfect way to get some exercise and take in Cape Cod's best asset—the sea. Because the hike is short, we recommend it in any kind of weather. Throw on your raincoats and take the hike. Upon returning to the museum, enjoy an afternoon of indoor fun; (508) 896-3867.

Skiing, Snowboarding, and Cross-Country Skiing. There are several family-friendly ski resorts worth noting in Massachusetts. Jiminy Peak in the Berkshires (three hours from Boston, about two-and-a-half hours from New York City) is an especially popular ski resort in this neck of the woods. And for good reason: It's got an ambitious Ski Wee program, more than 10 trails, a great base lodge (with a Pizza Hut), and a clean, comfortable hotel. Bonus: A new detachable cable car will debut soon. The kid's program at Jiminy Peak is organized. However, because of its enormous popularity (especially since it is a quick jaunt from the New York City area), during peak ski times (such as school holidays) there can be a shortage of ski instructors, pushing the children/instructor ratio to the limit—and beyond. Still, for better skiers, this is a very containable resort for older kids who can ski the mountain themselves. All trails end in one place. On spring days, plant yourselves at one of the outdoor picnic tables at Christiansen's Tavern, order up a plate of hot or garlic Buffalo wings, a steamy cocoa, and watch as your children ski down the slope; (888) 454-6469.

Jiminy Peak and Brodie used to be competitors, but the two ski resorts recently merged. Brodie is the smaller, less polished of the two sister resorts. In fact, its marketing director said it best, "Skiers in the lodge at Brodie read the *Boston Herald* and *New York Post* while skiers at Jiminy Peak read the *Wall Street Journal* and the *New York Times.*" But its smaller size and laidback atmosphere have won the hearts of many loyal fans. In fact, my son much preferred Brodie to Jiminy Peak. First, because it is less popular than Jiminy, the ski school tends to have less children. My son and one other boy ended up with one instructor all to themselves for the day. It doesn't get better than that. The chair lift lines tend to be nonexistent (and we visited during President's Day weekend.) We love this place also for its huge fireplace in the super-casual lodge. Come here on St. Patrick's Day and you'll ski on green slopes. Brodie is Irish to the bone, thanks to its former owners; (413) 443-4752.

Whale-Watching. Thar she blows! Whale-watching doesn't get any better than in Massachusetts. In fact, The World Wildlife Fund named the Bay State one of the world's top ten whale-watching spots. Most whale-watching excursions depart from the Cape and the Islands, although some depart from Boston and points north such as Gloucester and Rockport. April through October is prime whale-watching season in this neck of the woods.

The place to see whales: The Stellwagen Bank, about four miles off Provincetown on the outer Cape. We've taken whale-watching excursions out of P-town and Hyannis (mid-Cape). Both were rich in whale sightings. The P-town trips allow for shorter boat rides with more time spent at Stellwagen Bank, while the Hyannis trips are longer boat rides (because it takes that much longer to reach the Stellwagen Bank). It's worth taking a whale-watching trip out of Provincetown if you also plan to spend time exploring this funky, seaside town. Otherwise, the traffic can be unbearable on summer weekends, so you might opt to go out of Hyannis. But, if you combine a whaling trip with a dune-buggy tour, gallery hopping, boutique browsing, and some of the best chowdah in the Cape at Sylva's, a whale watch out of P-town is well worth any traffic snare-ups you may encounter.

In Provincetown, try Dolphin Fleet (phone (800) 826-9300) and Provincetown Whale Watch, Inc. (phone (800) 992-9333). In Hyannis, go with Hyannis Whale Watcher (phone (800) 287-0374). Out of Nantucket, go with Nantucket Whale Watch Cruises (phone (800) 942-5464), which depart from the end of Straight Wharf on Tuesdays during July and August. There are whale-watching excursions offered out of Boston. The New England Aquarium's cruises leave right from the aquarium (children under age 3 are not permitted; phone (800) 973-5281). Tip: If the weather is moody, rough seas can make for an unpleasant whale-watching experience, especially for children. In fact, a whale-watching excursion is really not appropriate for toddlers in even the best conditions. You'll spend more time watching your little ones than the whales.

Calendar of Festivals and Events

February

Washington's Birthday Celebration, Old Sturbridge Village, Sturbridge. Step back to Washington's time to celebrate his birthday; (508) 347-3362.

Winter Week, Hancock Shaker Village, Pittsfield. Ice-harvesting, sleigh rides, a winter farm, crafts and activities, and guided tours; (413) 443-0188.

Family Day at Williams College Museum of Art, Williamstown. Art activities, performances, and workshops; (413) 597-2429.

Family Fun Days, Sturbridge Village. Week of activities for kids, including puppets and storytelling; (800) SEE-1830.

Longfellow's Birthday Celebration, Cambridge. Tours, poetry readings, children's programs, and wreath laying at Longfellow's grave. Longfellow National Historic Site, Brattle Street; (617) 876-4491.

March

Saint Patrick's Day Parade, South Boston. (617) 268-8525. Put on your green and celebrate St. Paddy's day in this Irish part of town.

New England Spring Flower Show. World's third-largest flower show. More than five acres of colorful exhibits, demonstrations, activities, and competitions; (617) 536-9280.

April

Annual Lantern Celebration, Old North Church. Commemoration of the hanging of two lanterns on April 18, 1775, alerting Paul Revere that British troops were advancing up the Charles River to Lexington; (617) 523-6676.

Patriot's Day Celebration, Lexington. Boston's Freedom Trail hosts an array of family events April 15 through April 25. Paul Revere regales with stories of his life as a silversmith and patriot, plus scavenger hunts, Mother Goose spinning tales to kids at the State House, and eighteenth-century characters dramatizing the Revolution along the red-brick trail; (617) 227-8800.

Boston Marathon. This is the oldest American marathon, a 26-mile race; (508) 435-6905.

Daffodil Festival, Nantucket Island. An annual spring celebration with an antique car parade, a tailgate picnic, a shop-window decorating contest, and a flower show; (508) 228-1700.

May

Heritage Breeds and Heirloom Seeds, Plimouth Plantation. Heritage animal breeds from around New Engalnd, heirloom plants and herb garden walks, animal and craft decorations, and children's activities. Route 3, Plymouth; (508) 746-1622.

Dexter Rhododendron Festival, Heritage Plantation. Celebrate the blooming season of thousands of this plantation's famous plants; peak lasts from late May until mid-June. Pine and Grove Streets, Sandwich (on Cape Cod); (508) 888-3300.

Ducklings Day Parade. Festivities on Boston Common celebrating the classic children's story "Make Way for Ducklings."

June

Bunker Hill Days, Charlestown Navy Yard, Bunker Hill Monument. Commemorating the victory at Bunker Hill; (617) 242-5601.

Hyannis Harbor Festival, Bismore Park, Hyannis, Cape Cod. Blessing of the fleet, boat races, seafaring demonstrations, a kids' fair, and clam-shucking and pie-eating contests; (508) 775-2201.

Blessing of the Fleet, MacMillan Wharf, Provincetown, Cape Cod. The town gathers for the annual blessing of all the fishing boats; (508) 487-3424.

July

Boston Harborfest, Boston. Festival celebrating the maritime history of Boston with fireworks and concerts, a chowderfest, and historic reenactments; (617) 227-1528; (617) 536-4100.

Boston Pops Fourth of July Concert, Charles River Esplanade, Boston. Outdoor concert and fireworks; (617) 266-1492.

Yankee Homecoming Days, Newburyport. Waterfront concert, house tours, entertainment, parades, craft fair, antique car parade, lobsterfest, and fireworks; (978) 462-6680.

Barnstable County Fair, East Falmouth, Cape Cod. Animal judging, horse pulls, crafts, a petting zoo, and food; (508) 563-3200.

Independence Day Celebration and Parade, Old Sturbridge Village, Sturbridge. Historical parade, picnic on the Common, and reading of the Declaration of Independence; (508) 347-3362.

Your Hometown America Parade, Pittsfield. This is one of the largest Fourth of July parades in America; (413) 499-3861.

August

Gloucester Waterfront Festival, Gloucester. Yankee lobster bake, pancake breakfast, crafts, entertainment, and whale watches; (978) 283-1601.

Plymouth Lobster Festival, Plymouth. Plenty of succulent shellfish for everyone; (508) 746-8500.

Sand Castle and Sculpture Day, Jetties Beach, Nantucket. Families, individuals, and teams build castles and sculptures in the sand. Pre-registration is required; (508) 228-1700.

September

Cambridge River Festival, Memorial Drive, Cambridge. Music, dance, visual and participatory arts, handcrafts, children's activities, and international foods. Memorial Drive, Cambridge; (617) 349-4380.

Harwich Cranberry Harvest Festival, Harwich. Festival with family beach party, country-western jamboree, arts and crafts festival, fireworks, and a parade; (800) 441-3199.

Tub Parade, Lenox. Parade of carriages decorated with flowers and harvest vegetables re-creates an annual event from the 1890s. Historic Lenox Village, Route 7A, Lenox; (413) 637-3646.

Striped Bass and Bluefish Derby, Martha's Vineyard. Annual shore and boat fishing tournament with daily, weekly, and grand prizes; (508) 693-0728.

A Taste of the Berkshires, Great Barrington. Outdoor event celebrating the bounty of the Berkshires with farms, restaurants, and caterers offering samples, tours of local farms, and workshops on farm life. Band Stand Green in Great Barrington; (413) 528-1947.

October

Head of the Charles Regatta, Charles River, Cambridge/Boston. One of the biggest rowing events in the country with championship races for youth, veterans, and lightweights; (617) 864-8415.

Haunted Happenings, Salem. Scary stuff at Salem's infamous Halloween extravaganza, with a parade, haunted harbor cruises, witch trials, a psychic fair, and more; (978) 744-0013; (978) 744-0004.

November

Plimoth Plantation Thanksgiving Celebration, Plymouth. Visit the Colonists in the 1627 Pilgrim Village (reservations are required for Thanksgiving dinner); 508-746-1622.

Old Sturbridge Village Thanksgiving Day Celebration, Sturbridge. Stroll through Village homes and attend Meetinghouse services to see how families celebrated Thanksgiving more than 150 years ago (reservations are required for dinner in the Bullard Tavern); (508) 853-6015.

December

Boston Common Tree Lighting, Boston Common. More than 50 trees are lit, choral groups rejoice; (617) 635-4505.

Nantucket Noel and Christmas Stroll, Nantucket Island. (508) 228-1700.

First Night Boston. A grand New Year's Eve celebration; (617) 542-1399.

Cape Cod, Martha's Vineyard, and Nantucket

Miles of unspoiled, undeveloped beaches; weathered, shingled clam shacks; a bounty of lively fishing piers; whale-watching excursions; roadside antiques shops; rose-covered trellises and white picket fences . . . Cape Cod and her sister islands, Martha's Vineyard and Nantucket, have the stuff that dreams of old-fashioned summers are made of. Couple the simplicity of the Cape with upscale-yet-understated resorts, inns, and cabins, and you'll see why it's New England's pride and joy.

Cape Cod

Grab a couple of beach chairs, pails, and shovels and sink your toes into this back-to-basics, saltwater-kissed destination. Shaped like a large, muscular arm, with **Chatham** at the elbow and **Provincetown** (called P-town) at the wrist, the Cape has won the adoration of famous writers for decades. Henry David Thoreau spent a lot of time here and eventually went on to write about a book called *Cape Cod.* The more developed areas include **Dennisport** and **Hyannis** (not to be confused with **Hyannisport,** where the Kennedy family is based). You'll find a density of shops (including a mall) and accommodations in this neck of the woods. The farther you travel toward P-town, the less commercial the Cape becomes. You'll come across **Chatham** and **Harwich**—both quintessential New England hamlets with village greens and quaint shops—and sleepy seaside towns, such as **Truro** (with its quiet beaches) and **Wellfleet** (the art center of the Cape and home to many fine galleries; look in the local paper for listings of gallery openings when wine-and-cheese receptions welcome new exhibits—and, yes, kids).

Summer on Cape Cod is reserved for lazy, hazy days by the sea. Come fall, when the crowds thin and Indian summer days are the exception, not

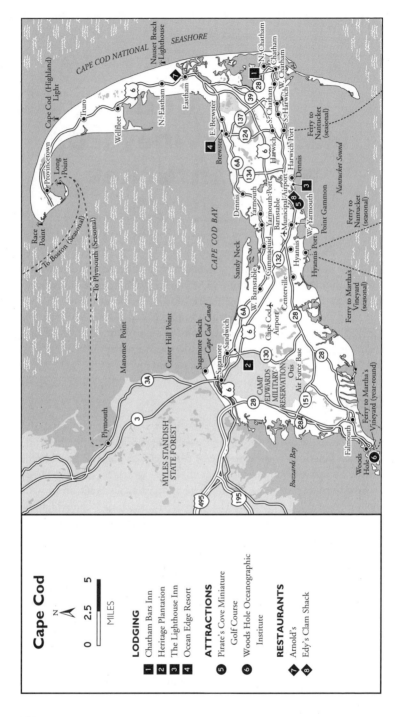

Cape Cod

N

0   2.5   5
MILES

LODGING

1 Chatham Bars Inn
2 Heritage Plantation
3 The Lighthouse Inn
4 Ocean Edge Resort

ATTRACTIONS

5 Pirate's Cove Miniature
  Golf Course
6 Woods Hole Oceanographic
  Institute

RESTAURANTS

7 Arnold's
8 Edy's Clam Shack

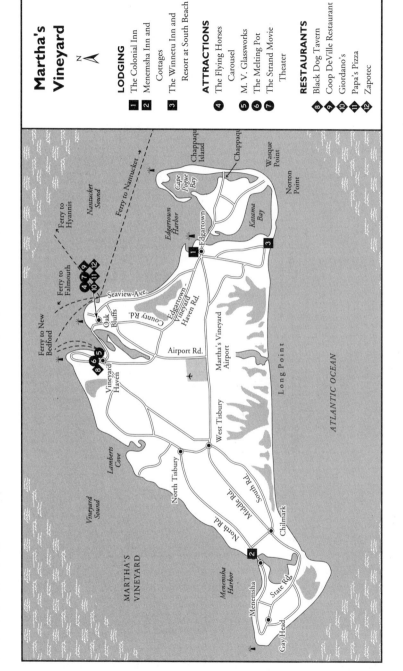

Martha's Vineyard

N

LODGING

1. The Colonial Inn
2. Menemsha Inn and Cottages
3. The Winnetu Inn and Resort at South Beach

ATTRACTIONS

4. The Flying Horses Carousel
5. M. V. Glassworks
6. The Melting Pot
7. The Strand Movie Theater

RESTAURANTS

8. Black Dog Tavern
9. Coop DeVille Restaurant
10. Giordano's
11. Papa's Pizza
12. Zapotec

LODGING

1. Accommodations Et Al
2. The Beachside at Nantucket
3. The Harbor House
4. Jared Coffin House
5. Nantucket Inn
6. The Wauwinet

ATTRACTIONS

7. Hinchman House Natural Science Museum
8. Maria Mitchell Aquarium
9. Maria Mitchell Observatory
10. Nantucket Life-Saving Museum
11. The Whaling Museum

RESTAURANTS

12. Arno's at 41 Main St.
13. The Atlantic Cafe
14. Brotherhood of Thieves
15. The Downeyflake Restaurant
16. Faregrounds Restaurant and Pudley's Pub
17. The Rose & Crown
18. SeaGrill
19. The Tap Room at the Jared Coffin House
20. Vincent's

Nantucket

N

0 ——————— 3

MILES

Nantucket Sound

Nantucket Harbor

Wauwinet

Nantucket Cliffs

Eel Point Rd.

Cliff Rd.

Coatue Point

Nantucket Town

Quidnet

Madaket Rd.

Massasoit Rd.

Hummock Pond

Polpis Rd.

Sesachacha Pond

New South Rd

Milestone Rd.

Hummock Pond Rd.

South Shore

Miacomet Pond

Cisco

Old South Rd.

New South Rd

Beach Rd.

Nantucket Memorial Airport

Surfside

the rule, cool nights make for cuddling under wool blankets. Winter is for recluse types—make no mistake about it, Cape Cod is a seasonal destination, and many hotels, restaurants, and attractions close for the winter from mid-October through mid-April. Of course, if you dig moody weather, the Cape beaches in the winter are breathtakingly still and beautiful.

If you're looking for a place where childhood memories will linger for generations, Cape Cod delivers. My own childhood memories of summer vacations are of digging for horseshoe crabs in a salty marsh in Chatham. The owner of the property gave me two steamers for every horseshoe crab I picked out of his clam bed. Memories of hours riding the waves at the beaches—despite the oft-cold water temperatures—were captured on

---

Something's Fishy

In the afternoon, between 3 and 4 p.m., when your bathing suits are still damp, head straight from the beach to the Chatham Fish Pier to admire the salty Cape Cod fishermen as they bring in their catch, drawing not only seagulls but kids of all ages. You'll spy nets full of cod, haddock, flounder, and halibut from a visitors balcony. This has been one of my son's favorite afternoon adventures since he was a toddler. There's also a fish market, so if you're staying at a cottage with a kitchen, you can purchase fresh-plucked-from-the-sea fish and seafood. Shore Road and Bar Cliff Avenue, Chatham.

---

home movies. And I can taste the sand, the sea, and the s'mores at the clambakes we often had at the beach with our dear friends. A swim after the sun curtsied into the sea was the most thrilling—the air and water temperature were almost the same, and the phosphorous in the water that would show up on our fingertips was as mysterious as the Chatham fog that rolled in later those evenings. You'll note vacations on the Cape aren't the man-made sort—the beaches provide most of the fun for families. If you don't adore beaches, the Cape isn't where you want to spend your vacation. The Cape's imprints of nature in the form of its stretches of sand and surf have put it on the map as an idyllic family holiday spot.

For more about Cape Cod's parks and beaches, see the Best Beaches and Parks section on page 119. For other Cape Cod activities, see the Family Outdoor Adventures section on page 125.

Martha's Vineyard

A good friend, Stephen Gronda, who travels from New York to Martha's Vineyard each summer with his young daughter Kelsey, has come to know the Vineyard better than anyone I know. This is his expert take on the very best of the Vineyard's family offerings.

Often, when icicles cling like crystalline stalactites to the edges of my roof in New York, I think about the salubrious waves of salt air that have washed over me in Martha's Vineyard. During these moments my thoughts tend to be crowded with smiling children's faces as they go round and round on the carousel in **Oak Bluffs,** with the bright yellow sunlight of a beach day, or the wooden echo of a sanded floor in a **West Tisbury** shop. Martha's Vineyard, with its wonderful necklace of bisque-colored beaches peppered with brightly striped umbrellas and din of vacationing children, is certainly one of our favorite places during the summer months. We have spent lots of time here and have come to love it not so much for what we can do there, although there is plenty, but for the sheer amount of nothing that we can get done—after all, isn't that what vacations are for?

We have come to especially love the sand that dusts our feet, the stately charm of sixteenth-century captains' homes, the historic setting, and, of all things, the homemade ice cream that has become synonymous with summer vacation. Martha's Vineyard is about the history of New England, the Civil War, sea-faring captains, and the whaling industry. The contemporary visitor to Martha's Vineyard can see the clean lines of whaling captains' homes, now painted bright white, that proudly flank the harbor in **Edgartown,** the pretty gingerbread houses of Oak Bluffs, and the famous cliffs of **Aquinah,** formerly Gay Head.

For more about Martha's Vineyard's beaches, see our Best Beaches and Parks section on page 119.

Nantucket

A car is not necessary on Nantucket, as the town is rather small and contained. Rental bicycles are readily available, as are motorized vehicles. Nantucket Regional Transit Authority Shuttles travel from one end of the island to the other, and this is a safe, convenient, and relatively inexpensive mode of transport—and children under the age of 6 ride free. The Shuttle runs from June 1 to September 30 from 7 a.m. to 11:30 p.m. All Shuttle buses are disabled accessible and have bicycle racks. Stops are located along each route at the gray posts with red and maroon stripes. Route maps are available at the Nantucket Island Chamber of Commerce office at 48 Main Street; call (508) 228-7025 or send an e-mail to nrta@nantucket.net.

My dear friend and colleague, William P. DeSousa, a transplanted Long Islander who cherishes his new life on Cape Cod, is to Nantucket what the Statue of Liberty is to New York—a welcoming symbol and guiding light for all those seeking its shores. Here is the best of Nantucket for families through Bill's 20/20 vision:

Nantucket's known as The Gray Lady, a nod either to its infamous fogs or, some say, its ubiquitous gray-shingled cottages. No matter the appellation, Nantucket is a timeless place, steeped in history and blessed with an enviable geography, temperate clime, and a bevy of family-friendly lodgings, eateries, museums, beaches, and activities.

Nantucket is a treasure to share. Parents delight in their children's ecstasy as they discover and revel in the warm sands and playful surf at Jetties Beach, climb the steep cliff at Sankaty Head, or have desultory meetings with the myriad dogs that cruise Main Street, shadowing their masters past The Expresso Cafe.

For more about Nantucket's beaches, see our Best Beaches and Parks section on page 119.

Wellfleet Drive-In

Take a trip down memory lane with a visit to the Cape's only drive-in movie theatre. Wear the little ones out at the play area before the flicks begin. A restaurant and snack bar are on site. Nightly double features start at sunset. Movies run from May through September and cost $6.50 for adults and $4 for ages 5–11. Route 6 on the Eastham/Wellfleet border; (508) 349-7176.

Cape Cod Family Lodging

Chatham Bars Inn

Cape Cod's most elegant inn just so happens to have an ambitious children's program—free of charge. This Chatham inn has the requisite sweeping porch with rocking chairs and views of Pleasant Bay across the way. There are rooms in the main inn, but families usually opt for one of the cottages spread out in this rambling resort. The Main Dining Room is a bit stiff—certainly for impatient youngsters—and expensive, but The Tavern at the Inn is more family-friendly. In the summer, the perfect eating spot for families is down by the pool and beach at the Beach House Grill, the lobster roll is to die for. Kids can eat with new-found friends, and on Friday nights the older kids have the privilege of strolling down into downtown Chatham with the counselors to visit the Chatham Candy Store (think paper bags that kids can fill with penny candies). Finally, enjoy the Friday night band concert at Kate Gould Park—a must for every Cape Cod visitor. But expect crowds! Shore Road, Chatham; (800) 527-4884.

The Lighthouse Inn

Several notches down on the luxury scale from Chatham Bars and Ocean Edge, this resort in West Dennis Beach nonetheless is one of Cape Cod's most popular family resorts. Smack on the Nantucket Sound, it's got a great location for beach lovers and a great kids program too. This is the kind of musty place you'd expect from a more budget-conscious beach resort—a cribbage table in the antiques-strewn living room with mismatched couches, wood paneling, an eclectic china collection (ships, lighthouses), and cranberry artifacts in the lobby. Every night the kids program features a different event, such as a magic show. There are several game rooms featuring Ping-Pong, air hockey, and pool. Kids can eat dinner in the spacious, cool kids room downstairs while parents enjoys their meals in peace upstairs. There's an outdoor pool with a miniature golf course next to it. There's also the only privately owned lighthouse recognized by the U.S. Coast Guard. There are no lifeguards at the pool or beach at this fam-

Cape Cod Potato Chip Factory

Come to this self-guided tour with an appetite. You can watch while Mr. and Mrs. Potato Head are super-transformed into a Cape Cod chip—they don't come any crunchier! You'll get a free sample bag of chips. Crunch! The tour is disabled accessible, and there's no admission fee. 100 Breed's Hill Road, Hyannis; (508) 775-7253.

ily resort. Rates start at $125 per night. Lighthouse Inn Road, Box 128, West Dennis; (508) 398-2244.

Ocean Edge Resort

Ocean Edge rivals Chatham Bars Inn for its superb kids program. The kids program here isn't complimentary but it is incredible, and it just so happens to be my son's favorite. Ocean Edge is more of an enclosed village than Chatham Bars Inn, with townhouses (complete with kitchens, washers, and dryers) down the road and across the street from the main property. Bonus: Sign your child up for private swimming lessons at Fletcher Pool, a huge indoor and outdoor pool complex (there's a toddler pool here too). There's another kids' pool by Mulligans, one of the casual restaurants. Make no mistake about it: in addition to catering to conferences and weddings, this resort loves families. Every Thursday is Family Night at the Reef, one of the three restaurants on property. On Tuesday afternoons the resort holds a sand castle competition; on Wednesday nights there's a kite-flying contest for families; on Thursday evenings there's a family croquet game for kids ages 10 and up and a family beach fire with marshmallows for roasting. The kids program, the Ocean *Edge* Venture, is broken into three age groups: 4 and 5, 6–8, and 9–12. The fee is $30 for a half-day session or $55 for the full day. There is also a teen program two days a week for 13- to 17-year olds, including such activities as a low ropes course, problem-solving initiatives, and orienteering. Fee is $40 and includes lunch. One of the nice things about this kids program is that while there are structured activities, there is also built-in flexibility. For instance, when my son showed up with his mitt in hand, one of the male counselors read that as a cue and summoned Alex out to play catch with him. This is, in fact, one of the children's programs that I had trouble getting Alex to leave. Tennis anyone? Sign your tennis or golf loving kids (11–14 years old) for junior tennis and golf camp, Monday through Friday from 9 a.m. to noon. Fee is $30 per child per day. Another bonus: Parent's Night Out for 4–12 year olds from 6 to 9 p.m. Fee is $25 per child. Many families rent the two- or three-bedroom villas by the week in July and August. In the mansion, there are 90 rooms. The beach is a shuttle-bus ride away from the townhouses, and there are no life-

Jump Right In
Any child age 6 or older who enjoys swimming will most probably find the tangle of tanned arms and legs along Sengekontacket Pond to be one of the most inviting sites on the island. Although, jumping from the small bridge adjacent to the Joseph Sylvia State Beach is discouraged, I have never driven along the beach road and not seen handfuls of children lined along it in various stages of a jump.

guards on the beach. Still, kids love to explore the tidal pools for little creatures. Rates begin at $175 per night. Route 6A, Brewster; (508) 896-9000.

Martha's Vineyard Family Lodging

The Colonial Inn of Martha's Vineyard, Edgartown

Location, location, location. Smack in the center of town, amid all the hoopla, and within walking distance of a nice beach, this 1911 inn operates more like a hotel. If you stay on the fourth floor you have immediate access to a secret roof deck from which you can watch the boats parade in the harbor and the tourists meander about town. Breakfast is included in the room rate, and you can take yours outside in a central courtyard (nothing fancy) or inside. The suites with kitchenettes are great for families. This is where you'll want to stay for an affordable room in the thick of Edgartown. However, if it is privacy and seclusion you're after, do not book a room here. Rates begin at about $150 for a standard room and $275 for a suite per night. The hotel is closed January through March. 38 N. Water Street, Edgartown; (800) 627-4701.

Menemsha Inn and Cottages

A venerable institution on the Vineyard, this dreamy spot has been in operation for 77 years and counting. With 27 rooms and cottages, many with gorgeous water views and fireplaces, and TVs and VCRs, you'll be tempted to hole up on this property and never leave. Tucked among 11 acres of woodlands and gardens, it's a short stroll to Dutcher Dock, a 300-year-old fishing wharf. Double-room rates begin at $175 per night. North Road, Box 38, Menemsha; (508) 645-2521.

The Winnetu Inn and Resort at South Beach

This beach beauty is a spanking new resort on Martha's Vineyard. It's pricier than the Colonial Inn, but it's on the beach and is family-friendly with kitchenettes that include a small refrigerator, two-burner stove, sink and microwave. All the rooms are named for lighthouses on the Vineyard.

A studio with a kitchenette sleeps two adults and two children comfortably. The rate is $275 per night in the high season (with a three- to four-night minimum stay required). That is the cheapest room—there are also suites and even full condos, with living rooms, dining rooms, and huge decks and patios, beginning at about $525 per night. Rates include a children's day camp for kids ages 3 (toilet trained) to preteen. There is also an evening kids camp for an additional fee (perfect for parents to enjoy their evening alone). Tip: Make reservations way in advance—this newcomer on the Vineyard is already very popular. It's open April through October 31. 270 Katama Road, Edgartown; (978) 443-1733.

Nantucket Family Lodging
ACCOMMODATIONS ET AL

This collection of period Greek Revival buildings is located in the town center. The Roberts House Inn, Manor House Inn, Periwinkle Guest House, Linden House, and Periwinkle Cottage are all beautifully renovated. Each guest room is furnished with antiques and reproductions, and most feature king or queen canopy beds, private baths, telephones, and air conditioning. In several buildings, there are suites of rooms and family suites, which are particularly comfortable lodgings for families with young children. There are also several adjoining rooms that share a bath between them—just perfect for mom and dad and the little ones (and the children will feel so grown up in their "own" room). Children are welcome in all of the buildings. Rates begin at $129 per night. 11 India Street; (800) 588-0078.

The Beachside at Nantucket

Just a short walk from Main Street and Jetties Beach, The Beachside is a perfect family accommodation. As Manager Mary Malavase puts it, "We welcome families! The children bring their parents." With a beautiful outdoor pool, white wicker tables and chairs, and sprawling lawns, flowers and plantings, this inn lets parents while away the afternoon while the little ones play contentedly. Continental breakfast is served each morning. Each room has its own rubber ducky for the kids. Rates begin at about $150 per night. 30 North Beach Street; (800) 322-4433.

The Harbor House

This resort features more than 100 rooms and cottages, a lovely dining room, tennis courts, nightly entertainment (in-season), and a swimming pool. Surprisingly, for a larger hotel, there are many antiques among the guest rooms, and the decor is decidedly traditional, with canopy beds to top off the historical ambiance. Rates begin at $150 per night. It's open April–December. S. Beach Street; (800) ISLANDS.

Jared Coffin House

This 60-room inn (open year round) features lodging in several adjacent buildings in the town center. The inn heartily welcomes children. In fact, it has one accommodation in Swain House that features bunk beds and another in Harrison Grey House with a queen canopy bed and a ship's ladder by which children reach the two twin beds in the loft. The inn's restaurant, The Tap Room, also has a children's menu. This property is one spot where the children will enjoy people-watching in the grand but understated entry hall and parlor. Most rooms offer televisions. Rates begin at $150 per night. 29 Broad Street; (800) 248-2405.

Nantucket Inn

This warm, welcoming property features more than 100 rooms overlooking three beautifully landscaped courtyards. There are indoor and outdoor pools, tennis courts, a fitness center, and a full-service restaurant featuring fresh local seafood and hearty fare. Its location at the airport makes arriving and departing a snap—and the complimentary shuttle service makes the inn just minutes away from town or the beach. 27 Macy's Lane; (800) 321-8484.

The Wauwinet

If you've got the money to spend—and children who are age 12 and older— this nineteenth-century resort delivers the goods. It'll pick you up at the ferry, scuttle you into town (eight miles away), and take you on a jeep tour of the Great Point reserve. Tennis courts, croquet, a library, and a gourmet restaurant put it over the top. Remember to pack pink and green clothing—things tend to get preppy here. The cottages are best for families. Rates begin at $400 per night, including a full breakfast. Wauwinet Road; (800) 426-8718.

Cape Cod Attractions

Heritage Plantation

Off Route 6A at Grove and Pine Streets, Sandwich; (508) 888-3300

Hours: Mid-May–October, daily 10 a.m.–5 p.m.; closed late October to mid–May

Admission: $8 adults; $4 children ages 6–18

Appeal by Age Groups:

Pre-school	Grade School	Teens	Young Adults	Over 30	Seniors
★★★★	★★★★	★★★	★★	★★★★	★★★★

Touring Time: Average 2 hours; minimum 1 hour

Rainy-Day Touring: OK for indoors but not for outdoors

Services and Facilities:

Restaurants Yes	Lockers No
Alcoholic beverages No	Pet kennels No
Disabled access No	Rain check No
Wheelchair rental No	Private tours Yes
Baby stroller rental No	

Descriptions and Comments There's a lot to learn in the museum, the carousel is sweet fun, and the gardens and trails are gorgeous. But kids love this place for one reason: the carousel. My son rode it five times and would have gone on five more times. (Kids age 5 and under need an adult to ride with them). I loved it for the landscape and grounds—76 acres that are exquisite for strolling and admiring. Along with pretty gardens, there are wood trails that flank the Upper Shawme Lake. There's also a Shaker-designed round barn that is home to an ambitious collection of antique cars; kids are given an activity sheet with clues about the cars they can try to locate. Other museums on the premises house an antique miniature military exhibit, firearms, and antiquated tools. We both loved the outdoor restaurant: Try the lobster Caesar salad with Cape Cod potato chips.

Pirate's Cove Miniature Golf Course

934 Route 28, South Yarmouth; (508) 394-6200

Hours: Call for hours

Admission: Call for admission

Appeal by Age Groups:

Pre-school	Grade School	Teens	Young Adults	Over 30	Seniors
★★	★★★	★★★★	★★	★★	★★

Touring Time: Average 1 hour; minimum 1 hour

Rainy-Day Touring: No

Services and Facilities:

Restaurants No	Lockers No
Alcoholic beverages No	Pet kennels No
Disabled access No	Rain check No
Wheelchair rental No	Private tours No
Baby stroller rental No	

Description and Comments This is a really fun miniature golf course with a couple of caves, lively pirate music, and the requisite pirate ship and pirates. It's not recommended for babies and toddlers. It tends to get quite crowded, so it's best to play at off-times (for example, before dinner rather than after).

Rainy-Day Fun on Martha's Vineyard

Even the thought of a rainy day on an island like the Vineyard might cause panic to set in. But fear not: while cloudy, damp days are not as welcome as sun-drenched beach days, you do have viable options.

The Melting Pot, Vineyard Haven   During one notably heavy rain day, we parlayed our disappointment into hand-glazed ceramics pieces here. Kids happily spend the better part of a morning or afternoon choosing glazes and applying them in a variety of ways to the coffee mug, dish, or platter you have just purchased. The Melting Pot then fires your finished pieces, and you can pick them up a few days later or have them packaged and sent to you. I still smile every time I see the yellow sun at the bottom of the coffee cup that says, "I Love You." Call (508) 693-6768.

The Strand Movie Theater, Oak Bluffs   Rainy days mean matinees, and this theater delivers. Arrive early. Lots of other parents have the same brilliant idea; (508) 696-8300.

M.V. Glassworks, Vineyard Haven   OK, it's raining, but you could consider the glass half full rather than half empty by visiting M.V. Glassworks. It is fascinating to watch glass being blown into colorful, artistic creations; (508) 693-6926.

The Flying Horses Carousel, Oak Bluffs   This carousel is responsible for as many smiling faces as any other attraction on the Vineyard. It is the oldest operating carousel in the United States and it is a national landmark. Its horses were hand-carved in New York in 1876. Amazingly, without all of the razzle-dazzle of a computerized pinball machine (which can be found across the street), the Flying Horses Carousel provides joyful entertainment for youngsters day after day, night after night. For $1, or $8 for a book of ten tickets, your child can go round and round, each time grabbing a ring from the shoot (yes, there is a brass ring). Let it rain: There are other amusements in the same building. To top it all off, on the next corner there is a Mad Martha's Ice Cream Shop that you can run to, dodging raindrops along the way. The carousel is open Easter Sunday through Columbus Day; (508) 693-9481.

Woods Hole Oceanographic Institute

15 School Street (off Water Street), Woods Hole; (508) 289-2252

Hours: Late May–early September, Monday–Saturday 10 a.m.–4:30 p.m.,
Sunday noon to 4:30 p.m.; call for off-season hours (closed
January–March)

Admission: $2 donation suggested for adults

Appeal by Age Groups:

Pre-school	Grade School	Teens	Young Adults	Over 30	Seniors
★	★★★	★★★	★★★★	★★★	★★★

Touring Time: Average 1½ hours; minimum 1 hour

Rainy-Day Touring: Yes

Services and Facilities:

Restaurants No	Lockers No
Alcoholic beverages No	Pet kennels No
Disabled access No	Rain check No
Wheelchair rental No	Private tours Yes
Baby stroller rental No	

Description and Comments   One-hour walking tours are recommended
for those who want to get as much as possible out of this research institution dedicated to marine science (reservations are necessary). Stop in the
visitors center beforehand for the informative video about the institute's
research. Little tykes will be bored; this is best for school-age kids and
up—it's specially thrilling for children interested in marine science.

Nantucket Attractions

Hinchman House Natural Science Museum

7 Milk Street, Nantucket; (508) 228-0898

Hours: June through the fall for self-led tours; call for hours

Admission: Call for admission

Appeal by Age Groups:

Pre-school	Grade School	Teens	Young Adults	Over 30	Seniors
★★	★★★★	★★★	★★	★★	★★

Touring Time: Average 2 hours; minimum ½ hour

Rainy-Day Touring: Yes

Services and Facilities:

Restaurants No	Lockers No
Alcoholic beverages No	Pet kennels No
Disabled access Yes	Rain check No
Wheelchair rental No	Private tours Yes
Baby stroller rental No	

Description and Comments Hinchman House is an ambitious museum on the natural history of Nantucket, with collections of many living island reptiles and preserved birds and fauna. Displays also include freshly cut wildflowers and plants. Natural science programs, such as children's nature classes and bird and nature walks, are administered by the staff. Kids can get hands-on learning about this very special island and its indigenous animals and plants.

Maria Mitchell Aquarium

28 Washington Street, Nantucket; (508) 228-5387

Hours: June–August, Tuesday–Saturday 10 a.m.– 4 p.m.

Admission: $1

Appeal by Age Groups:

Pre-school	Grade School	Teens	Young Adults	Over 30	Seniors
★★	★★★	★★★	★★	★★	★★

Touring Time: Varies depending on whether a family marine ecology trip is taken

Rainy-Day Touring: Yes

Services and Facilities:

Restaurants No	Lockers No
Alcoholic beverages No	Pet kennels No
Disabled access Yes	Rain check No
Wheelchair rental No	Private tours Yes
Baby stroller rental No	

Description and Comments Where but Nantucket could you find a real marine aquarium in a quaint waterfront shack? On the harbor, the Aquarium exhibits Nantucket's fresh- and saltwater marine life. The marine organisms of Nantucket's salt marshes, harbors, and nearshore waters await your acquaintance. Marine ecology trips can be scheduled; reservations are recommended. Friendly science interns are on hand to answer all your questions about mollusks, crustaceans, and fin fish, and there are hands-on exhibits for children.

A Good Read

Whether on a seashell-strewn strand or inside your cottage on a moody weather day, a good book is as important to an island vacation as sunscreen, pails, and shovels. Here are the best places to pick up a good read—for adults and kids.

Nantucket Atheneum. The recently renovated Nantucket Atheneum on India Street, one of the oldest libraries in continuous service in the United States, is housed in an elegant and historic Greek Revival structure (1847). It's a free public library, and its holdings number more than 40,000 volumes plus a collection of historic paintings, sculpture, ship models, and scrimshaw. The new, light-filled Weezie Wing for Children is an exciting and charming library for young readers. The Atheneum offers a Story Hour; call (508) 228-1110 for the schedule.

Maria Mitchell Association Science Library. The Maria Mitchell Association operates a science library with a cheery children's nook. The association is named for America's first woman astronomer, and it pursues a mission to educate adults and children in astronomy, environmental science, and Nantucket history. The association comprises five study centers: the Aquarium, Maria Mitchell Birthplace, Hinchman House, Maria Mitchell Observatory, and Science Library. It's located at 2 Vestal Street, Nantucket; (508) 228-9198; www.mmo.org.

Some of Nantucket's bookstores offer children's activities and book signings by authors of children's books. Children find such signings very exciting and often cherish these books long after their childhood, passing these revered volumes along to their own children and grandchildren.

Maria Mitchell Observatory

Vestal Street Observatory, 3 Vestal Street; Loines Observatory, Milk Street Extension, a short walk away; (508) 228-9273

Hours: October–May, Wednesdays and Fridays at 8 p.m., tours Saturday 11 a.m.; June–September, Monday, Wednesday, and Friday at 8 p.m., tours every day Tuesday–Saturday 11 a.m. (open nights take place at Loines, and the tours take place at Vestal Street)

Admission: $10 adults, $6 children

Lighthouses

Lighthouses engender romance and mystery. Your children may well enjoy *Hardy Boys* stories in which lighthouses play important roles. Today, lighthouses, even those that have been decommissioned by the U.S. Coast Guard, still have tremendous allure. They are associated with a guiding light—beacons of help—for the mariner. They are also picturesque and come in many shapes and sizes. Nantucket has a long, proud maritime past, and three lighthouses guard the island's northern tip, eastern shoreline, and harbor. These are proud, stalwart reminders of the days when Nantucket's main harvests were from the oceans. Great Point Light, Sankaty Head Light, and Brant Point Light safely guided thousands of sailors home to the protection of Nantucket's harbor, helping them avoid the terrible and harrowing shoals and guiding them through Nantucket's infamous fogs. These are wonderful venues for storytelling and photo opportunities.

Great Point Light is on the northern tip of the island, overlooking many miles of splendid beaches. Sankaty Head Light is perched way atop Sankaty Bluff in the east, presiding over one of the island's finest golf courses. Brant Point Light is the most well-known of all Nantucket's lighthouses, as it welcomes the thousands of visitors arriving on the island by boat. The original structure was built in 1746, and it was the second lighthouse built in America.

Appeal by Age Groups:

Pre-school	Grade School	Teens	Young Adults	Over 30	Seniors
★	★★★	★★★	★★★	★★★	★★★

Touring Time: Average 1 hour; minimum 1 hour

Rainy-Day Touring: Yes

Services and Facilities:

Restaurants No	Lockers No
Alcoholic beverages No	Pet kennels No
Disabled access Yes	Rain check No
Wheelchair rental No	Private tours Yes
Baby stroller rental No	

Description and Comments There are two observatories here—Vestal Street and Loines observatories. Both observatories offer research facilities

Other things to Do on Nantucket

Take a Tour   Tour the island by bicycle, van, bus, or on foot, but tour it you must! There are several tour operators available, but only one that features a sixth-generation native—Gail's Tours. Gail stops for pictures too. Pickup is at Chestnut Street. Tours are given at 10 a.m., 1 p.m., and 3 p.m. daily year round. Call (508) 257-6557.

Go Fish   Families can charter a family-fishing expedition aboard fishing boats or with surf-casting guides. Most guides and charters provide all the requisite equipment and training for children and adults. Families can also join the crew of the Friendship sloop *Endeavor* and sail into Nantucket Sound or set sail with chanteyman Steve Sheppard on a "Songs and Stories of the Sea" excursion. All depart from Straight Wharf, and a parent must accompany children. Call (508) 228-5585. Another good option is a fishing excursion with Harbor Cruises (Motor Yacht) on the *Anna W II*. Bonuses: Children's ice cream cruises as well as seal-watch and lobstering cruises.

Enroll in Day Camp   Some children's camps have enrollment requirements, but all happily accept vacationing children. Children's camp programs include full-day and specialized camps for soccer, Little League baseball, field hockey, lacrosse, and basketball. Try: Murray Camp, 25½ Bartlett Road, (508) 325-4600; Nantucket Community School, 10 Surfside Road, (508) 228-7257; Strong Wings, 30 Surfside Road, (508) 228-1769.

Swing   There are several playgrounds on Nantucket—with the usual accoutrements—swing sets, slides, and climbing equipment. If the little ones need to hit the swings, these are the hot spots: Children's Beach (just west of Steamship Wharf), Jetties Beach (a half-mile west of Children's Beach on North Beach Street) and the Nantucket Elementary School.

Play Miniature Golf   What child could possibly not thrill to hitting the green? Nobadeer Mini Golf is open all day long and features a very attractive setting, with lovely gardens, ponds, and a waterfall. It even has a free shuttle service from downtown. It's on Sun Island and Nobadeer Farm roads; (508) 228-8977.

Soak up History   The Nantucket Historical Association was founded in 1894 to preserve the island's historical treasures. Museums and historical houses are situated throughout Nantucket town and illustrate the lives of Nantucketers from the seventeenth-century farming com-

Other things to Do on Nantucket (continued)

munity to the whaling capital of the world during the eighteenth and nineteenth centuries. The historic properties are open June 15–Labor Day 10 a.m.–5 p.m., with curtailed hours during spring and fall. Admission is charged at each site, but all-inclusive passes can be purchased for $10 adults and $5 children ages 5–14 (free admission for children under age 5); (508) 228-0925.

Take an Art Class Budding artists will appreciate Nantucket—the light here is incredible and titillates artists the world over. There are many locations where children can study art on the island. The following offer classes in drawing, painting, ceramics, mixed media, basketry, jewelry making, art, and nature: Nantucket Island School of Design and the Arts, 23 Wauwinet Road, (508) 228-9248, www.nantucket.net/art/nisda; Artists' Association of Nantucket, Gardner Perry Lane; (508) 325-5251.

Go Out on the Town During the summer, Murray Camp offers a Kids Night Out program for ages 5–13 from 6-9 p.m. Parents leave the children and pick them up downtown. Camp counselors entertain the youngsters with theater performances, ghost walks, miniature golf, crabbing trips, and more. Call (508) 325-4600.

Try Thespian Pursuits The Actors Theatre of Nantucket offers a Children's Theater Program from mid-July through August. Young actors and actresses perform in professionally produced versions of well-known plays and musicals. Methodist Church, 2 Centre Street; (508) 228-6325, atnrmc@aol.com.

Color Nantucket Mary Miles has been a resident of Nantucket for more than a decade. She has written a number of books for Nantucket children, including *Color Nantucket #1* and *Color Nantucket #2, Nantucket Etcetera, What's So Special About Nantucket?*, and *Nantucket Gam*. She has four grown children and three grandchildren who are "laptop consultants" for storytelling. You can pick these up in one of the island's bookstores.

Go Fly a Kite Many Nantucket stores sell kites—from the basic to the "Cadillac." Just pick your kite and string, head for the beach (where there always seems to be a good breeze), and watch it soar into the wild blue yonder. The best spots to buy a kite are Nantucket Kiteman, 14 S. Water Street; (508) 228-7089, and Sky's the Limit, at the Courtyard, Straight Wharf; (508) 228-4633.

to astronomers and interns. The education program includes children's astronomy classes and popular public viewing nights at Loines Observatory, which is open year round. Climb a ladder to the eyepiece of a fine, old telescope and sample the sights of the distant heavens. Astronomy has changed since the days when Maria Mitchell swept the skies for comets, but the observatory at 3 Vestal Street is still a place of discovery. Widely known for its program of supervised undergraduate research, the observatory hosts internships for young scientists investigating topics of current interest in astronomy using both telescopes on the site and the best radio and optical telescopes in the nation. Year-round tours at the Vestal Street Observatory feature an outdoor scale-model of the solar system, a planar sundial, sunspot observations (when clear), and a permanent astronomy exhibit. In the summer, public programs also include children's classes in astronomy and talks by visiting and resident astronomers. There are also half-hour educational interactive shows. A professional astronomer, Dr. V. Strelnitski, and primary school teachers of science (Michael Girvin) and drama and dance (Marjory Trott) combined their experiences and ideas in order to achieve a high level of aesthetic attractiveness, scientific truth, and educational effectiveness of the show.

Nantucket Life-Saving Museum

158 Polpis Road, Nantucket; (508) 228-1885

Hours: June 15–Columbus Day weekend, daily 9:30 a.m.–4 p.m.; tours at other times by special arrangement

Admission: $4 for adults, $2 for children age 6 and older, free for children age 5 and under

Appeal by Age Groups:

Pre-school	Grade School	Teens	Young Adults	Over 30	Seniors
★	★★	★★★	★★★	★★★	★★★

Touring Time: Average 1 hour; minimum ½ hour

Rainy-Day Touring: Yes

Services and Facilities:

Restaurants No	Lockers No
Alcoholic beverages No	Pet kennels No
Disabled access Yes	Rain check No
Wheelchair rental No	Private tours Yes
Baby stroller rental No	

Description and Comments This outstanding museum is dedicated to the human drama of man's efforts against the relentless sea and is testimony to those early Nantucket natives who saved hundreds of lives in and near the island's treacherous shores and shoals. It is an authentic replica of the original 1874 U.S. Life-Saving Service Station at Surfside, one of four such Nantucket stations. It tells the stories of people pitted against the angry demands of the sea, people who risked their lives to rescue others, people who knew and understood the little-known motto of the U.S. Life-Saving Service and the United States Coast Guard: "You have to go out, but you don't have to come back." This is a little heavy for the younger set but interesting and humbling for kids old enough to appreciate and respect the sea.

The Whaling Museum

13 Broad Street, Nantucket; (508) 228-1894

Hours: June–September, daily 10 a.m.–5 p.m.; call for off-season hours

Admission: $5 adults, $3 children ages 5–14

Appeal by Age Groups:

Pre-school	Grade School	Teens	Young Adults	Over 30	Senior
★	★★★	★★★	★★★	★★★	★★★

Touring Time: Average 1 hour; minimum ½ hour

Rainy-Day Touring: Yes

Services and Facilities:

Restaurants No	Lockers No
Alcoholic beverages No	Pet kennels No
Disabled access Yes	Rain check No
Wheelchair rental No	Private tours Yes
Baby stroller rental No	

Description and Comments   This building, formerly a candle factory, presently exhibits an outstanding collection of whaling artifacts, paintings, scrimshaw, and (kids love this) a skeleton of a 43-foot finback whale. An extremely interesting lecture on the history of whaling is presented three times daily.

Cape Cod Family-Friendly Restaurants

ARNOLD'S LOBSTER AND CLAM BAR

Route 6, Eastham; (508) 255-2575

Meals Served: Lunch and dinner
Cuisine: Seafood
Entree range: $2.75–35
Children's menu: No, but has some kids' favorites

Reservations: Not accepted
Payment: Cash only

For the best fried clams on the Cape, not to mention milky clam chowder and golden fried onion rings, steer your bike or car to Arnold's. That's right, bike. This roadside seafood place has a great location on the Cape Cod Bike Trail and it makes the perfect stop for families who've worked up an appetite on two wheels. During peak season you may have to wait in line (this spot feeds thousands of people a day in the summer), but the line moves quickly and efficiently, thanks to the efforts of the meticulous owner, Harrison Ford-lookalike Nate Nickerson. Dine on picnic tables under pretty pine trees or on the open-air patio. All fish and shellfish is caught and purchased daily from local waters. The prices are affordable—hamburgers are $2.75, lobster rolls are $10.95. Splurge for one of the lobster dinners (from $15.95), which include the works (corn on the cob and chowder; for $18.95 you can get some of the most succulent steamers around). There's also a raw bar (think Wellfleet oysters) available from 5 to 8 p.m. Wine and beer are available. There is not a children's menu, but there are items that kids love—hamburgers, hot dogs, and grilled cheese. It's open one week before Memorial Day until one week after Labor Day, daily from 11 a.m. until 10 p.m.

EDDY'S CLAM SHACK

Route 28, Yarmouth; no phone

Meals Served: Lunch and dinner
Cuisine: Seafood
Entree range: $5.95 and up
Children's menu: No, but the chicken tenders and grilled cheese are favorites
Reservations: Not accepted
Payment: All types accepted

Tired and worn around the edges, this roadside restaurant is the perfect stop before or after playing a round of mini-golf at Pirate's Cove just down the street. Note: Lots of other people think so, too, so be prepared to wait. We recommend the clams—lightly battered and not greasy. It's open year round.

Martha's Vineyard Family-Friendly Restaurants

BLACK DOG TAVERN

Beach Street Extension (on the harbor), Vineyard Haven; (508) 693-9223

Meals served: Breakfast, lunch, and dinner

Cuisine: Seafood and great desserts
Entree range: $9.95 and up
Children's menu: Yes, for dinner
Reservations: No
Payment: All types accepted

You've no doubt seen this restaurant's signature black Lab T-shirt, so now try the food. Home-cooking (think seafood), yummy pies, and the you've-got-to-try-it Eggs Galveston for breakfast make this salty, no-frills restaurant an island institution. It's located a seashell's throw from the ferry—so you might want to plan your ferry ride accordingly (in other words, build time in for a meal at the Black Dog before you board or after disembarking).

COOP DEVILLE RESTAURANT

Dockside Marketplace, Oak Bluffs Harbor; (508) 693-3420

Meals served: Lunch and dinner
Cuisine: Chicken wings, seafood, raw bar
Entree range: $8.95 and up
Children's menu: Yes
Reservations: Not accepted
Payment: All types accepted

Excellent burgers and fries and spicy chicken wings are favorites here, but there's also an outdoor raw bar where you can enjoy clams on the half-shell before indulging in a New England clambake dinner or overstuffed lobster roll. Kids who shun seafood can munch on jumbo hot dogs and chicken fingers. The restaurant has a wonderful setting with a view of the harbor and sunsets worthy of applause.

GIORDANO'S

107 Circuit Avenue, Oak Bluffs; (508) 693-0184

Meals served: Lunch and dinner
Cuisine: Italian
Entree range: $7.95 and up
Children's menu: No (but there's pizza)
Reservations: Not accepted
Payment: No credit cards

Giordano's offers take-out pizza and very good Italian fare. We spent the beginning of at least one evening at Giordano's and enjoyed the kid-friendly atmosphere and staff. You'll find its location convenient for a night of merriment with children too. It's near the carousel.

PAPA'S PIZZA

158 Circuit Avenue, Oak Bluffs; (508) 693-1400

Meals served: Lunch and dinner
Cuisine: Pizza and other Italian dishes
Entree range: $1.50–8
Children's menu: No
Reservations: No
Payment: All Types

It's affordable, it's easy, and believe it or not there's something about a slice of pizza by the sea—it just tastes better! You can also get subs, chicken fingers, mozzarella sticks, and Italian dishes.

ZAPOTEC

10 Kennebec Avenue, Oak Bluffs; (508) 693-6800

Meals served: Lunch and dinner
Cuisine: Mexican and Southwestern
Entree range: $7 and up
Children's menu: Yes
Reservations: Not necessary
Payment: All types accepted

Got a hankering for Mexican food in New England? It happens to the best of us. You can get decent Mexican food (and Mexican beer) here and enjoy it in a casual setting. You can also order take out and head for the beach.

Nantucket Family-Friendly Restaurants

ARNO'S AT 41 MAIN STREET

41 Main Street; (508) 228-7001

Meals served: Breakfast, lunch, and dinner
Cuisine: Eclectic
Entree range: $12 and up
Children's menu: Yes
Reservations: Recommended
Payment: All types accepted

This unassuming storefront facing the passersby on Main Street specializes in family dining, serving breakfast, lunch, and dinner. The breakfasts are bountiful, the lunches inventive, and the dinners delectable. Soaring brick walls and muralesque paintings by artist Molly Dee evoke a gentler, bygone era. The portions are decent, and the food is priced fairly. It's closed January through March.

THE ATLANTIC CAFE

15 S. Water Street; (508) 228-0570

Meals served: Lunch and dinner
Cuisine: Seafood, appetizers
Entree range: $15 and up
Children's menu: Yes
Reservations: Not accepted
Payment: All types accepted

Casual, comfortable, and congenial. The food is quite good, and the chowder is legendary. This cafe has won awards for being the best inexpensive place to eat on the island. Seafood dishes, hearty appetizers (the nachos win our vote!), pub fare, plus the special children's menu—and even high chairs—make this a particularly welcoming place for family dining.

BROTHERHOOD OF THIEVES

23 Broad Street; no listed phone

Meals served: Lunch and dinner
Cuisine: Sandwiches, burgers
Entree range: $7.95 and up
Children's menu: Yes
Reservations: Not accepted
Payment: No credit cards

Read the menu—it begs the question, "How will I ever choose?" Despite its boisterous nature, it is a good place for the whole family. It has wonderful ambiance, with low ceilings, oak beams, candle-lit rooms (it's so dark inside, candles are required even in full daylight—that will appeal to the little ones). Extra thick sandwiches, burgers, chowder, Brotherhood shoestring fries are a few things to try. The wait can be considerable.

THE DOWNEYFLAKE RESTAURANT

18 Sparks Avenue; (508) 228-4533

Meals served: Breakfast and lunch
Cuisine: Pancakes, sandwiches, doughnuts
Entree range: $4 and up
Children's menu: Yes

Reservations: Not accepted
Payment: No credit cards

This unassuming and beloved little cottage restaurant is an institution on this island of institutions. For several decades, islanders and visitors alike have raved about its wonderful baked goods, blueberry pancakes, and legendary doughnuts. The Flake serves breakfast and lunch seven days a week from a menu of favorites and daily specials for good food and fast, friendly service in a relaxed atmosphere. Breakfast is served until 2 p.m. daily (noon on Sunday). Look for the big doughnut outside.

FAREGROUNDS RESTAURANT AND PUDLEY'S PUB

27 Fairgrounds Road; (508) 228-4095

Meals served: Lunch, dinner, and late-night snacks
Cuisine: You name it
Entree range: $5 and up
Children's menu: Yes
Reservations: Yes
Payment: All types accepted

This is a great place to take the children. The ambiance is cozy, and the dinner menu is diverse and affordable. Faregrounds offers the largest appetizer menu on the island—the 40 starter offerings include everything from nachos and potato skins to seafood burritos and homemade crab cakes. There are nightly surf-and-turf specials and daily all-you-can-eat specials. After dinner or for lighter fare, cross the hallway for Pudley's Pub, where lunch is served and more than 60 items are offered until midnight. It's open seven days a week year round.

THE ROSE & CROWN

23 S. Water Street; (508) 228-2595

Meals served: Lunch and dinner
Cuisine: Seafood, burgers, sandwiches
Entree range: $10 and up
Children's menu: Yes
Reservations: No
Payment: All types accepted

This is the perennial favorite of islanders, offering a traditional pub atmosphere. Fresh seafood and lobster, chowder, steaks, salads, burgers, sandwiches, and their famous hand-cut French fries are favorites. The restaurant offers

Get It to Go

Provisions in Harbor Square at Straight Wharf offers gourmet take-out and picnics to go. Think pâtés, cheeses, homemade muffins, bagels, scones, baguettes, croissants, specialty salads, hearty soups, chowders and coffees, espresso and cappuccino. Outstanding, awesome, and delectable sandwiches will make your mouth water. If you can leave Provisions without downing your sandwich, you'll be in the minority. Call or stop in to have Provisions prepare your picnic or beach lunch (and someone should get the Muffaletta sandwich—hauntingly delicious); (508) 228-3258.

early bird specials. Bonus: The tables are covered with paper so little doodlers can doodle away.

SEAGRILLE

45 Sparks Avenue; (508) 325-5700

Meals served: Lunch and dinner
Cuisine: Seafood and some meat
Children's menu: Yes
Entree range: $15.95 and up
Reservations: Yes (preferred)
Payment: All types accepted

A hand-painted mural sets a nautical theme for this wonderful spot for seafood, which, as the name indicates, is the house specialty. The chef's interpretation of local and regional seafood dishes are both traditional and creative. The specials—quesadilla salad and bouillabaisse—are mongo-sized. SeaGrille sports an award-winning wine list.

THE TAP ROOM AT THE JARED COFFIN HOUSE

29 Broad Street; (508) 228-2400

Meals served: Lunch and dinner
Cuisine: Pub fare
Entree range: $5–15
Children's menu: No, but kid-friendly food is on the menu
Reservations: No
Payment: All types accepted

Just like the name says, this place is a reminder of those affable pubs from days of yore. Fine food and spirits are offered daily in a casual atmosphere for lunch and dinner, and it's fun for the whole family. Smoking is permitted in the bar.

VINCENT'S

21 S. Water Street; (508) 228-0189

Meals served: Lunch, dinner, late-night snacks
Cuisine: Italian, seafood
Entree range: $7 and up
Children's menu: Yes
Reservations: Yes
Payment: All types accepted

Who doesn't love pasta? You can get it here, along with seafood platters, stuffed lobster, lobster rolls, grilled seafood, and a host of Italian specialties at lunch and dinner. Come late-night for appetizers and pastries along with espresso and cappuccino. Take out is available.

Boston and Cambridge

The romantic city of **Boston** is also idyllic for families looking for cultural attractions, green spaces, first-class restaurants, and affordable hotels all wrapped up in a tidy, compact package. The beauty of this very civil city with old European charm is that it is a walking town. You can reach most of the hot spots by foot; if you tire, jump on the T, which is also easily accessible from anywhere in the city.

Cambridge is a stone's throw across the Charles River and home to Harvard and MIT. A stroll or bike ride along the Charles (either on the Boston or Cambridge side) is a perfect way to while away a couple of hours, and there are several small bridges you can safely cross by foot to reach either Boston or Cambridge. There's more to Cambridge than academia; there are many cafes scattered about the tight and narrow streets, as well as shops (you'll have plenty of opportunities to buy Harvard T-shirts and sweatshirts). You can also tour Harvard Yard if you wish. Several good family hotels are also here. Remember to book early if you're coming around college graduation times. That's a good rule of thumb for booking hotels in Boston, too, as Boston University, Boston College, and Northeastern are located in Beantown. Families vie for hotel rooms come graduation each spring (as well as during alumni weekends and other major events).

Many visitors spend a couple days in Boston and Cambridge before or after visiting Vermont, Maine, New Hampshire, Rhode Island, and Cape Cod and the islands of Martha's Vineyard and Nantucket. Consider Boston the hub, and the other states and destinations the spokes in the wheel. In fact, whenever we visit New England, we will almost always visit Boston, for a couple of days, an overnight, or just a few hours to take in a game at Fenway Park or indulge in an ice cream cone at one of the outdoor spots along trendy Newbury Street. You can also day trip from Boston to

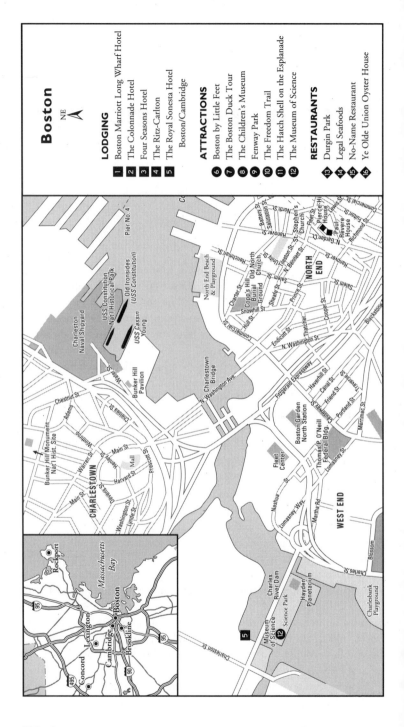

Boston

NE

LODGING
1. Boston Marriott Long Wharf Hotel
2. The Colonnade Hotel
3. Four Seasons Hotel
4. The Ritz-Carlton
5. The Royal Sonesta Hotel Boston/Cambridge

ATTRACTIONS
6. Boston by Little Feet
7. The Boston Duck Tour
8. The Children's Museum
9. Fenway Park
10. The Freedom Trail
11. The Hatch Shell on the Esplanade
12. The Museum of Science

RESTAURANTS
13. Durgin Park
14. Legal Seafoods
15. No-Name Restaurant
16. Ye Olde Union Oyster House

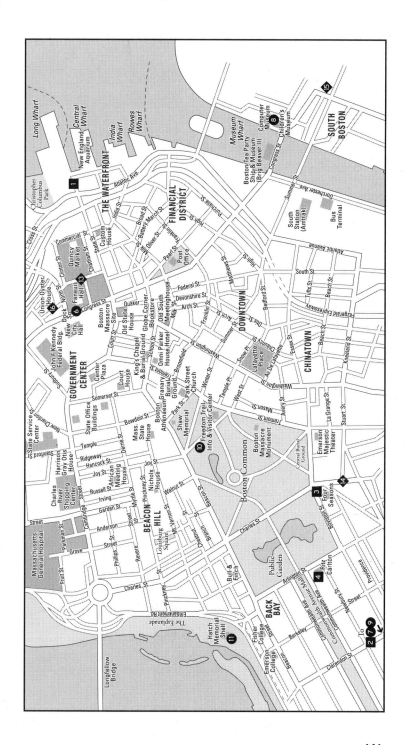

places such as Cape Cod and Salem; ferries frequently depart Boston in summer months to these destinations.

Family Lodging

Boston Marriott Long Wharf Hotel

This huge, 400-room property has a fun, busy location right on the water and not far from the aquarium. Kids love the indoor pool, saunas, whirlpools, and game room. Caveat: Some of the guest rooms overlook the Big Dig—make sure you request a room overlooking the harbor instead of the street or your wake-up call may be a backing-up bulldozer (beep, beep, beep). Double-room rates begin at $200 per night but inquire about discounted weekend packages. 296 State Street, Boston; (800) 228-9290.

The Colonnade Hotel

This large hotel, across the street from the Hynes Convention Center complex, wows kids at check-in with a fanny pack filled with things such as binoculars, crayons, and sunglasses as part of the Kids See & Do weekend package. The package also includes four passes (two adults and two children) to the Science Museum or Aquarium and parking. Another thing kids and parents love is the outdoor rooftop pool. The hotel's central location puts you within walking distance of most attractions, including Fenway Park and Faneuil Hall. Brasserie Jo, the hotel's restaurant, is reminiscent of a Paris bistro, and the food is *tres bien*. The package is $189 per night. 120 Huntington Avenue, Boston; (800) 962-3030.

Four Seasons Hotel

As expensive as the Ritz-Carlton, this hotel has less glitz but with just much, if not more, sophistication. You can't beat the service at the Four Seasons—you'll want for nothing. Want to go to Legal Seafoods in town for dinner? They don't take reservations, and the wait can be upwards of two hours on a busy night. But don't worry—the concierge at the Four Seasons will call over and get you priority seating. Another thing the hotel has going for it is its location directly across the street from the Public Garden. Come winter, mosey out the door with skates in tow and glide around Frog Pond before heading back for afternoon tea at your home away from home. You also can't beat the central location, the service, and the penthouse pool. If you can afford it, this is where you want to stay. Rates begin at $300 per night. 200 Boylston Street, Boston; (617) 338-4400.

The Ritz-Carlton

Save your pennies. A stay at this Boston gem—one of the oldest hotels in town dating to 1927—will cost you, but, as the saying goes, you get what

---

Dog Days

Can't bear to leave Rover in the kennel? Don't whimper. Several Boston hotels allow dogs, including: The Four Seasons, The Ritz-Carlton, The Seaport Hotel (phone (877) SEAPORT), The Sheraton Boston Hotel & Towers (phone (800) 325-3535), Le Meridien Boston (phone (800) 543-4300), The Westin Copley Place Boston (phone (800) WESTIN), the Howard Johnson Hotel-Boston/Kenmore (phone (800) 654-2000), and the Fairmont Copley Plaza (phone (800) 527-4727).

---

you pay for. One of the most unique features of this small hotel is a special children's room, which has been furbished by FAO Schwartz, the famous toy store. We're talking a loft bed, Nintendo Center, games, and toys for every age group. The kids' room (there is only one in the hotel) is connected by a door to another room, presumably the parents' (although we're told it's often used for the nanny). The friendly elevator operators often let the kids take over. Another bonus: The Ritz is directly across from the Public Garden and Frog Pond, where the swan boat rides are a huge hit with kids. Rates begin at $200 per night. 15 Arlington Street, Boston; (800) 241-3333.

The Royal Sonesta Hotel Boston/Cambridge

In the shadow of Boston—just across the Charles River—sits this family-friendly hotel, within magnifying-glass distance of the Science Museum. The hotel has a great indoor pool and a whirlpool, but there's no lifeguard. Make sure you reserve a room with a view, as the views of Boston from this hotel are renowned. Other accolades: the Charles River is just outside the hotel's doorstep, with a lovely walking path for a stroll or jog. Take advantage of the hotel's picnic-to-go—you'll get a Land's End cooler stocked with fresh fruit, yummy sandwiches, drinks, tablecloths, salt, pepper . . . the only thing missing is the ants. Rates begin at $175 per night. Go for one of the summer packages that include admission to such attractions as the Science Museum. 5 Cambridge Parkway, Cambridge; (800) SONESTA.

Attractions

Boston by Little Feet

Meet at the statue of Samuel Adams on the Congress Street side of
  Faneuil Hall; (617) 367-2345

Hours: Saturday at 10 a.m., Sunday at 2 p.m., and Monday at 10 a.m.

Fenway Park

If you're in town when the Red Sox are playing, you're in luck! But if they're not, you haven't totally struck out. Take the Fenway Park tour. You'll see the famed Green Monster in left field, stop at the press box and the "600" Club (a Red Sox private suite), and take a stroll around the playing field via the warning track. Kids love this tour—especially starry-eyed Little Leaguers. It's disabled accessible, and there is a fee. Gate D, Yawkey Way and Van Ness Street, Boston; (617) 236-6666 (for the tour) or (617) 267-8661 for game tickets.

Admission: $6

Appeal by Age Groups:

Pre-school	Grade School	Teens	Young Adults	Over 30	Seniors
	★★★★				

Touring Time: Average 1 hour; minimum 1 hour

Rainy-Day Touring: Yes

Services and Facilities:

Restaurants No	Lockers No
Alcoholic beverages No	Pet kennels No
Disabled access No	Rain check No
Wheelchair rental No	Private tours No
Baby stroller rental No	

Description and Comments   What a great way for 6- to 12-year-olds to explore the Freedom Trail (description follows). You won't see it all—but that's exactly the point. Consider this tour the Cliff Notes version of the Freedom Trail.

The Boston Duck Tour

101 Huntington Avenue, Prudential Center, Boylston Street side, Boston; (800) 226-7442

Hours: Open daily 9 a.m.–a half hour before sunset (rain or shine)

Admission: $21 general, $18 seniors and students, $11 children ages 4–12, 25¢ children age 3 and under

Appeal by Age Groups:

Pre-school	Grade School	Teens	Young Adults	Over 30	Seniors
★★	★★★★	★★★★	★★★★	★★★★	★★★

Fun in Any Season

For a fun summer afternoon, grab some sandwiches to go at one of a handful of take-out spots along Newbury Street. Then stroll the couple of blocks or so to the Public Garden, and set out your picnic spread on the banks of Frog Pond. After you've satiated your kids' appetites for lunch and for running around, take the relaxing 15-minute ride on the Swan Boats. Perfection.

For an afternoon of winter fun, forgo the picnic and opt instead to eat at one of Newbury's casual cafes. Then, stroll to Frog Pond with skates over your shoulders (bring your own or rent them.) There's something so absolutely magical about gliding along this frozen pond on a burly winter day in Boston. Toes numb? Head across the street to the Four Seasons Hotel for afternoon tea, held daily from 3 to 4:30 p.m. Tip: Make reservations for tea in advance; (617) 338-4400. Bliss.

Touring Time: Average 1 hour; minimum 1 hour
Rainy-Day Touring: Yes
Services and Facilities:

Restaurants No	Lockers No
Alcoholic beverages No	Pet kennels No
Disabled access No	Rain check No
Wheelchair rental No	Private tours No
Baby stroller rental No	

Description and Comments This tour is lots of fun and a fresh, exciting look at Boston's history. You can't help but quack up on this unique tour that has you riding a World War II amphibious tank through the streets of Boston before finally settling into the Charles River. This is great fun for every family member—and educational, too. (Note: not appropriate for babies).

The Children's Museum

300 Congress Street, Boston; (617) 426-8855
Hours: Daily 10 a.m.–5 p.m., Friday until 9 p.m.
Admission: $7 adults, $6 children and seniors, $2 for children age 1 and under; on Fridays between 5 and 9 p.m. admission is $1 for everyone
Appeal by Age Groups:

Pre-school	Grade School	Teens	Young Adults	Over 30	Seniors
★★★	★★★★	★	★	★	★

Touring Time: Average 1 hour; minimum 1 hour

Rainy-Day Touring: Yes

Services and Facilities:

Restaurants No	Lockers No
Alcoholic beverages No	Pet kennels No
Disabled access No	Rain check No
Wheelchair rental No	Private tours No
Baby stroller rental No	

Description and Comments   Innocent, rainy-day fun! Kids can dress up in Grandma's Attic, run amuck in a giant playspace full of toys, and climb a two-story-high maze. Note: Try to steer clear of school holidays; if it's too crowded it can be unpleasant for adults and kids alike.

The Freedom Trail

147 Tremont Street and at the Bunker Hill Pavilion in the Charlestown Navy Yard Visitor Center; (617) 242-5601

Hours: Open daily 9 a.m.–5 p.m. This is a self-guided tour so you can set your own hours.

Admission: None

Appeal by Age Groups:

Pre-school	Grade School	Teens	Young Adults	Over 30	Seniors
★	★★★	★★★	★★★	★★★	★★★

Touring Time: Average depends on how much of the trail you want to cover. For the entire trail, plan on 3 hours; minimum as little time as you care to spend

Rainy-Day Touring: No

Services and Facilities:

Restaurants Along the way	Lockers No
Alcoholic beverages Yes	Pet kennels No
Disabled access Yes	Rain check No
Wheelchair rental No	Private tours Yes
Baby stroller rental No	

Description and Comments   Wow, this is great fun for families because you can do it at your own pace, packing in a lot of history and stopping along the way at kid-friendly places like ice cream stores. Sites on the Freedom Trail include: Boston Common, America's oldest public park; the Boston Globe Store, the meeting place of authors Emerson, Hawthorne, Holmes, and Stowe; the Bunker Hill Monument, a 221-foot monument commemorating the first battle in Boston, the Battle of Bunker Hill; Faneuil Hall,

You Want a What?

Not only is there the infamous New England accent to contend with, but there's also a unique language in this neck of the woods, especially when it comes to food. For instance, when ordering soda such as Coca Cola, you'd better ask for "tonic." When requesting sprinkles on an ice cream cone, ask for "jimmies." Crave a milkshake? Ask for a "frappe" (pronounced frap).

built in 1742 as a town meeting place and public market; several burying grounds of such notables as Paul Revere, Samuel Adams, John Hancock, and Cotton Mather; King's Chapel and Burying Ground, Boston's first Anglican Church; Old North Church, Christ Church, Boston's oldest church building built in 1723 (services are still held); the Old State House; Park Street Church, where the hymn *America* was sung for the first time in a public space in 1831; Paul Revere's house; and the USS *Constitution,* the world's oldest warship, known as Old Ironsides. A three-mile, red-painted path connects Boston's historic sights from the Boston Common to the Bunker Hill Monument. You can get free maps, brochures, and info at the Boston Common Visitor Center, (617) 536-4100.

The Hatch Shell on the Esplanade

The Esplanade; (888) SEE-BOSTON

Hours: Friday evenings; varies, call for times

Admission: Free

Appeal by Age Groups:

Pre-school	Grade School	Teens	Young Adults	Over 30	Seniors
★★★	★★★★	★★★★	★★★★	★★★	★★

Touring Time: Average length of the movie; minimum N/A

Rainy-Day Touring: No

Services and Facilities:

Restaurants No	Lockers No
Alcoholic beverages No	Pet kennels No
Disabled access Yes	Rain check No
Wheelchair rental No	Private tours No
Baby stroller rental No	

Description and Comments   It's free, it's fun, it's summertime, and the living is easy at this outdoor amphitheater. Traditionally used for concerts

---

Faneuil Hall Marketplace

This is one of the best spots in town to eat lunch or dinner. It's an attractive, brick-walled food court with everything you could possibly want, from chowder to chicken to Chinese. It's inexpensive, and we guarantee you won't hear a complaint from your children that they can't find anything to eat here.

(the July Fourth fireworks concert by the Boston Pops is the Cadillac of concerts), on Friday evenings this venue on the Esplanade is a movie-lovers paradise. Bring a picnic, and spread out on the sprawling lawn in front of the Hatch Shell and catch a family movie. It's a great freebie! Tip: Arrive early and stake out your spot.

The Museum of Science

O'Brien Highway, Boston; (617) 723-2500

Hours: Saturday–Thursday 9 a.m.–5 p.m., Friday 9 a.m.–9 p.m.

Admission: $10 adults, $3 children ages 3–7 and seniors

Appeal by Age Groups:

Pre-school	Grade School	Teens	Young Adults	Over 30	Seniors
★★	★★★	★★	★★	★★	★★

Touring Time: Average 2 hours; minimum 1 hour

Rainy-Day Touring: Yes

Services and Facilities:

Restaurants Yes	Lockers No
Alcoholic beverages No	Pet kennels No
Disabled access Yes	Rain check No
Wheelchair rental No	Private tours Yes
Baby stroller rental No	

Description and Comments   The exhibits in the museum are OK, but what really sets this science museum apart from others in its league is the Omni Theatre—a very cool experience for school-age kids. We saw the Michael Jordan film on a Saturday night—a great way to spend an evening. And also worth the price of admission is The Planetarium—low key and informative, again especially appropriate for school-age kids. It doesn't touch New York's new planetarium in terms of scale and quality, but it offers a nice explanation of stars, comets, and other space stuff.

Family-Friendly Restaurants

DURGIN PARK

30 N. Market Street (Faneuil Hall); (617) 227-2038

Meals served: Lunch and dinner
Cuisine: Seafood
Entree range: $10–20
Children's menu: No
Reservations: No
Payment: All types accepted

This tourist spot smack in the middle of lively Faneuil Hall is reputed as much for its good food as for its no-nonsense (but efficient) wait staff. Order the bread pudding for dessert.

LEGAL SEAFOODS

26 Park Square; (617) 426-4444

5 Cambridge Center, Kendall Square, Cambridge; (617) 864-3400

Meals served: Lunch and dinner
Cuisine: Seafood
Entree range: $10–20
Children's menu: Yes
Reservations: No
Payment: All types accepted

Legal Seafoods is atypical of chain restaurants. Each location dishes up just-plucked-from-the-sea seafood. The kids' menu offers a whole or half lobster for kids who want to see if they like it without breaking Mom and Dad's budget. The lobster meat is thoughtfully taken out and put back into the shell before it is served to make it easy on kid fingers. The staff is super friendly, the pace is kid-friendly, and the ambiance is casual. Note: You may have to wait hours for a table. If you are staying at a hotel with a concierge, enlist his or her help in securing a table. While Legals doesn't take reservations, it helps to have a hotel concierge make a call on your behalf and it will most certainly reduce your waiting time—considerably, in most cases.

NO-NAME RESTAURANT

Rock and Roll

Plymouth Rock is a must-see for all kids who are familiar with the story of the Pilgrims, and it's a chance for those not familiar to become so. Don't get your hopes up too high—this rock is small compared to its legendary status and it is well protected so kids won't be able to climb upon it. Plan to visit the rock when you visit Plimoth Plantation (it's about three miles away) and the *Mayflower II*, berthed just a short stroll from Plymouth Rock. See page 172 for a sidetrip to Plymouth.

---

15 Fish Pier, Boston; (617) 338-7539

Meals served: Lunch and dinner
Cuisine: Seafood
Entree range: $7.95 and up
Children's menu: No
Reservations: Not accepted
Payment: No credit cards

This was a favorite haunt of mine when I went to college in Boston. It's not easy to find, which makes it that much more special. The crowds tend to grow quickly and you'll dine with others at big tables, but you couldn't find a more laid-back and fun spot to eat in Boston. There's no kids' menu, but there are hamburgers and chicken on the menu, and you are also welcome to share your plate with your child. Believe us, this is a friendly, accommodating, come-on-in-and-have-a-good time restaurant. Caveat: Because of this spot's great reputation, it's super popular. Try to arrive as early as possible, especially if you've got impatient little ones.

YE OLDE UNION OYSTER HOUSE

41 Union Street; (617) 227-2750

Meals served: Lunch and dinner
Cuisine: Seafood and fish
Entree range: $10–20
Children's menu: Yes
Reservations: No
Payment: All types accepted

Here, in one of the country's oldest restaurants (1826), you can cozy right up to the oyster bar where Daniel Webster used to hang, or for a more family- friendly experience, sit upstairs in a booth in one of the darkly lit

---

Mayflower II

This is a full-scale replica of the type of ship that brought the Pilgrims from England to America in 1620. It is fascinating for kids, especially because of its *small* size. Actors walk its decks describing the Pilgrims' life aboard the ship, and kids love the adventure of being able to board and explore. During the summer months, expect crowds. Admission is $5.75 for adults, $3.75 for children ages 6 to 12. However, you can purchase admission to both the *Mayflower II* and Plimoth Plantation for $18.50 adults, $16.50 seniors, and $11 children ages 6 to 12. Kids younger than 6 get in free. It's open April through November, daily from 9 a.m. to 5 p.m. See Plymouth Side Trip on page 172.

---

rooms. Try and get a window seat that overlooks the Holocaust Memorial Wall (sobering, yes, but it's interesting to watch the throngs of people). Another thing this restaurant has going for it is that it's smack on The Freedom Trail, so work up an appetite and dig in. There is a kids' menu: the thick peanut butter and jelly sandwich is served with a slice of melon, tomatoes, fries, and a bowl of coleslaw. Coloring books, placemats with the story of the Oyster House, and a compact map of the Freedom Trail entertain and educate.

Side Trip: Lexington and Concord

Go west, young man. Boston's neighbors to the west are just as keen on history as the big city. Take Route 2A about 20 minutes west of Boston, to visit the **homes of Louise May Alcott, Nathaniel Hawthorne, Ralph Waldo Emerson,** and the site of **Henry David Thoreau's cabin.** The first battle of the Revolutionary War took place in Lexington, and history buffs will want to visit the Minuteman statue and village green. Henry David Thoreau put Concord on the map, more specifically its pond, **Walden Pond,** where Thoreau took time out to write and contemplate his life. Walden Pond is hugely popular with families, thanks to its tranquil waters. Take a short hike to a replica of Thoreau's modest cabin. It's open Memorial Day to Labor Day from 1 to 8 p.m.; call for spring and fall hours. Parking costs $2. Route 126; (978) 369-3254. While you can spend the night in Lexington and Concord, we recommend you visit these areas as day trips out of Boston.

Side Trip: Plymouth

While you can stay in the town of Plymouth, we recommend visiting the attraction as part of a day trip either from Boston (it's a 45-minute trip without traffic) or Cape Cod (it's about 15 minutes from the Cape). Most children learn about Plymouth Rock and the Pilgrims in school, so a visit to Plymouth is an educational trip.

ATTRACTIONS
Plimoth Plantation

Route 3, Plymouth; (508) 746-1622

Hours: April–November, daily 9 a.m.–5 p.m.

Admission: $18.50 adults, $16.50 seniors, $11 children ages 6–17

Appeal by Age Groups:

Pre-school	Grade School	Teens	Young Adults	Over 30	Seniors
★★	★★★★	★★★	★★	★★	★★

Touring Time: Average 3–4 hours; minimum 1½ hours

Rainy-Day Touring: Yes

Services and Facilities:

Restaurants	Yes	Lockers	No
Alcoholic beverages	No	Pet kennels	No
Disabled access	Yes	Rain check	No
Wheelchair rental	No	Private tours	Yes
Baby stroller rental	No		

Description and Comments Step back in time to see and do what the Pilgrims did in the 1600s. This re-created 1627 village doesn't stray much from the period—the re-enactors behave much as the real Pilgrims would have when this community thrived in the 17th century. They stay in character as they talk to visitors and answer kids' questions. Expect to walk a lot (they didn't have autos back then, remember); comfortable shoes for adults and kids are recommended.

Side Trip: Salem and Rockport

Gloucester and its more refined sister fishing village of **Rockport** have always drawn tourists to their shores. But the salty coastal towns are drawing more crowds than ever these days, thanks to *The Perfect Storm,* a true tale about the disappearance of the swordfishing boat *Andrea Gail.* The movie was shot on location, so many tourists want to see the town where the movie was made. These North Shore villages are an easy day trip from Boston (you can take a train or drive) or a great place to lie low for a couple of days.

If you decide to skip a visit to the **Witching Village** of Salem it may come back to haunt you—the kids will love the spookiness of it all (especially Harry Potter fans who are fascinated by wizardry and witchcraft). You can easily do Salem in a day by taking a day cruise from Boston. But there are two reasons you'll want to spend a night here. First, **The Salem Inn** is family friendly and has a really cool basement for breakfast (included in the rate). And second, there is a floating restaurant in the middle of the harbor (on a small barge), accessible only by boat. The food is good, the ambiance is super casual, and the kids are encouraged by the manager to throw the leftovers overboard to the hungry fish that scamper to chow it down.

Manchester-by-the-Sea is a darling village that is right on the commuter rail to Boston, and, alas, many Bostonians flee the hot city concrete in summer for the squeaky "singing" sands of **Singing Beach** here. It's not a huge beach, but it's lovely and there are lifeguards, snack bars, and rest rooms. Of course, if your itinerary calls for Boston only, you might want to consider taking a day trip to Singing Beach. You can get there on the train or, of course, by driving. But take note: You must park in the train parking lot, and it is about $15 per day and a half-mile walk to the beach—okay for teens and preteens but too far for little ones. Manchester-by-the-Sea is about nine miles northeast of Salem and 28 miles northeast of Boston. Take Route 127, and you can't miss it.

FAMILY LODGING

The Salem Inn

For an authentic New England experience, opt to stay in this neat inn with three linked properties. Two are former ship captain's homes and are listed on the National Register of Historic Places. There is also the Peabody House, perfect for families, with suites and kitchenettes. The inn is within walking distance of all Salem attractions, and there is a lovely patio out back for sipping sherry and refreshments (compliments of the house). The basement-level restaurant is really cool for kids—dungeon-like with stone walls and low ceilings, it is where the complimentary breakfast is served each morning. Rates begin at about $100 per night, including breakfast. 7 Summer Street, Salem; (800) 446-2995.

ATTRACTIONS

The House of Seven Gables

54 Turner Street, Salem; (978) 744-0991

Hours: May–November, daily 10 a.m.–5 p.m.; December–April, daily 10 a.m.–5 p.m. and Sunday noon to 5 p.m.; closed the first two weeks in January.

Admission: $8 adults, $5 children 6–17, free for kids under age 6

Appeal by Age Groups:

Pre-school	Grade School	Teens	Young Adults	Over 30	Seniors
★★★	★★★	★★★★	★★★★	★★★★	

Touring Time: Average 1 hour; minimum 1 hour

Rainy-Day Touring: Yes

Services and Facilities:

Restaurants Yes	Lockers No
Alcoholic beverages No	Pet kennels No
Disabled access No	Rain check No
Wheelchair rental No	Private tours Yes
Baby stroller rental No	

Description and Comments   This pretty home on the water was the inspiration for Nathaniel Hawthorne's novel of the same name. Kids love the secret staircase. There is a short, kid-friendly tour of the house, and then you are welcome to tour Hawthorne's birthplace (which was moved to this location) on your own.

The Salem Trolley

Trolley Depot, 191 Essex Street, (978) 744-5469

Hours: May–October, daily 10 a.m.–5 p.m. (extended hours July and August); March and April, weekends only 10 a.m.–4 p.m.

Admission: $9 for all ages

Appeal by Age Groups:

Pre-school	Grade School	Teens	Young Adults	Over 30	Seniors
★★★	★★★★	★★★★	★★★	★★★	★★★

Touring Time: Average 1 hour; minimum 1 hour

Rainy-Day Touring: Yes

Services and Facilities:

Restaurants No	Wheelchair rental No
Alcoholic beverages No	Baby stroller rental No
Disabled access Yes	Rain check No
Lockers No	Private tours Yes
Pet kennels No	

Description and Comments   Take a trolley tour when you first arrive in

Salem; it's a great way to get your bearings about town. You'll get a narrated tour of the sights, and you can also use the trolley as a shuttle between attractions.

The Salem Wax Museum

288 Derby Street, Salem; (978) 740-2WAX

Hours: November–April, daily 9 a.m.–5 p.m.; May–June and September, daily 9 a.m.–6 p.m.; July–August and October, daily 9 a.m. to 7 p.m.

Admission: $4.50

Appeal by Age Groups:

Pre-school	Grade School	Teens	Young Adults	Over 30	Seniors
★★	★★★★	★★★★	★★★★	★★★	★★★

Touring Time: Average 45 minutes; minimum 30 minutes

Rainy-Day Touring: Yes

Services and Facilities:

Restaurants No	Lockers No
Alcoholic beverages No	Pet kennels No
Disabled access Yes	Rain check No
Wheelchair rental No	Private tours No
Baby stroller rental No	

Description and Comments   It's not a world-class wax museum, but if you lower your expectations you'll find this smallish museum interesting. Hands-on activities include gravestone rubbing. Tip: Don't purchase the Salem Hysteria Pass, which gives you admission to the Salem Wax Museum and the adjacent Salem Witch Village. You can skip the Witch Village altogether—it's not worth the price of admission. So just buy single admission to the Wax Museum.

Salem Willows

160–180 Fort Avenue, Salem; (978) 745-0251

Hours: Call for hours

Admission: Free, but you'll need to buy tickets for the rides and arcades

Appeal by Age Groups:

Pre-school	Grade School	Teens	Young Adults	Over 30	Seniors
★★★	★★★★	★★★★	★★	★	★

Touring Time: Average 1 hour; minimum ½ hour

Rainy-Day Touring: Yes

Services and Facilities:

Restaurants Yes	Lockers No
Alcoholic beverages No	Pet kennels No
Disabled access Yes	Rain check No
Wheelchair rental No	Private tours No
Baby stroller rental No	

Description and Comments   This old, no-frills amusement park with an ambitious video arcade is a nice diversion from the dark witch trials of Salem. The rides are simple, and that's the appeal. Near the water, it's an easy amusement park to "do," and you can also fill up on cotton candy, popcorn, and hot dogs.

The Salem Witch Museum

Washington Square, Salem; (978) 744-1692

Hours: Daily presentations are made every half hour; September–June, 10 a.m.–5 p.m.; July–August 10 a.m. to 7 p.m. (closed Thanksgiving, Christmas, and New Year's days)

Admission: $4.50

Appeal by Age Groups:

Pre-school	Grade School	Teens	Young Adults	Over 30	Seniors
★★	★★★★	★★★★	★★★	★★★	★★★

Touring Time: Average 1 hour; minimum 1 hour

Rainy-Day Touring: Yes

Services and Facilities:

Restaurants No	Lockers No
Alcoholic beverages No	Pet kennels No
Disabled access Yes	Rain check No
Wheelchair rental No	Private tours No
Baby stroller rental No	

Description and Comments   This museum offers fascinating and visually exciting commentary on the Salem Witch Trials of 1692. This exhibit helps to put all the events surrounding the trials into perspective. It can be scary for really young children, as the presentation is done in a dark room.

FAMILY-FRIENDLY RESTAURANTS

HELMUT'S STRUDEL

69 Bearskin Neck, Rockport; (978) 546-2824

Meals Served: Breakfast and snacks
Cuisine: Strudel, cinnamon buns, muffins, croissants, coffee
Reservations: Not accepted
Payment: No credit cards

Plan your day around a stop at this darling shop with one of the best porch views in town. What to order? Strudel, of course, and a cup of coffee. The kids will love it. It's open daily from mid-May through the end of October.

THE ROCKMORE RESTAURANT

Salem Harbor (board at Pickering Wharf), Salem; (978) 740-1001

Meals Served: Lunch and dinner
Cuisine: Fish and seafood
Entree Range: $10–20
Children's menu: Yes
Reservations: No
Payment: All types accepted

Skip the land version of this restaurant (service is painfully slow) and opt instead to jump aboard the little boat at Pickering Wharf to this floating restaurant in the middle of Salem Harbor. The food is good, and the views can't be beat. We had a great time here, especially feeding the fish our leftovers. This is a unique experience the kids will remember long after memories of the Salem witchcraft museums fade. It's open daily from Memorial Day through Labor Day weekend.

Interior Massachusetts: The Berkshires, Deerfield, Sturbridge Village

This region's wealth of culture and mountainous beauty puts it on the map as a fabulous family vacation destination. Many of the towns found in **The Berkshires** and **Deerfield** are typecast New England villages—white clapboard homes gingerly protected by white picket fences and the requisite Irish setter on the front porch. It's all straight out of a Norman Rockwell painting, and no wonder. Rockwell lived in **Stockbridge,** and a museum in that town houses his paintings and his studio.

The Berkshire hills are alive with the sound of music in the summer thanks to **Tanglewood,** an ambitious outdoor musical event that takes place June through August. Pack a picnic (most of the delis in town will oblige) and spread your fare on one of the sloping hills to enjoy the music. Dance is also celebrated in the summer at **Jacob's Pillow,** an outdoor stage.

Come winter, the icing on the cake comes in the form of snow, when the hills are blanketed with the white stuff kids dream of. There are several great ski resorts in the area (see **Jiminy Peak** and **Brodie** in our Family Outdoor Adventures section on page 125).

The colors that sweep the Berkshire hills in autumn rival Rockwell's palette. This is leaf-peeping territory, although for some reason it is not as popular as Vermont but certainly just as glorious and much closer for folks traveling from the south (the Berkshires are a two-and-a-half-hour drive from New York City).

Sturbridge Village is an enormously popular attraction in interior Massachusetts (about 10 miles from the Connecticut border) and is really a destination unto itself. While there is a bona-fide town called Sturbridge, it is not what draws people here. The real magnet is the re-created nineteenth-century village.

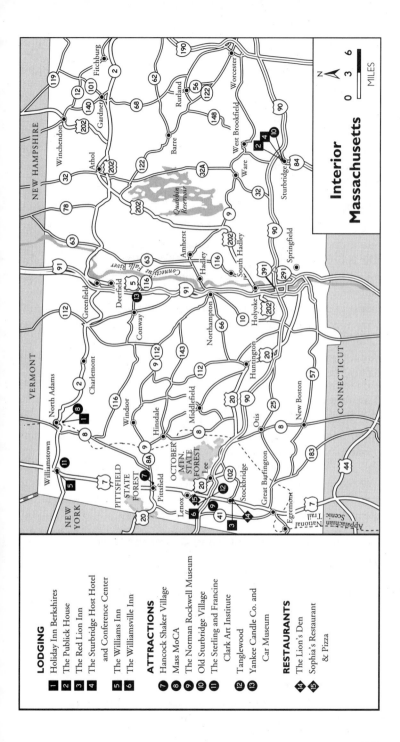

LODGING

1. Holiday Inn Berkshires
2. The Publick House
3. The Red Lion Inn
4. The Sturbridge Host Hotel and Conference Center
5. The Williams Inn
6. The Williamsville Inn

ATTRACTIONS

7. Hancock Shaker Village
8. Mass MoCA
9. The Norman Rockwell Museum
10. Old Sturbridge Village
11. The Sterling and Francine Clark Art Institute
12. Tanglewood
13. Yankee Candle Co. and Car Museum

RESTAURANTS

14. The Lion's Den
15. Sophia's Restaurant & Pizza

Family Lodging

Holiday Inn Berkshires

This 86-room full-service chain hotel has a restaurant, a health club, an indoor pool, a sauna, and a Jacuzzi. It's also got a central location for exploring Mass MoCA, the Sterling and Francine Clark Institute, and Williamstown. Double-room rates begin at $125 per night. 40 Main Street, North Adams; (800) HOLIDAY

The Publick House

The biggest hotel located On The Common (right in the thick of it all) in Sturbridge Village is The Publick House, a historic inn and motor lodge. The Publick House actually houses two inns (the bed and breakfast inn is a mile off the property) and a country lodge motel as well as several restaurants and a delicious bakery. There are 10 dining rooms in the Publick House and a tavern (smoking is allowed in the tavern so be forewarned.) Rates vary—the inn's rates begin at $160 per night (for a suite, suitable for a family of four) to the country motor lodge, which begins at $100 (two double beds). The bed and breakfast inn has a suite that begins at $150 per night. 295 Main Street, Sturbridge; (800) PUBLICK.

The Red Lion Inn

The sweeping porch at this established Berkshire inn welcomes guests with open arms. The rooms can be on the smallish side (and some don't have private baths), but there are others that are very accommodating for families. The inn is centrally located if you want to explore the Normal Rockwell Museum and take in a Tanglewood concert. However, it is almost an hour to the northernmost sections of the Berkshires. Rates begin at $100 per night. Main Street, Stockbridge; (413) 298-5545.

The Sturbridge Host Hotel and Conference Center

The Sturbridge Host Hotel and Conference Center on Main Street is popular accommodation for visitors to Sturbridge Village. It has 237 rooms, and rates that begin at $129 per night for a room with two double beds. This property is across the street from Sturbridge Village and has an indoor pool, an outdoor lake and beach, a fitness center, several restaurants, and outdoor entertainment on weekend evenings. 366 Main Street, Sturbridge; (800) 582-3232.

The Williams Inn

Set in the perfect college town, Williamstown, this inn is located in the very northern tip of the Berkshires. The 150-room inn is family-friendly, with an indoor pool and hot tub to lure the kids after a full day of skiing at nearby Brodie and Jiminy Peak mountains (about a 20-minute drive away). Williams College dominates Williamstown, but there is also a small main street that is home to a coffee shop (with couches and a fireplace), a toy store (called Where'd Ya Get That?), and several clothing stores. The inn has a pricey restaurant you can skip, opting instead for the friendly tavern with a fireplace and decent children's menu. The rooms are clean and tastefully decorated in floral wallpaper. Double-room rates begin at $120 per night. 1090 Main Street, On the Village Green, Williamstown; (800) 828-0133.

The Williamsville Inn

This totally unpretentious, rambling 16-room inn, owned by an actress, is a magnet for theater types in the Berkshires. Yes, families can and do stay here. However, you don't have to stay here to enjoy dinner and storytelling on Sunday evenings. Note: Not all storytelling nights are appropriate for kids, so call ahead. This is a real treat. Route 41, West Stockbridge; (413) 274-6118.

Attractions

Hancock Shaker Village

Route 20, Pittsfield; (800) 817-1137

Hours: April–mid-May and late October–November, daily 10 a.m.–3 p.m. (guided tours only); mid-May–late October, daily 9:30 a.m.–5 p.m. (self-guided tours only); December–March, guided tours by appointment only

Admission: $10 for guided tour (good for two consecutive days); $13.50 for self-guided tour (ticket good for 10 consecutive days)

Appeal by Age Groups:

Pre-school	Grade School	Teens	Young Adults	Over 30	Seniors
★★★	★★★★	★★★	★★	★★	★★

Touring Time: Average 2 hours; minimum 1 hour

Rainy-Day Touring: Yes

Services and Facilities:

Restaurants Yes	Lockers No
Alcoholic beverages No	Pet kennels No
Disabled access Yes	Rain check No
Wheelchair rental No	Private tours Yes
Baby stroller rental No	

Description and Comments　Twenty historic buildings located within a working heritage farm give the kids plenty of roaming room and action. This is a very hands-on attraction—kids can make crafts in the Discovery Room and listen to first-person portrayals of life in the olden days.

Mass MoCA, the Massachusetts Museum of Contemporary Art

87 Marshall Street, North Adams; (413) 664-4481

Hours: June–October, Sunday–Thursday 10 a.m.–5 p.m., Friday–Saturday 10 a.m.–7 p.m.; November–May, Tuesday–Sunday 10 a.m.–5 p.m.

Admission: $8 adults, $3 ages 6–16, free for kids age 5 and under

Appeal by Age Groups:

Pre-school	Grade School	Teens	Young Adults	Over 30	Seniors
★	★	★★★	★★★	★★★	★★★

Touring Time: Average several hours; varies on whether you take in the performances as well as exhibits; minimum 1 hour

Rainy-Day Touring: Yes

Services and Facilities:

Restaurants Yes	Lockers No
Alcoholic beverages Yes	Pet kennels No
Disabled access Yes	Rain check No
Wheelchair rental No	Private tours Yes
Baby stroller rental No	

Description and Comments　A 13-acre campus of more than 150,000 square feet of exhibition and performance space—you'll want to devote an entire morning or afternoon to this ambitious, new attraction. The focus here is on contemporary and modern works of art.

Old Sturbridge Village

Route 20, Sturbridge; (800) SEE-1830

Hours: April–October, daily 9 a.m.–5 p.m.; October–March, daily 9 a.m.–4 p.m.

Admission: $18 adults, $17 seniors, $9 children ages 6–15, free for kids under age 6; admission is good for two consecutive days

Appeal by Age Groups:

Pre-school	Grade School	Teens	Young Adults	Over 30	Seniors
★★★	★★★★	★★★	★★★	★★	★★★

Touring Time: Average full day; minimum a half day

Rainy-Day Touring: Yes
Services and Facilities:

Restaurants Yes	Lockers No
Alcoholic beverages Yes	Pet kennels No
Disabled access Yes	Rain check No
Wheelchair rental No	Private tours Yes
Baby stroller rental No	

Description and Comments   Sturbridge Village is the main attraction in this part of the state—in fact, it is *the* attraction. Just 55 miles southwest of Boston (do it as a day trip or spend the night), this is central Massachusetts' centerpiece with about two dozen historic buildings showcased on a sprawling 200 acres. Interpretive discussions about the nineteenth century are available in some of the homes and shops. There's a riverboat ride and a village store. My friend Phil, who lives just outside of Boston, travels to Sturbridge Village every so often just for the chocolate chip cookies at the bakery at the Publick House restaurant. If you decide to spend the night, you'll have a handful of options; see our Family Lodging section on page 180 for two options.

The Norman Rockwell Museum

Route 183, Box 308, Stockbridge; (413) 298-4100
Hours: May–October, daily 10 a.m.–5 p.m.; November–April, weekdays
   10 a.m.–4 p.m., weekends and holidays 10 a.m.–5 p.m.
Admission: $9 adults, $2 children ages 6–18, $20 family
Appeal by Age Groups:

Pre-school	Grade School	Teens	Young Adults	Over 30	Seniors
★★	★★★	★★★★	★★★★	★★★★	★★★★

Touring Time: Average 1 hour; minimum ½ hour
Rainy-Day Touring: Yes
Services and Facilities:

Restaurants No	Lockers No
Alcoholic beverages No	Pet kennels No
Disabled access Yes	Rain check No
Wheelchair rental No	Private tours Yes
Baby stroller rental No	

Description and Comments   This small museum offers a fascinating peek at Rockwell's depiction of Americana. Kids love to visit Rockwell's studio out back (which was moved here from its original location), especially climbing the life-size sculptures strewn throughout the grounds.

Yankee Doodle Candle

Tucked in the heart of what is known as Pioneer Valley, Deerfield is a quintessential New England village with a white steepled church and a tree-lined promenade flanked by period homes that are now museums. While the guided tours are delightful for adults, the same cannot be said for kids.

What does excite children is the Yankee Candle Company and Car Museum in South Deerfield. This is where you'll want to stock up on Christmas gifts and candles for back home on those dark and stormy powerless nights. Kids can dip their own candles, and the car buffs will love the 70-plus American and European cars on display in the museum. The candle shop and museum are located on US 5, Route 10 in South Deerfield; (413) 665-2929. It's open daily from 9:30 a.m. to 6 p.m.; holiday schedules vary. Admission to the museum is $5, and the candle shop is free.

The Sterling and Francine Clark Art Institute

225 South Street, Williamstown; (413) 458-9545

Hours: September–June, Tuesday–Sunday 10 a.m.–5 p.m.; July–August, Tuesday–Sunday, 10 a.m.–5 p.m. (open until 8 pm on Tuesday)

Admission: $5 adults, free for students and ages 17 and younger; free to everyone on Tuesday from November through June

Appeal by Age Groups:

Pre-school	Grade School	Teens	Young Adults	Over 30	Seniors
★	★★	★★★	★★★★	★★★★	★★★★

Touring Time: Average 2 hours; minimum ½ hour

Rainy-Day Touring: Yes

Services and Facilities:

Restaurants	Yes	Lockers	No
Alcoholic beverages	No	Pet kennels	No
Disabled access	Yes	Rain check	No
Wheelchair rental	No	Private tours	Yes
Baby stroller rental	No		

Description and Comments This museum not only houses a collection of French Impressionist, American, and Old Master paintings, but it is also itself a piece of art. We visited on a sunny winter morning the day after a new snow had fallen, and the 122 acres that surround the museum were blanketed in white. Younger children will love admiring nature's artworks outside the museum, while grade school kids and teens will enjoy the art inside.

Tanglewood

West Street, off Route 183, Lenox; (617) 266-1492 or (413) 627-1600

Hours: Vary depending on concert schedule; open mid-June through Labor Day

Admission: Ticket prices vary depending on the concert

Appeal by Age Groups:

Pre-school	Grade School	Teens	Young Adults	Over 30	Seniors
★	★★	★★★	★★★★	★★★★	★★★★

Touring Time: Average N/A; minimum N/A

Rainy-Day Touring: Yes

Services and Facilities:

Restaurants No	Lockers No
Alcoholic beverages No	Pet kennels No
Disabled access Yes	Rain check No
Wheelchair rental Yes	Private tours Yes
Baby stroller rental No	

Description and Comments   Tanglewood is the summer home of The Boston Symphony Orchestra under the direction of Seiji Ozawa. Performances at this outdoor stage are held from late June through Labor Day. The 5,000-seat main shed is the stage for large concert events, while the Seiji Ozawa Hall, which seats 1,200, is used for more intimate recitals. For families with older children (or young kids who will fall asleep) there is nothing sweeter than packing a blanket and a picnic supper and opting to sit on the lawn under the stars. You can buy lawn or seat tickets online at www.bso.org or call (800) 274-8499 outside of Boston or (617) 266-1200 in Boston. Concerts sell out early so reserve ahead of time.

Family-Friendly Restaurants

THE LION'S DEN

The Red Lion Inn, Main Street, Stockbridge; (413) 298-5545

Cuisine: Pub fare
Entree range: $6–15

Children's menu: Yes
Reservations: No
Payment: All types accepted

This lively, casual basement restaurant (it's located in the Red Lion Inn) is a lot of fun. It has a courtyard out back where you can dine in the summer. The menu is standard pub-type fare—burgers, grilled chicken sandwiches—but there are hearty New England chowders and stews on the menu too. At night there is music and no cover charge.

SOPHIA'S RESTAURANT & PIZZA

Routes 7 and 20; (413) 499-1101

Meals served: Lunch and dinner
Cuisine: Pizza, sandwiches, pasta
Entree range: $3.50 and up
Children's menu: No
Reservations: No
Payment: All types

This is a great kids' spot because it's relaxed and unpretentious. Besides, what kid doesn't love pizza or spaghetti? Try the Greek salad or a grinder.

Part Four

New Hampshire

The Granite State can best be summed up by its state motto "The road less traveled." It takes this saying from one of its most famous resident poets, Robert Frost, whose home in **Derry** is now a state park and open to visitors. The roads that Frost alludes to will take you along the seacoast to a pristine lake, up **Mount Washington** through quintessential New England villages and deep forests. New Hampshire is compact—only 100 miles at its widest and a mere 200 miles from north to south—so you can take in a lot of it over the span of your vacation. It's only about two hours tops from most of New Hampshire's eastern to western borders, and a four- to four-and-a-half-hour drive from south to north. Enjoy breakfast by the sea in **Portsmouth** and then head north for lunch and swimming in **Lake Winnipesaukee.** Let the kids grab a nap in the car as you head for the **White Mountains.**

The 6,288-foot Mount Washington has put New Hampshire on the map for visitors—and, in fact, it's the highest mountain in the Northeast. It's extremely popular with skiers and climbers alike, and you've probably spied a bumper sticker that reads, "This car climbed Mt. Washington." While there are a handful of small towns in New Hampshire, this state is best known for its rural beauty and the Great Outdoors.

GETTING THERE

By Car. Interstates 89, 93, and 95 conveniently serve many destinations in New Hampshire. A free State Highway Map is available at Welcome and Information Centers throughout the state or by calling (800) FUN-IN-NH. Tip: If traveling from the south, opt not to take I-95 and instead take Route 1A from Hampton Beach to Portsmouth. The seacoast views of sandy strands are worth the detour.

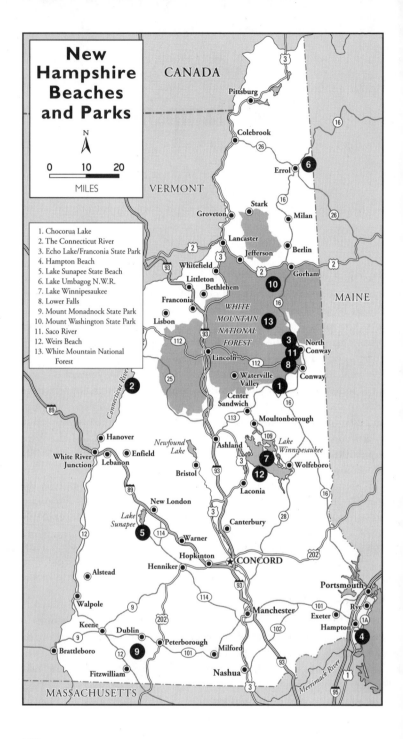

New Hampshire Beaches and Parks

N

0   10   20
MILES

1. Chocorua Lake
2. The Connecticut River
3. Echo Lake/Franconia State Park
4. Hampton Beach
5. Lake Sunapee State Beach
6. Lake Umbagog N.W.R.
7. Lake Winnipesaukee
8. Lower Falls
9. Mount Monadnock State Park
10. Mount Washington State Park
11. Saco River
12. Weirs Beach
13. White Mountain National Forest

CANADA

VERMONT

MAINE

MASSACHUSETTS

Pittsburg

Colebrook

Errol

Stark

Groveton

Milan

Lancaster

Jefferson

Berlin

Whitefield

Littleton

Gorham

Bethlehem

Franconia

WHITE MOUNTAIN NATIONAL FOREST

Lisbon

Lincoln

North Conway

Conway

Waterville Valley

Center Sandwich

Moultonborough

Hanover

Newfound Lake

Ashland

Lake Winnipesaukee

Wolfeboro

White River Junction

Enfield

Lebanon

Bristol

Laconia

New London

Lake Sunapee

Warner

Canterbury

Hopkinton

CONCORD

Alstead

Henniker

Walpole

Portsmouth

Rye

Keene

Dublin

Manchester

Exeter

Hampton

Brattleboro

Peterborough

Milford

Fitzwilliam

Nashua

Connecticut River

Merrimack River

Fun New Hampshire Facts

- State nickname: The Granite State
- State capital: Concord
- Statehood: June 21, 1788 (ninth state)
- State motto: Live free or die
- Highest point: 6,288 feet (Mount Washington)
- Lowest Point: Sea level
- State flower: Purple lilac
- State fish: Brook trout, striped bass
- The windiest place on earth is atop Mount Washington, the highest peak in New England, where the National Weather Service operates a climate research station. On April 12, 1934, this station's instruments registered a world-record wind speed of 231 miles per hour. (Normally, winter gusts on Mount Washington range between 120 to 160 miles per hour.)
- Captain John Mason named New Hampshire after Hampshire, his home county in England.
- The first presidential primary in the nation is held in New Hampshire every four years.

By Plane. There are three major airports that serve New Hampshire. They are: Manchester Airport in Manchester, (603) 624-6539; Logan International Airport in Boston, (800) 235-6426; and Portland International Airport in Portland, Maine, (207) 775-5809. Boston and Portland are about an hour away. You can rent a car at all three airports. The Lebanon Municipal Airport in Lebanon is a regional airport served by commuter airlines such as USAir Express out of Boston, Philadelphia, and New York's LaGuardia Airport.

By Train. There is currently no train service into New Hampshire. However, you can take Amtrak to South Station in Boston or White River Junction in Vermont and then reach New Hampshire by car or bus. Concord Trailways busline has a terminal within walking distance of Boston's South Station. Note: You really should rent a car to see New Hampshire, as it is spread out and there is no public transportation in most tourist regions. Many of the roads throughout the state are especially scenic. Be sure to take some of the Special Scenic Drives and Cultural and Scenic Byways during your visit (we'll tell you where they are in this chapter).

How to Get Information before You Go

The Official New Hampshire tourism site: www.visitnh.gov.

Fall Foliage Reports provided by The New Hampshire Division of Travel & Tourism Development (September through October); (800) 258-3608.

Daily Ski Conditions (November through March): Cross-Country and downhill provided by The New Hampshire Division of Travel & Tourism Development; (800) 258-3608.

Snowmobile Trail Conditions provided by The New Hampshire Division of Travel & Tourism Development (November through April); (603) 743-5050.

Weekly New Hampshire Events provided by The New Hampshire Division of Travel & Tourism Development (April through August); (800) 258-3608.

To receive a year-round Vacation Kit provided by The New Hampshire Directory of Travel & Tourism, call (800) 386-4664.

The Best Beaches and Parks

Crawford Notch State Park. It's swimming-hole central at this six-mile unspoiled gem. It's also got serious white-water rafting thanks to the Saco River, which rushes through the notch's ravines in spring. It's got some decent hiking, too. Bonus: Views of the Presidential Range from some of the hiking trails are unparalleled. One of the tallest waterfalls in New Hampshire, Arethusa Falls, is a short hike away. Located along Route 302, 12 miles north of Bartlett; (603) 374-2272.

Chocorua Lake. In the southern part of Mount Washington Valley, there are two sandy beaches on the east side of this pretty lake, one of which is open to the public (the other is for private residents only.) It's located along Route 16; (800) 367-3364.

Echo Lake. This giant park's pristine mountain lake within Franconia Notch State Park is great for swimming and picnicking. At the base of White Horse Ledge, the mountain views are awesome. There are also hiking trails. Two miles west of North Conway on Old West Side Road; (603) 356-2672.

Leaf Peeping Hotline

Want to know where the most brilliant foliage is? Here are some tips: Around mid-September the mountaintops and the swamp maples in the lowlands turn a fiery red (although there may be some sneak previews to the main performance as early as late August). Generally speaking, from the end of September through the first week in October, you can expect to spy the hottest of colors in the far northern reaches of the state, while the southern environs follow suit in early October to mid-month. For the latest in peak foliage reports, call (800) 258-3608 or (800) 262-6660. This service is updated twice a week from mid-September through October. You can also discover the best foliage spots on the web at www.visitnh.gov.

Dixville Notch State Park. A wow-look-at-that gorge, cool waterfalls, and hiking trails that lead to Table Rock entertain the kids, not to mention the spooky historic gravesite. Located on Route 26 in Dixville; (603) 323-2087.

Franconia Notch State Park. Perhaps there is no greater spokesperson for New Hampshire than the Great Stone Face, the Old Man of the Mountain in Franconia Notch State Park. Carved by nature a thousand years ago, this natural stone profile juts out from a cliff 1,200 feet above aptly named Profile Lake. This phenomenon is formed by five separate ledges and measures 40 feet from chin to forehead. Tip: Bring binoculars to get the best view. A gift shop and visitor center are on site; (603) 823-8800.

The Great North Woods. The Northern White Mountains Chamber of Commerce in Berlin hosts Moose Tours in the Great North Woods—you'll spy the moose grazing along roadsides and in swampy areas. The majority of the land is owned by timber companies, but its also home to more state parks than any other region in the state. This is an especially popular camping spot. Call (603) 752-6060 for information about camping and moose tours. Northern Forest Heritage Park, a remote neck of the woods in the Great North Woods, stretches so far north you're just as likely to hear French spoken as English.

Hampton Beach. Life is a beach—and much more—at Hampton Beach. You'll find a new supervised playground, a waterslide, fireworks, free band concerts, a dog track, and a historic boardwalk, not to mention swimming, parasailing, Jet-Skiing, and a separate beach for surfers.

Lake Sunapee State Beach. A 700-foot sandy stretch of beach on the gorgeous shores of the 4,085-acre Lake Sunapee. The beach has a bathhouse and snack bar. Located in Newbury, on NH 103; (603) 763-5561.

Lake Winnipesaukee. This is New Hampshire's largest lake with 183 miles of shoreline and 274 habitable islands. It is surrounded by three mountain ranges. One of the most popular ways to see the lake is by cruise on the M/S *Mount Washington.* Daytime cruises depart from Weirs Beach (the main port), Wolfeboro, Alton Bay, and Center Harbor. For more information call (888) THE-MOUNT.

Lower Falls. This popular swimming spot along The Kancamagus, a National Scenic Byway, offers both fast- and slow-moving water, a pailful of sandy beaches, picnic tables, and changing rooms. It's located seven miles from Conway; (800) FIND-MTS.

Mount Monadnock State Park. This park offers one of the most frequently climbed mountains in the world, with 40 miles of trails, many of which lead to the mountain's 3,165-foot summit. Located off Route 124, four miles west of Jaffrey; (603) 532-8862. Bonus: There's a perfect family resort at the foot of Mount Monadnock called Inn at East Hill Farm; (800) 242-6495.

Pisgah State Park. At 13,500 acres, this is New Hampshire's largest state park. Hiking, mountain biking, fishing are natural fits. It can be accessed in Chesterfield, Hinsdale, and Winchester, off routes 63, 199, and 10; (603) 239-8153.

Weirs Beach. More a destination than a beach, this parent-dreaded, kid-adored spot woos kids with bumper cars, arcades, go-carts, miniature golf, waterslides, candlepin bowling, and, oh yeah, a beach. Endicott Beach at Weirs Beach is on Lake Winnipesaukee and very family friendly, but it's a popular swimming spot, so plan to come early in the day, as the parking lot tends to fill up by late morning. Call (800) 521-2347.

White Mountain National Forest. It's estimated that between 94 and 97 percent of New Hampshire's land is undeveloped, and a good part of that vast wilderness can be found in White Mountain National Forest. There are more than 250 hiking trails and more than 100 waterfalls in the glorious, 790,000-acre White Mountains. The falls are often the reward after a hike, but some can be seen from the road (such as Silver and Flume Cascades in Crawford Notch, which can be enjoyed from Route 302). The highest peak in the White Mountain National Forest, and in the Northeast, is Mount Washington, snow-capped practically year-round and a magnet for

Cool Websites for New Hampshire–Bound Kids

America's Stonehenge: www.stonehengeusa.com

Attitash Bear Peak: www.attitash.com

Canterbury Shaker Village: www.shakers.org

Celebrate New Hampshire Culture: www.festivalnh.org

Children's Museum of Portsmouth: www.childrens-museum.org

Christa McAuliffe Planetarium: www.starhop.com

Conway Scenic Railroad: www.conwayscenic.com

Greater Laconia/Weirs Beach Chamber of Commerce:
www.laconia-weirs.org

Hampton Beach Chamber of Commerce: www.valleynet/-
han_area_chamber

Heritage—New Hampshire: www.heritagenh.com

Loon Mountain: www.loonmtn.com

Lost River: www.findlostriver.com

M/S Mount Washington: www.msmountwashington.com
or cruiseNH.com

Mount Washington Observatory: www.mountwashington.org

Museum of New Hampshire History: www.NHHistory.org

New Hampshire Stories: www.nhstories.org

Northern White Mountain Chamber of Commerce:
www.northernwhitemountains.com

Portsmouth Harbor Cruises: www.portsmouthharbor.com

Portsmouth Harbour Trail: www.seacoastnh.com

Portsmouth: www.portsmouthnh.com

Santa's Village: www.santasvillage.com

Six Gun City: www.sixguncity.com

Ski New Hampshire: www.skinh.com

Squam Lakes Natural Science Center: www.slnsc.org

Story Land: www.storylandnh.com

Strawberry Banke: www.strawberrybanke.com

Waterville Valley: www.waterville.com

The Weather Discovery Center: www.mountwashington.org

Weirs Beach: www.weirsbeach.com

White Mountains Trail: www.whitemountainstrail.com

Yogi Bear's Jellystone Park: www.jellystonenh.com

New Hampshire's Not-to-Be-Missed Attractions

Seacoast
- Hanging out at Hampton Beach
- Strawberry Banke Museum, Portsmouth
- The Children's Museum of Portsmouth
- A day trip to Concord to visit the Christa McAuliffe Planetarium

Lake Winnipesaukee
- Weirs Beach on Lake Winnipesaukee
- Hart's Turkey Farm Restaurant, Meredith
- Touring the lake on the M/S Mount Washington
- Leaf peeping along the Kancamagus Highway

The White Mountains
- The Old Man in the Mountain, Franconia Notch State Park
- The Robert Frost Place, Franconia Notch
- Hiking, driving or taking the cog railway to the top of Mount Washington
- Story Land, Glen
- Heritage-New Hampshire, Glen
- Balsams Grand Resort Hotel, Dixville Notch.

---

the most Type-A hikers. The Mount Washington State Park sits atop 52 acres of this wonderland, where the highest land wind velocity in the world was clocked at 231 mph.

For those of us not interested as much in gravity-defying activities, you can access the mountain by the ever-popular cog railroad and by car (hence the "This car climbed Mt. Washington" bumper stickers). The Mount Washington Observatory at the top is viewable when the mountain isn't shrouded in clouds. The White Mountains' Presidential Range is equally impressive—a series of granite peaks. There are 86 peaks in the Presidential Range, and notches are the only way to traverse them.

Family Outdoor Adventures

Biking. When the snow has melted, Loon Mountain blooms with wild-flowers and family fun thanks to a mountain-bike center for all ages and abilities. Teens and experienced riders will be thrilled with the prospect of taking their bikes to the summit of Loon via the Mountain Skyride Gondola. Younger or less-skilled riders will want to stick to the 13-mile paved bike path to experience the beauty of Franconia Notch State Park. Other kid thrills include New Hampshire's longest aerial gondola skyride, Glacial Caves, horseback riding, and a skate park. (603) 745-8111, ext. 5400.

The Balsams Mountain Bike and Nature Center in Dixville Notch is cycling heaven. Grab your bikes (or rent them here) and head out for the miles of marked and annotated trails that curl and twist throughout this 15,000-acre private estate. You can rent mountain bikes and other equipment, as well as purchase bikes and have repairs done. Take advantage of one of the guided tours or take a self-guided tour; (603) 255-3921.

The Conway Recreation Trail in Mount Washington Valley, behind the police station, is perfect for biking. Well-marked, it parallels the Saco River and is great for beginners and families.

Canoeing/Rafting. Canoeing doesn't get any better than on Lake Umbagog National Wildlife Refuge, providing prime osprey, otter, and eagle sightings. Rent canoes from Saco Bound Northern Waters white-water school for less than $30 a day; (603) 447-2177.

The gentle Saco River is ideal for canoeing or swimming. It's not far from North Conway Village (turn west on River Road and park at the roadside near the first bridge). Tip: Bring a jug to fill it up with fresh mountain water. Note: Jumping and diving from the bridge is prohibited.

Cross-country Skiing. Many of the resorts listed in our Skiing section (page 197) offer cross-country and snowshoeing trails. Odiorne State Park in Rye puts a unique twist on cross-country skiing—the trails are the snow-covered beach along the chilly but beautiful Atlantic Ocean.

Cruises. At the Lake Squam Natural Science Center during July and August, take the small cruise to learn about the loons and this undeveloped lake. There's also a place just for kids—Gordon Children's Center with plenty of climbing and crawling opportunties. Kirkwood Gardens showcases plants especially planted to attract birds and butterflies. Route 113, Holderness; (603) 968-7194.

Hiking. The Appalachian Mountain Club offers guided hiking trips through the White Mountains, including stays in full-service mountain huts (bunks and meals). Contact the Appalachian Mountain Club, Pinkham Notch Visitor Center and Lodge, Route 16, Box 298, Gorham, NH 03581.

There are more than 250 hiking trails and more than 100 waterfalls in the glorious, 790,000-acre White Mountain National Forest. The falls are often the reward after a hike, but some can be seen from the road (such as Silver and Flume Cascades in Crawford Notch, which can be enjoyed from Route 302). A short, quarter-mile hike will take you to Beecher and Pearl Cascades farther west on Route 302. Nothing beats Diana's Falls on a steamy summer day (a rarity in New Hampshire but even a warm day will do); to reach these falls take River Road from North Conway onto the Bartlett section of West Road, where you'll find the entrance to a relatively easy two-mile hike. The highest peak in the White Mountain National Forest, and in the Northeast, is Mount Washington, snow-capped practically year-round and a magnet for the most Type-A hikers. The Mount Washington State Park sits atop 52 acres of this wonderland, where the highest land wind velocity in the world was clocked at 231 mph.

Crawford Notch State Park has some decent hiking, too. Views of the Presidential Range from some of the hiking trails are unparalleled. One of the tallest waterfalls in New Hampshire, Arethusa Falls, is a short hike away. Located along Route 302, 12 miles north of Bartlett; (603) 374-2272.

Monadnock State Park houses Mount Monadnock, whose summit is 3,165 feet. There are 40 miles of trails, many of which lead to the summit. Year-round camping is also available. Off Route 124, four miles west of Jaffrey; (603) 532-8862.

Ice Sports. The Lakes Region, with 273 lakes and ponds that freeze over when the temperatures plummet, is idyllic for ice skating, ice fishing, ice sailing, and even auto ice racing.

Snowmobiling. New Hampshire boasts more than 6,000 miles of inter-connecting trails statewide! Throughout the state there are more than 120 snowmobiling clubs that maintain these trails. There's even a museum dedicated to the sport—The New Hampshire Snowmobile Museum at Bear Brook State Park in Allenstown; (603) 271-3254.

Snowtubing. This popular winter sport is available at many New Hampshire ski areas including, Cannon Mountain in Franconia Notch, Pat's Peak in Hennker, Snowhill at Eastman in Grantham, Whaleback Ski Area in Lebanon, Gunstock in Gilford, McInteyre in Manchester, Cranmore Mountain Resort in North Conway, King Pine in East Madison, Loon Mountain in Lincoln, Ragged Mountain in Danbury, and Tenney Mountain in Plymouth. Call (800) 88-SKINH.

Skiing. White Mountain National Forest lays claim to over half of New Hampshire's downhill and cross-country ski resorts, thanks to the 780,000-acre White Mountain National Forest.

The majority of the resorts are in the Mount Washington Valley region, with seven alpine and six Nordic ski areas within a 25-mile radius. About 15 minutes north of North Conway, the lovely town of Jackson, in the White Mountains National Forest, is home to a necklace of groomed cross-country ski trails. Jackson is also home to Black Mountain Ski Resort.

Attitash Bear, Peak Route 302, Bartlett; (800) 223-7669. This resort keeps getting bigger and bigger and bigger. Located in the heart of Mount Washington Valley, it's got two interconnected mountains with 60 trails and glades and 12 lifts, including three quads. Brand new is the Ground Zero 500-foot in-ground half-pipe.

Black Mountain, Route 16B/Five Mile Circuit, Jackson; (800) 1-SKI-NOW. A ski resort since 1935, Black Mountain has a peak that soars to 3,303 feet, affording skiers bird's-eye views of Mount Washington and the Presidential Range. There are 40 trails for skiing and a ski school that's been around for 60 years. This is family skiing at its best. To get there, travel through the covered bridge on Route 16B/Five Mile Circuit in Jackson.

Bretton Woods Ski Area and the Bretton Woods Cross Country Center, Route 302, Bretton Woods; (800) 258-0330. This ski area has the new West Mountain with 24 trails and glades serviced by a new quad chair. Bonus: A Mount Washington Cog Railway passenger coach on top of the mountain serves as a warming hut at the summit. At the Cross Country Center, there's also a new warming hut, as well as a lighted cross-country loop for nighttime cross-country skiing.

Cannon Mountain, Exits 2 and 3 on I-93 (the Franconia Notch Parkway), Franconia; (603) 823-8800. A new beginner area, including the Brookside Learning Slope and Children's Center, complements New Hampshire's greatest vertical drop at this ski resort. In addition, there is a new high-speed quad chairlift and two new triple chairlifts.

The Great Glen Trails Outdoor Center. With 1,100 acres at the base of Mount Washington in Pinkham Notch, this is an encompassing outdoor receration area area, winter and summer. In winter, there is a full-time cross-country ski school, a child care center, a sit-down deli, and an Outfitters shop. Open every day from 8:30 a.m. to 5 p.m. Located at Rt. 16, Pinkham Notch; 603-466-2333.

The King Pine Ski Resort, Route 153, Madison; (800) FREE-SKI, is my Boston-based friend Kerry Sullivan's favorite New Hampshire ski resort. "What I appreciate most about it," says Kerry, "is that it is small and your kids are never too far off—it's easy to keep track of them." There are ski lessons by qualified instructors, babysitting, night skiing, tobaggoning, skating, snow-mobiling. Just 20 minutes from North Conway, it's in a perfect location, away from North Conway's traffic jams but close enough to enjoy the outlet stores.

Loon Mountain, Exit 32 off I-93, Lincoln; (603) 745-8111 ext. 5400. Smack in White Mountain National Forest, Loon Mountain is a winter wonderland of fun—not just skiing. Yes, there are miles and miles of trails for cross-country skiing, snowshoeing and downhill skiing. Plus, there's ice skating, night and day snowtubing (kids absolutely thrill to this!), and— get this—winter horseback riding. Intermediate skiers and expert skiers rejoice at this resort; the snowtubing park is a magnet for kids.

Waterville Valley, Exit 28 off I-93, then 11 miles via Route 39 to Waterville Valley; (800) GO-VALLEY. Alpine skiing, cross-country skiing, snowboarding, snowshoeing—it's all here. And the best part: for beginners or kids who want to hone their skills, there is a snowsports ski school. Off the slopes, families enjoy the horse-drawn sleigh rides and indoor ice-skating arena in the middle of the Waterville Valley Town Square. There are a number of lodging options, including staying in a condo at the Waterville Valley Town Square (call (888) 462-9887) or in the Black Bear Lodge, where one-bedroom suites with full kitchens sleep up to six, and there is an indoor pool (call (800) 349-2327).

Calendar of Festivals and Events

May

Annual Chili Challenge. Love chili? Indulge at this annual event that features some of the best chili around. Waterville Valley region; (603) 236-8175.

July

Annual Lake Winnipesaukee Antique Classic Boat Show, Weirs Beach and Wolfeboro. This two-day show at the end of the month will float your boat; (603) 524-0348 or (603) 569-2212.

August

Annual Celebrate Your Lakes Day, Meredith. New Hampshire's lakes are worth celebrating, and this daylong event with lots of family activities is the perfect place to do it; (603) 528-8703.

Moose Festival. Activities and events that celebrate New Hampshire's beloved Moose population. Throughout towns in the Great North Woods region; (603) 237-8939.

Hampton Beach Children's Festival, Hampton Beach. Five fun-filled days for families and kids, including magic shows, clowns, storytellers, sand-castle contests, and a parade at which every child gets a prize; (800) GET-A-TAN.

September

Annual Seafood Festival, Hampton Beach. A street fair with seafood and other eats from more than 50 participating restaurants; (603) 926-8717.

Bark in the Park, North Conway. This is northern New England's largest pet expo, and kids love it; (603) 356-5701.

October

Annual Quilt Show, Laconia. With winter on its way, this quilt showcase comes at the perfect time; (603) 524-8813.

Wool Arts Tour. A self-guided tour of New Hampshire's sheep farms and wool studios during the height of the foliage season. Events are held throughout the state; (603) 428-7830.

December

Annual Candlelight Stroll, Strawbery Banke Museum, Portsmouth. Stroll through Portsmouth's lovely streets, which are lighted with more than 1,100 candles in the spirit of the holidays; (603) 433-1100.

Inn to Inn Holiday Cookie Tour, Mt. Washington Valley. Got milk? Cookies galore make this tour worth while for kids who are old enough to behave on a tour of holiday-decorated inns; (603) 356-5701.

First Night Portsmouth. Bring in the New Year by joining in the citywide festivities that begin in the afternoon of December 31 and culminate at midnight with fireworks; (603) 436-1118.

The Seacoast

Welcome to the pocket-size Seacoast region of the state, with 18 miles of shoreline. Skip the boring and fast-moving I-95, opting instead for Route 1A when traveling from **Hampton Beach** to **Portsmouth.** You'll be rewarded with gorgeous views of sandy strands, stately homes, and adorable summer cottages. Portsmouth is only one hour from Boston, so you might want to keep that in mind if you're pining to visit Beantown. One of the best ways to explore pretty Portsmouth is by horse and carriage; call (603) 427-0044. Portsmouth is a working port (and has been for three centuries). Visitors will find a seaport town that is complemented by lovely historic homes, fine art galleries, and coffeehouses.

Hampton Beach is all about children, with nightly entertainment, fireworks, water slides, parades, sand-castle contests, swimming, parasailing, Jet-Skiing, surfing (there's a separate beach for surfers), and a historic boardwalk for old-fashioned strolling. Phew, if Hampton Beach doesn't wear out your kids nowhere will.

Family Lodging

Anchorage Inn

Easy access to town, attractions, and shopping is the name of the game at this 93-room "inn." There are four suites that come with a living room and a refrigerator and microwave, and there's an indoor heated pool at the inn with a whirlpool spa and hot-rock sauna. The cafe serves a complimentary continental breakfast each morning (a great way to cut costs; eating breakfast out each morning for a family of four can really put a kink into a tight budget). Don't expect a remote property. This is a city property, although the "city" is a very lovely, historic one. Double-room rates begin at $100 per night. 417 Woodbury Avenue, Portsmouth; (603) 431-8111.

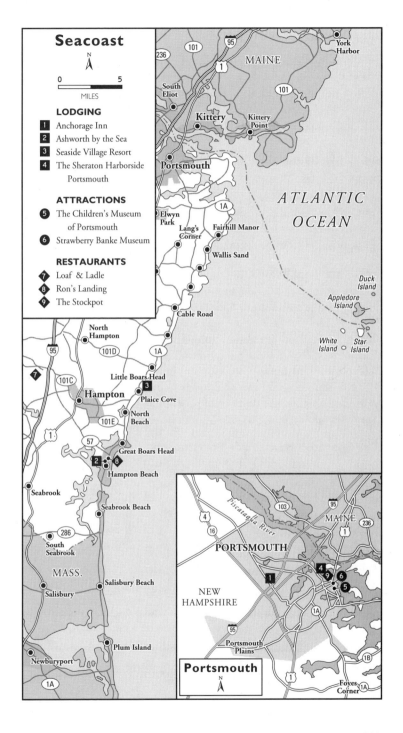

Seacoast

N

0 _____ 5
MILES

LODGING

1 Anchorage Inn
2 Ashworth by the Sea
3 Seaside Village Resort
4 The Sheraton Harborside
   Portsmouth

ATTRACTIONS

5 The Children's Museum
   of Portsmouth
6 Strawberry Banke Museum

RESTAURANTS

7 Loaf & Ladle
8 Ron's Landing
9 The Stockpot

MAINE

York
Harbor

South
Eliot

Kittery

Kittery
Point

Portsmouth

ATLANTIC
OCEAN

Elwyn
Park

Lang's
Corner

Fairhill Manor

Wallis Sand

Duck
Island

Appledore
Island

Cable Road

White
Island

Star
Island

North
Hampton

Little Boars Head

Hampton

Plaice Cove

North
Beach

Great Boars Head

Hampton Beach

Seabrook

Seabrook Beach

South
Seabrook

MASS.

Salisbury Beach

Salisbury

Plum Island

Newburyport

Piscataqua River

MAINE

PORTSMOUTH

NEW
HAMPSHIRE

Portsmouth
Plains

Portsmouth

N

Foyes
Corner

Seacoast Lodging Options
There are many motels and hotels in Hampton Beach. Call (800) GET-A-TAN for more options.

Ashworth by the Sea

With an oceanfront location, an indoor/outdoor pool, and a central location near Hampton Beach's ongoing frenzy of activities, this spot is popular with families. Most rooms have private sundecks that peer out over the ocean, and there are several restaurants on the property. Double-room rates begin at $79 per night. 295 Ocean Boulevard, Hampton Beach; (800) 345-6736.

Seaside Village Resort

If you want a beach location, this unassuming resort is smack on the sandy strand. It is the only hotel in New Hampshire that's directly on the beach. You must rent by the week in peak season; some units have kitchenettes that make them feel like home. North Hampton Beach is within walking distance (you'll cross some dunes). Families tend to make friends for life here, planning return summer vacations around one another's schedules. Tip: Not all rooms have air conditioners (only those in the newer, slightly more expensive cottages do), but all have ceiling fans. 1 Ocean Boulevard, North Hampton; (603) 964-8204.

The Sheraton Harborside Portsmouth

Smack in the city, this hotel allows you to explore pretty Portsmouth by foot. This 205-room hotel has everything, including an indoor pool, a sauna, and a fitness room. Double-room rates begin at $125 per night. 250 Market Street, Portsmouth; (800) 325-3535.

Attractions

The Children's Museum of Portsmouth

280 Marcy Street, Portsmouth; (603) 436-3853

Hours: Tuesday–Saturday 10 a.m.–5 p.m., Sunday 1–5 p.m.; open
   Mondays 10 a.m.–5 p.m. during summer and school vacations

Admission: $4 adults and kids, free for ages 2 and under

Appeal by Age Groups:

Pre-school	Grade School	Teens	Young Adults	Over 30	Seniors
★★★	★★★				

Touring Time: Average 1½ hours; minimum 45 minutes

Rainy-Day Touring: Yes

Services and Facilities:

Restaurants No	Lockers No
Alcoholic beverages No	Pet kennels No
Disabled access No	Rain check No
Wheelchair rental No	Private tours No
Baby stroller rental No	

Description and Comments   The Children's Museum provides totally hands-on fun: computers and dinosaurs for grade-schoolers and a space shuttle cockpit and lobster boat for the littlest set (under age four). This is a good rainy-day diversion for young kids.

Strawberry Banke Museum

Marcy and Hancock streets, Portsmouth; (603) 433-1100

Hours: Late April–October, daily 10 a.m.–5 p.m.; open a couple of weekends in December for special events; walking tours throughout the winter

Admission: $12 adults, $8 kids ages 7–17, free for ages 6 and under; $28 for a family

Appeal by Age Groups:

Pre-school	Grade School	Teens	Young Adults	Over 30	Seniors
★★	★★★★	★★★	★★	★	★

Touring Time: Average a full day; minimum a half-day

Rainy-Day Touring: Yes (bring an umbrella)

Services and Facilities:

Restaurants Yes	Lockers No
Alcoholic beverages No	Pet kennels No
Disabled access Yes	Rain check No
Wheelchair rental Yes	Private tours Yes
Baby stroller rental No	

Descriptions and Comments   Strawberry Banke is great for the elementary-age gang to early teen crew. Put on your walking shoes—there are 42 historic buildings in a 10-acre area of downtown Portsmouth (in fact, this is one of New England's largest museums). Costumed interpreters and period gardens provide an up-close and personal insight into how early settlers lived. Visit in the summer and board an old-fashioned sailboat. In the winter, the museum gets decked out for its annual Candlelight Stroll with 1,000 candles and luminarias and four centuries of festivities.

Family-Friendly Restaurants

LOAF & LADLE

9 Water Street, Exeter; (603) 778-8955

Meals served: Breakfast, lunch, and dinner
Cuisine: American
Entree range: $5.50 and up
Children's menu: No
Reservations: No
Payment: Major credit cards accepted

The Loaf and Ladle offers kid-friendly, cafeteria-style chowders, soups, stews, and huge sandwiches on homemade bread. For dinner, the menu is more ambitious, with pastas, chicken, and more. The restaurant overlooks the river, so sit on the outside deck if you can. There's no children's menu, but bet the little ones will dig the Fluffernutter sandwich!

RON'S LANDING

379 Ocean Boulevard, Hampton Beach; (603) 929-2122

Meals served: Lunch and dinner
Cuisine: Seafood, chicken, pasta
Entree range: $5 and up
Children's menu: Yes
Reservations: Yes
Payment: All types accepted

Locals love this place as much as the tourists, who loyally come back year after year. While the menu is diverse, your best bet is the fish and seafood (this is a beach town, after all.) Children will enjoy grilled chicken, tuna salad, a veggie wrap, pizza, and pasta. Note: There is a dress code here called proper formal (translation: no ripped jeans).

THE STOCKPOT

53 Bow Street, Portsmouth; (603) 431-1851

Meals served: Lunch and dinner
Cuisine: American
Entree range: $3 and up
Children's menu: Yes

Reservations: No (come early for the best view of the river)
Payment: All types accepted

Inexpensive homemade goodies such as sandwiches, soups, and salads are the main fare here. At dinner, try the steaks and chicken. Always arrive early: in summer, to sit out on the deck for a view of the river; in winter, if you'd like to sit by a window with a water views.

Side Trip: Merrimack Valley Region (Concord/Manchester/Salem)

This diverse and populated region is where New Hampshire's government has been seated for 200 years. The state capital is **Concord,** home to one of New Hampshire's most fabulous attractions, the **Christa McAuliffe Planetarium,** which pays homage to Christa McAuliffe, an astronaut on the ill-fated space shuttle *Challenger.* McAuliffe was a teacher in Concord. Home to two other large cities, **Nashua** and **Manchester,** the Merrimack Valley Region isn't frequented by overnight tourists as much as the other regions of the state. But it is worth a short visit before heading to the seacoast or White Mountains. Because New Hampshire is small enough to reach several regions in one day, plan a day trip to Concord to visit the following two attractions.

ATTRACTIONS

America's Stonehenge

Mystery Hill, Haverhill Road, North Salem; (603) 893-8300

Hours: Daily 9 a.m.–5 p.m.

Admission: $8 adults, $6 kids ages 13–15, $5 ages 6–12, free for ckids under age 6

Appeal by Age Groups:

Pre-school	Grade School	Teens	Young Adults	Over 30	Seniors
★★	★★★	★★★	★★★	★★★	★★★

Touring Time: Average 1½ hours; minimum 1 hour

Rainy-Day Touring: No

Services and Facilities:

Restaurants No	Lockers No
Alcoholic beverages No	Pet kennels No
Disabled access No	Rain check No
Wheelchair rental No	Private tours Yes
Baby stroller rental No	

Description and Comments This is considered one of the oldest megalithic (stone-constructed) sites in North America—and the largest. Reminiscent of England's Stonehenge, this phenomenal structure was built by people well versed in astronomy and is still used to predict specific solar and lunar events during the year. Archaeological excavation of the site has unveiled historic artifacts. Take the one-hour self-guided tour and explore the chambers (caves). Kids love the caves.

The Christa McAuliffe Planetarium

3 Institute Drive (I-93 to Exit 15E) Concord; (603) 271-STAR

Hours: Tuesday–Sunday (closed Mondays and the three weeks following Labor Day)

Admission: $6 adults, $3 children; advance tickets are recommended for the shows

Appeal by Age Groups:

Pre-school	Grade School	Teens	Young Adults	Over 30	Seniors
★	★★★★	★★★	★★	★	★

Touring Time: Average 1 hour; minimum 1 hour (the shows are 1 hour long)

Rainy-Day Touring: Yes

Services and Facilities:

Restaurants No	Lockers No
Alcoholic beverages No	Pet kennels No
Disabled access No	Rain check No
Wheelchair rental No	Private tours Yes
Baby stroller rental No	

Description and Comments Christa McAuliffe, a teacher from Concord, was one of the astronauts aboard the ill-fated space shuttle *Challenger.* Hour-long cosmic shows excite and educate kids of all ages, although they're best suited for grade-schoolers. The Planetarium features 92 unidirectional seats in a theater with a 40-foot, three-dimensional domed screen. The star database contains more than 9,000 stars and can simulate travel up to 600 light years from Earth.

FAMILY-FRIENDLY RESTAURANTS

MARGARITA'S: A MEXICAN RESTAURANT AND WATERING HOLE

Bicentennial Square, Concord; (603) 224-2821

Meals served: Dinner (but opened seasonally for lunch; call for hours)
Cuisine: Mexican
Entree range: $6.95 and up
Children's menu: Yes
Reservations: No
Payment: All types accepted (even pesos!)

Even if kids don't love Mexican food, this restaurant's location—in the historic Concord police station and jail—will have them shouting olé quicker than a Mexican jumping bean. The dining room is divided into cells, and the theme of this restaurant is fun, fun, fun. The kids' menu features chicken, hamburgers, tacos, nachos, and quesadillas. It's about a 15-minute walk from the Christa McAuliffe Planetarium.

MARKIS LOBSTER AND STEAKHOUSE

354 Sheep Davis Road, Route 106, Concord; (603) 225-7665

Meals served: Lunch and dinner
Cuisine: Seafood and steak
Entree range: $8.95 and up
Children's menu: Yes
Reservations: No
Payment: All types accepted

Near the Christa McAuliffe Planetarium, this family-friendly restaurant satisfies hungry adults with an ambitious lobster and steak menu, and the little ones with chicken tenders, grilled cheese, spaghetti, and hamburgers.

The Lake
Winnipesaukee Region

If the stillness and beauty of a grand lake floats your boat, this is the spot to vacation. This lake region has something for everyone—from the amusements and diversions of **Weirs Beach** to the shopping of **Laconia, Meredith,** and **Center Harbor** to the more subdued **Squam** and **Newfound Lake** regions. The historic village of **Wolfeboro** is said to be America's first summer resort. Also on hand in this region are a handful of covered bridges and 274 habitable islands with such kid-captivating names as Bear and Beaver. Views of **Mount Washington** and sister mountains are bonuses. If you'll be traveling from Portsmouth, take Route 16 and then divert to routes 153, 125, and even smaller local roads around **Milton** and **Wakefield,** or take Route 28 E. to Wolfeboro. What's appealing about the region for families? How about jumping into temperate lake waters on a hot summer day? Spending a lazy day sailing the lake's calm waters? Roasting marshmallows, singing campfire songs, skinny dipping? Aside from loving the simplistic lake life, the other kid-style attraction in this region is the aforementioned Weirs Beach—thanks primarily to its bounty of amusement rides (including a waterslide) and arcades. But in a word, this region is all about lakes.

Family Lodging

There are a gazillion places to stay along Lake Winnipesaukee, namely cottages that you can rent. For more info on renting a cottage on the lake, call (800) 60-LAKES.

The Inn at Bay Point

A lakeside stunner surrounded by 2,000 feet of a lakefront park, this inn offers super views. Many of the guest rooms have private lakeside balconies and fireplaces. A dock is the perfect place to perch and watch sailboats glide by. On rainy days, mosey next door to the Mill Falls Inn & Marketplace, where you'll find 18 shops, a tavern, and several restaurants. Double-room rates begin at $109 per night. 312 Daniel Webster Highway, Meredith; (603) 279-7006.

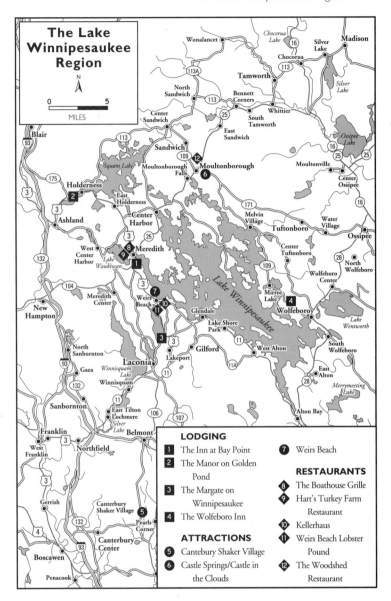

The Lake Winnipesaukee Region

N

0   5
MILES

LODGING

1 The Inn at Bay Point
2 The Manor on Golden Pond
3 The Margate on Winnipesaukee
4 The Wolfeboro Inn

ATTRACTIONS

5 Cantebury Shaker Village
6 Castle Springs/Castle in the Clouds

7 Weirs Beach

RESTAURANTS

8 The Boathouse Grille
9 Hart's Turkey Farm Restaurant
10 Kellerhaus
11 Weirs Beach Lobster Pound
12 The Woodshed Restaurant

The Manor on Golden Pond

While this is one of New Hampshire's most romantic inns, it's also a super family spot with swimming at a private beach, croquet, volleyball and Ping-Pong. Right on Squam Lake, the inn also offers canoeing in summer and cross-country skiing and snowshoeing on the frozen lake in winter. Children must be age 12 and older. There are rooms in the Manor House and cottages, and the cottages are better suited for families. Double-room rates begin at $125 per night. Route 3, Box T, Holderness; (800) 545-2141.

The Margate on Winnipesaukee

This lakeside beauty is open year round and features 146 air-conditioned rooms and a central location near attractions and outlet shopping. Kids stay and eat free. The private, 400-foot, white-sand beach really appeals to kids. There are also tennis courts, a health club, pedal boats, rowboats, and a playground. Double-room rates begin at $100 per night. 76 Lake Street, Laconia; (800) 396-3796.

The Wolfeboro Inn

This large, 44-room inn gives families the best of both worlds—inn ambiance in a place that's big enough so that you don't feel you have to constantly pester the children to stop touching, to keep their voices down, and to stop running. There's a private beach (albeit the size of a postage stamp) and a 150-passenger boat, the *Winnipesaukee Belle.* Double-room rates begin at $89 per night. 90 N. Main Street, Wolfeboro; (800) 451-2389.

Attractions

Note: Because most attractions in this region center around the lake and outdoor adventures, we've listed many of them in Family Outdoor Adventures on page 195.

Canterbury Shaker Village

288 Shaker Road, Canterbury (take Exit 18 off I-93); (800) 982-9511

Hours: May–October, daily 10 a.m.–5 p.m.; November, December, and April, weekends 10 p.m.–3 p.m.; closed January, February, and March.

Admission: $10 adults, $5 kids ages 6–15, free for kids under age 6

Appeal by Age Groups:

Pre-school	Grade School	Teens	Young Adults	Over 30	Seniors
★	★★★★	★★★	★★	★	★

Touring Time: Average 2 hours; minimum 1 hour

Rainy-Day Touring: Yes

Services and Facilities:

Restaurants Yes	Baby stroller rental No
Alcoholic beverages Yes; dinner only	Lockers No
	Pet kennels No
Disabled access Yes; but not everywhere	Rain check No
	Private tours Yes
Wheelchair rental No	

Descriptions and Comments   School-age kids love to discover life as the Shakers lived it from the 1780s to today. This private, nonprofit historic village and museum features 24 original buildings on 694 acres of open fields, woods, and ponds. There are tours where you can see craftsmen make Shaker crafts and learn about the organic vegetable gardens and herb and flower gardens. There are also ongoing workshops, such as basket making, and festivals. Plan your visit right before dinner, and then eat strictly by candlelight (Friday and Saturday nights) at The Creamery Restaurant, where the chef captures over 200 years of Shaker cooking techniques. Many of the ingredients are grown and raised at the village. The furniture is also reflective of the simple Shaker style. There is a gift shop on the premises. The Creamery is also open for lunch.

Castle Springs/Castle in the Clouds

Route 171, Moultonborough; (800) 729-2468

Hours: Mid-May–mid-June, Saturday and Sunday 9 a.m.–5 p.m.; mid-June–Labor Day, daily 9 a.m.–5 p.m.; Labor Day–mid-October, daily 9 a.m.–4 p.m.; closed November–April

Admission: $11 adults, $10 seniors, $8 students, free for ages 6 and under

Appeal by Age Groups:

Pre-school	Grade School	Teens	Young Adults	Over 30	Seniors
★	★★★★	★★★	★★	★	★

Touring Time: Average 2 hours; minimum 1 hour

Rainy-Day Touring: No

Services and Facilities:

Restaurants Yes; snack shop	Lockers No
Alcoholic beverages No	Pet kennels No
Disabled access No	Rain check No
Wheelchair rental No	Private tours Yes
Baby stroller rental No	

Take the Mailboat to the Islands

You can reach nine of the islands in Lake Winnipesaukee, but you'll need to jump aboard the *Sophie C,* a floating mailboat, to do so. Kids love to see reach these offshore islands via the mailboat. Mail service began on the lake in 1892, but it wasn't until 1914 that an Act of Congress designated the mailboat as a U.S. Post Office. It not only sells stamps, but also postcards and ice cream. (In a typical season, the *Sophie C* delivers 30,000 pieces of mail.) Call (800) 60-LAKES.

Description and Comments   Skip the tour of the mansion that commands over 5,200 acres of the Ossipee Mountains (unless you have a budding interior decorator in your midst) and opt instead to spend a couple of hours on the grounds at your own pace. Fall is an especially glorious time to visit. Bring a panoramic camera if you have one—the views of Lake Winnipesaukee and the mountains are stunning. Hike along the well-marked trails. Take the tram-ride up the tree-topped mountain lane to the spring site where Castle Springs water rises naturally to the surface in a mountain glen. This is also the site of the Castle Springs Premium Mountain spring-water bottling facility, as well as a new microbrewery of Castle Springs Brewery Co., where premium, handcrafted Lucknow beers and ales are brewed.

Family-Friendly Restaurants

THE BOATHOUSE GRILLE

Routes 3 and 25, Meredith; (603) 279-2253

Meals served: Lunch and dinner
Cuisine: Seafood, meat, pasta
Entree range: $7.95 and up
Children's menu: No
Reservations: No
Payment: All types accepted

Overlooking Lake Winnipesaukee, The Boathouse Grille offers panoramic views of the pretty lake and an ambitious menu. If you choose, you can boat to the restaurant, as there is available dock space. There's no children's menu, but you can order small portions of cheese pizza, grilled chicken breast, and steak.

HART'S TURKEY FARM RESTAURANT

Route 3, Meredith; (603) 279-6212

Meals served: Lunch and dinner
Cuisine: American
Entree range: $9.50 and up
Children's menu: Yes
Reservations: No
Payment: All types accepted

This is *the* place for turkey lovers—every day is Thanksgiving. You'll also find a full American menu. It's a great spot for kids—loud, busy, dim lighting, and great service (turnovers are quick). Don't expect much in the way of decor but rather a homespun, Yankee appeal.

KELLERHAUS

Route 3, two blocks from Weirs Beach; (603) 366-4466

Meals served: Breakfast and snacks
Cuisine: Ice cream and waffles
Entree range: $2.95 and up
Children's menu: No, but can order half portions
Reservations: No
Payment: All types accepted

Calling all kids—this 4,500-square-foot gift shop is also home to one fine ice cream buffet—pick a flavor at the register and then peruse the 15 toppings that you put on. Kellerhaus is also open for breakfast, and the specialty of the house is Belgian waffles (there are also eggs and the usual breakfast fare on the menu). The waffle concept is similar to the ice cream—you order your waffle (kids can order half a waffle) at the register and then slop on your favorite toppings at the buffet. How sweet it is!

WEIRS BEACH LOBSTER POUND

US Route 3, Weirs Beach; no phone

Meals served: Lunch and dinner
Cuisine: American
Entree range: $8.95 and up
Children's menu: Yes
Reservations: No

Payment: All types accepted

This great spot is open only from late spring through early fall. Everything's good, but we say skip the chicken and steak and go for, what else, the lobster! Kids' meals cost five cents for every pound of their body weight (lobster is not on the kids' menu).

THE WOODSHED RESTAURANT

Lee's Mill Road, Moultonborough; (603) 476-2311

Meals served: Dinner
Cuisine: Seafood, steak
Entree range: $11 and up
Children's menu: Yes
Reservations: Yes
Payment: All types accepted

A legend in the Lakes Region for more than two decades, The Woodshed is in an 1860s farmhouse and post-and-beam farm setting. House specialties include prime rib, lobster, and Alaskan king crab. The homemade bread baked in a flowerpot is very popular. The children's menu has the standard hot dogs and chicken, but the more daring child can order king crab legs, spare ribs, and steak. All kids' meals come with salad and potato.

The White Mountains

The White Mountains region is New Hampshire in all its glory! The White Mountains are to New Hampshire what the Adirondacks are to New York—a gorgeous mecca for outdoor-loving vacationers. The White Mountains are the main attractions in this neck of the woods—naturalists and lovers of old-fashioned vacations love to spend the days discovering the waterfalls, admiring the stunning views, and hiking. In the southern stretch is action-packed **North Conway,** which combines sandy beaches with great shopping at factory outlets, miniature golf courses, and movie theaters. Farther north is **Crawford Notch**—the antithesis of North Conway—with several waterfalls that kids will love. Still farther north is **Bretton Woods**—fabulous for skiing and home to one of the world's oldest railways.

Franconia Notch bears witness to nature's wonders with the awe-inspiring **Old Man of the Mountain** geologic formation, carved by nature thousands of years ago. This natural stone profile protrudes from a sheer cliff 1,200 feet above Profile Lake in Franconia Notch State Park.

Mount Washington is the highest mountain in the northeast. Visitors either drive their cars up the steep road to the top or traverse it by the cog railway (not for the faint of heart). Of course, you can hike it if you hear that calling.

Loon Mountain, in the southwestern corner of the White Mountains and about 25 miles north of Waterville Valley, endears mountain bikers in the summer months, but it remains relatively quiet even so. In the winter months visitors ski, snow tube, and even horseback ride this mountain. (For more about Loon Mountain, see Family Outdoor Adventures, page 195.)

In a state where nature abounds, **Waterville Valley** is the antithesis of natural. This is a planned community, including a cookie-cutter Town Square, with few shops of interest and a restaurant and grocery store/deli. But we loved the lift-serviced mountain biking and fireworks over the small-ish lake at this self-contained valley resort when we visited on Fourth of July

The White Mountains

N

LODGING

1. The Franconia Inn
2. The Mount Washington Hotel & Resort
3. The Purity Spring Resort
4. Rockhouse Mountain Farm
5. The Spalding Inn
6. Whitney's Inn

ATTRACTIONS

7. Clark's Trading Post
8. Conway Scenic Railroad
9. Heritage New Hampshire
10. Lost River Gorge
11. Mt. Washington Cog Railway
12. Mt. Washington Weather Discovery Center
13. Santa's Village
14. Six Gun City & Fort Splash Water Park
15. Story Land

RESTAURANTS

16. Bellini's
17. Polly's Pancake Parlor
18. Stonehurst Manor
19. Wild Coyote Cafe

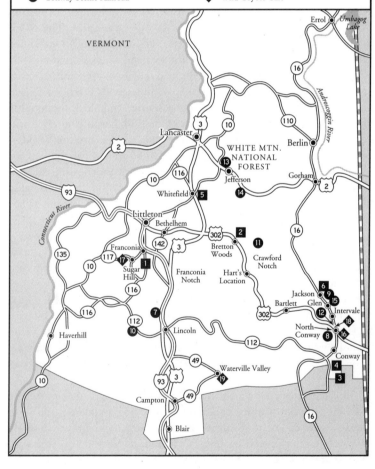

weekend. Our accommodations, though uninspired, were a short stroll to the Town Square. Still, some families love Waterville Valley, at the foot of the White Mountains, for its low-key ambiance and easy handling. Besides, it offers an ambitious summer recreation program with an open gym and kids' night-out programs, plus an athletic club and inexpensive rates. Call (800) GO-VALLEY for information.

Family Lodging

The Franconia Inn

Need inspiration in your life? This historic inn affords guests with the same views of Franconia Notch that inspired the poetry of Robert Frost, namely The Road Not Taken. With quintessential New England architecture— white clapboard, green shutters—this 34-room inn is the perfect getaway. Its features rival the awesome views—a library, a cross-country ski center, a riding stable, a heated swimming pool, bicycles, a sauna, and movies. Rates begin at $89 per night. Easton Road, Franconia; (800) 473-5299.

The Mount Washington Hotel & Resort

Location, location, location. At the foot of the Presidential Range, this Grande Dame packs in the guests. Since it opened in 1902, the resort habitually hibernated for the long winter months, but the new millennium changed all that and now it's open year round. Families can downhill ski (at Bretton Woods; see Skiing on page 197), cross-country ski, sleigh ride and snowshoe on the property. Luring families in summer are 27 holes of PGA golf, 12 red-clay tennis courts, horseback riding, indoor/outdoor swimming pools, and hiking, not to mention the 900-foot wrap-around veranda.

The resort is easily accessible from many of the White Mountains' top attractions, including the Mount Washington Cog Railway in North Conway. Organized children's programs win big points with kids and vacation-starved moms and dads. Luxury doesn't come cheap, but room rates include breakfast and dinner. Rates begin at $229 per night. NH Route 302, Bretton Woods; (800) 258-0300.

The Purity Spring Resort

Open year-round, this family-owned property down the road from the King Pine Ski Resort offers an indoor pool, cross-country skiing on groomed trails, and packages with the King Pine Ski Area, including ski for free midweek, except holiday periods. It's about 20 minutes from North Conway, a nice respite from the buzz at the outlet stores and a snowball's throw from great skiing. In summer, there's hiking, tennis, water-skiing, a climbing wall, a fitness center, childcare, and a pretty lake. Double room rates begin at $100 per night. NH Route 153, East Madison. Call (800) FREE-SKI.

Rockhouse Mountain Farm

Got an only child? Head here, where kids get to sleep in the same room with other kids staying at the farm—in bunk beds, no less. At the foot of the White Mountains, this working farm (kids get to milk cows and collect eggs) sprawls over 450 acres. There are organized activities, such as hikes, but for the most part, your little cowhands have the run of the place. Some of the rooms (there are 15 total) have shared bathrooms, so if a private bath is important to you, inquire ahead. Per-night rates begin at $68 per adult, $40 per child age 12 and older, $34 per child age 6–11, and $28 per child age 1–5. Rates include breakfast and dinner. Rockhouse Mt. Road, Eaton Center (6 miles south of Conway); (603) 447-2880.

The Spalding Inn

Let 'em loose! Over 200 acres of freedom lures families to this unassuming inn with four clay tennis courts, a heated swimming pool, and family suites and cottages. It's near Six Gun City and Santa's Village. Bonus: Fido is welcome. Rates begin at $100 per night. 199 Mountain View Road, Whitefield; (800) 368-VIEW.

Whitney's Inn

Adjacent to the Black Mountain Ski Area and loaded with cross-country ski trails, this is back-to-basics family vacationing. While there is a main building with lovely guest rooms, families should opt to stay in one of the eight suites (housed together in a separate building) or one of the two cottages. Frozen toes are thawed inside while sipping hot cocoa and playing board games. In summer, you can enjoy the pond and hiking. While you'll feel you're in the country (and make no mistake about it, you are), the town of Jackson is about a mile down the road. Kids age 12 and under stay and eat free in the family suites. Rates begin at $89 per night. NH Route 16B, Jackson; (800) 677-5737.

Attractions

Clark's Trading Post

NH Route 3, Lincoln; (603) 745-8913; www.clarkstradingpost.com

Hours: Mid-May–mid-June and early September–mid-October, weekends only; mid-June–early September, daily 9 a.m.–6 p.m. (ticket office closes at 5 p.m.)

Admission: $9 ages 6 and older, $8 senior citizens (ages 65 and older), $3 ages 3–5, free for kids under age 3

Appeal by Age Groups:

Pre-school	Grade School	Teens	Young Adults	Over 30	Seniors
★	★★★★	★★★	★★	★	★

Touring Time: Average 2 hours; minimum 1 hour

Rainy-Day Touring: Yes

Services and Facilities:

Restaurants No	Lockers No
Alcoholic beverages No	Pet kennels No
Disabled access No	Rain check No
Wheelchair rental No	Private tours Yes
Baby stroller rental No	

Description and Comments Part circus, part train excursion, this attraction has been around for 70 years. Kids love the North American Bear Show. During the summer months the Grimmy Family Circus mesmerizes the children with juggling and acrobatics. The White Mountain Central Railroad excursion across a covered bridge is a thrill. With an 1884 Fire Station and bumper boats, there's something for everyone (except maybe Mom and Dad.) Actually the candle and gift shops are good souvenir stops.

Conway Scenic Railroad

NH Route 16. Norcross Circle in the heart of North Conway Village; (800) 232-5251

Hours: Valley train: April–mid-May and November and December, weekends only; mid-May–late October, daily. Notch Train, June 20–September 9, Tuesday–Saturday; September 12–October 13, daily.

Admission: $9 ages 6 and older, $8 seniors, $3 ages 3–5, free for kids 2 amd under

Appeal by Age Groups:

Pre-school	Grade School	Teens	Young Adults	Over 30	Seniors
★★★	★★★★	★★★	★★	★	★★

Touring Time: Average 1–5 hours, depending on trip you choose; minimum 1 hour

Rainy-Day Touring: Yes

Services and Facilities:

Restaurants Yes; dining car on board (kids under age 4 eat and ride free at lunch)	Baby stroller rental No
	Lockers No
	Pet kennels No
Alcoholic beverages Yes	Rain check No
Disabled access No	Private tours Yes
Wheelchair rental No	

Description and Comments   This is a fun and pretty way to see the gorgeous White Mountains. The Valley Train offers rides to Conway and Bartlett, and the Notch Train traverses stunning Crawford Notch. Tip: Reservations on the Notch Train are recommended for the fall because it is foliage peeping time. The quickest trip is one hour, perfect for preschoolers. There are longer trains—the longest is five hours up to Crawford Notch, ideal for elementary school kids and older. There are also dinner excursions.

Heritage-New Hampshire

NH Route 16, Glen, adjacent to Story Land; (603) 383-4186

Hours: Mid-June–mid-October, 9 a.m.–5 p.m.

Admission: $10 adults, $4.50 children ages 6 to 12, free for children under age 6

Appeal by Age Groups:

Pre-school	Grade School	Teens	Young Adults	Over 30	Seniors
★	★★★★	★★★	★★★	★	★

Touring Time: Average 1–5 hours, depending on trip you choose; minimum 1 hour

Rainy-Day Touring: Yes

Services and Facilities:

Restaurants Yes; snack shop	Lockers No
Alcoholic beverages No	Pet kennels No
Disabled access No	Rain check No
Wheelchair rental No	Private tours Yes
Baby stroller rental No	

Descriptions and Comments   Here you'll get a cool peek at New Hampshire's glory days, spanning 350 years. First you'll set sail from 1634 England with the promise of the new land. Once ashore you'll explore at your own pace. You can bet that grandmother's 1850s kitchen doesn't have a microwave. Then take a simulated rail trip through Crawford Notch at peak foliage season. Since it's an indoor attraction, save it for a rainy day.

Lost River Gorge

NH Route 112, Kinsman Notch in North Woodstock; (603) 745-8031

Hours: Mid-May–mid-October, weather permitting

Admission: $10 adults, $4.50 kids age 6–12, free for children under age 6

Appeal by Age Groups:

Pre-school	Grade School	Teens	Young Adults	Over 30	Seniors
★	★★★★	★★★	★★	★	★

Touring Time: Average 2 hours; minimum 1 hour

Rainy-Day Touring: No

Services and Facilities:

Restaurants No	Lockers No
Alcoholic beverages No	Pet kennels No
Disabled access No	Rain check No
Wheelchair rental No	Private tours Yes
Baby stroller rental No	

Description and Comments This natural attraction, created by glaciers, digs deep into the past. Kids love to traverse the narrow, steep-walled gorge and explore the caverns and waterfalls. Bridges make it all the more fun to explore. There is a self-guided tour, which takes about an hour. Kids love the Hall of Ships, the Lemon Squeezer, and to stand under Guillotine Rock. Also check out the Lost River Mining Company to pan for gemstones and minerals (separate fee).

Mount Washington Cog Railway

NH Route 302, Bretton Woods; (800) 922-8825

Hours: Call for hours and to make reservations (advance ticket purchase is recommended)

Admission: Varies (call for rates)

Appeal by Age Groups:

Pre-school	Grade School	Teens	Young Adults	Over 30	Seniors
★★★	★★★★	★★★★	★★	★	★

Touring Time: Average 3 hours; minimum 3 hours

Rainy-Day Touring: Yes

Services and Facilities:

Restaurants Yes; at the Marsh-field Base Station at the summit	Baby stroller rental No
	Lockers No
	Pet kennels No
Alcoholic beverages No	Rain check No
Disabled access No	Private tours No
Wheelchair rental No	

Description and Comments   This century-old steam engine chugs up the slope of the tallest mountain on the East Coast—to the summit of 6,288-foot Mount Washington. Yes, the views are extraordinary (on a clear day you can see forever . . . or at least Canada and the Atlantic Ocean). If you love moody weather, take the train on a cloudy day and you'll climb above the clouds. Some people choose to drive up Mount Washington, but the Mount Washington Cog Railway is less taxing on your engine—and your nerves. This is not a ride for the faint of heart, as it is reputed to be one of the steepest railways anywhere. The littlest of kids (age five and under) sit on adult laps and ride free of charge.

The Mount Washington Weather Discovery Center

NH Route 16, North Conway (north of the village); (603) 356-2137

Hours: Daily 10 a.m.–5 p.m.

Admission: $2 adults, $1 children, free for kids age 5 and under

Appeal by Age Groups:

Pre-school	Grade School	Teens	Young Adults	Over 30	Seniors
★	★★★★	★★★	★★★	★★★	★★★

Touring Time: Average 3 hours; minimum 3 hours

Rainy-Day Touring: Yes

Services and Facilities:

Restaurants No	Lockers No
Alcoholic beverages No	Pet kennels No
Disabled access Yes	Rain check No
Wheelchair rental No	Private tours Yes
Baby stroller rental No	

Description and Comments   The Mount Washington Observatory has been the center of weather observation, research, and recording for more than 50 years. In fact, Mount Washington holds the world record for surface wind speed at 231 miles per hour in 1934. You'll learn all about the summit observatory, and kids will have the chance for hands-on activities

The Road Less Traveled

Revered American poet Robert Frost found his road less traveled in New Hampshire. A dilapidated metal mailbox and a field of lupines mark the place the Frosts called home from 1915 to 1920 and where they summered for 18 years thereafter.

The Robert Frost Place sits high on a ridge in Franconia Notch. Here, the poet laureate composed some of his most enduring works. In a yard filled with sugar maples and wildflowers, Frost found inspiration for such great poems as *Mending Wall, Evening in a Sugar Orchard,* and *The Tuft of Flowers.*

In 1976, Franconia purchased the farmhouse as part of its bicentennial celebration. In 1977, the town voted to select a poet-in-residence to live in the modest white farmhouse each summer. Frost's benevolent spirit endows resident poets with creative energy and inpsiration. Since 1979, the Festival of Poetry on the site has drawn poets for readings and classes, some open to the public.

The Robert Frost Place is open to visitors from Memorial Day through mid-October. You can explore the woods while enjoying the verses of his poetry posted along the paths, and you can tour the farmhouse where the poet lived with his family. The Robert Frost Place is located off NH Route 116 in Franconia; (603) 823-5510.

—*William Raymond*

to teach them about weather observation tools and weather technology. They'll walk away with a greater appreciation of weather and a strong fascination with how weather shapes our world.

Santa's Village

NH Route 2, Jefferson; (603) 586-4445

Hours: Mid-June–Labor Day, daily 9:30 a.m.–5 p.m.; Memorial Day–mid-June and Labor Day–early October, weekends 9:30 a.m.–5 p.m.; open at Christmas time, of course, 9:30 a.m.–5 p.m.

Admission: $17 per person, $15 seniors age 62 and older, kids age 3 and under get in free; admission includes all rides and shows

Appeal by Age Groups:

Pre-school	Grade School	Teens	Young Adults	Over 30	Seniors
★★★★	★★★★	★★	★★	★	★

The White Mountain Trail

The White Mountains Trail was designated a national scenic and cultural byway in 1998. The trail is a loop that you can drive in less than a day, or you can opt to spend your entire vacation exploring its mountains, rivers, wetlands, woodlands, 18th- and 19th-century buildings, and historic sites. The trail snakes past popular family attractions, including the Cannon Mountain Aerial Tramway and the historic Mount Washington Cog Railway, as well as the state's natural stone profiles, including The Indian Head and the Old Man of the Mountain. The trail also traverses the Kancamagus Highway, a National Scenic Byway, from the shopping town of North Conway to the ski town of Lincoln. Stay overnight at one of the campgrounds along the route or at one of the handful of great family resorts and inns. The trail begins and ends at the White Mountains Visitor Center in North Woodstock. Happy trails! For more information, call (888) 944-8368.

Touring Time: Average a full day; minimum a half day

Rainy-Day Touring: No

Services and Facilities:

Restaurants Yes	Lockers No
Alcoholic beverages No	Pet kennels Yes
Disabled access No	Rain check Yes
Wheelchair rental Yes	Private tours Yes
Baby stroller rental Yes	

Descriptions and Comments   Christmas in July? Absolutely! Kids adore this nutty amusement park, so much fun even Scrooge would give it a thumbs up. Lots of fun rides and slides and entertaining shows make this a magical park. The rides have whimsical names such as the Yule Log Flume ride and Rudy's Rapid Transit roller coaster. Kids love becoming a Santa's helper at the North Pole Workshop. Grin and bear it, moms and dads—and consider using this park as a bribe for that nice quiet evening you're longing for back at the resort. As if!

Six Gun City & Fort Splash Water Park

NH Route 2, Jefferson; (603) 586-4592

Hours: Memorial Day–mid-June, weekends only; mid-June–Labor Day, daily 9 a.m.–6 p.m.

Admission: $15.45 for ages 4 and older, free for ages 3 and under

Appeal by Age Groups:

Pre-school	Grade School	Teens	Young Adults	Over 30	Seniors
★★	★★★★	★★	★★	★	★

Touring Time: Average a full day; minimum a half day

Rainy-Day Touring: No

Services and Facilities:

Restaurants Yes; snack bar	Lockers No
Alcoholic beverages No	Pet kennels No
Disabled access No	Rain check No
Wheelchair rental No	Private tours No
Baby stroller rental No	

Descriptions and Comments   Right down the street from Santa's Village is this Western-themed, two-in-one attraction with a miniature horse show, 13 rides and waterslides, cowboy skits, and a frontier show. Little ones especially like this park, thanks to the opportunity to help round-up "the bad guys," the chance to spy cowboys and bank robbers, and the laser-tag game. Pack a picnic lunch to save a penny.

Story Land

NH Route 16, Glen (about ten miles north of North Conway and adjacent to Heritage-New Hampshire); (603) 383-4186

Hours: Mid-June–Labor Day, daily 9 a.m.–6 p.m.; Labor Day–Columbus Day, weekends 9 a.m.–6 p.m.

Admission: $18 for all guests age 4 and older (admission covers unlimited rides, the picnic area, and parking), free for kids age 3 and under

Appeal by Age Groups:

Pre-school	Grade School	Teens	Young Adults	Over 30	Seniors
★★★★	★★★	★★	★★	★	★

Touring Time: Average a full day; minimum a half day

Rainy-Day Touring: No

Services and Facilities:

Restaurants Yes; snack bar	Lockers No
Alcoholic beverages No	Pet kennels No
Disabled access Yes	Rain check No
Wheelchair rental Yes	Private tours No
Baby stroller rental Yes	

Description and Comments   Carousels, a Sprayground, a flume ride, a Polar Coaster, a talking tree house, Cinderella's Castle, and a raft ride put this on the map as a don't-miss family spot. There are 16 theme rides featured at this 35-acre park. There's also a cool educational attraction, A Child's Visit to Other Lands (Africa, Holland, Antartica, and even outer space.) And kids love the kooky interactive show at the Tales of Wonder Theater. There are shaded picnic areas, so pack a lunch and save a penny. Worth noting: If you visit after 3 p.m., you'll have to pay full admission but will receive a pass for any other day in the current season.

Family-Friendly Restaurants

BELLINI'S

33 Seavey Street, North Conway; (603) 356-7000

Meals served: Dinner
Cuisine: Italian
Entree range: $10 and up
Children's menu: Yes
Reservations: No
Payment: All types accepted

Checkerboard floors, striped awnings, and *Cinzano* umbrellas enliven this North Conway restaurant with a festive atmosphere. An excellent Italian menu will make the whole family happy. It's closed Monday and Tuesday.

POLLY'S PANCAKE PARLOR

Hildex Farm, Route 117, Exit 38 off I-93, Sugar Hill; (603) 823-5575

Meals served: Breakfast and lunch
Cuisine: Pancakes
Entree range: $5 and up
Children's menu: Yes
Reservations: No
Payment: All types accepted

The homemade pancakes, waffles, and French toast are all made with home-ground flours and served with pure maple syrup. Yum! The menu also offers soups, salads, quiche, sandwiches, and homemade bread, but it's the pancakes that vie for best vacation memory. Bonus: Panoramic views of the White Mountains. It's closed in the winter months.

STONEHURST MANOR

Route 16, North Conway; (800) 525-9100

Meals served: Dinner
Cuisine: Wood-oven pizza and American specialties
Entree range: $9.95 and up
Children's menu: Yes
Reservation: Yes
Payment: All types accepted

In the summertime, opt to sit on the screened-in porch overlooking the pretty garden. Be sure to indulge in a gourmet, wood-fired pizza—Stonehurst is on the map for its fabulous pies. But it also dishes up creative specials, including duck, prime rib, and fish. The kids' menu has cheese pizza, pasta, grilled chicken breast, and even prime rib.

WILD COYOTE CAFÉ

Waterville Valley Resort & Conference Center, Exit 28 off I-93, then 11 miles on Route 49; (603) 236-4919

Meals served: Lunch and dinner
Cuisine: American and Mexican
Entree range: $5.95 and up
Children's menu: Yes
Reservations: No
Payment: All types accepted

The pickins are slim for eats at Waterville Valley. Your best bet: the second floor of the athletic center at the Waterville Valley Resort & Conference Center. You can walk or bike to the athletic center from many of the accommodations at Waterville Valley. We enjoyed our meals here (two nights; it's practically the only game in town). The mood is easy-going and friendly.

Side Trip: The North Country

Not many tourists make it this far north, but the lucky few that do are rewarded with a vast wilderness of lakes, streams, rivers, and acres upon acres of undeveloped woods. The North Country is idyllic for wildlife spotting: moose, eagles, and deer are common sightings. The **Great North Woods** has the largest moose population in the state. Visit during mid-June through mid-October and participate in the Moose Tour, which leaves from the Gorham Information Booth in the pretty town of **Gorham,** traveling north through **Berlin** into the Great Woods Region. Make reservations for this tour; call (800) 992-7480. There are few towns—Berlin is the largest and most prominent. Northwest Maine, northeastern Vermont, and the southernmost part of Quebec are neighbors of the Great North—don't be surprised to hear French spoken. **Dixville Notch** is home to New Hampshire's most remote resort—**The Balsams.** This is the place to come when you're ready to say "See ya" to your normal routine and are looking for a fabulous vacation escape from it all.

Don't expect any man-made diversions in this neck of the woods. Instead, throw caution to the wind and head out of doors and let it all hang out. Northern Forest, Heritage Park, and Dixville Notch State Park are wilderness wonderlands that adventurous families wil love to explore. See our Family Outdoor Adventures section (page 195) and The Best Beaches and Parks section (page 190) for information.

FAMILY LODGING

The Balsams Grand Resort Hotel

This year-round resort is *raison d'etre* many families make the journey to the North Woods of New Hampshire. The resort houses 15,000 acres, with golf, tennis, swimming, and mountain-bike trails. In summer there's a kids' camp program, and when the temperatures dip there's downhill and cross-country skiing, skating, snowboarding, and snowshoeing. This resort has an all-inclusive concept, so everything (accommodations, meals, and activities) are included in one rate. Rates begin at $200 per night. Dixville Notch; (800) 255-0600; in New Hampshire, (800) 255-0800.

Part Five

Rhode Island

This tiny state has one of the best coastlines in the Northeast. It's also got a handful of tony mansions in **Newport.** What it doesn't have that many of its sister New England states do is winter skiing. You'll want to travel to Rhode Island in the spring, summer, and fall—but especially during the summer when the water is as warm as it's going to get all year and everything is open.

Providence is Rhode Island's largest city, and what a difference its face-lift has made. Having undergone a major transformation, this renaissance city with a river running through it is a great family destination. You can explore this compact city by foot, taking in Waterplace Park and the Providence Riverwalk, the Fleet Skating Center at Kennedy Plaza, and dozens of shops, art galleries, and restaurants. Cross the Providence River and you're in the historic East Side, home to Brown University.

The sandiest, splashiest strands in Rhode Island can be found in the **South County** region, where you'll happily discover 400 miles of coastline, stretching from **Narragansett** to **Watch Hill.** (Statewide, there are more than 100 beaches!) Bonus: Rhode Island waters tend to be warmer than those in neighboring New England states. Of course, August is the month with the warmest water.

Rhode Island is considered this country's first vacationland, thanks to the beauty of Narragansett Bay, one of the largest saltwater recreational areas in New England. It apparently earned this distinction in 1524, when Italian navigator Giovanni da Verazzano, an explorer for France, lingered a fortnight after becoming entranced by the beauty of Narragansett Bay—the origin of the first two-week vacation with pay on record. No doubt, Giovanni paid a modest sum compared to what you'll pay today: Rhode Island's most popular beach resorts, including Watch Hill, Newport, and Block Island, are not cheap. But you get what you pay for—and what you

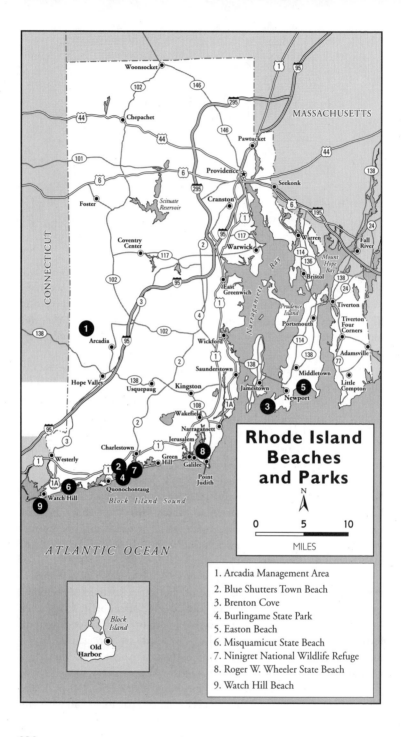

Rhode Island Beaches and Parks

N

| 0 | 5 | 10 |

MILES

1. Arcadia Management Area
2. Blue Shutters Town Beach
3. Brenton Cove
4. Burlingame State Park
5. Easton Beach
6. Misquamicut State Beach
7. Ninigret National Wildlife Refuge
8. Roger W. Wheeler State Beach
9. Watch Hill Beach

Fun Rhode Island Facts

- Rhode Island enacted the first law against slavery in North America on May 18, 1652.

- Touro Synagogue in Newport is the oldest Jewish house of worship in America, established in 1763.

- The Narragansett Pacer, a saddle-horse bred during the Colonial days in Rhode Island, was the first breed of American horse.

- The first street in America to be lighted by gaslight was Newport's Pelham Street, in 1806.

- Watch Hill Resort in Westerly operates the nation's oldest carousel, dating back to 1850.

- President John F. Kennedy and Jacqueline Bouvier were married in St. Mary's Church in Newport in 1952.

- Newport is celebrated as the Sailing Capital of the World and was home to the America's Cup for 53 years.

---

can expect are some of the prettiest beaches anywhere, with a laid-back, old-fashioned charm devoid of much commercialism. Good things really do come in small packages! (See The Best Beaches and Parks section on page 233 for information about the beaches.)

GETTING THERE

By Car. Compact Rhode Island is easily accessible by car. Providence is bisected by Interstates 95 and 195. It is 183 miles from New York City and 45 miles from Boston. Newport is 20 miles south of Providence. Note: Block Island is the only part of Rhode Island that is not accessible by car.

By Plane. T.F. Green Airport (PVD) has recently expanded and is a gateway to New England. The airport is a 12-minute drive to downtown Providence and 25 minutes to Newport. Call (401) 737-8222; www.pvd-ri.com.

By Train. Providence is on Amtrak's Washington to Boston, Northeast Corridor main line. A high-speed rail service, the *Acela,* is finally on track, making access to Providence quicker than ever. Call (800) USA-RAIL.

State Symbols

- State flag's motto: Hope
- State's nickname: The Ocean State
- State flower: Violet
- State bird: Rhode Island Red Hen
- State tree: Red Maple
- State shell: Quahog

- State mineral: Bowenite, a close relative of jade, found in northern Rhode Island
- State rock: Cumberlandite, a dark brown or black with white markings. Interesting note: it will attract a magnet. It is found on both sides of Narragansett Bay but not north of Cumberland.

By Ferry. Block Island Ferry services Block Island from Point Judith, Providence, and Newport as well as New London, Connecticut. Call (401) 783-4613. The Viking Fleet, (631) 668-5700, runs from Mantauk, New York, to Block Island.

How to Get Information before You Go

Block Island Chamber of Commerce, Water Street, Block Island, RI 02807; (401) 466-2982.

East Bay Chamber of Commerce, 654 Metacom Avenue, Suite 2, Warren, RI 02885; (888) 278-9948; www.eastbaychamber.org.

Newport County Convention and Visitors' Bureau and the Visitor Information Center, 23 America's Cup Avenue, Newport, RI 02840; (800) 976-5122; www.gonewport.com.

Providence Warwick Convention & Visitors' Bureau, 1 West Exchange Street, Providence, RI 02903; (800) 233-1636; Visitor Information Center (401) 751-1177; www.providencecvb.com.

Rhode Island Tourism Division, 1 West Exchange Street, Providence, RI 02903; (800) 556-2484; www.VisitRhodeIsland.com.

South County Tourism Council, 4808 Tower Hill Road, Wakefield, RI 02879; (800) 548-4662; www.southcountyri.com.

Cool Websites for Rhode Island–Bound Kids

Astors' Beechwood Mansion: www.astors-beechwood.com
Feinstein IMAX Theater Providence Plaza:
    www.imax.com/providence
Fleet Skating Center: www.fleetskating.com
Newport Guide: www.newportri.com
Newport Mansions of the Preservation Society: www.newportman-
    sions.org
Pawtucket Red Sox: www.pawsox.com
Providence Convention and Visitors Bureau:
    www.Providencecvb.com
Providence Cultural Arts: www.caparts.org
Rhode Island School of Design Museum: www.risd.edu
Roger Williams Park Zoo: www.rwpzoo.org
State Beach information: http://state.ri.us/dem
South County: www.southcountyri.com
Tourism Info: www.VisitRhodeIsland.com
Waterfire Providence: www.waterfire.orgwww.soea.com

The Best Beaches and Parks

Blue Shutters Town Beach. Sandy and clean, this is a popular beach with families, although at times the surf can be moderate to heavy. There is a concession stand. It's located on East Beach Road, off Route 1 in Charlestown.

Brenton Cove. If you've got toddlers, this sandy stretch in Newport is the swimming spot for you. One side of this cove has a lifeguard and a roped-off area just for young swimmers.

Burlingame State Park. This is one of the state's finest places to picnic, bike, boat, and camp. A swimming pond is on site. Note: There is a modest admission fee for cars in the summer. It's located off Prosser Trail, off Route 1 in Charlestown, South County; (401) 322-7994.

Easton Beach. Newport's most family-friendly beach stretches for more than a mile, and the waters are relatively calm. But enough about the sand and surf: a carousel, snack bars, a bathhouse, and even an aquarium bait families to come here.

Rhode Island's Best Bets

Providence
- Waterplace Park
- The Roger Williams Park & Zoo
- Canoeing along the revitalized riverfront

South County
- The Flying Horse Carousel, Watch Hill
- Napatree Point, Watch Hill
- Water Wizz, Westerly
- Ninigret National Wildlife Refuge, Charlestown
- Blue Shutters Beach, Charlestown
- Burlingame State Park, Charelstown
- Misquamicut Beach, Charlestown
- A day trip to Newport to walk the Cliff Walk and see the mansions

Block Island
- Building sandcastles and biking about Block Island
- Mohegan Bluffs, Block Island

Misquamicut State Beach. This seven-mile strand is Rhode Island's largest state beach—and much more than sand and surf. An amusement park, a carousel, a miniature golf course, and waterslides make this spot as family central. There is parking for 3,000 cars so you don't have to get up at the crack of dawn to secure a spot. It's on Atlantic Avenue in Westerly; (800) SEA-7636.

Roger W. Wheeler State Beach. A nice, clean, sandy beach with no undertow and no rough surf, thanks to a jetty. Plop your beach chairs, towels, and sun-ready selves and call it a day. There are snack bars and a bathhouse. Located at Sand Hill Cove Road, off Route 108, Narragansett.

Watch Hill Beach. It's tiny so you better arrive early. With minimum waves and soft sand, this is a popular beach as much for those reasons as for its location within walking distance of the ever-popular Flying Horse Carousel. It's on Bay Street in Watch Hill.

Family Outdoor Adventures

Birding. There are some great spots throughout the state for spying warblers, goldfinches, osprey, herons, and egrets. Some of the best perches are: Trustom Pond Wildlife Refuge in Charlestown, (401) 364-9124; Kimball Wildlife Refuge in Charlestown, (401) 231-6444; Block Island; Ninigret National Wildlife Refuge, on Route 1, just south of the Ninigret Park exit in Charlestown, (401) 334-6244; and the Great Swamp Management Area in Charlestown, (401) 789-0281. To get to the Great Swamp, take Exit 3A off I-95 to Route 138 E. Turn right onto Liberty Lane just before the junction of Route 110.

Camping. Burlingame State Park is one of the state's finest places to camp, bike, picnic, and swim in the swimming pond. It's located off Prosser Trail, off Route 1 in Charlestown, South County; (401) 322-7994.

Cross-country Skiing. In Ninigret National Wildlife Refuge, you'll find cross-country skiing plus fabulous year-round birding. This is a former World Water II Naval Station. There are also one- to two-hour hikes. Note: No biking is allowed. Located Route 1 just south of Ninigret Park exit.

Arcadia Management Area has cross-country ski trails snaking through its 13,817 acres—it's Rhode Island's largest public land. (401) 789-3094.

Cruises. One of the prettiest ways to take in Providence is a 40-minute ride along the Woonasquatucket and Providence rivers in a gondola. A basket of cheese and crackers, an ice bucket, and glasses are provided (translation: you bring your favorite bottle of vino.) *The Cynthia Julia* and *The Cynthia Jacob* are powered by a gondolier and a 16-foot oar. Italian music is provided or you can even request an accordion player. This is most appropriate for families with teenagers. Price is $60 for the first two persons and $15 for each additional person; (401) 421-8877.

Hiking. Ninigret National Wildlife Refuge offers some one- to two-hour hikes that are good for families. Route 1, Charlestown; (401) 334-6244.

Calendar of Festivals and Events

January

First Night Celebration, Providence. Ring in the New Year at this city-wide celebration; (800) 233-1636.

May

May Breakfasts, Statewide. This annual statewide event began in 1867. It showcases Rhode Island's specialty dishes in various locations throughout the state, including bird sanctuaries and schools; (800) 556-2484.

June

Annual Schweppes Great Chowder Cook-Off, Newport. Over 25 restaurants and caterers vie for the accolade of "Best Chowder in New England." There is music, a children's area, and more. It's held at the Newport Yachting Center, 4 Commercial Wharf, Newport; (401) 846-1600.

Annual Newport to Bermuda Race, Newport. An exciting international ocean-racing event with 150 sailboats. You can watch the start at Castle Hill in Newport, but you'll have to travel to St. Georges, Bermuda, to see the finish; (401) 423-0528.

Block Island Race Week. The largest sailing event on the entire East Coast. One hundred and twenty boats dock in New Harbor and race off Block Island throughout the week. Lots of family activities are planned around the event; (800) 338-BIRI.

July

Newport Music Festival. World-renowned musicians present over 55 concerts in various Newport mansions; (401) 846-1133.

August

Newport Folk Festival, Fort Adams State Park. Nationally known and rising stars perform as part of this festival; (401) 847-3700.

Newport Jazz Festival. An international event that attracts top jazz talent to Fort Adams State Park; (401) 847-3700.

September

Annual Rhode Island Heritage Festival, Providence. Thirty ethnic groups celebrate their culture with music, song, dance, and, of course, food. On the State House Lawn; (401) 222-2678.

October

Annual Oktoberfest. Weekend-long affair with Bavarian music, a biergarten, weingarten, and German marketplace. Newport Yachting Center, 4 Commercial Wharf, Newport; (401) 846-1600.

December

Annual Christmas in Newport. A holiday festival that's celebrated citywide in mansions, churches, and colonial homes. Includes a Festival of Trees, a Holly Ball, candlelight tours, and visits from Santa; (800) 326-6030.

Providence

Wow, has this capital town ever undergone a renaissance—thanks in part to a downtown waterfront that has been completely refurbished to include pedestrian walkways along the Providence River and a series of auto and foot bridges connecting downtown Providence to the city's historic East Side (think Venice). The hit TV drama series *Providence* has also helped put this town on the map. **Waterplace Park** is a gathering spot in the shadow of Rhode Island's **State House** and is the place for summer concerts in the outdoor amphitheater. This park is also the beginning and end of **The Banner Trail**—designated for visitors to explore the neighborhoods and sites on foot (most sites are within a one-mile radius of the park).

Providence is about 45 miles from Boston, so it's easy to visit both cities in one fell swoop—especially if you'll be driving from points south, such as New York City. Providence is also accessible from popular South County destinations (about a 45-minute drive) so consider a day trip to this interesting and exciting New England city.

Family Lodging

Holiday Inn Downtown

Located three blocks from the city, this business hotel is a hit with families, thanks to the indoor pool with an outdoor patio and Jacuzzi. It's also somewhat easier on the budget than some of the other Providence hotels—although not much. But it's worth the extra dollars to stay in one of the nicer hotels in town, and you can get special weekend packages. Waterplace Park and historical Federal Hill "Little Italy" are nearby. Room rates begin at $175 per night for the first adult, a second adult is charged $10; children age 19 and under stay free with parents. 21 Atwells Avenue, Providence; (401) 831-3900.

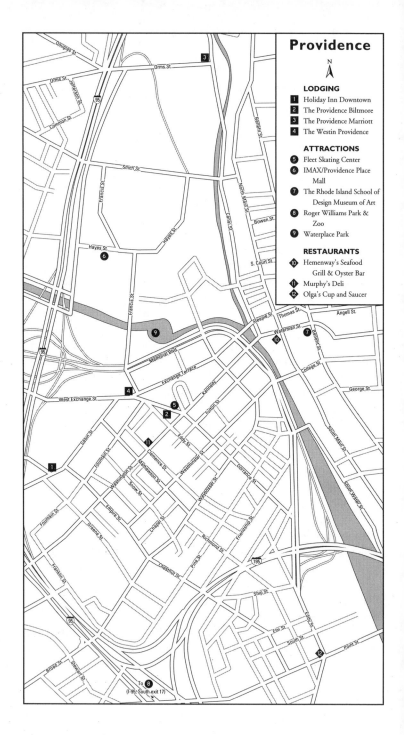

Providence

N

LODGING
1 Holiday Inn Downtown
2 The Providence Biltmore
3 The Providence Marriott
4 The Westin Providence

ATTRACTIONS
5 Fleet Skating Center
6 IMAX/Providence Place Mall
7 The Rhode Island School of Design Museum of Art
8 Roger Williams Park & Zoo
9 Waterplace Park

RESTAURANTS
10 Hemenway's Seafood Grill & Oyster Bar
11 Murphy's Deli
12 Olga's Cup and Saucer

The Providence Biltmore

Known as the Grande Dame, this landmark hotel has graced the ever-changing city since 1922. It epitomizes old world elegance, yet offers modern amenities travelers have come to expect from a fine city hotel. These amenities include a fitness center, spacious junior suites, and a concierge floor. The hotel is centrally located in the downtown area, so expect to see a lot of business travelers. It's got one of Providence's popular restaurants, Davio's. There is not a swimming pool. Double room rates begin at $165 per night for a standard room; a junior suite costs $215 per night. 111 Dorrance Street, Providence; (800) 294-7709.

The Providence Marriott

Just north of downtown Providence, this hotel lures families with its indoor-outdoor pool with sauna and whirlpool, as well as an outdoor poolside deck. It's a large hotel—345 rooms, each with in-room movies—that caters to the business crowd. Double room rates begin at $199 per night. Charles and Orms Streets, Providence; (800) 228-9290.

The Westin Providence

This is Providence's nicest downtown hotel, but it's pricey. The indoor pool is a plus for kids, as is the in-room Nintendo. This is a chain hotel smack in the middle of the city so don't expect much New England charm. Rates begin at $150 per night. 1 W. Exchange Street, Providence; (800) WESTIN-1.

Other Options

There are a handful of reasonably priced hotels, some in Providence, others within 10 minutes of downtown. Try the Courtyard by Marriott, (401) 272-1191; Days Hotel on the Harbor, (401) 272-5577; and Holiday Inn, (401) 831-3900.

Attractions

The Rhode Island School of Design Museum of Art

224 Benefit Street, Providence; (401) 454-6500

Hours: Tuesday–Sunday 1–5 p.m., third Thursday each month open until 9 p.m.

Admission: $5 adults age 19 and older, $4 seniors, $1 kids ages 5–18, free for kids under age 5

Appeal by Age Groups:

Pre-school	Grade School	Teens	Young Adults	Over 30	Seniors
★	★	★★★	★★★	★★★	★★★

Fun Things to Do in Providence

Play at Waterplace Park   This ambitious, four-acre public square, considered the hub of Providence, features a one-acre pond and fountain, cobblestone and brick river walks, and an amphitheater that sets the stage for summer concerts. The story behind it is fascinating—two rivers, the Moshassuck and the Woonasquatucket, were literally rerouted to follow the natural routes they once took before urban development shifted and filled them. The park is a gathering place in the shadow of Rhode Island's State House, just steps from the Rhode Island Convention Center. Waterplace Park is a super place for kids to let off steam.

Watch Baseball   The Pawtucket Red Sox is the Red Sox AAA team and first base for many major-league hitters. The season starts in May and runs through the end of August. Rhode Islanders are great baseball fans, and attending a ballgame here is as thrilling as Boston's Fenway Park (well, almost!). They play at McCoy Stadium, Ben Mondor Way, Pawtucket, a baseball-throw from Providence (if you're Pedro Martinez, that is.) For a schedule and tickets, call (401) 724-7300.

Go Skating   If you're visiting in the winter, there is no better activity on a frosty night than ice-skating at the Fleet Skating Center. Twice the size of the Rockefeller Center rink in New York City, this rink offers ice-skating from early October through March. In the spring and summer, it's roller-skating time. Lockers, skate rentals, a snack bar, and a full-service restaurant make this a one-stop destination. Cost for admission and skate rental is $9 for adults and $8 for kids. The use of helmets is free. Located at 2 Kennedy Plaza, Downtown Providence; (401) 331-5544.

Touring Time: Average 2–3 hours; minimum 1 hour
Rainy-Day Touring: Yes
Services and Facilities:

Restaurants Yes	Lockers No
Alcoholic beverages No	Pet kennels No
Disabled access Yes	Rain check No
Wheelchair rental No	Private tours Yes
Baby stroller rental No	

Fun Things to Do in Providence (continued)

Watch Bonfires If you're visiting Providence any time between March and November, even just for a day, don't even *think* about leaving town until well after sunset. That's when 97 bonfires are lighted on the river that runs through Providence, accompanied by music that ranges from original compositions to ritual chants from all over the world. This attraction pleases all the senses—the bright glow from the fires is beautiful to behold, the music stirs the soul, and the sweet smell of the burning wood lingers (recycled cedar fencing, as well as oak and pine is used to create the fires). The bonfires are put out at midnight. This is a really cool and magical experience for kids, and it's free of charge. Note: The bonfires are not lighted in the event of rain. Call (401) 272-3111 (any cancellations are announced on this information line before noon on the day of the event.)

See IMAX Seems most big cities have one, and, yep, Providence does too. The IMAX Theater seats 400 people and is housed in the spanking new Providence Place Mall in the heart of downtown Providence. Movies change frequently. Call (401) 453-2100.

Description and Comments More than 65,000 works of art grace this museum, from Greek sculpture to French Impressionist paintings to eighteenth-century American decorative art. This is a great way to spend a rainy morning, if you have older kids who appreciate art.

Roger Williams Park & Zoo

1000 Elmwood Avenue, ten minutes from downtown Providence (Exit 16 traveling north off I-95; Exit 17 traveling south); (401) 785-3510

Hours: Labor Day–Memorial Day, daily 9 a.m.–4 p.m.; Memorial Day–Labor Day, daily 9 a.m.–5 p.m.; closed Christmas Day

Admission: $6 adults, $3.50 kids ages 3–12 and seniors, free for kids age 3 and under

Appeal by Age Groups:

Pre-school	Grade School	Teens	Young Adults	Over 30	Seniors
★★★	★★★★	★★★	★★	★★	★★

Touring Time: Average 4 hours; minimum 2 hours

Rainy-Day Touring: Yes
Services and Facilities:

Restaurants Yes	Lockers No
Alcoholic beverages No	Pet kennels No
Disabled access Yes	Rain check No
Wheelchair rental Yes	Private tours Yes
Baby stroller rental Yes	

Description and Comments   While visiting the 900 animals here, make time to say hello to Norton and Trixie, the zoo's resident polar bears. A carousel and a miniature train woo kids, and paddleboats and tennis make it a well-rounded destination for families.

Family-Friendly Restaurants

Providence has a strong Italian influence, and nowhere is this felt more than on Federal Hill, referred to as Providence's "Little Italy." Italian restaurants flank the streets in this spirited section of town. Another good place with a conglomeration of restaurants is The Arcade, a glorified food court including a McDonald's. The coolest thing about this venue is the building—a Greek Revival structure that's a National Historic Landmark. Eat on the lower level and visit the shops upstairs. It's at 65 Weybosset Street; (401) 456-5403.

HEMENWAY'S SEAFOOD GRILL & OYSTER BAR

One Old Stone Square, Providence; (401) 351-8570

Meals served: Lunch and dinner
Cuisine: Seafood and steak
Entree range: $12.95 and up
Children's menu: Yes
Reservations: Yes
Payment: All types accepted

Families are welcome at this nice-looking spot known for fresh seafood and an extensive oyster bar. The chowder has won awards. If you want crayons and paper, ask and you shall receive. The children's menu covers the bases with pasta, chicken fingers, hamburgers, cheeseburgers, and fish 'n' chips.

MURPHY'S DELI

55 Union Street, Providence; (401) 421-1188

Meals served: Lunch and dinner
Cuisine: Sandwiches and side dishes
Children's menu: No
Entree range: $5.95 and up
Reservations: No
Payment: All types accepted

Around since 1929, and tucked behind the Biltmore Hotel, this is where kids with insatiable appetites can order Murphy's famous Mountain High deli sandwich. While there is no children's menu, there are chicken fingers and other kid-friendly items that you can order in half-portion sizes.

OLGA'S CUP AND SAUCER

103 Point Street, Providence; (401) 831-6666

Meals served: Breakfast, lunch, and dinner
Cuisine: Creative sandwiches and more
Entree range: $5.95 and up
Children's menu: No
Reservations: No
Payment: Credit cards accepted

Located in the Jewelry District, this is a favorite spot of locals, who crave Olga's creative sandwiches and to-die-for desserts. No kids' menu, but there's plenty on the menu to satisfy even picky eaters.

South County: Watch Hill and Narragansett

My friend Stephen Gronda knows this southeastern corner of Rhode Island especially well. Here is his take for family-gracious Watch Hill and its environs:

Watch Hill seems to shout, "This is what you always thought summer should feel like!" With its stately, clapboard homes trimmed in white, its rolling green lawns yawning into thickets of magenta rugosa rose, and the splashing waves of the Atlantic beyond, it can't help but fill your senses with the essence of summer. Having been fortunate enough to summer near Watch Hill for many seasons, come May, I found myself yearning for that sweet effusion coming from those same rose thickets as I stepped off the corner of Bay Street onto the rock-strewn sand path and onward to the water's edge. Here the visitor will find one of the small remaining public sections of beach to the east of **Watch Hill Lighthouse.**

Stretching west from the lighthouse is **Napatree Point,** an appendage of beach that arches gently for a mile into Little Narragansett Bay. Parking is extremely limited and first-come, first-served. Public restrooms are located across from the carousel and are open through Labor Day from 10 a.m. to 6 p.m.

The downtown area is blessed with nearly 50 wood structure shops and galleries, still sporting wood screen doors that slap their jambs as though applauding each time you enter or exit. The main parking lot is between Bay Street and the Yacht Club and is available for shoppers. On the bend in Bay Street, there is a perennial favorite of young children, a **"Flying Horse" carousel.** No ordinary carousel, its hand-carved, hand-painted horses go-round on chains that suspend them from above. Built around 1880, it arrived with a carnival and never left. It has undoubtedly brought smiles to many faces.

Reach for the brass ring and then stop into the **Book & Tackle Shop** next door and choose from among the eclectic items, including forgotten sand toys, flip-flops, or an honest to goodness, old fashioned ice cream cone.

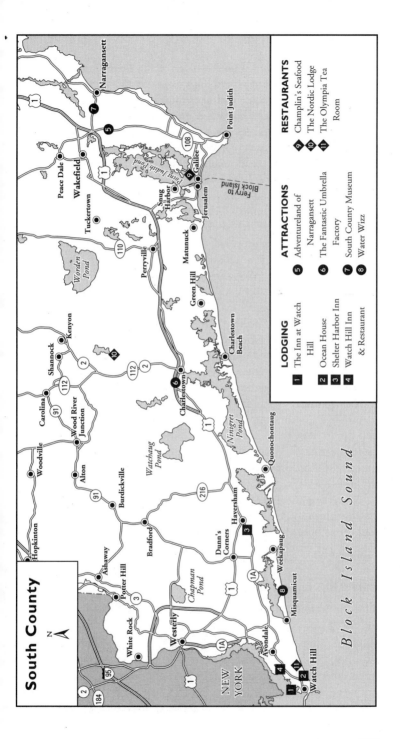

South County

N

LODGING

1 The Inn at Watch Hill
2 Ocean House
3 Shelter Harbor Inn
4 Watch Hill Inn & Restaurant

ATTRACTIONS

5 Adventureland of Narragansett
6 The Fantastic Umbrella Factory
7 South County Museum
8 Water Wizz

RESTAURANTS

9 Champlin's Seafood
10 The Nordic Lodge
11 The Olympia Tea Room

Block Island Sound

Watch Hill was thinned-out considerably by the Hurricane of 1938, which virtually demolished anything in its path. Where there were once seven wooden hotels, in the trail of the hurricane, only one remained. It, the **Ocean House,** is now considered the Grand Dame of hotels in these parts. The floors fairly echo your presence with every footstep, and nowhere will you ever wish, "if only these walls could talk," so fervently again. This old and graceful hotel has withstood more than a century of weather and seems to get better with age. There is a rolling lawn from the open-air deck to the sand at the leading edge of beach. Sam, the lifeguard, may still make this his home during summers, though on my last visit he hadn't returned yet. Yet, the whole package of bright yellow hotel at the crest of a grass and beach-rose laden hill, wooden decks that sound like the back of a guitar when you walk on them, and eclectic furnishings from a grand time in America makes this a "have to see" even if you don't stay.

Charlestown is all about secluded beaches. First inhabited by Native Americans, the Narragansetts, Charlestown is often called "the best-kept secret in Rhode Island." Shhhh! It is home to **Ninigret Park** and **Ninigret Wildlife Refuge,** both fabulous spots for hiking, bird-watching and playing. The Frosty Drew Nature Center at Ninigret Park allows kids to explore nature in a coastal setting. **Burlingame State Park** is also in Charlestown and is super for hiking and biking.

Narragansett is home to the **Port of Galilee,** the second-largest fishing port in New England and a fun spot to explore, shop, and eat. You can also hop the ferry to Block Island from Galilee. Narragansett's **Point Judith Lighthouse** has been a guiding light on the rocky Rhode Island coast since the early 1800s. Today, visitors can tour the lighthouse grounds and take in the birds-eye view.

Westerly is home to **Misquamicut State Beach,** Rhode Island's largest. An amusement park, a new pavilion, waterslides, a carousel, and mini-golf round out Westerly as an idyllic family spot. About five miles south of Westerly lies Watch Hill.

Family Lodging

The Inn at Watch Hill

On Bay Street, the main street of the village, this inn has 16 rooms. The village of Watch Hill is within walking distance, as is the beach. This inn has a best-of-both-worlds location: on the main strip near the carousel and just a short stroll from Napatree Beach. Double room rates begin at $150 per night. It's open May to October. 115 Bay Street, Watch Hill; (401) 596-0665.

Ocean House

A well-preserved example of late 19th-century summer resort hotel, this 59-room charmer was built in 1868. The resort seems to echo its past while the ocean waves below curl in a hypnotic mantra. Most rooms offer a view of the ocean or bay. There are also fabulous open-air and glassed-in porches for dining and cocktails in the ocean breeze. The kiddies can play on the sprawling lawn below. The private beach is a definite bonus. It's open late June to Labor Day. Double-room rates begin at $205 per night, including breakfast and dinner; extra-person rates (ages 7–18) are $55 per night. 1 Bluff Avenue, Watch Hill; (401) 348-8161.

Shelter Harbor Inn

This nineteenth-century farmhouse with 24 units welcomes children. It's in an off-the-beaten-path country setting about 10 minutes from Westerly town center. It has a private beach, although you have to take a shuttle to reach it. The shuttle runs on weekends only; during the week you'll get a pass for parking at the beach. Kids will enjoy the croquet, paddle-tennis courts, and rooftop whirlpool. Double-room rates begin at $75 per night, breakfast included. Route 1, 10 Wagner Road, Westerly; (800) 468-8883.

Watch Hill Inn & Restaurant

A perfect place for families, this 16-room, year-round inn is located in middle of the village of Watch Hill with views of Little Narragansett Bay. Fabulous sunsets, perhaps the best the area has to offer, are best seen from the dining deck. The restaurant offers a variety of casual dining choices that are very appealing to families with children. Double-room rates begin at $200 per night. 38 Bay Street, Watch Hill; (800) 356-9314, (401) 348-6300.

Attractions

Adventureland of Narragansett

Pt. Judith Road, Narragansett; (401) 789-0030

Hours: Mid-June–Labor Day, daily 10 a.m.–10 p.m.

Admission: Call for rates

Appeal by Age Groups:

Pre-school	Grade School	Teens	Young Adults	Over 30	Seniors
★★	★★★★	★★	★★	★★	

Touring Time: Average 3–4 hours; minimum 1 hour

Rainy-Day Touring: No

The Fantastic Umbrella Factory

This unique shopping venue contains a handful of eclectic shops. It's a great spot for kids, thanks to the tiny animal farm (sheep and geese) and lovely nursery. There are four buildings here; three house shops, the other a small vegetarian restaurant. This is a nice place to shop, combined with a visit to nearby Ninigret Park. It's located at the Ninigret Park/Tourist Info exit, off Route 1 in Charlestown; (401) 364-6616.

Services and Facilities:

Restaurants No	Lockers No
Alcoholic beverages No	Pet kennels No
Disabled access No	Rain check No
Wheelchair rental No	Private tours No
Baby stroller rental No	

Description and Comments   Bumper boat rides, go-cart rides, a miniature golf course (a great one), and a batting cage—let 'em loose! While the younger set might enjoy riding on a go-cart with you and playing minature golf, this attraction is really geared toward school-aged kids.

South County Museum

Canonchet Farm, RI Route 1A, Narragansett; (401) 783-5400

Hours: May–October, Wednesday–Sunday 11 a.m.– 4 p.m.

Admission: $4 adults; $2 children, free for kids age 6 and under

Appeal by Age Groups:

Pre-school	Grade School	Teens	Young Adults	Over 30	Seniors
★★★	★★★	★★	★★	★★	★★

Touring Time: Average 2 hours; minimum 1 hour

Rainy-Day Touring: Yes

Services and Facilities:

Restaurants No	Lockers No
Alcoholic beverages No	Pet kennels No
Disabled access No	Rain check No
Wheelchair rental No	Private tours No
Baby stroller rental No	

Love a Lighthouse

The Point Judith Lighthouse in Narragansett has been guiding ships away from the rocky Rhode Island coast since the early 1800s. The present lighthouse dates back to 1857 and was rebuilt twice. Kids love lighthouses, and the views of the Atlantic are awesome. It's located at the end of Ocean Road in Narragansett. Tip: Park your car (there's plenty of parking) and bicycle the Ecotrail.

Description and Comments   The museum is a good rainy-day diversion. It houses more than 15,000 artifacts dating from 1800 to 1930 in a main exhibit building and four workshop buildings, including a blacksmith and print shop. For nice days, there are also an outdoor live animal farm exhibit (cows and goats), places to picnic, and nature trails.

Water Wizz

Atlantic Avenue, Westerly; (401) 322-0520

Hours: Mid-June–Labor Day, daily 10 a.m.–10 p.m.

Admission: Call for rates

Appeal by Age Groups:

Pre-school	Grade School	Teens	Young Adults	Over 30	Seniors
★★★★	★★★★	★★★	★★	★★	

Touring Time: Average 3–4 hours; minimum 1 hour

Rainy-Day Touring: No

Services and Facilities:

Restaurants Yes	Lockers No
Alcoholic beverages No	Pet kennels No
Disabled access No	Rain check No
Wheelchair rental No	Private tours No
Baby stroller rental No	

Description and Comments   This water park is located on Misquamicut Beach. Water lovers can jump out of the sea right into a giant 35-foot waterslide, 50-foot high-speed slides, a kiddie slide, or the Serpentine slide. Kids of all ages thrill to this park, and you'll have fun, too. You can take the littlest ones down the slides.

Family-Friendly Restaurants

CHAMPLIN'S SEAFOOD

256 Great Island Road, Galilee; (401) 783-3152

Meals served: Lunch and dinner
Cuisine: Seafood
Entree range: $8 and up
Children's menu: No, but there are hamburgers, hot dogs, and chicken fingers
on the menu
Reservations: No
Payment: Credit cards accepted

Grab a seat and watch all the action—the Block Island ferry maneuvering
Galilee's tight channel and the fishing fleets coming and going. You can
expect great seafood—lobster, fish, clams, mussels—in a rustic setting.

THE NORDIC LODGE

178 Pasquisett Trail, Charlestown; (401) 783-4515

Meals served: Dinner
Cuisine: Lobster
Entree range: See prices below
Children's menu: Yes
Reservations: No
Payment: Credit cards accepted

To sum it up: all-you-can-eat lobster buffet. Need we say more? Prices are
$47 for adults, $30 for ages 10–12, $20 ages 6–9, and $10 for ages 2–5.

THE OLYMPIA TEA ROOM

Bay Street, Watch Hill; (401) 348-8211

Meals served: Breakfast, lunch, and dinner
Cuisine: Seafood/American
Entree range: $10 and up
Children's menu: No
Reservations: No
Payment: Credit cards accepted

Having opened in 1916, the Tea Room still bears the ambiance of that era with its black-and-white checked floor, high-backed wooden booths, marble counter, and soda fountain. If you're in the mood for pancakes and eggs at breakfast, the Tea Room is your place. Lunch offers fish, sandwiches, and burgers. Evening diners will be excited to find more creative fare on the menu, such as pistachio grilled salmon with lemongrass sauce, grilled pork tenderloin, or poached scallops.

Side Trip: Newport

Arguably the most upscale destination in all of New England, this seasonal beach resort is all about mansions and yachts. The mansion tours are big doings in Newport, and while adults love to the chance to peek at opulence at its best, kids couldn't care less. Further, most of the mansions don't allow strollers. There is one exception to the kids-hate-mansions rule: **The Beechwoods.** A local theater group conducts the tour while re-enacting life in the late 1800s, when the Beechwoods summered in the mansion (more information under Attractions, page 252).

Newport is also a very popular spot for college kids, who take "shares" in cottages (many are from Boston and its environs who have tired of summering on Cape Cod). As a result, Newport (especially Thames Street, the main artery) can be very congested during peak summer months so don't even think of driving about; this is a walking-friendly town. One of the most popular ambles is the **Cliff Walk,** a three-and-a-half-mile trail that runs along the Atlantic Ocean and past a couple of the mansions; there are benches along the path for resting. However, this trail is not totally kid-friendly because of steep sections, so consider it only if you can put the baby in a backpack or have older children and teens.

FAMILY LODGING

Newport is an extremely expensive destination, and many of the properties don't accept children under the age of 12, with a few exceptions. If you're bent on staying in the Newport area and are budget-conscious, consider staying three miles south of Newport, in Middletown, where you'll find the less-expensive options such as Courtyard Newport/Middletown; (800) 321-2211.

Castle Hill Inn & Resort

This gem dates to 1874 and has recently been chosen as one of the top 25 small hotels in North America by *Conde Nast Traveler* magazine. The hotel

---

For Sail

Visiting Newport without setting foot on a boat is like visiting Paris and never once setting foot in a cafe. You simply must. One of the best boating experiences for families is to sail off into the sunset, literally, with a two-hour sail on authentic America's Cup 12-meter yachts. The sails are offered from May through the end of October. Cost is $60 adults and $30 for children. Call (401) 846-9886.

---

has undergone an extensive $7 million renovation project over the past three years. You can't beat the location on a 40-acre peninsula along Ocean Drive. It has mansion rooms overlooking Narragansett Bay, secluded rooms in Harbor Houses, and sprawling guest rooms in the Beach House. Children under age 12 are not permitted in the main house but are welcome in the Harbor House and Beach House accommodations. If you don't stay here, you should consider visiting for lunch, dinner, or Sunday brunch. Double room rates begin at $145 per night, including breakfast. Closed January and open only on weekends in the off-season. 590 Ocean Avenue, Newport; (888) 466-1355.

Cliffside Inn

If you have teenagers, this is a special place to stay in Newport, thanks to the fireplaces in the rooms and Jacuzzis. Children under age 13 are not allowed. There are only a dozen or so rooms, some of which are suites. You may want to reserve the suite with the Jacuzzi and state-of-the-art showerheads (the hotel will know which one you're talking about). The history of this inn is told through the paintings that adorn the walls—many of them are self portraits of Beatrice Turner, a woman who rebelled against her over-protective parents by shutting out the world and painting (she could have done worse things, no?). If you stay here, plan your days exploring Newport, but be back for afternoon tea at the inn—you won't want to miss it. Double room rates begin at $250 per night, including breakfast. Located at 2 Seaview Avenue, Newport; (800) 845-1811.

ATTRACTIONS

The Astors' Beechwood Mansion

580 Bellevue Avenue, Newport; (401) 846-3772

Hours: Summer, daily 10 a.m.–4 p.m.; off-season, weekends only
   10 a.m.–4 p.m.

> ## See Newport on Foot
>
> One of the kid-friendliest tours in Newport is one that spills tales about haunted houses and graveyards with visits to a haunted burial ground. This tour is best suited for kids in fourth grade and older, although kids in strollers and backpacks are also welcome (they usually conk out!), says the proprietor. The tours range from 75 to 90 minutes. Cost is $7 for adults and free for kids age 12 and under. Other tours focus on Colonial Newport. Tours are given April through October and leave from the Gateway Visitor Information Center, 23 America's Cup Avenue. Call Newport on Foot at (401) 846-5391 for tour times.

Admission: $10 adults, $8 children ages 6–13, free for kids age 5 and under; family plan: $30 for two adults and two or more children

Appeal by Age Groups:

Pre-school	Grade School	Teens	Young Adults	Over 30	Seniors
★★	★★	★★★	★★★	★★★	★★★

Touring Time: Average 45 minutes for the guided tour; minimum 45 minutes

Rainy-Day Touring: Yes

Services and Facilities:

Restaurants No	Lockers No
Alcoholic beverages No	Pet kennels No
Disabled access First floor only	Rain check No
Wheelchair rental No	Private tours Yes
Baby stroller rental No	

Description and Comments   This is the most kid-friendly mansion tour in Newport, thanks to actors from around the country hired to narrate the tour. It's not suitable for youngest of kids (strollers are allowed in but there are many stairs). Special events are scheduled, including a Children's Day in June; call for details.

International Tennis Hall of Fame

194 Bellevue Avenue, Newport; (401) 849-3990

Hours: Daily 9:30 a.m.–5 p.m.

Admisssion: $8 adults, $6 seniors and military, and $4 children age 16 and under; family rate: $20 for two adults and all kids age 16 and under

Appeal by Age Groups:

Pre-school	Grade School	Teens	Young Adults	Over 30	Seniors
★	★★★	★★★	★★★	★★★	★★★

Touring Time: Average 1½ hour; minimum 45 minutes

Rainy-Day Touring: Yes

Services and Facilities:

Restaurants Yes	Lockers Yes
Alcoholic beverages Yes	Pet kennels No
Disabled access Yes	Rain check No
Wheelchair rental No	Private tours Yes
Baby stroller rental No	

Description and Comments   This formidable attraction is love/love for budding tennis players and fans of the game. Lots of memorabilia and interactive exhibits entertain kids and tennis buffs. But this is much more than a museum: renowned tournaments are played here, and there are also tennis courts that are open to the public. To reserve a court time or for more information about visiting the attraction, call the number above. The on-site restaurant, La Forge Casino, can be reached at (401) 847-0418.

FAMILY-FRIENDLY RESTAURANTS

BRICK ALLEY PUB

140 Thames Street; (401) 849-6334

Meals served: Lunch and dinner
Entree range: $12 and up
Cuisine: You name it: burgers, pizza, salads
Children's Menu: Yes, for kids under age nine
Reservations: Yes
Payment: All types accepted

Everything and anything goes here. You'll find loads of families and locals sampling the fare and hanging in the game room where there are video games and a pool table. The decor is as eclectic as the cuisine. The kids menu has old standbys like grilled cheese and PB&J. It's a good place for families to gather for lunch or dinner.

SCALES AND SHELLS

527 Lower Thames Street, Newport; (401) 846-3474

Meals served: Lunch and dinner
Cuisine: Seafood
Entree range: $10 and up
Children's Menu: No
Reservations: Yes, recommended
Payment: No credit cards

If you don't love fish, don't eat at this very casual restaurant. Expect huge portions of some of the freshest fish and seafood around. While there's no kid's menu, the restaurant is happy to appease kids with pasta and butter, pizza, or half-orders of anything on the menu.

Side Trip: Block Island

Block Island is just 12 miles off Rhode Island's coast, but it seems a world away. With the 250-foot Mohegan Bluffs, miles of beaches, and a harbor for every day of the week, Block Island (all 11 square miles of it) beckons families. Hiking, biking, boating, and kayaking—this dot in the Atlantic is an outdoor lovers' paradise. New Englanders flock to Block Island each summer via ferry from Point Judith in Rhode Island. But it's equally popular with New Yorkers, thanks to a ferry that runs from Montauk Point to Block Island. In a word: beach. There are no attractions on this island other than sand, sea, and a lighthouse. If a beach doesn't do it for you, whatever you do, don't board the ferry.

There is only one bona fide town on the island, **Old Harbor,** where you'll find many homes, shops, hotels, and restaurants. Old Harbor is the place where the ferries dock. The best way to get around is by foot and bicycle. Cars are allowed on the island, and some of the ferries will accommodate your car, but the beauty of Block Island is that you don't need your car. Block Island is refreshingly devoid of any man-made attractions, unless you consider the two lighthouses. The **Southeast Lighthouse,** a couple miles south of Old Harbor, was designated a National Historic Landmark in 1997. A visit will cost you $5. A second lighthouse, the **North Lighthouse,** is in Old Harbor and now houses an interpretive center of Block Island's history; part of the fun of visiting it is to stroll the rocky beach to reach it.

> ### Parasailing
>
> Got a kid who loves to defy gravity? Block Island Parasail enables kids who think they're Superman to take off and land on a 28-foot boat (they can choose from three different heights). It's open May through Columbus Day. Cost is between $50 and $70. Make reservations at Town Dock in Old Harbor; (401) 466-2474 or (401) 864-2474.

FAMILY LODGING

Atlantic Inn

If the scaled-down version of the inn that's a playhouse for kids doesn't steal your heart, the views from the inn's sweeping porch will. With just 21 rooms, this almost-intimate inn also has croquet and tennis. Children age 12 and under stay free in their parents' room. Double room rates begin at $120 per night, breakfast included. It's closed November through April. High Street, Block Island; (800) 224-7422.

The 1661 Inn & Hotel Manisses

If you have children 12 and older, you are invited to stay at the very upscale and refined Hotel Manisses. If you don't, you won't suffer in the hotel's sister property, the lovely 1661 Inn, including a couple of cottages and a guest house, all of which take kids of all ages. All of the rates include a buffet breakfast each morning, a wine and nibble hour each afternoon, and island tours. Kids love visiting the animal farm with llamas, goats, swans, geese, and Scottish highland steer. Rates vary considerably depending upon the accommodation. One Spring Street, Block Island; (800) MANISSE.

The Surf Hotel

The playground is a dead give away—no doubt about it, this is a family-friendly spot. It's a little salty around the edges (translation: not elegant), but for families on a budget it's a decent choice. Not all of the guest rooms have private baths. It's got a beach, but it's also in the center of town so don't expect much in the way of privacy. Bonus: Hearty breakfasts. Rates begin at $150 per night. Dodge Street, Block Island; (401) 466-2241.

FAMILY-FRIENDLY RESTAURANTS

BALLARD'S

42 Water Street, Old Harbor; (401) 466-2231

Meals served: Lunch and dinner
Cuisine: Seafood
Entree range: $10 and up
Children's menu: Yes
Reservations: No
Payment: All types accepted

Plan to dine here on a sunny day because you'll want to sit out on the terrace that overlooks the beach. This place is easy to enjoy, thanks to a casual ambiance, an ambitious menu, and nice views. It's within walking distance of the ferry.

DEAD EYE DICKS

Payne's Dock, New Harbor; (401) 466-2654

Meals served: Lunch and dinner
Cuisine: Seafood
Entree range: $12.95 and up
Children's menu: No
Reservations: No
Payment: No credit cards

Fun-loving seafood restaurant with an edge.

MOHEGAN CAFÉ

Water Street, Old Harbor; (401) 466-5911

Meals served: Lunch and dinner
Cuisine: American, seafood
Children's menu: Yes
Entree range: $12.95 and up
Reservations: No
Payment: All types accepted

Right across the street from the ferry in Old Harbor, this very popular eatery satisfies hungry, just-off-the-boat families. The kids' menu has burgers, grilled chicken breast, and chicken fingers; the main menu has the same and a lot more, including fried clams, chowder, and daily specials. Kids can doodle with supplied crayons, and tables can be put together for large parties.

THE OAR

West Side Road; (401) 466-8820

Meals served: Breakfast, lunch, and dinner
Cuisine: Pancakes to buffalo wings to swordfish
Entree range: $8 and up
Children's menu: No
Reservations: No
Payment: Credit cards accepted

Block Island is all about water, and the water views from this casual spot steal hearts. Oars galore hang on the walls, but, again, the views of Great Salt Pond rival the restaurant's decor. The menu has a little bit of everything from lobster rolls to burgers to fun finger foods. At night the menu is a little more ambitious, with fish and steak dishes.

Part Six

Vermont

You won't find a coastline in this Green Mountain State, but what you can expect is a curvaceous landscape dotted with farmland and valleys. Strawberry festivals, old-fashioned swimming holes, quaint country stores, and Ben & Jerry's Holstein-studded ice-cream stores are the exclamation points in easy-going Vermont. Yet the state has a sophisticated side, too. **Burlington,** on the banks of Lake Champlain, is a university town with great restaurants and cafes and a buzz of activity.

While Vermont beckons with perfect summer temperatures (warm, low-humidity days coupled with cool evenings), its popularity peaks concurrently with the fall foliage. Leaf peeping is big in the Green Mountains, and you'll need to plan your visit way in advance, as inns and resorts book up early.

Winter is another poetic and popular time of year in Vermont, thanks to the skier-friendly **Green Mountains** and the fabulous ski resorts that cater to families. You'll need to book ahead to get an accommodation at the ski resorts during the Christmas and winter breaks (usually February). My son learned to ski at Okemo Mountain in **Ludlow,** where white-frosted mountains have buffered many young children's falls.

The award-winning Smugglers' Notch resort up north in **Jeffersonville** is Mecca to families who return year after year, no matter the season, to celebrate the wonders of the family vacation. Farther north, the **Northeast Kingdom** is a blueprint for cross-country skiing and snowshoeing and other winter-fun activities that are dependent on Ol' Man Winter's snow-making potential.

The Great Outdoors is adored in Vermont, thanks in part to the wealth of hiking, biking, and camping activities in the Green Mountains and Taconic Mountain range. In fact, Vermont beckons outdoors enthusiasts with 50 state parks, 35 of which welcome day visitors and some of which welcome camping. *Caveat:* Black-fly season is in May and June. These nasty,

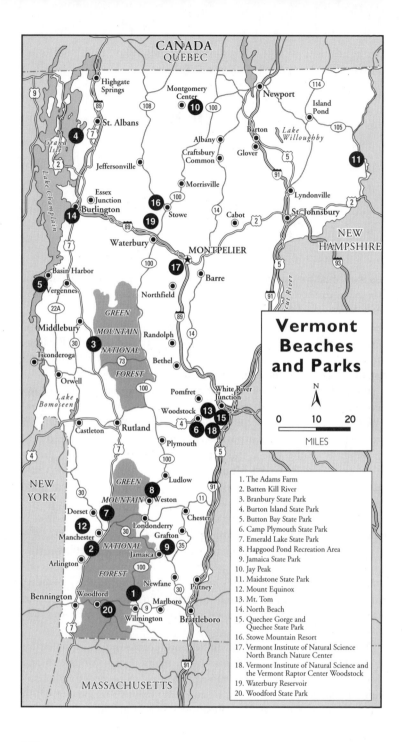

Vermont Beaches and Parks

N

0   10   20

MILES

1. The Adams Farm
2. Batten Kill River
3. Branbury State Park
4. Burton Island State Park
5. Button Bay State Park
6. Camp Plymouth State Park
7. Emerald Lake State Park
8. Hapgood Pond Recreation Area
9. Jamaica State Park
10. Jay Peak
11. Maidstone State Park
12. Mount Equinox
13. Mt. Tom
14. North Beach
15. Quechee Gorge and
    Quechee State Park
16. Stowe Mountain Resort
17. Vermont Institute of Natural Science
    North Branch Nature Center
18. Vermont Institute of Natural Science and
    the Vermont Raptor Center Woodstock
19. Waterbury Reservoir
20. Woodford State Park

blood-sucking flies can take a real bite out of your vacation. But Vermonters don't let anything get in the way of their enjoying the lay of the land.

We've divided Vermont into several regions, focusing on the areas that are most conducive to family vacations (although we also cover all of the major ski resorts in the state). Southern Vermont is especially popular with New Yorkers who yearn to reach the tranquility of Vermont without having to travel too far. There are lovely resorts in this region, as well as great skiing and fantastic outlet shopping. Next up: Woodstock, the quintessential New England village with a town green. There are plenty of skiing opportunities in town, as well as in the region, and some cool museums and cultural attractions. About 20 miles to the east is Killington, a super ski resort in winter; in summer, the mountain blooms with family fun activities, including mountain biking. Farther north, Lake Champlain beckons, as do the glorious Northern Green Mountains the mysterious Northeast Kingdom. While this region is all about wilderness and the Great Outdoors, there are a handful of family-oriented museums and the fabulous city of Burlington, smack on Lake Champlain, with funky stores, galleries, and restaurants.

GETTING THERE

By Car. Coming from the south (as most visitors do), you'll want to take I-91, from Hartford, Connecticut, north along the Vermont/New Hampshire border before veering inland through northern Vermont. Interstate 89 and Vermont Route 100 (the fabled skiers highway) also cut through the state, south to north. A pretty way to reach the Burlington region in the north is to take the scenic route through the Adirondack Mountains in New York State and then take the car ferry from Port Kent in New York across Lake Champlain to Burlington.

By Plane. Fly into Burlington International Airport or other gateways, including Albany, New York (less than an hour's drive from southern Vermont); Boston, Massachusetts (about an hour-long drive to southern Vermont); Hartford, Connecticut (a two-hour drive to southern Vermont)—it all depends on where in Vermont you want to travel. You can also fly into Montreal, Quebec, in Canada if you'll be traveling to northern areas (about an hour drive to Burlington).

By Train. There are two Amtrak routes through Vermont—The Amtrak Vermonter begins in Washington, D.C., making stops through Philadelphia, Hartford, and finally Vermont, stopping at about a dozen Vermont towns before ending at St. Albans, just north of Burlington. The Ethan Allen Express begins in New York City and disembarks in Rutland, Vermont, mak-

Fun Vermont Facts
Vermont has more than 100 covered bridges, most of which were constructed before 1912, and all of which are protected by law. Vermont leads the country in maple-syrup production.

ing stops primarily in New York towns along the route. Both trains offer specially fitted bike racks. Call (800) USA RAIL; www.amtrak.com.

HOW TO GET INFORMATION BEFORE YOU GO

Alpine and Nordic Resorts, Ski Vermont, (800) VERMONT, Ext. 068; www.skivermont.com *and* www.ridevermont.com.

Lake Champlain Regional Chamber of Commerce, 60 Main Street, Suite 100, Burlington, VT 05401; (802) 863-3489, www.vermont.org.

Ludlow Area Chamber of Commerce, P.O. Box 333, Ludlow, VT 05149; (802) 228-5830; www.vacationinvermont.com.

Manchester and the Mountains Regional Chamber of Commerce, 5046 Main Street, Suite 1, Manchester Center, VT 05255; (802) 362-2100; www.manchestervermont.net.

Mount Snow/Haystack Region Chamber of Commerce, P.O. Box 3, Wilmington, VT 05363; (802) 464-8092.

Vermont Chamber of Commerce, P.O. Box 37, Montpelier, VT, 05601; (802) 223-3443; www.vtchamber.com.

Vermont Department of Tourism and Marketing, 134 State Street, Montpelier, VT 05602; (800) VERMONT; www.travel-vermont.com.

The Best Beaches and Parks

There are no bona fide beaches in Vermont, as the state does not border the ocean. Still, there are more than a handful of swimming and sunning spots and old-fashioned swimming holes at some of the lakes, including Lake Champlain—far too many to list here. Here are some best, along with great Vermont parks.

The Adams Farm. There are 700 dairy farms throughout the state. One of the best is this educational farm in Wilmington (in Southern Vermont). The new Livestock Barn theater lets visitors learn about farming in the Green Mountains, rain or shine, and it also features 100 of the farm's animals that

State Symbols

- State nickname: Green Mountain State
- State capital: Montpelier
- Statehood: March 4, 1791 (14th state)
- State motto: Freedom and Unity
- Highest point: Mount Mansfield, 4,393 feet above sea level

- Lowest point: Lake Champlain, 95 feet above sea level
- State flower: Red clover
- State tree: Sugar maple
- State bird: Hermit thrush
- State fish: Brook trout, walleye pike

you can feed. There's also a petting zoo, indoor pony rides, hayrides, and a farmers market. Kids can gather eggs from the chicken coop and milk a goat. Call (802) 464-3762.

Batten Kill River. Beginning in Dorset, this river runs all the way into New York State's Hudson River and is the setting for a summer swim. One of the most popular river pastimes is fishing. The Orvis Company in Manchester has a wealth of information about fishing this river and also gives classes. Canoeing is another favorite activity on the Batten Kill, (802) 362-3750.

Branbury State Park. In central Vermont, this park is bosomed at the base of Mt. Moosalamoo on Lake Dunmore. It's got sandy beaches, hiking trails, a nature museum and naturalist programs, a playground, and a gorgeous picnic area. Bonuses: food concessions and boat rentals.

Burton Island State Park. Way up near the Canadian border in northern Vermont is where you'll seek out this sprawling 253-acre park on Lake Champlain. The coolest part is that you can arrive only by ferry. Hiking and biking is easy on this island thanks to its flat terrain, and there's swimming at the shale beach (sorry no sandy beaches on this island). Call (800) 252-2363.

Button Bay State Park. The Button Island Natural Area at this park is where kids will want to check out fossilized corals, snails, and other prehistoric animals in the limestone. It's on a bluff in Ferrisburgh along Lake Champlain. Call (802) 475-2377.

Camp Plymouth State Park. Hey, gold diggers! Kids will love panning for gold at this gem of a park in the town of Plymouth on the east shore of Echo Lake. Call (802) 228-2025.

Cool Websites for Vermont-Bound Kids

Adams Farm: www.adamsfamilyfarm.com

Ascutney Resort: www.ascutney.com

Ben & Jerry's Ice Cream Factory Tours: www.benjerry.com

Billings Farm: www.billingsfarm.com

Blueberry Hill: www.blueberryhillinn.com

Bolton Valley Resort: www.boltonvalleyvt.com

Bromley Mountain Resort: www.bromley.com

Catamount Family Center, Inc.: www.catamountoutdoor.com

Fairbanks Museum: www.fairbanksmuseum.org

Hildene Ski Touring Center: www.hildene.org/scski.htm

Jay Peak Resort: www.jaypeakresort.com

Killington Resort: www.killington.com

Mad River Glen Ski Area: www.madriverglen.com

Middlebury College Snow Bowl:
www.middlebury.edu/~sports/snow_bowl.html

Montshire Museum: www.montshire.net

Mount Snow: www.mountsnow.com

Okemo Mountain: www.okemo.com

Rural Vermont: www.ruralvermont.com

Shelburne Museum: www.shelburnemuseum.org

Simon Pearce Glassworks: www.simonpearce.com

Skiing in Vermont: www.skivermont.com

Smugglers' Notch Area Chamber of Commerce:
www.smugnotch.com

Snowboarding: www.ridevermont.com

Snowshoeing: www.tubbssnowshoes.com

Stowe Mountain Resort: www.stowe.com

Stratton Mountain Resort: www.stratton.com

Sugarbush Resort: www.sugarbush.com

Suicide Six Ski Area/Woodstock Inn: www.woodstockinn.com

The Equinox Ski Touring Center: www.equinoxresort.com

The Spirit of Ethan Allen II (Lake Champlain cruise):
www.soea.com

Cool Websites for Vermont-Bound Kids (continued)

This is Vermont: www.thisisvermont.com

Tracks of Vermont: www.exploreVT.com

Trapp Family Lodge XC Ski Area: www.trappfamily.com

Vermont Association of Snow Travelers, Inc. (VAST): www.vtvast.org

Vermont Life: www.vtlife.com

Vermont Snowmobile Tours: www.vermontsnowmobiletours.com

Vermont State Parks: www.vtstateparks.com

Vermont Teddy Bear Company: www.vermontteddybear.com

Vermont: www.vermont.com

Vermont's Northeast Kingdom: www.vermonter.com/nek

Woodstock Ski Touring Center: www.woodstockinn.com

Emerald Lake State Park. Alongside Dorset Mountain is where you'll happily discover this 430-acre, user-friendly park with a darling small lake and sandy swimming beach (shade is also available thanks to some trees nearby). A snack bar, a playground, and boat rentals are available. It's in the Manchester region near the Equinox Hotel.

Hapgood Pond Recreation Area. This pretty pond, part of the sprawling Green Mountain National Forest in the lower part of the state, beckons families for swimming and fishing. It's on Route 11 in Weston, just north of Peru.

Jamaica State Park. Kayaking and canoeing is superior at this park on Route 30 on the banks of the West River in southern Vermont. Amble along the nature trail to Hamilton Falls. It's not far from Manchester and Bromley. Call (802) 874-4600 or (802) 479-4280.

Maidstone State Park. This park in St. Johnsbury in the Northeast Kingdom is home to Maidstone Lake, one of the clearest, most stunning lakes in the state. It's great for fishing: 25-pound lake trout, landlocked salmon, rainbow trout, and brook trout can be taken. Call (802) 676-3930 or (802) 479-4280.

Mount Equinox. This is the highest peak in the Taconic Range (3,835 feet), located in Manchester. On a clear day you can see forever—or at least New York State, New Hampshire, Massachusetts, and Quebec. Take the pretty, five-mile Skyline Drive and stop along the way at the viewing spots with

Vermont's Not-to-Be-Missed Attractions

Southern Vermont
- Leaf peeping
- Skiing at Okemo Mountain
- Shopping the outlets in Manchester
- Playing chess and sipping Shirley Temples at Marsh Tavern at the Equinox Resort

Woodstock Region
- Leaf peeping
- Hanging out at the Woodstock Village Green
- Cross-country skiing and outdoor fun at The Woodstock Inn and Resort, Woodstock
- Vermont Institute of Natural Science and Raptor Center, Woodstock
- Staying at Blueberry Hill Inn in Goshen (or at least cross-country skiing its groomed trails)
- Quechee Gorge, Quechee
- Killington Adventure Zone, Killington

Lake Champlain, the Northern Green Mountains, and the Northeast Kingdom
- Leaf peeping
- Cruising Lake Champlain on the Spirit of Ethan Allen II, Burlington
- Al's French Fries, Burlington
- Licking an ice cream cone at the Ben & Jerry's factory in Waterbury
- Shelburne Museum, Shelburne
- Biking Isle La Motte on the Champlain Islands
- Skiing and staying at Smuggler's Notch, Jeffersonville

picnic tables. There are also many well-marked trails, some more difficult than others. Call (802) 362-1115.

Mt. Tom. A gentle hill overlooking the pretty village of Woodstock, this is a great hiking spot for families. You can take the trail up to a clearing where you can sit and admire the village of Woodstock, or keep going to the summit for a more panoramic peek at Woodstock and the Green Mountains.

North Beach. Close to downtown Burlington, this is the largest and most populated of Lake Champlain beaches in the area. This is a beach with a view—of the rolling Adirondack Mountains. Lifeguards, picnic tables, rest rooms, and a snack bar are available.

Quechee Gorge and Quechee State Park. One of Vermont's more popular natural attractions near Woodstock is this mile-long, 200-foot wide, 165-foot deep gorge. You can hike to a great vantage spot for viewing the Ottauquechee River or admire the cascading falls from either side of the bridge. Route 4, Quechee; (802) 295-7600.

Stowe Mountain Resort. Eureka! This terrain park is a kid's paradise—with mud holes, boulders, and other extreme challenges located at the base of the Mt. Mansfield Gondola. Call (800) 253-4SKI.

Vermont Institute of Natural Science (VINS) North Branch Nature Center. In Montpelier, the meadows and trails are perfect for children and adults who want to while away the afternoon admiring wildflowers and warblers. Call (802) 457-2779.

Vermont Institute of Natural Science (VINS) Woodstock. Here you'll find 78 acres of self-guided nature tours and exhibits of snakes, bees, and woods turtles. Flight demonstrations of raptors and birds of prey entertain kids of all ages. Call (802) 457-2779.

Waterbury Reservoir. Rent a paddleboat, kayak, or canoe. Pick your own private beach for a picnic, explore for ancient clay babies, and check out the 1937 dam built by the Civilian Conservation Corps. Located at the State Park at Waterbury Center. Call (802) 253-2317.

Woodford State Park. In Southern Vermont, less than ten miles from Bennington, this park has the highest elevation of any state park in Vermont: 2,400 feet. There's also a swimming hole, Adams Reservoir. Call (802) 447-7169.

Family Outdoor Adventures

Vermont is perfect for outdoor adventures in fall, winter, and summer (you can skip the spring, a.k.a. mud season). Most of the attractions in the state are of the natural, outdoor variety.

Boating. For boating opportunities, see Jamaica State Park and Waterbury Reservoir in The Best Beaches and Parks section on page 262.

Camping. Most Vermont State Parks open mid-May, and there are many camping opportunities in the parks. But you must reserve early. How early? Believe it or not, January 2 is when camping reservations for the summer season are taken. Some of the best family-oriented campgrounds are at Groton State Forest (Stillwater, New Discovery, Big Deer, and Ricker). The campgrounds have swimming, easy hikes, a recreation trail that traverses an old railroad bed, interpretive programs, and kid-friendly entertainment. For a list of state parks and more information, call the Vermont Department of Forests, Parks and Recreation at (802) 241-3655.

Christmas-Tree Chopping. Many families head to Vermont in December with one goal: to cut down their family Christmas tree. The Vermont balsam fir is the most popular of the trees in New England. Vermont Fresh & Natural Christmas Tree Month usually begins in mid-November and runs through mid-December. Special packages are available that include such things as lodging, breakfast, and a tree. For more info call (802) 223-3443.

Climbing. When the kids start climbing the walls, jump in the car and head for a spot where they have permission to do so. Several of the ski resorts offer climbing walls, including: Killington (call (800) 621-MTNS), Mount Snow (call (800) 245-SNOW) and Stratton (call (800) STRATTON).

Cross-Country Skiing. Vermont was the first state in the nation to develop a network of trails on public and private lands, and today cross-country skiers (and snowshoers) can traverse Vermont's on over 280 miles of trails. Thanks to the Catamount Trail Association, you'll come across small Nordic centers with pot-bellied stoves, hot chocolate, friendly staff, and groomed and tracked trails. In fact, the Catamount Trail that cuts through Vermont is pristine for cross-country skiing. For more info on cross-country skiing, call (802) 223-2439. For info on snowshoeing, call (800) 882-2748.

The Woodstock Ski Touring Center has a necklace of trails that snake through Marsh-Billings-Rockefeller National Historic Park. The park was opened in 1998, when the ever-generous Laurance Rockefeller donated his land and home in Woodstock to the National Park Service. In the winter, cross-country ski buffs especially enjoy this park. In the summer, the park becomes a playground for hikers; (800) 448-7900.

Downhill Skiing. Skiing is such a big deal in Vermont that we had to give the sport special attention. See pages 270–76 for details of the ski resorts.

Fishing. For fishing opportunities, the Batten Kill River reigns supreme. The Orvis Fly Fishing School in Manchester is a great outlet for fishing the Batten Kill. Tuition ranges from $370 to $430 and includes lunch, instruction, a fishing license, equipment, and access to the river before and after classes. The school also has a special package at the Inn at Willow Pond in Manchester. Call (800) 235-9763.

Hiking. With the Northern Vermont Llama Company, you can hike in style—on a llama—up into the Green Mountains; (802) 644-2257. For other hiking opportunities, see Branbury State Park, Burton Island State Park, Mount Equinox, Mt. Tom, Quechee State Park, and others in The Best Beaches and Parks section on pages 262–67.

Leaf Peeping. Fall foliage doesn't get any better than in Vermont. Why? Because more than 30 percent of the forest is home to sugar maple trees, whose leaves turn brilliant orange and startling scarlet. Other trees paint the forest with yellows.

You can bet your life that there will be gorgeous fall foliage throughout the state each and every year. The real challenge is figuring out when it peaks, in other words, when is the best viewing time. During the first week of October is a good hedge, as that is when it most consistently peaks. But not always. The fall foliage show is not just a one-act play, though, and there are several acts until the curtain drops. So if you travel to Vermont anywhere from the last week in September through the end of October, even into the first couple of days of November, chances are you'll be in for a treat.

The best spots to spy the parade of colors? All of the major state highways will afford you good opportunities—especially I-89 between White River Junction and St. Albans—but these are not the most interesting ways to enjoy the show. You'll have to go off the beaten path.

For the most up-to-date foliage information beginning in mid-September through mid-October, call the Vermont Fall Foliage Hotline at (800) VERMONT or (802) 828-3239.

Mountain Biking. At Jay Peak resort, an aerial tram will whisk older kids and their bikes up the mountain—it's all downhill from there. Call (802) 988-2611. Killington Resort's mountain-bike trails are a lot of fun to cruise in the summer months. In fact, you can take your bikes up to the summit in a gondola. You can do this on your own or as part of a tour. This is not for young kids but is suitable for able-bodied teens. Younger kids can test out the dry ski-snowboard deck. Call (800) 621-MTNS. In summer, Mount Snow offers lift-accessed mountain biking and a mountain-biking school. In-line skating and skateboarding are also accommodated. Call (800) 245-SNOW.

Snowmobiling and Other Winter Sports. While Vermont is the skiing capital of New England thanks to the bounty of ski resorts, Vermont's state parks are no slouches in the winter-fun category. While the facilities at these parks usually hibernate for the winter, the trails and woods still beckon winter-loving souls. And you won't have to pay a fee, as is required when the parks are open in the spring, summer, and fall). Snowmobiling is huge in Vermont, and many of the state parks and state forests contain the biggest network of snowmobile routes, maintained by the Vermont Association of Snow Travelers (VAST). Further, cross-country skiers and snowshoe aficionados will find some of the best paths and trails along some of the state park roads. State park ponds and lakes are often accessible for ice fishing, ice boating, and skating. Caveat: Parking can be a test of your creative genius, as most of the parking lots are not plowed in the winter. For more information or maps on VAST trails call (802) 229-0005.

Skiing. Skiers rejoice! With more than 5,700 acres of terrain served by nearly 170 lifts, Vermont skiers have plenty of choices when it comes to schussing the slopes. Annual snowfall averages 250 inches, and yet 70 percent of Vermont's lift-served terrain is covered by snowmaking machines. Many of the ski resorts cater to snowboarders, with terrain parks, halfpipes, and the latest and greatest Superpipe. For information on any of Vermont's 16 resorts and ski areas, contact the Vermont Ski Areas Association at (802) 229-6917.

Ascutney Mountain Resort

About six miles off I-91, Ascutney is easy to get to. With 100 percent slopeside skiing, southern Vermont's "Mountain on the Rise" is an easy resort for families to navigate and enjoy. There's a new North Peak Express mile-long, high-speed quad, six new trails (for a combined 56), an increased vertical drop from 1,530 feet to 1,800 feet, and lots of kids activities and events. One of the most popular is for kids ages 4 to 10: Cheddar's Happy Hour from 5 to 8 p.m. every Saturday in the Monadnock Room. Cheddar, a mouse, and his partners entertain the kids with face-painting, pizza, and dancing, capped off with a movie. Midweek there is Midweek Music Munchie Madness. During holiday weeks there are special group swims, treasure hunts, family-themed dinners, and fireworks. The Snowdance Learning Center's philosophy is that learning to ski should be fun for every age level and ability. The Center also features The Flying Ducks Childcare Program and Mini and Young Olympians, as well as private and group lessons. There's also a magic carpet surface lift and a separate 10-acre Learning Park. Nordic skiing is available. Brownsville; (800) 243-0011.

Bromley Mountain

Bromley woos families with an expanded base lodge and Mighty Moose & Pig Dog Pup (mascots of the award-winning Learning Center). The resort is a snowball's throw from Vermont's liveliest shopping town, Manchester. New groomers and snowmaking guns have made more trails accessible in warmer temperatures. A new trail, Sunset Pass, on the west side of the mountain, is perfect for schussing down the slopes while admiring the sun as it takes its final bow each evening. Bromley is the only New England mountain with southern exposure, so bring your sunscreen—there's nothing like a day on a sun-kissed snowy slope. Note: There is no Nordic skiing at Bromley. Manchester; (800) 865-4786.

Jay Peak Resort

Jay Peak gets more natural snow than any other eastern ski resort, with an average 340 inches thanks to Orographic lift, a meteorological phenomenon that's responsible for much of the snowfall and is often called Jay's Cloud. Die-hard skiers who love to cut fresh tracks will be able to do so without having to travel west. For nature lovers, guided tours are offered at the summit of the mountain. Families staying at the Hotel Jay and Jay Peak condominium get free nursery and day care from 9 a.m. to 4 p.m. at Jay Peak's Child Care Center (located at the base area), with indoor activities for kids age 2 to 7. For families not staying at Jay Peak, all-day childcare is $30; half day is $15. There is also free lodging for kids age 14 and under staying in the same room as their parents at the Hotel Jay and Jay Peak Condominiums. The Kinderschool Ski program, a half-day morning or afternoon ski program is great for beginners (free skiing for kids age 6 and under staying in the same room with parents at the Hotel Jay and Jay Peak condominiums). There are programs for older kids, including Mountain Adventureland, a kids-only ski area in the woods with a snow hut and obstacle course for kids who know how to ski. Jay Peak naturalists give one-and-a-half-hour snowshoe tours by moonlight through Jay Peak's woods and cross-country trails (boots, Tubbs snowshoes, and headlamps are provided, if needed). Families can enjoy a visit to a working dairy farm, a ride in a grooming machine up the side of a mountain, night sledding and marshmallows around a bonfire, and ice skating under the lights. Teens, listen up: movie and bowling nights, snow volleyball, skating parties, a teen club dance nights, and bonfires are just for you. There is Nordic skiing at Jay Peak. Jay; (800) 451-4449.

Killington Ski Resort

Killington has one of the most extensive snowmaking systems in the country. This means that the ski season here is one of the longest in Vermont—typically from October to June. And this resort, with 200 trails that stretch over seven mountains, is known for other accolades as well. The Superpipe (think bigger-than-life halfpipe) has walls reaching 13 to 15 feet high. This resort always has some great gimmick for families, such as its recent Kids Ski and Snowboard Free Program, which allows children 12 and younger to ski or ride free the same number of days as their parents when parents purchase a lift ticket for five or more consecutive days. The Ground Zero Fun Park at the K-1 Base Lodge is packed with action for energized kids. Open Wednesday and Saturday nights, it has a luge track, a 450-foot lit halfpipe, and lighted areas for tubing, ice skating, and snowshoeing by moonlight. Killington is a terrific place for kids to learn to ski and snowboard, as it's one of three Vermont ski resorts to use the Perfect Turn program in its instruction. The Perfect Turn clinics are all taught by ski school pros, and the emphasis is on individual ability. Note: There is no Nordic skiing at Killington. Hate to ski but the kids love it? You can still experience the mountain. Killington has two high-speed, eight-passenger gondolas with heated cabins. You'll get to the top of the mountain in six minutes flat. Killington; (800) 621-6867.

Mad River Glen Ski Area

Mad River Glen is where you'll want to ski if you hate sharing the slopes with snowboarders. Snowboarding is banned at this resort, where skiing is a sport not an industry. Skiing is serious stuff here. Still, Mad River Glen loves families and just completed a new lift and area, the "Ski It if You Can" mountain, designed solely for first-time skiers and kids. There's also the Mad River's Cricket Club Daycare center. The resort also has an interchangeable lift ticket with Sugarbush Resort (four miles away); a shuttle bus connects the two. No Nordic skiing. Waitsfield; (800) 82-VISIT.

Middlebury College Snow Bowl

Here you'll find back-to-basics skiing and snowboarding at a good price. Some of the trails were cut in the 1940s and 1950s and still follow their original lines. There are usually no crowds. Middlebury; (802) 388-7951.

Mount Snow

Mount Snow is a 130-trail resort over five mountain faces and was the East's first snowboard park. Kids love it for its two halfpipes, four terrain parks, and family-fun activities. Parents love its value-friendly ski packages. Bonus: Mount Snow's tubing park is open day *and* night. Double Bonus: The Gut at Mount Snow is Vermont's longest lift-serviced halfpipe. Wheeeeeeee! When the kids are all skied out, Mt. Snow has a Snowseum at its base, a full-color, interactive museum that showcases the history of skiing and riding in the United States from the 1880s to the present. Admission is free. Note: There is limited Nordic skiing at Mt. Snow. West Dover; (800) 245-SNOW.

Okemo Mountain Resort

Okemo is a great place for kids to learn to ski. Snow Stars is the name of Okemo's ski and snowboard instruction for kids ages 4 to 7 of all ability levels. There are morning or full-day sessions. The Young Mountain Explorers program takes kids ages 7 to 12 and is offered as either a full-day program (except for beginners) or as a single lesson. The Young Riders program (as in snowboarders) is available as a full-day package on weekends and holidays for snowboarders who can use a chairlift and ride lower mountain terrain. The Get Altitude Adventure Clinics speaks to teens (ages 13 to 16, intermediate level and up), by encouraging them to meet friends and cut loose in a class of their own. Snow Tracks, a nature program integrated into the Cutting Edge Learning Center, gives kids of every age the opportunity to check out the indigenous wildlife, thanks to a special map that shows the locations of don't-miss sites in the Okemo Nature Zone. Okemo also has an instructional ski and snowboard program for disabled skiers, including a private lesson.

For nonskiing kids and kids who need a break (ages 6 weeks to 8 years), there's the on-premise Penguin Playground Day Care Center. The center offers a one-hour skiing instruction for ages 3 and 4 and also has arts and crafts, storytime, circle games, movies, and a kids night out with movies and pizza (extra cost). The day-care rate is $55 per child per day; half-day rate is $33. The Okemo Valley Nordic Center has cross-country trails that snake in and around the Okemo Valley Golf Course and miles of snowshoeing trails, too. No snow? No problem—Okemo has extensive snowmaking capability. Ludlow; (802) 78-OKEMO.

Smugglers' Notch

Smugglers' Notch is Vermont's—no, strike that—New England's premier family ski resort. It's the standard by which all other family ski resorts are compared and is consistently voted number one by *SKI* magazine and parenting magazines. The kids camp is the big reason, although the skiing on the resort's three big mountains isn't bad either. There are Mom & Me and Dad & Me ski programs where an intermediate skiing parent and a young ski bunny are coached on how to ski together. The instructors are trained Snow Sport University Guides who oversee Snow Sport University's Discovery Dynamo ski camps for 3- to 5-year-olds and Adventure Rangers ski camps for 6- to 12-year-olds. There's a slope-side village that is party central, with non-stop action for kids and families alike. Bonus: A swimming pool! Teens like navigating the bumps and chutes while night tubing on Sir Henry's Hill at Smugglers' Notch. Family activities include karaoke, torchlight parades, fireworks, snowshoe treks, outdoor ice skating, bonfires with hot cocoa, family game nights, and snowmobile tours.

Stowe and Smugglers' Notch resorts are in the same neck of the woods, so resort guests can take advantage of the Smugglers'-Stowe Connection, allowing them to ski or snowboard over the mountain pass to enjoy a day of skiing at a different resort. There is Nordic skiing at Smugglers' Notch. The Snowflake Bentley Weather Center meshes weather information with close-up photos of snow crystals. A nature trail gives kids an up-close experience with animals in their habitats. Jeffersonville; (800) 451-8752.

Stowe Mountain Resort

Stowe, on Vermont's highest peak, beckons beginner snowboarders with the Learn to Ride (LTR) program used to accelerate the learning curve so that students can link turns in the very first lesson and hit the slopes in record time. Way cool! Night skiing, two snowboard parks, and a half pipe are also a hit with the kids. Childcare is a hit with the parents. Of course, there's also a full-service ski school. Nordic skiing is available. Stowe; (800) 253-4SKI.

Stratton Mountain Resort

This resort is on Stratton Mountain, southern Vermont's highest peak. It offers great skiing on 90 trails, halfpipes, a Superpipe, and terrain parks, and also has a lot to offer when the stars shine at night. The Tubing Zone offers night tubing under the lights, and moonlight snowshoe treks, ice-skating, and sleigh rides make this one ambitious winter getaway. There's also a slope-side village complete with shops and restaurants. Nordic skiing is available here, as is the Stratton Mountain Resort's Tubbs Snowshoe Adventure Center with an expanded network of backcountry snowshoe trails. Stratton Mountain; (800) STRATTON.

Sugarbush Resort

Sugarbush has 115 trails that descend from six interconnected mountains with 2,650 feet of vertical drop. But don't let the size fool you—Sugarbush is also known as a great beginner family resort with sleigh rides and ice-skating. Family Adventure Land is a 75-acre designated mountain area for families only. And the Perfect Turn learn to ski program was expanded to include Perfect Kids for kids ages 3 to 16. There is no Nordic skiing at Sugarbush. Warren; (800) 53-SUGAR.

Suicide Six

Despite its ominous name, this ski resort, which is owned by Laurance S. Rockefeller, who also owns the Woodstock Inn, is one of the gentlest ski resorts in Vermont, thanks to a modest vertical drop. Suicide Six's claim to fame: This is the site of American's first chairlift. Just two miles from Woodstock, Suicide Six is a big hit with beginners and families because of

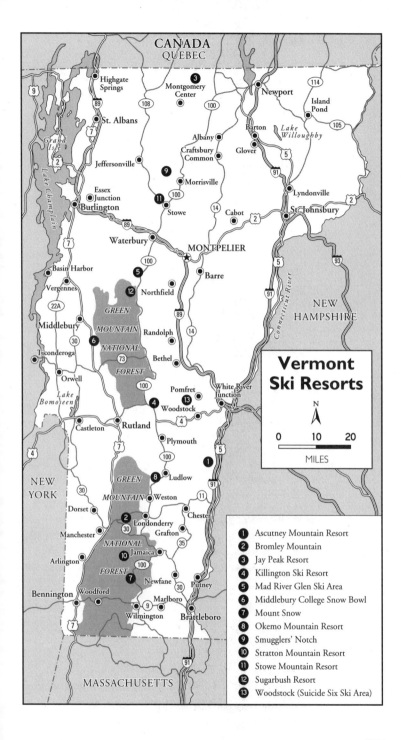

CANADA
QUEBEC

Highgate Springs
Montgomery Center
Newport
Island Pond
St. Albans
Albany
Barton
Lake Willoughby
Jeffersonville
Craftsbury Common
Glover
Morrisville
Lyndonville
Essex Junction
Burlington
Stowe
Cabot
St. Johnsbury
Waterbury
MONTPELIER
Basin Harbor
Barre
Vergennes
Northfield
NEW HAMPSHIRE
GREEN MOUNTAIN NATIONAL FOREST
Middlebury
Randolph
Ticonderoga
Bethel
Orwell
Pomfret
White River Junction
Lake Bomoseen
Woodstock
Castleton
Rutland
Plymouth
Ludlow
NEW YORK
GREEN MOUNTAIN
Weston
Dorset
Chester
Manchester
Londonderry
Grafton
NATIONAL
Jamaica
Arlington
FOREST
Newfane
Putney
Bennington
Woodford
Marlboro
Wilmington
Brattleboro

MASSACHUSETTS

Vermont Ski Resorts

N

0   10   20
MILES

1 Ascutney Mountain Resort
2 Bromley Mountain
3 Jay Peak Resort
4 Killington Ski Resort
5 Mad River Glen Ski Area
6 Middlebury College Snow Bowl
7 Mount Snow
8 Okemo Mountain Resort
9 Smugglers' Notch
10 Stratton Mountain Resort
11 Stowe Mountain Resort
12 Sugarbush Resort
13 Woodstock (Suicide Six Ski Area)

The Teen Scene

For teens who want to be on the scene, here are the state's most happening teen nightclubs at the many ski resorts.

Ascutney: Sidewinders

Okemo: Altitude After Dark

Killington Resort: Bumps

Smugglers' Notch Resort: Millennium Zone

Mt. Snow: Planet 9

---

its laid-back ambiance, easy trails, and compact size. Beginner skiers especially enjoy the mountain, and intermediate skiers can find some challenging trails among the 23 total. Expert skiers, you won't find Suicide Six ambitious enough; (800) 448-7900.

Calendar of Festivals and Events

June

The Kids Maritime Festival, Lake Champlain Maritime Museum, Ferrisburgh. An educational and fun way to spend a day. Power a ferry horse with your own legs, paddle a kayak or a canoe, enjoy maritime stories, or participate in a shipwreck simulation; (802) 475-2022.

Yellow Barn Music School and Festival, Putney. A series of 30 events, including chamber ensemble concerts, children's concerts, public master classes, composers' nights, and tours; (800) 639-3819.

Vermont Heritage Weekend, Heritage Festival, Cabot Creamery, Cabot. Entertainment, food tastings, tours, and cheese-making exhibits. In addition, the Vermont Historical Society in Montpelier and more than 35 community historical societies in central and northeastern Vermont open their museums, historical buildings, and exhibit rooms; (888) TRY-CABOT.

"A Day in the Country" Showcase of Agriculture, Morgan Horse Complex, Shelburne. Morgan Horse demonstrations, food samples, agricultural exhibits, animal petting, and butter making; (802) 985-8665.

July

Manchester Music Festival, Manchester. From July through August, there are chamber music and orchestral music concerts; (802) 362-1956.

Peacham's Ghost Walk, Peacham. Dramatizations of the past by adults and children in period dress, with pretty Peacham Cemetery as a backdrop.

Actors stand by the tombstone of the person they represent and share anecdotes; (802) 592-3432.

Annual Middlebury Festival On-the-Green, Middlebury. A long-time summer tradition, this festival features a week of entertainment under a tent on the village green; (802) 388-0216.

August

Vermont Festival of the Arts in the Mad River Valley, Waitsfield. This ten-day festival spotlights more than 50 events, including visual arts, dance, music, and the written and spoken word; (802) 496-7907.

September

Champlain Valley Fair, Essex Junction. This is one of Vermont's biggest hoopla festivities, with free entertainment, agricultural education, exhibits, and competitions. It's also Vermont's largest craft show and sale, and the kids will love the giant sand sculpture; (802) 878-5545.

Killington Stage Race, Killington. The largest bicycle stage race in the country, featuring Tour de France-style teams and pros who compete in this three-day race (rated the most difficult in the United States). The course provides 278 miles of spectator viewing as the riders snake through 40 towns in central Vermont. It happens on Labor Day weekend; (800) 621-MTNS.

Northeast Kingdom Fall Foliage Festival, Marshfield, Cabot, Walden, Plainfield, Peacham, Barnet, Groton, and St. Johnsbury. Learn the history and meet the residents of eight Northeast Kingdom towns during the peak of the foliage season. Each town has its own day and features events characteristic to itself; (802) 563-2472.

October

Vermont Farm & Food Fair at Hildene, Manchester. A family-oriented event with activities that include a tractor-pull, a horse and ox pull, turkey calling, a petting zoo, and a children's play tent; (802) 362-1788.

Haunted Forest, Huntington. A traditional Halloween celebration with an outdoor community theater set in a dark forest; (802) 434-3068.

December

Woodstock Wassail Celebration, Woodstock. A spirited annual holiday event during which visitors enjoy the classic English grog as well as parades and dances; (802) 457-3555.

First Night Burlington. Lots of family activities are planned to wind down the old year and kick off the New Year. The fun begins at 2 p.m., and the event culminates with fireworks at midnight; (802) 863-6005.

Southern Vermont

Just an hour and a half to two hours from Boston, this lush region of the Green Mountain State can be enjoyed alone or coupled with a trip to other New England destinations.

In southern Vermont, as well as in each region of the state, the ski resorts are the major players in terms of accommodations, no matter the season. Many of the resorts have more lodging options than you'd expect, including slope-side rooms and condominiums. Of course, there are also lovely country inns and bed-and-breakfast inns in the ski regions and elsewhere around the state, and we will cover those in these pages.

Vermont is one of New England's most laid-back spots, but that doesn't mean there's nothing happening. *Au contraire.* It's one of the busiest states in terms of tourism, thanks to the aforementioned ski resorts (there are more here than any other New England state) and stunning fall foliage. It's the attitude of the locals that gives Vermont its super-casual and easy-going MO. Even in its most upscale areas you won't wish you had packed your high heels and pashmina.

Take a quintessential New England town like **Manchester** and marry it with the upscale outlet shopping in **Manchester Center,** and you've defined a lively place that lures tourists with its bargains and nearby skiing. Once a rich playground of such prominent figures as Mary Lincoln Todd and Julia Boggs Dent (wife of Ulysses S. Grant), Manchester bears evidence of that past today, namely with Federal-period homes along its quiet side streets.

While **outlet shopping** is the bait for many visitors to Manchester, the **Orvis Fly Fishing School** in Manchester (call (802) 362-3750) is equally alluring. So are **Stratton Mountain** and **Bromley Mountain Ski Resort,** both less than a half-hour's drive from Manchester (see our Skiing section on page 270). Bromley is less of a scene and a great place for beginners, and it's got the only southern-facing slopes so the sun tends to warm hearts and toes. Stratton is one of Vermont's more splashy ski resorts; it's a much bigger resort

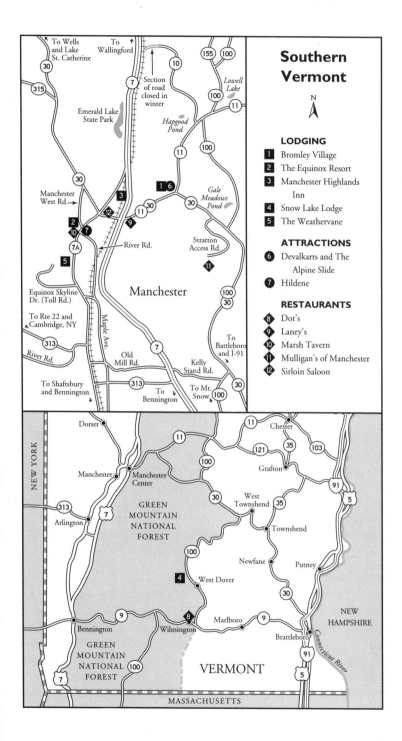

Southern Vermont

N

LODGING

1 Bromley Village
2 The Equinox Resort
3 Manchester Highlands Inn
4 Snow Lake Lodge
5 The Weathervane

ATTRACTIONS

6 Devalkarts and The Alpine Slide
7 Hildene

RESTAURANTS

8 Dot's
9 Laney's
10 Marsh Tavern
11 Mulligan's of Manchester
12 Sirloin Saloon

and more expensive. Snowboarders will especially love Stratton; in fact, snowboarding was invented on these slopes. To the southeast in West Dover, you'll find Mt. Snow, an equally popular Green Mountains ski resort.

At the heart of Manchester—in spirit and literally—is the famous **Equinox Resort.** Its casual **Marsh Tavern** is a great gathering place with warm fireplaces, chess sets, a lively bar, and music. My son took on several inn-mates his age in spirited chess matches. If you don't stay at the Equinox (although it is a great base for families and we recommend you do so), do at least enjoy one evening at Marsh Tavern.

Family Lodging

Bromley Village

Serious about skiing? Opt to book a slope-side condo (one to four bedrooms) at Bromley Village. They're fully equipped with kitchens, fireplaces, cable TV, and VCRs. There's also a fitness center on site. Rates begin at about $475 midweek with lodging, lifts, and lessons; weekend rates begin at about $555 for lodging only. The best part of all—mountain skiing is right outside your door. In summer, rates begin at $385 for a three-night stay in a one-bedroom condo. Bonus: An outdoor heated pool. Route 11, Peru; (800) 865-4786.

The Equinox Resort

The centerpiece of Manchester Village, this historic resort is a family winner, especially the townhouse rooms in the back of the property. Caveat: If reserving a townhouse room, make sure to reserve a room on the top floor—occupants on the first floor hear every thud from up above. Kids like this resort for its heated indoor pool, family-friendly pub, and kids room with Nintendo. The resort also runs the Orvis Inn next door, but it is not as suitable for families and is pricey. Double room rates begin at $179 per night; (800) 362-4747. Route 7A, Manchester Village; (800) 362-4747.

Manchester Highlands Inn

Have a hankering for a quintessential New England-inn experience but afraid you won't find one child-friendly enough? This 15-room, hilltop beauty, with classical music and the scent of baked goods permeating the air, loves kids. And kids love the inn—especially Humphrey the cat, who's likely to be curled up on the sofa. There's a game room, a pub, a sun-drenched wicker room, a pool, and the perfect lawn for croquet. The inn's porch is perfectly positioned for watching the sun set over Mt. Equinox. Breakfast is special: think lemon-souffle pancakes and Morning Glory muffins. Later in the afternoon, home-baked goodies lure guests back to the inn after a day of exploring. Room rates begin at $100 per night. Ask about the three-day, midweek, all-inclusive Stay and Play package for $333 per person. Highland Avenue, Manchester; (800) 743-4565.

Snow Lake Lodge

Stay near the base of Mt. Snow in this budget-friendly, 92-room lodge that affords guests great views of the mountain. The rooms are basic—two double beds and cable TV. A shuttle bus transports guests the short ride to the mountain. There's also a small video/game room. Double room rates begin at $87 per night. 199 Mountain Road, Mount Snow; (800) 664-6535.

The Weathervane

This is a classic resort motel tucked beneath Mount Equinox, with great views of the Green and Taconic mountains. Rooms have refrigerators and coffee makers. The heated outdoor pool and putting green entertain the kids. Continental breakfast is included in the rate. Double room rates begin at $100 per night; Route 7A, Manchester Village; (802) 362-2444.

Attractions

Devalkarts and The Alpine Slide

Bromley Mountain, Route 11; (802) 824-5522

Hours: Memorial Day–mid-June, weekends 9:30 a.m.–6 p.m.; mid-June–August, daily 9:30 a.m.–6 p.m.; September–October, daily 10 a.m.–5 p.m.

Admission: $6, free for ages 7 and under

Appeal by Age Groups:

Pre-school	Grade School	Teens	Young Adults	Over 30	Seniors
★★	★★★★	★★★★	★★★	★★	★

Touring Time: Average 3–4 hours; minimum 1 hour

Rainy-Day Touring: No

Services and Facilities:

Restaurants	No	Lockers	No
Alcoholic beverages	No	Pet kennels	No
Disabled access	No	Rain check	No
Wheelchair rental	No	Private tours	No
Baby stroller rental	No		

Description and Comments Take the chairlift up Bromley Mountain and ride down on the Alpine Slide. The slide features three ability tracks—slow, fast, or easy-does-it—so all ages can get in on the fun. Devalkarts are similar to go-carts, but they're gravity-driven and have brakes built into the steering mechanisms. They're especially cool for kids age 10 and up; helmets are a must.

Hildene

Route 7A, Manchester; (802) 362-1788

Hours: Mid-May–October, daily 9:30 a.m.– 4 p.m.; grounds close at 5:30 p.m.

Admission: $8 adults, $4 children, free for ages 6 and under

Appeal by Age Groups:

Pre-school	Grade School	Teens	Young Adults	Over 30	Seniors
★★	★★★	★★★	★★★	★★★	

Touring Time: Average 1½ hour; minimum 1 hour

Rainy-Day Touring: Yes

Services and Facilities:

Restaurants No	Lockers No
Alcoholic beverages No	Pet kennels No
Disabled access No	Rain check No
Wheelchair rental No	Private tours Yes
Baby stroller rental No	

Description and Comments. At the home of Robert Todd Lincoln, you'll get a personal peek at the lifestyles of the 1800s to 1890s, when Lincoln lived. This is not a high-five attraction for kids, unless they're history nuts or aspire to be President someday. There's a mold of President Lincoln's hand that kids love to size their hands up against. The saving grace for active types is that there are nature trails on the grounds. You might want to pack a picnic, for there is a pretty picnic area on the perfectly manicured grounds. In winter, when the home is officially closed, come anyway with your cross-country skis.

Family-Friendly Restaurants

DOT'S

W. Main St., Wilmington; (802) 464-7284

Meals served: Breakfast, lunch, and dinner
Entree range: $2.75 and up
Cuisine: Authentic diner grub

Children's menu: No
Reservations: No
Payment: All types accepted

Near Mt. Snow in the southeastern corner of the Green Mountains, Dot's has been packing 'em in for years. Blue-plate specials keep customers coming back for more, but it's the breakfasts that most visitors seek out; you can get the usual pancakes and eggs, or live it up and order a skillet breakfast. There is no kids' menu, but the offerings certainly are kid-friendly (and the prices are friendly the wallet). There's a second Dot's in Dover, but this one is the real enchilada with checkerboard linoleum and pine paneling.

LANEY'S

Junction of Routes 11 and 30; Manchester; (802) 362-4465

Meals served: Dinner
Cuisine: Brick-oven pizza, ribs, chicken
Entree range: $9 and up
Children's menu: Yes
Reservations: Yes
Payment: All types accepted

Laney's is one of the friendliest of family restaurants: it's loud, it's casual, it's lots of fun, and the portions are generous. You'll sit real close to other families and make friends, as we did with a family en route to Okemo Ski Resort in Ludlow; they told us they always stop at Laney's for dinner on the way to Okemo. We liked this place so much we ate here two nights in a row. Order the ribs, they're finger-licking good!

MARSH TAVERN

Route 7A, Manchester Village; (800) 362-4747

Meals served: Lunch and dinner
Entree range: $10 and up
Cuisine: Hearty New England fare
Children's menu: Yes
Reservations: Yes
Payment: All types accepted

Come in jeans and a turtleneck or dress up a bit; either way you'll be comfortable in this tavern at the 225-year-old Equinox Resort. One of four restaurants at the resort, this is the most family-friendly, and it's a must.

The ambiance is quintessential New England, with low ceilings, a fireplace, and cozy chairs in the lounge area. The food, hearty New England fare, is the best around.

MULLIGAN'S OF MANCHESTER

Route 7A, Manchester Village; (802) 362-3663

Meals served: Lunch and dinner
Entree range: $7.95 and up
Cuisine: American
Children's menu: Yes
Reservations: No
Payment: All types accepted

Located right outside of town (between the Equinox and the Orvis Fly Fishing School), you'll find Mulligan's turn-of-the-century atmosphere welcoming. The kids' menu includes standard stuff (grilled cheese, hot dogs, macaroni and cheese); the "adult" menu runs the gamut from fish to pasta to steak. Shop 'til you plop at the Manchester outlet stores and then relax over a meal here.

SIRLOIN SALOON

Routes 11 and 30, Manchester Center; (802) 362-2600

Meals served: Lunch and dinner
Entree range: $10 and up
Cuisine: Steak, seafood
Children's menu: Yes
Reservations: No
Payment: All types accepted

This Vermont steakhouse has been around almost 40 years, and it still packs in hungry customers. Expect a Western-theme ambiance and very kid-friendly noise level. In addition to steak, you'll find prime rib, a great salad bar, and seafood, including Maine lobster.

Woodstock Region

You want a rich, storybook New England experience? Your search will take you directly to Woodstock. A picture-perfect village green, darling town with galleries and boutiques, and many homes that are on the National Register of Historic Places create a vacation experience unlike any other you'll experience in Vermont. Woodstock is an especially upscale village, thanks to the Rockefellers who have embellished it with big bucks. The snow white **Woodstock Inn** is home base for many visitors exploring the region, and in winter months it is a base for skiers at **Killington** (20 miles east; see our Skiing section on pages 270–275). The Woodstock region is one of Vermont's most popular spots, so you can expect crowds and tour buses at certain times of the year, namely during peak foliage season in the fall.

Quechee is five miles east of Woodstock and is a popular spot for families to visit, thanks to the **Quechee Gorge,** Vermont's "Little Grand Canyon." Woodstock is also near Norwich, a sleepy, off-the-beaten-path town along the Connecticut River with a popular family attraction, the **Montshire Museum of Science.** This area of Vermont is very close to the New Hampshire border, and many visitors cross the border to Hanover, New Hampshire, home of Dartmouth College.

Family Lodging

The 1830 Shire Town Inn

If you crave a quaint New England inn experience, consider this 1830 home on the National Register of Historic Places. Rooms have antiques and private baths. The property offers an outdoor skating rink, access to cross-country ski trails, and a one-block stroll the village. A hearty New England country breakfast is served each morning, included in the rate. Double-room rates begin at $70 per night. 31 South Street, Route 106, Woodstock; (802) 457-1830.

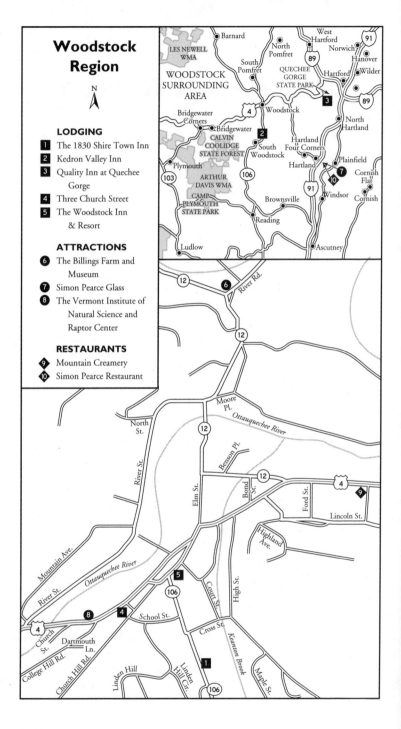

Woodstock Region

N

LODGING

1. The 1830 Shire Town Inn
2. Kedron Valley Inn
3. Quality Inn at Quechee Gorge
4. Three Church Street
5. The Woodstock Inn & Resort

ATTRACTIONS

6. The Billings Farm and Museum
7. Simon Pearce Glass
8. The Vermont Institute of Natural Science and Raptor Center

RESTAURANTS

9. Mountain Creamery
10. Simon Pearce Restaurant

Kedron Valley Inn

About five miles from Woodstock, the Kedron Inn has three buildings—the inn (some rooms have fireplaces), the brick building (rooms are reminiscent of the inn and some have fireplaces), and the log cabin (all rooms have fireplaces, but the rooms are similar to hotel rooms rather than quaint inn rooms). Kids of all ages are welcome (as are pets, but do let them know ahead of time). Bonus for kids: a swimming pond out back. Double-room rates begin at $227 per night, including breakfast and discounted admission to a nearby fitness center with an indoor pool. Note: There is an additional charge of $7.50 each morning per child for breakfast. Route 106, South Woodstock; (800) 836-1193.

Quality Inn at Quechee Gorge

This hotel is about one mile from the bridge at Quechee Gorge. There are fabulous family packages available November through May at this affordable hotel with a full-service restaurant and cross-country ski trails on the premises. Rooms include cable TV and in-room coffee makers, and there is guest laundry on the premises. You can take advantage of the Quechee Club indoor pool and fitness center for a small extra charge per person. Double-room rates begin at $65 per room (no charge for extra person). Call for package information. US Route 4, Quechee; (800) 732-4376.

Three Church Street

This 11-room inn, at one end of the Woodstock Green, sits on over two acres of gardens and lawns—perfect for kids to run around on. The inn is within walking distance of Woodstock village. It's antique-filled and has a music room as well as a library with a fireplace. A tennis court and swimming pool will entertain the kids, and pets are welcome. Double-room rates begin at $75 per night. 3 Church Street, Woodstock; (802) 457-1925.

The Woodstock Inn & Resort

You can't miss this inn. It's directly across from the village green, and it's got a formidable, stately presence. Unlike other classic Vermont inns, this inn dates back only to the 1960s. It's a full-service resort with a Robert Trent Jones-designed golf course (at the Woodstock Country Club, also owned by the inn), an indoor and outdoor swimming pool, a fitness center (tennis, squash, racquetball, and steam rooms), nature trails, and 36 miles of groomed cross-country ski trails. Kids love the game rooms (when the weather is frightful) and putting greens (when the sun shines). Double-room rates beign at $175 per night. 14 The Green, Woodstock; (800) 448-7900.

The inn is owned by the same Rockefeller who owns the nearby, family-friendly Suicide Six ski area. Woodstock is also 20 minutes north from Ascutney Mountain Resort, a popular family ski resort, in Brownsville. The Woodstock Inn & Resort also encompasses the Woodstock Ski Touring Center with a necklace of trails that snake through the new Marsh-Billings-Rockefeller National Historic Park. The park was opened in 1998, when the ever-generous Rockefeller donated his land and home in Woodstock to the National Park Service. In the winter, cross-country ski buffs will especially enjoy this park. In the summer, the park becomes a playground for hikers; (800) 448-7900.

Attractions

The Billings Farm and Museum

Woodstock, less than half-mile north of town; (802) 457-2355

Hours: May–October, daily 10 a.m.–5 p.m.

Admission: $8 adults, $7 seniors, $6 children ages 13–17, $4 children ages 5–12, $1 children ages 3–4

Appeal by Age Groups:

Pre-school	Grade School	Teens	Young Adults	Over 30	Seniors
★★	★★★	★★	★★	★★	★★

Touring Time: Average 3 hours; minimum 1½ hour

Rainy-Day Touring: Not recommended

Services and Facilities:

Restaurants No	Lockers No
Alcoholic beverages No	Pet kennels No
Disabled access No	Rain check No
Wheelchair rental No	Private tours No
Baby stroller rental No	

Description and Comments Kids love this place. Kids can milk prize Jersey cattle, plus churn butter and perform other chores of farm life in the late 1800s. There are lots of demonstrations, including rug hooking and wool spinning. The petting zoo is a big hit.

Simon Pearce Glass

The Mill, Main Street, Quechee; (802) 295-2711

Hours: Daily 9 a.m.–9 p.m.

Admission: Free

Appeal by Age Groups:

Pre-school	Grade School	Teens	Young Adults	Over 30	Seniors
★	★★	★★★	★★★	★★★	★★★

Touring Time: Average 1 hour; minimum ½ hour

Rainy-Day Touring: Yes

Services and Facilities:

Restaurants Yes	Lockers No
Alcoholic beverages Yes	Pet kennels No
Disabled access Yes	Rain check No
Wheelchair rental No	Private tours Yes
Baby stroller rental No	

Description and Comments What excites kids here are the glass-blowing demonstrations. You can watch artisans at work and purchase some of the wonderful glass items.

The Vermont Institute of Natural Science and Raptor Center

RR 2, Box 532, Woodstock; (802) 457-2779

Hours: Memorial Day–October, daily 9 a.m.–5 p.m.; November–April, Monday–Saturday 10 a.m.–4 p.m.

Admission: $6 adults, $3 students ages 12–18, $2 kids ages 5–11, free for kids under age 5

Appeal by Age Groups:

Pre-school	Grade School	Teens	Young Adults	Over 30	Seniors
★★	★★★	★★★	★★★	★★★	★★★★★

Touring Time: Average 45 minutes; minimum ½ hour

Rainy-Day Touring: Yes

Services and Facilities:

Restaurants No	Lockers No
Alcoholic beverages No	Pet kennels No
Disabled access Yes	Rain check No
Wheelchair rental No	Private tours Yes
Baby stroller rental No	

Description and Comments Animal and nature lovers will enjoy this educational avian rehabilitation center for about two dozen birds, including bald eagles and snowy owls. Before arriving here, the birds were wounded seriously enough that they can never be returned to the wild. The birds are housed in very large outdoor cages that are displayed along a horseshoe path.

The Quechee Gorge

About five miles east of Woodstock, Quechee Gorge is a natural wonder that tempts many visitors with its spectacular scenery, especially during fall foliage season. The best viewing of the gorge is from the bridge on Route 4, from which you will see the cascading waters of the Ottauquechee River tumble 165 feet below. For another vantage point, take the stairs near the parking lot (there's a gift shop here) to a path that runs along the river—you'll spy an old mill along the way. This flat path is fine for young kids to hike. Also make time to visit Quechee Gorge Village, where you'll find an antiques mall and an arts and crafts center, as well as miniature steam train rides and antique carousel rides. For more information call (800) 438-5565.

Family-Friendly Restaurants

MOUNTAIN CREAMERY

33 Central Street, Route 4, Woodstock; (802) 457-1715

Meals served: Lunch and dinner
Entree range: $5 and up
Cuisine: Salads, sandwiches, pies, and homemade ice cream
Children's menu: Yes
Reservations: No
Payment: All types accepted

Tell the kids if they behave they'll be rewarded with homemade ice cream. And if they're *really* good, they can choose the make-your-own-sundae entry off the menu. The ambiance here is very family-friendly with booths and kid-palatable food such as deli sandwiches. You can also get take-out, which you might consider for a picnic. Then again, that make-your-own-sundae probably won't travel well . . .

SIMON PEARCE RESTAURANT

The Mill, Quechee; (802) 295-1470

Meals served: Lunch and dinner

Entree range: $18 and up (dinner), $6.95 and up (lunch)
Cuisine: Continental
Children's menu: No
Reservations: Yes
Payment: All types accepted

The ambiance can't be beat at this restaurant that's housed in a 19th-century woolen mill with very Vermont-like wide pine floors and wooden tables and chairs. Meals are served on (what else?) Simon Pearce glassware and pottery (see Attractions, page 288), and you can even buy your dinnerware if you care to. The menu is eclectic, featuring everything from duck to salmon to steak prepared with a creative bent that is only fitting in this artsy spot. Lunch is more family-friendly since there's no children's menu.

Side Trip: Killington

Welcome to New England's most ambitious ski resort. It's got Vermont's second-highest mountain, which you can ski in the winter and hike in the summer. Lodging can be pricey during peak times—namely ski season—when it has its most captive audience. Budget-friendly Rutland is just a couple of miles away, and many families choose it as a base and travel to Killington to ski during the day.

Killington's owner, the American Skiing Company, bought the resort and others to form one huge conglomerate in New England. It also purchased the runt of the ski resorts in Vermont, Killington's neighboring slope, Pico, and combined the two resorts. Because of the enormity of this ski resort, we don't suggest you let your kids loose with a plan to meet at the base of a trail or at the lodge. It's too easy to get lost. Tip: Walkie-talkies or two-way radios are especially helpful for families who want to separate. There are many lodging options in the region, but many skiers rent condominium units. For more info renting a condo or alternate accommodations, including motels and inns, call the Killington Lodging and Travel Bureau, (800) 621-6867.

Another viable option is to stay in **Rutland,** about 11 miles away and very accessible to Killington. Vermont's second-largest city, Rutland has a vital downtown with restaurants, movie houses, and shopping. Just north of Rutland, along Route 7, is **Pittsford,** home to four of Vermont's signature items (no, not maple syrup): covered bridges. You'll come across the **1840 Depot Bridge** (just off Route 7 on Kendall Hill Road), the **1843 Hammond Bridge** (off Route 7 on Florence Road), the **1849 Cooley Bridge** (off Proctor Road), and the **1841 Gorham Bridge** (also off Proctor Road).

FAMILY LODGING

Killington Ski Resort has a dizzying number of lodging options, including the new **Killington Grand Resort Hotel and Conference Center** with 200 rooms, studios, and one-, two-, and three-bedroom suites. This is a full-service, slope-side property with an outdoor heated swimming pool, health club, day-care center, and restaurant and cafe. Caveat: Expect to pay top dollar for these amenities. More family-friendly, easy-on-the-wallet options at Killington include **Whiffletree,** one-to-four bedroom condominiums across the street from a ski-home trail (you can board a shuttle for a fast ride to the slopes). Whiffletree's condos have fireplaces and central washer/dryer locations. Another affordable family resort is the **Pico Resort Hotel and Condominiums,** perfect for families looking for ski-in, ski-out accommodations. It's located in Pico Village, at the base of Pico Mountain at Killington, and units range in size from studios to three-bedroom condos with lofts. Most units have fireplaces or woodstoves. It's also a good spot if you want to take advantage of an in-village location, and you'll have access to the Pico Health Club too.

Killington offers many packages that vary depending on the resort you choose and the season. For more information, call (877) 4-KTIMES (toll-free), or you can book online by visiting www.killington.com. Up and down Killington Road, there are more condominium complexes than you can count, though these not operated by the resort.

If you don't have to be near all the action in Killington but certainly want to be accessible to skiing Killington (and if you want to experience Vermont without all the commercialism of Killington), we recommend you stay at Blueberry Hill (see below) or the Woodstock area (about a 20-minute drive). If you opt to stay in Rutland, a free shuttle bus connects Rutland to Killington Road throughout the day. However, we recommend you have a car for more flexibility in exploring the area.

Blueberry Hill

My son and I fell head over skis in love with this kid-friendly and remotely located inn, whose nearest "big" city is Middlebury. It's a great base if you plan to alpine ski Middlebury College Bowl or even Killlington, Sugarbush, and Mad River Glen. If you're interested in the best cross-country skiing in Vermont, look no farther.

The inn is a back-to-basics retreat with some of the best cross-country skiing in Vermont right outside the door. In fact, there's a cross-country ski center adjacent to the inn, where you can rent skis and benefit from the expertise of the ski experts on staff. A skating pond is out back, with a sauna cottage tucked behind the pond. Hot-from-the-oven chocolate chip cookies continually fill up a cookie jar (and that's no easy feat as these cookies are adored). Tony Clark, innkeeper extraordinaire, will make you feel as if you were staying with relatives. Families eat at long tables in the dining room, and gorgeous cheese platters are enjoyed in front of the fire in the living room beforehand. Note: The inn does not have a liquor license but you're welcome to bring your own wines and spirits.

There are a number of accommodations here—the best for families are the rooms with lofts and entrances off a greenhouse. There are no televisions or phones in the rooms, but there is one in the main inn. Blueberry Hill is so idyllic you'll be tempted to let the battery run out on your cell phone for the duration of your stay. Board games will help you while the time away when you're not outdoors exploring. Don't even think of staying anywhere else when visiting this region—Middlebury is just five miles away, the historic village of Brandon is seven miles away, and the inn is surrounded by 22,000 acres of Moosalamoo, a nature preserve within the Green Mountain National Forest. RR 3, Forest Service Road, #32, Goshen; (800) 448-0707; www.blueberryhillinn.com. P.S. If you can't stop thinking of those chocolate chip cookies, call (800) 448-0707 to order some for delivery.

ATTRACTIONS

The main attractions in Killington center around the Killington resort (activities are listed above in The Best Beaches and Parks, page 262; Family Outdoor Adventures, page 268; and Skiing, page 270). Besides skiing, area attractions include wall-climbing and mountain biking (you can take your bikes up the mountain on a gondola and coast down). For younger kids, there's a dry ski/snowboard deck to test out. And the Killington Adventure Center thrills kids of all ages.

For rainy-day fun, enjoy the Wednesday matinee of Broadway hits performed by The Green Mountain Guild at the Snowshed Base Lodge at Killington Ski Resort.

FAMILY-FRIENDLY RESTAURANTS

CASEY'S CABOOSE

Killington Road, Killington; (802) 422-3800

Meals served: Lunch and dinner
Cuisine: American

Entree range: $9 and up
Children's menu: Yes
Reservations: Yes
Payment: All types accepted

Kids love this place, if for nothing else, for the fact that it's housed in a caboose. There's a snowplow car, to boot. The best bet for families is the observation-deck compartment in the raised snowplow car, which seats six. Anticipate whimsical menu names, such as the Locomotive (a 16-ounce prime rib). This is a fun, upbeat spot for kids, with burgers, steak, pasta, and lobster on the menu.

THE GRIST MILL

Killington Road, Killington; (802) 422-3970

Meals served: Lunch and dinner
Cuisine: American
Entree range: $10 and up
Children's menu: Yes
Reservations: Yes
Payment: All types accepted

The Grist Mill has a waterwheel to entertain the kids. Plus it has the bigger-than-life Fieldstone fireplace, lots of antiques, and nice location on Summit Pond. The menu features American favorites like soup, salad, steak, seafood, and chicken.

Lake Champlain, the Northern Green Mountains, and the Northeast Kingdom

Welcome to wilderness. This region is a huge expanse of verdant forest encompassing most of the northeastern corner of the state from the Connecticut River on the east to the Green Mountains on the west. While Vermont is known for its mountains, this reach of the state is known as much for its lakes as its peaks. **Lake Champlain** is the biggest lake in Vermont, with over 600 miles of shoreline and 70 islands. The major ski resort is **Jay Peak** (see Skiing, page 270), and there are notable museums such as the **Fairbanks Museum and Planetarium, Shelburne Farms and Shelburne Museum,** and **The Vermont Teddy Bear Museum.**

Burlington is Vermont's hippest, most vibrant town, thanks to the University of Vermont, which uses downtown Burlington as its campus (since it really doesn't have a city-type campus to call its own). Right on the banks of Lake Champlain, this is a walking town, so park your car and foot it. You'll want to hit **Church Street Marketplace,** a colorful, brick-and-cobblestone pedestrian mall. Grab a cappuccino at one of the outdoor cafes, and you'll have a front-row seat for the many street performers and musicians. Teens will love the hippie feel of this college town.

The main attraction in Burlington, especially for young kids, is Lake Champlain. You can enjoy it down at the **Burlington Waterfront,** where you'll find the **Burlington Community Boathouse.** You can jump aboard one of the ferries that cruise the lake, even taking one over to New York state. Consider renting bikes to enjoy the eight-mile **bike path** that snakes along Lake Champlain and connects the city's lakeside parks and beaches. Visit **Leddy Arena,** an indoor ice rink at **Leddy Park,** or just hang in the park, where there are basketball and tennis courts and a small beach.

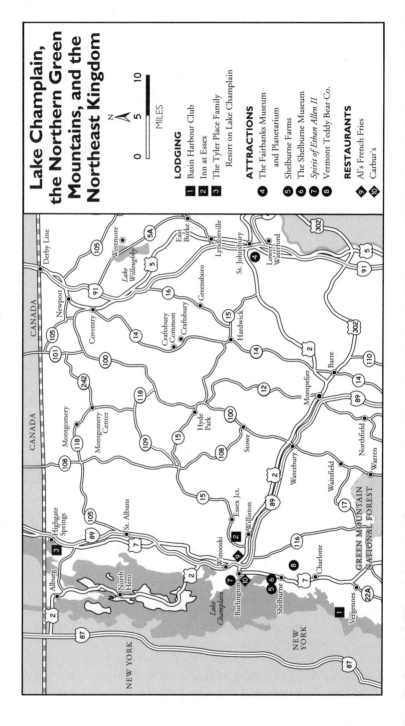

Lake Champlain, the Northern Green Mountains, and the Northeast Kingdom

LODGING

1. Basin Harbour Club
2. Inn at Essex
3. The Tyler Place Family Resort on Lake Champlain

ATTRACTIONS

4. The Fairbanks Museum and Planetarium
5. Shelburne Farms
6. The Shelburne Museum
7. *Spirit of Ethan Allen II*
8. Vermont Teddy Bear Co.

RESTAURANTS

9. Al's French Fries
10. Carbur's

Family Lodging

Basin Harbor Club

A member of the prestigious Historic Hotels of America, this resort takes the prize in upscale family accommodations. On the shores of Lake Champlain, it has more than 700 acres of nature trails plus gardens, golf, tennis, water sports, hiking, biking, and a children's program. The Lake Champlain Maritime Museum, dedicated to the exploration and preservation of Lake Champlain, is on the resort's grounds. Children who are guests of the resort can take advantage of the museum's ambitious summer program. Accommodations include 38 guest rooms in three guesthouses, as well as 77 cottages, each of which has a deck or screened porch, refrigerator, and wet bar. Double room rates begin at $200 per night; also inquire about affordable packages. Open mid-May to mid-October. Basin Harbor Road, Vergennes; (800) 622-4000.

Inn at Essex

My son and I stayed at this lovely country-style inn about 20 minutes from downtown Burlington, and we got the best of both worlds—the rolling countryside of Vermont and easy access to exploring Burlington's shopping and restaurants. Another great reason to stay here is the food—the resort functions as a satellite campus of the Montpelier-based New England Culinary Institute. The inn also has an art gallery, an outdoor pool, a library, and pretty gardens and paths. Double room rates begin at $170 per night. 70 Essex Way, Essex; (800) 727-4295.

The Tyler Place Family Resort on Lake Champlain

This lakefront resort celebrates the family vacation with family-friendly cottages and suites and rates that include all meals and sports. Kids eat separately (some parents love this, others frown upon it). There are programs for everyone from toddlers to teens, and there's even infant care. Activities include tennis, windsurfing, biking, canoeing, sailing, kayaking, and golf (down the road). Opt for one of the 27 fireplace cottages if you're visiting in the winter. If visiting in summer, book one of the family suites with screened-in porches and separate bedrooms for the kids. During the months of May, June, and September (shoulder season), there are very affordable packages, which begin at $190 per adult per night and $150 per child per night. Highgate Springs; (802) 868-4000.

Attractions

The Fairbanks Museum and Planetarium

Main and Prospect Streets, St. Johnsbury; (802) 748-2372

Hours: Monday–Saturday 10 a.m.–4 p.m., Sunday 1–5 p.m.; open until
6 p.m. during summer months

Admission: $5 adults, $4 seniors, $3 children age 5–17, free for kids under
age five, $12 per family (maximum three adults, no limit on kids)

Appeal by Age Groups:

Pre-school	Grade School	Teens	Young Adults	Over 30	Seniors
★★	★★★	★★★	★★	★★	★★

Touring Time: Average 1 hour; minimum ½ hour

Rainy-Day Touring: Yes

Services and Facilities:

Restaurants No	Lockers No
Alcoholic beverages No	Pet kennels No
Disabled access Yes	Rain check No
Wheelchair rental No	Private tours Yes
Baby stroller rental No	

Description and Comments   Home to Vermont's only public planetarium
and the largest natural science museum north of Boston, this museum
entertains kids with mounted animals (even a polar bear) and a cool "bug
art" exhibit. You'll also see antique tools and toys, dolls and dinosaurs, and
artifacts indigenous to Vermont. You can watch weather in the making at
the Northern New England Weather Center that's on the premises. You
could spend as little as a half-hour just taking in one part of this eclectic
museum, or take your time and take it all in.

Shelburne Farms

Bay and Harbor Roads, Shelburne; (802) 985-8686

Hours: Mid-May–mid-October, daily 10 a.m.–5 p.m. (guided tours
offered five times a day)

Admission: $5 adults, $4 seniors and kids ages 3–14, free for kids under
age 3

Appeal by Age Groups:

Pre-school	Grade School	Teens	Young Adults	Over 30	Seniors
★★★★	★★★	★★	★	★	★

Play Ball! The Vermont Expos

This Single-A farm team for the Montreal Expos is a lot of fun to watch. The team's lake monster mascot, Champ, gets the crowds cheering in this intimate, old-fashioned stadium. The season runs mid-June through early September. Tickets are $6 reserved, $4 for general admission, $3 for seniors, and $1 for children age 12 and under. Purchase tickets by phone or at the park; call (802) 655-6611. Games are played at the University of Vermont's Centennial Field in Burlington.

Touring Time: Average full day; minimum a half day

Rainy-Day Touring: Not recommended

Services and Facilities:

Restaurants Yes	Lockers No
Alcoholic beverages Yes	Pet kennels No
Disabled access Yes	Rain check No
Wheelchair rental No	Private tours Yes
Baby stroller rental No	

Descriptions and Comments It's fun to amble about this 1,400-acre farm, designed by Frederick Law Olmstead, who also designed Central Park. Spend the day exploring the 19th-century buildings and formal gardens. There is a gorgeous inn at Shelburne Farms, should you decide you never want to leave, and the Marble Restaurant, a showcase for local Vermont ingredients, for breakfast and dinner. A nice complement to the Farms is a trip to the Shelburne Museum, about one mile east.

The Shelburne Museum

US 7, Shelburne; (802) 985-3346

Hours: Late May–late October, daily 10 a.m.–5 p.m.; April–late May and mid-October–early December, museum open daily 1–4 p.m., store open noon–5 p.m.

Admission: $8.75 adults, $3.50 kids ages 6–14, free for kids under age 6

Appeal by Age Groups:

Pre-school	Grade School	Teens	Young Adults	Over 30	Seniors
★★★★	★★★	★★★	★★★	★★★	★★★

Touring Time: Average full day; minimum a half-day

Chocolate

Chocaholics will love the Lake Champlain Chocolate Factory. This retail shop and chocolate-making factory lets you see the secret makings of the sweet stuff from an observation deck. 750 Pine Street, Burlington; (802) 864-1808.

Rainy-Day Touring: Not recommended

Services and Facilities:

Restaurants Yes	Lockers No
Alcoholic beverages Yes	Pet kennels No
Disabled access Yes	Rain check No
Wheelchair rental No	Private tours Yes
Baby stroller rental No	

Descriptions and Comments This 45-acre museum is to Vermont what the Smithsonian is to Washington, D.C. There are almost 40 exhibit buildings, a lighthouse, and more than 80,000 objects of American folk art and Americana, including quilts, carriage, and circus memorabilia. The Owl Cottage Family Center at this museum is especially fun, offering new exhibits each week, such as butter churning and stenciling. Kids adore riding on Shelburne's c. 1920 carousel—let them pick their favorite steed.

Spirit of Ethan Allen II

Burlington Community Boathouse, College Street, Burlington; (802) 862-8300

Hours: May–October, departs daily at 10 a.m., noon, 2 p.m., and 4 p.m.

Admission: $8.95 adults, $3.95 kids ages 3–11, free for kids under age 3

Appeal by Age Groups:

Pre-school	Grade School	Teens	Young Adults	Over 30	Seniors
★★★	★★★★	★★★	★★★	★★★	★★★

Touring Time: Average 90 minutes (narrated cruise tour); minimum 90 minutes

Rainy-Day Touring: No

Services and Facilities:

Restaurants Dinner cruises	Wheelchair rental No
Alcoholic beverages Yes	Baby stroller rental No
Disabled access Yes	

Lockers No	Rain check No
Pet kennels No	Private tours Yes

Description and Comments   Cruise Lake Champlain on this 500-passenger, triple-deck boat. Kids love it because they have a chance to spy "Champ," the legendary serpent that lurks in the waters of Lake Champlain. They also love to feed the sea gulls that escort the boat (depending on how plentiful the handouts are). Note: Meal and theme cruise rates vary considerably, from $9.95 for adults and $4.95 for kids on the Sunset cruise to $35.95 for adults and $25.95 for kids on the Lobster on the Lake dinner cruise.

Vermont Teddy Bear Company

6655 Shelburne Road, Shelburne; (800) 829-BEAR, www.vtbear.com

Hours: Monday–Saturday 9 a.m.–6 p.m., Sunday 10 a.m.–5 p.m.

Admission: $1 adults, free for children under age 12

Appeal by Age Groups:

Pre- school	Grade School	Teens	Young Adults	Over 30	Seniors
★★★★★	★★	★	★	★	★

Touring Time: Average 1 hour; minimum ½ hour

Rainy-Day Touring: Recommended

Services and Facilities:

Restaurants No	Lockers No
Alcoholic beverages No	Pet kennels No
Disabled access Yes	Rain check No
Wheelchair rental No	Private tours Yes
Baby stroller rental No	

Description and Comments   Take a tour of this teddy-bear factory and learn history and fun facts about teddy bears while you watch them being made. The Make a Friend for Life room is especially endearing—kids can watch a bear being "born" and decide how smart it will be, how it will dress, and how it will act. And then they get to keep it—at a cost. There's also a bear gift shop with lots of the cuddly guys for sale.

Family-Friendly Restaurants

AL'S FRENCH FRIES

1251 Williston Road, South Burlington; (802) 862-9203

Meals served: Lunch and dinner

Cuisine: Burgers and fries
Entree range: $3 and up
Children's menu: Yes
Reservations: No
Payment: No credit cards

Got a hankering for some awesome french fries (what kid doesn't)? This is the perfect low-key, pile-'em-on spot.

CARBUR'S

115 Saint Paul Street, Burlington; (802) 862-4106

Meals served: Lunch and dinner
Cuisine: Everything under the sun, 200 menu items
Entree range: $2.50–17
Children's menu: Yes
Reservations: Preferred seating (call ahead and when you arrive, if there's a wait, your name goes up top)
Payment: All types accepted

If you were scouting for a family restaurant for a movie location, Carbur's would be typecast. Peanut butter fluff sandwiches jump out from the ambitious 16-page menu for kids; for adults, it's the huge beer list that wets their whistle. Sandwiches, salads, steaks, ribs—you name it, Carbur's has it.

Side Trip: Stowe

Just 30 minutes from Burlington, Stowe encompasses two mountains, **Mount Mansfield** and **Spruce Peak.** Bosomed within these towering tops (although Mount Mansfield stands head and shoulders above Spruce Peak), is the darling village of Stowe, about five miles from the ski slopes. The requisite white-steepled church and general store give Stowe its Yankee definition. Very popular in the winter because of its fabulous downhill and cross-country skiing opportunities, Stowe is also a perfect summer getaway. In summer, Vermont's highest peak, Mount Mansfield (4,393 feet), lays out a welcome mat that's dotted with wildflowers and has myriad hiking, biking, and camping opportunities. If you're here to ski, you won't find much in the way of slope-side lodging (at least not as compared to some of the other heavy-hitter ski resorts in the state), but there are a handful of celebrated resorts in the area.

FAMILY LODGING

Green Mountain Inn

If you care to stay in something quaint and more intimate than the grand resorts in the area, this pretty inn, located smack in the center of Stowe, delivers. It has 76 rooms and suites, some with a fireplaces and Jacuzzi. There are two restaurants and bars, a health club, an outdoor pool, and a game room. Pets are allowed. Double room rates begin at $89 per night. Main Street, Stowe; (800) 253-7302.

Topnotch at Stowe Resort and Spa

Located at the foot of Mount Mansfield, this 120-acre upscale resort's most endearing assets are its 23,000-square-foot spa and year-round tennis facility. There are also nature trails, a children's center, and a huge indoor pool and whirlpool. Many of the rooms have Jacuzzis. Double room rates begin at $170 per night. 4000 Mountain Road, Stowe; (800) 451-8686.

Trapp Family Lodge

Think *Sound of Music,* and you'll know why the Trapp family name rings a bell. This Austrian-style resort has a super kids program, the Mountain Kids Club for ages 3 to 12, which has the kids out and about exploring the hills that are alive. This is a resort that also celebrates family together time—bingo, storytelling, and sing-alongs are regular fare. Come in the summer and enjoy the fishing stream, outdoor pool, and tennis court. Double room rates begin at $100 per night. 700 Trapp Hill Road, Stowe; (800) 826-7000.

ATTRACTIONS

The main attractions in Stowe center around Stowe Mountain Resort, no matter the season. In addition to the slopes, there's the Spruce Peak Alpine Slide and the Stowe Launch Zone (in-line skating, skateboards, and BMX bikes). For information on other activities, see the Skiing section on page 270.

For rainy-day fun, the Painting Place on Mountain Road has paint-your-own pottery. Choose a piece of pottery, paint it, and take it home for a souvenir; (802) 253-7753.

Side Trip: The Champlain Islands

There are 70 islands in Lake Champlain, most of which are inhabitable and are suitable primarily for day-trippers (think picnics), although there are scant accommodations. One of the most popular islands explored by

---

We All Scream for Ice Cream

Vermont is Ben & Jerry's country, and you won't want to miss the Ben & Jerry's tour at its ice cream factory in Waterbury, about 15 minutes from Stowe. This is one of Vermont's most popular attractions and no wonder—who doesn't love ice cream? Expect crowds if you visit during peak times, but the kids won't mind waiting for their tour. They'll be entertained by face painters and engaged in crafts. If the lines are really long or if your kids are very young or particularly antsy, forgo the tour (it includes a short video and peek at the factory) and just stop by for the ice cream and fun. Thirty-minute tours are given daily, every half-hour beginning at 10 a.m., with the last tour at 5 p.m. Tours include samples of ice cream. Cost is $2 adults, $1 for seniors, and free for kids age 12 and under. Tours are on a first-come, first served basis, although groups of 10 or more can make reservations. Note: Ben & Jerry's does not make ice cream on Sundays or holidays, although the factory and tour are open. If you are set on seeing ice-cream making in the works, you should not come on those days. Ben & Jerry's also has special promotions, including Snowshoe and Ice Cream, an event that includes a snowshoe trek with a guide through Ben & Jerry's 44-acre property, followed by a warm drink and free tour. Cost is $8 per person, including snowshoes and poles. Call (802) 253-2317. Ben & Jerry's Factory is located on Route 100 in Waterbury; (802) 244-TOUR.

---

families is **Burton Island,** with the formidable Burton Island State Park (see The Best Beaches and Parks on page 262). It is accessible only by boat.

North Hero is another popular island for day-tripping families, thanks to the Royal Lipizzan Stallions of Austria. The horses put on quite a show, delighting the children with their antics. For information, call (802) 372-5683.

Isle La Motte, at the northern tip of Lake Champlain, is a great place for a family biking trip. Rent bikes and soak in the scenery along the waterfront. You can even pedal past the island's fossil-reef formations. The Bike Shed rents several types of bikes, including road bikes, mountain bikes, and tandem bikes. Helmets and maps are available too. You'll find them at 1071 West Shore Road; (802) 928-3440. In June, September, and October, they're open weekends from 9 a.m. to 6 p.m. and other days by appointment. July through August, they're open Thursday through Monday from 9 a.m. to 6 p.m. Rentals are $5 an hour, $15 for a half day, or $20 a day.

Part Seven

New York

New York is vast—so vast that the country's largest city is but one small aspect of its personality. Sure, New York City gets worldwide attention and draws visitors from around the globe. But, think about the state's other aspects: one of the world's largest nature preserves at Adirondack Park; one of the most famous honeymoon spots at Niagara Falls; Baseball's Hall of Fame; a two-time Winter Olympic site at Lake Placid; the Hudson Valley, where a school of landscape painting was inspired; the cradling ground of the Women's Movement in Seneca Falls; Rochester, a city where photography for common folks first saw light; and engineering feats that changed the American lifestyle, like the Erie Canal and the Brooklyn Bridge. The list goes on. It's a huge state, and it offers so much to see and do that many vacations can be happily spent exploring it. Keep in mind that distances between sites are often vast: Niagara Falls is 410 miles from New York City and a three-hour drive from Albany; Lake Placid is nearly a five-hour drive from Manhattan; and while Rochester stands less than an hour from Syracuse and Buffalo, the northern tier area will require three to four hours to reach from most other parts of the state.

We start with the northwestern section, including **Buffalo, Niagara Falls,** and the state's far western corner. We continue our explorations in the central region—**Rochester** and **Syracuse**—and move on to the **Finger Lakes,** including **Cooperstown.** From there it's into the **Adirondacks** and the **Saratoga Springs** area, then down through the **Hudson Valley** and **Catskills** into **New York City** and finally east onto **Long Island.**

GETTING THERE

By Car. **Greater Buffalo** is accessed from the east and south by the New York Thruway (I-90); downtown can be reached via I-190 or the Kensington Expressway/State Route 33. Reach **Niagara Falls** from Buffalo on northbound I-190; when approaching from the east, take the I-290 bypass to I-190 northbound. To **Rochester** from the New York Thruway (I-90), take Exits 45, 46, or 47; I-490 branches into the metro area, and I-590 combines with Route 104 to form a freeway loop around town. I-590 continues north to the shores of Lake Ontario. To reach **Syracuse** from east or west, take the Thruway (I-90); from north or south, take I-81. To get to the **Finger Lakes Region** driving in from the south, approach via I-81 and Route 17; from the east and west, leave the New York State Thruway (I-90) and go south on I-81 to Route 20 west towards Auburn (if you're accessing the eastern lakes region), or at Seneca Falls and travel south along the lake of your choice. To get to **Albany,** the main thoroughfare is I-87, which runs north from Albany along the region's eastern edge. This highway provides direct access to **Saratoga Springs, Lake George,** and **Plattsburgh,** as well as reasonable access to **Lake Placid.** Reaching the more remote areas of the region requires two-lane driving and a good road map. Most of the **Catskills/Hudson River Valley** region can be reached by a two-and-a-half-hour drive from New York City. Follow the New York State Thruway (I-90) north; to reach the western sections of the Catskills, follow the Quickway, State Route 17. To get to **New York City** from the north, approach on the New York Thruway (I-87), which becomes the Major Degan Expressway when it passes into the Bronx. From the west, approaches are via I-78 through the Holland Tunnel to lower Manhattan; via NJ State Route 3 and I-495 through the Lincoln Tunnel to mid-town at 40th Street; or via I-80 across the George Washington Bridge to the upper west side at 178th Street. To get to **Long Island** from New York City, the main route is the Long Island Expressway, I-495, which runs to Riverhead. The Northern State Parkway runs between Queens and Hauppauge, while the Belt Parkway/Southern State Parkway runs from Brooklyn and Queens to Oakdale.

By Plane. **Buffalo Niagara International Airport** (call (716) 630-6000) is about 15 minutes east of downtown Buffalo; we recommend renting a car, particularly if you're traveling to Niagara Falls or the nearby beaches or mountains. The **Greater Rochester International Airport** (call (716) 464-6000) is located southwest of downtown Rochester. **Syracuse Hancock International Airport** (call (315) 454-3263) is on I-81. The Finger Lakes region can be accessed through the Rochester or Syracuse airports. The most common way to reach the Catskills and Hudson Valley by air is to fly into New York City airports (JFK, LaGuardia, or Newark, New Jersey) or into **Albany International Airport,** 875 Albany-Shaker Road, Albany (call (508) 869-3021).

Three airports serve New York City. **John F. Kennedy International Airport** (call (718) 244-4444) and **La Guardia Airport** (call (718) 533-3400) are both located in Queens. In nearby New Jersey, **Newark International Airport** (call (973) 961-6000) serves the city. To get to Long Island, **Long Island Islip MacArthur Airport** (call (631) 467-3210), centrally located on Long Island in Ronkonkoma, offers scheduled flights from nine airlines. JFK International and LaGuardia Airports are also convenient.

By Train. Amtrak provides daily service to **Niagara Falls;** the station is a ten-minute drive from Niagara Falls' lodging and attractions. Trains can get you to much of **Westchester County** and, in particular, the sites in Tarrytown, Sleepy Hollow, and cities along the Hudson River. Amtrak services **Albany** and **Saratoga** and stops farther north in the region at Fort Edward, Whitehall, Westport (from which connection can be made to **Lake Placid** by taxi or jitney service), and **Plattsburgh.** Call Amtrak at (800) 872-7245; www.amtrak.com. Also try Metro North, (800) 638-7646. **Manhattan** has two train stations. Penn Station is between 31st and 33rd streets at 7th Avenue. It's served by Amtrak, (call (800) 872-7245); MTA-Long Island Railroad (call (718) 217-5477); and New Jersey Transit (call (800) 772-2222). Grand Central Terminal, at 42nd Street and Park Avenue, serves points north and into Connecticut via Metro-North Railroad (call (800) 638-7646). Some NJ Transit trains require connection via the PATH (call 800) 234-7284), a subway that links northern New Jersey with Manhattan's west side. Many folks commute to and from Long Island on the Long Island Railroad (call 516) 822-5477), and the line offers a viable alternative to driving for many destinations.

By Bus. The Port Authority Bus Terminal, (call (212) 564-8484), is the country's largest bus station. Buses serve destinations throughout the United States and all major New York metro airports. Many parts of the state can be reached by bus. Contact Greyhound, (800) 231-2222; Trailways, (800) 858-8555; or Short Line, (800) 631-8405.

How to Get Information before You Go

Adirondack Regional Tourism Council, P.O. Box 2149, Plattsburgh, NY 12901; (800) 487-6867, (518) 846-8016; www.adk.com.

Campsite information and reservations statewide, (800) 456-2267.

Columbia County Tourism Department, 401 State Street, Hudson, NY 12534; (800) 724-1846, (518) 828-3375; www.columbiacountyny.com.

Fun New York Facts

- Total population: 18,976,457; third most in the nation

- The total area of New York State is 54,471.144 square miles (47,223.839 land and 7,247.305 inland water).

- There are 6,713 natural ponds, lakes, and reservoirs of one acre or more, 76 with an area of one square mile or more. There are 1,745 square miles of inland water, including some 4,000 lakes, ponds, and reservoirs. Oneida Lake is the largest lake completely within the state.

- At the site of Niagara Falls, the Niagara River spills 40 million gallons of water 180 feet downward each minute across a ragged ledge nearly two-thirds of a mile wide.

- The New York State Barge Canal System is the longest internal waterway system in any state (800 miles or 1,280 kilometers), carrying over two million tons per year.

- The first railroad in America ran between Albany and Schenectady, a distance of 11 miles.

- New York was the first state to (1) preserve a historic site (Washington's Headquarters at Newburgh); (2) establish a state park (Niagara Reservation); and (3) declare land "forever wild" (the Adirondack and Catskill forest preserves) in the State Constitution.

- Why is New York City called The Big Apple? The term "The Big Apple" was coined by touring jazz musicians of the 1930s who used the slang expression "apple" for any town or city. Therefore, to play New York City is to play the big time–The Big Apple.

Delaware County Chamber of Commerce, 114 Main Street, Delhi, NY 13753; (800) 642-4443, (607) 746-2281; www.delawarecounty.org.

Dutchess County Tourism Promotion Agency, 3 Neptune Road, Suite M-17, Poughkeepsie, NY 12601; (800) 445-3131, (914) 463-4000; www.dutchesstourism.com.

Finger Lakes Association, 309 Lake Street, Penn Yan, NY 14527; (800) 548-4386; www.fingerlakes.org.

Gore Mountain Region Chamber of Commerce, P.O. Box 84, Main Street, North Creek, NY 12853; (800) 880-4673, (518) 251-2612; www.goremtnregion.org.

State Symbols

- State nickname: The Empire State
- State capital: Albany
- Statehood: July 26, 1788 (11th state)
- State motto: *Excelsior* ("Ever Upward")
- Highest point: Mt. Marcy; 5,344 feet above sea level

- Lowest point: Sea level
- State flower: Rose
- State tree: Sugar maple
- State bird: Bluebird
- State fish: Brook trout
- State fruit: Apple
- State animal: Beaver

Greater Buffalo Convention & Visitors Bureau, 617 Main Street, Buffalo, NY 14203; (800) 283-3256 or (716) 852- 0511; fax (716) 852-0131; www.buffalocvb.org.

Greater Rochester Visitors Association, 126 Andrews Street, Rochester, NY 14604; (800) 677-7282 or (716) 546-3070; fax (716) 232-4822; www.visitrochester.com.

Greene County Promotion, Route 23B, P.O. Box 527, Catskill, NY 12414; (800) 355-2287, (518) 943-3223; www.greene-ny.com.

Hudson Valley Tourist Information Center, Palisades Center, 1000 Palisades Center Drive, Fourth Floor, West Nyack, NY 10994; (914) 429-7661.

Lake Champlain Visitors Center, RR1, Box 724, Bridge Road, Crown Point, NY 12928; (800) 447-5224.

Lake George Regional Chamber of Commerce, 2176 Route 9, P.O. Box 272, Lake George, NY 12845; (800) 705-0059, (518) 668-5755; www.lgchamber.org.

Lake Placid/Essex County Convention & Visitors Bureau, Olympic Center, Main Street, Lake Placid, NY 12946; (800) 447-5224, (518) 523-2999; www.lakeplacid.com.

Long Island Convention & Visitors Bureau, 330 Motor Parkway, Suite 203, Hauppague, NY 11788; (877) 386-6654 or (516) 951-3440; www.licvb.com.

New York State Department of Economic Development, P.O. Box 2603, Albany, NY 12220; (800) 225-5697; www.iloveny.state.ny.us.

Niagara Falls Convention & Visitors Bureau, 310 Fourth Street, Niagara Falls, NY 14303; (800) 421-5223 or (716) 285-2400; fax (716) 285-0809; www.niagara-usa.com.

NYC & Company, 810 7th Avenue, New York, NY 10019; (800) 693-8474 or (212) 484-1200; www.nycvisit.com.

Orange County Tourism, 30 Matthews Street, Suite 111, Goshen, NY 10924; (800) 762-8687, (914) 291-2136; www.orange-tourism.org.

Putnam County Visitors Bureau, 110 Old Route 6, Building 3, Carmel, NY 10512; (800) 470-4854, (914) 225-0381; www.visitputnam.org.

Rockland County Department of Tourism, 3 Main Street, Suite 2, Nyack, NY 10960; (800) 295-5723, (914) 353-5533; www.rockland.org.

Sullivan County Visitors Association, 100 North Street, Monticello, NY 12701; (800) 882-2287, (914) 794-3000; www.scva.net.

Syracuse Convention & Visitors Bureau, 572 S. Salina Street, Syracuse, NY 13202; (800) 234-4797; fax (315) 471-8545; www.syracusecvb.org or www.syracuse.ny.us.

Ulster County Tourism, 244 Fair Street, P.O. Box 1800, Kingston, NY 12401; (800) 342-5826, (914) 340-3566; www.co.ulster.ny.us.

Ulster County Tourism, City Office Building, 244 Fair Street, Kingston, NY 12401; (800) 342-5826; www.co.ulster.ny.us.

Westchester Convention and Visitors Bureau, 235 Mamaroneck Avenue, White Plains, NY 10605; (800) 833-9282, (914) 948-0047; www.westchesterny.com.

The Best Beaches and Parks

Adirondack Park. Covering six million acres as it does, it's a bit hard to describe this wonderland. It encompasses mountains, lakes, countryside, the entire western shore of Lake Champlain, villages, farms, museums, restaurants, artisan shops, and a wide variety of accommodations. Some land within its boundaries is private. Many of the attractions listed in the following pages sit inside the park. Within the so-called "Blue Line," as its boundary is called, lie more than 40 state-operated campgrounds, 2,000 miles of hiking trails, hundreds of miles of canoe routes, and 42 peaks that rise more than 4,000 feet in elevation. All manner of recreation is possible: hiking, fishing, white-water rafting, canoeing, mountain biking, road biking, sailing, and more. During the winter, alpine and Nordic skiing, snowmobiling, skating, dog sledding, and snowshoeing are common pastimes. For information, contact New York State Department of Environmental Conservation, Region 5 Headquarters, Route 86, Box 296, Ray Brook, NY 12977, (518) 897-1200; or Region 6 Headquarters, 317 Washington Street, Watertown, NY 13601, (315) 785-2263; or the Adirondack Regional Tourism Council, P.O. Box 2149, Plattsburgh, NY 12901, (518) 846-8016.

Allegany State Park. About an hour's drive south of Buffalo (follow State Route 17 east to Exit 19), Allegany holds 65,000 acres with 70 miles of hiking trails, 55 miles of equestrian trails, and a five-and-a-half-mile paved bike trail encircling Red Lake. Fish and boat on the lake, and camp in one of more than 300 campsites and 300 rental cabins. Rental equipment is available for most activities. Visit the Stone Tower at the Summit Cabin area for terrific views and to gape at the gargantuan boulders of Thunder Rocks. Route 1, Salamanca; (716) 354-9121.

Bear Mountain State Park. A busy park with playgrounds, hiking, ball fields, a rowing pond, an ice-skating rink, cross-country ski trails, a ski-jump complex, and the Bear Mountain Inn restaurant/hotel. It's along the shores of the Hudson with great views from the mountaintop tower. About an hour from New York City on Route 9 W., Bear Mountain; (914) 786-2701.

Beaver Island State Park. This 950-acre state park sits on the Niagara River nine miles north of Buffalo. You'll find a swimming beach, fishing, bike and nature trails, playgrounds, picnic areas, athletic fields, an 18-hole golf course, and a historic home in which President Cleveland spent his summers. In winter you can enjoy cross-country skiing, snowshoeing, sledding, and ice fishing. 2136 W. Oakfield Road, Grand Island; (716) 773-3500.

Central Park. Running from 59th Street to 100th Street and encompassing 840 acres, Central Park is smack in the middle of everything. Visit the famous statue of Alice in Wonderland, the antique carousel, and the gem of a zoo. Rent bikes or paddleboats, ice skate, or just people watch. You'll find near-sylvan walking paths, country-like meadows, biking and skating paths, and even a rowing lake. Free summertime concerts, Shakespeare-in-the-Park, endless softball fields, tennis courts, and a winter ice-skating rink round out its attractions; (212) 794-6564.

Fire Island National Seashore. A 20-mile section of this famous 32-mile barrier island features unspoiled beaches and the Otis Pike Wilderness Area, the only federal wilderness in New York. You'll also find the Sunken Forest, a 300-year-old holly forest, and a lighthouse you can tour. The westernmost six miles of the island make up Robert Moses State Park, which harbors excellent beaches. The park has picnic areas, an 18-hole pitch-and-putt golf

Cool Websites for New York–Bound Kids

New York State Kids Room: www.dos.state.ny.us/kidsroom/
nysfacts/factmenu.html

**Here on the Erie Canal: The Kids' Unofficial Guide to the Erie
Canal:** www.redsuspenders.com/~nms/middleschool/canal/ecb.html

The Statue of Liberty Photo Tour:
www.nyctourist.com/liberty1.htm

New York Underground: www.nationalgeographic.com/features/
97/nyunderground

The Empire State Building Coloring Book: www.esbnyc.com/
coloringbook

New York State Waterfalls: www.ecojb.fiu.edu/waterfalls.html

New York State Parks: www.nysparks.state.ny.us/next.html

course, food concessions, a playground, and organized recreational programs. 20 Laurel Street, Patchogue; (631) 289-4810; www.nps.gov/fiis.

Four Mile Creek State Campgrounds. Just a few miles from town and also
near Fort Niagara, this is the best place for campers to set up for a Niagara
Falls visit. It offers disabled access, 266 tent/trailer sites, a dump, recreation
activities and programs, hiking, fishing, and a playground. Lake Road,
Youngstown; (716) 745-3802.

Genesee Valley Park. This 800-acre park contains the Genesee River, Erie
Canal, and Red Creek and offers riverside bike and walking paths, canoe
rentals, ball fields, cross-country skiing, two 18-hole golf courses, a fully
enclosed ice rink, and an Olympic-sized swimming pool. Southwest of
downtown Rochester off I-390 at Exit 16A-B, with access via Elmwood
Avenue, E. River Road, and Crittenden Road; (716) 428-7005.

Harriman State Park. Just north of the New Jersey line off the Palisades
Parkway, Harriman is a bastion of nature just beyond the suburbs. It's great
for hiking, biking, camping, boating, and fishing, and there's a public
swimming pool open in summer. You'll find 31 lakes and reservoirs, 200
miles of hiking trails, three beaches, and two public camping areas. Palisades Park Commission, Bear Mountain; (914) 786-2701.

Hecksher State Park. With camping, beach swimming, pool swimming, windsurfing, 20 miles of hiking trails, and a playground, there's something for everyone at this state park. Also on-site are picnic areas, bathhouses, food concessions, a museum, and organized recreational programs. Heckscher Parkway, East Islip; (516) 581-2100.

Highland Forest. Located about 25 miles southeast of Syracuse, this 2,700-acre preserve boasts of being the "Adirondacks of Central New York." You can tour the Pioneer Museum and one of the region's last operating sawmills. Follow the self-guiding nature trail, ride horses or mountain bikes, and, in winter, enjoy horse-drawn sleigh rides. $1 per car entry fee. Route 80, Fabius; (315) 683-5550.

Jones Beach State Park. A 2,400-acre park with six miles of ocean beach, a bayfront beach, a two-mile boardwalk, a pool, a golf course, and outdoor concerts at the Marine Theater; Ocean Parkway, Wantagh on Long Island; (516) 785-1600.

Letchworth State Park. This park is known as the Grand Canyon of the East because the Genesee River cut cliffs that are as high as 600 feet. You'll find hiking, horseback riding, biking, two swimming pools, and programs covering nature, history, and the performing arts. There are also guided walks, whitewater rafting, kayaking, and hot-air ballooning. Winter activities include ice skating, snow-tubing, cross-country skiing, snow-mobiling, and horse-drawn sleigh rides. 1 Letchworth State Park, Castile; (716) 493-3600. It's 35 miles south of Rochester off I-390 Exit 7.

Long Beach. Located on the southern shore, Long Beach became a popular summer vacation spot for the rich and famous in the 1920s, and it remains a popular beachgoing spot today. It's a thriving small town, with many shops and restaurants in the downtown area, and a four-mile boardwalk lined with small shops and amusements. Daily beach admission is $5. Buy passes at the recreation center, Magnolia Boulevard and West Bay Drive. General information: 350 National Boulevard; (516) 432-6000.

Minnewaska State Park Preserve. Set along the rocky-ledged, dramatic, 2,000-foot Shawangunk Mountain ridge, this park is best known for its cross-country skiing and technical rock-climbing terrain. Its dense hardwood forest and two lakes also offer hiking, swimming, and horseback riding. Route 44 and 55, New Paltz; (914) 255-0752.

Mohonk Preserve. Near Minnewaska, this 6,400-acre site is New York State's largest privately funded nature preserve. Hike on 31 miles of trails, bike and walk on 25 miles of carriage roads, or technical rock climb. Stop

New York's Not-to-Be-Missed Attractions

Statewide

- New York State Park Niagara Reservation
- Corning Museum of Glass, Corning
- National Baseball Hall of Fame & Museum, Cooperstown
- Olympic Attractions, Lake Placid
- Hiking Prospect Mountain near Lake George
- U.S. Military Academy at West Point
- Empire State Building Observatories/New York Skyride, New York City
- Central Park, New York City
- Bronx Zoo, Bronx

Buffalo, Niagara Falls, and West

- Explore & More A Children's Museum
- Aquarium of Niagara
- New York State Park Niagara Reservation

Rochester

- Seabreeze Amusement Park & Raging Rivers Water Park, Rochester
- Strong Museum, Rochester

Syracuse

- MOST Milton J. Rubenstein Museum of Science & Technology, Syracuse

Finger Lakes Region

- Corning Museum of Glass, Corning
- National Baseball Hall of Fame & Museum, Cooperstown

Adirondacks and Lake Placid

- Adirondack Museum, Blue Mountain Lake
- Olympic Attractions, Lake Placid
- Hiking Prospect Mountain near Lake George

New York's Not-to-Be-Missed Attractions (continued)

Saratoga Springs and the Albany Area

- National Museum of Racing and Hall of Fame, Saratoga Springs
- New York State Museum, Albany

Catskills and Hudson Valley

- Old Rhinebeck Aerodome, Rhinebeck
- Phillipsburg Manor, Sleepy Hollow
- Sunnyside, Washington Irving Home, Tarrytown
- U.S. Military Academy at West Point
- Eagle Spotting at The Eagle Institute, Barryville

New York City

- Dining at the Culinary Institute of America, Hyde Park
- Empire State Building Observatories/New York Skyride, New York City
- Ellis Island Immigration Museum/Statue of Liberty National Monument, New York City
- American Museum of Natural History/Rose Center for Earth & Space, New York City
- Central Park, New York City
- Metropolitan Museum of Art, New York City
- Bronx Zoo, Bronx

Long Island

- Fire Island National Seashore, Patchogue
- Long Island Children's Museum, Garden City

in the visitors center for exhibits on the human and natural history of the Ridge. Lake Mohonk, New Paltz; (914) 255-0919.

Robert H. Treman State Park. While the Ithaca area abounds with gorgeous gorges, Treman Park offers one of the best and easiest gorge hikes, a two-and-a-quarter-mile scramble with spectacular rock formations and views. If someone is willing to play chauffeur and pick up the rest of the family at the bottom, the whole thing can be done downhill. Reach the park by following Route 13 south for five miles out of town to Route 327; Ithaca; (607) 273-3440.

Saratoga National Historical Park. The Wilkinson National Historic Trail runs four and a half miles through areas significantly associated with the Battles of Saratoga. There are also six miles of historic road suitable for hiking and wooded hiking trails. Cyclists are welcome to bike the paved roads. (518) 664-9821.

Watkins Glen State Park. Perhaps the best known of the Finger Lakes parks, this one is accessed right from the heart of Watkins Glen. The stream here drops some 500 feet in a 2-mile course, creating 19 waterfalls. The streamside path goes beside the water, sometimes crossing under a falls, sometimes over. The park houses a public swimming pool, picnic facilities, and a campground. Get there by following Route 14 north or Route 329 south into downtown Watkins Glen; the entrance road is on the left as you come north, on the right as you come south; (607) 535-4511.

Westhampton Beach. Quiet and upscale, this is a place to go if you're staying in the Hamptons and want nothing but pure beach, *sans* amusements and other distractions. The village shops and restaurants are within walking distance. Two pavilions with rest rooms are open from May to September. In the heart of town, a small park with a gazebo is the site of concerts. Beach information (summer only): (631) 288-6306.

Family Outdoor Adventures

Biking. Towpath Bike Shop is full-service shop along the Erie Canal that rents bikes, including those outfitted with tagalongs or kiddie trailers. Schoen Place, Pittsford; (716) 586-2808.

At Stewart Park, a fully equipped lakeside park in Ithaca, you'll find a paved walking/biking path, plus playing fields, playgrounds, etc. Bikes can be rented at Cayuga Mountain Bike Shop, 138 W. State Street, Ithaca, (607) 277-6821, or the Outdoor Store, 206 The Ithaca Commons, Ithaca, (607) 273-3891. Stewart Park is located at the junction of Routes 13 and 34 in Ithaca; (607) 273-8364.

The 10-mile Warren County Bikeway runs from the southern tip of Lake George to Queensbury, wandering through mountains away from auto traffic. The route is largely flat with some gently rolling hills. Bike rentals from Beach Road Outdoor Supply, (518) 668-4040.

Boating/Canoeing/Kayaking. Oak Orchard Canoe rents canoes and kayaks alongside the Erie Canal by the hour, day, or for multiple days. 40 State Street, Pittsford; (716) 586-5990.

Around Ithaca, boat rentals are available at: Owasca Marina in Auburn, (call (315) 253-0693); Taughannock Boat Rentals in Ithaca (call (607) 387-3311). Canoe, kayak, or rowboat rentals are available from: East Shore Sailing, Ithaca, (call (607) 273-2560), and Riverforest Marina & Campground, Weedsport, (call (315) 834-9458).

The northern Delaware River borders the western Catskills. Wild & Scenic River Tours in Barryville offers raft, kayak, canoe, or tubing trips in whitewater or calm water; call (800) 836-0366 or (914) 557-8783. Lander's River Trips in Narrowsburg runs water trips from ten locations and offers camping at four campgrounds along the Delaware River; (800) 252-3925.

Wetlands, open water, creeks, and rivers around Long Island can be a paddler's paradise. The Paddling Company rents kayaks and canoes and leads one-and-a-half-hour guided tours of local waters for $25 per person; Peconic; (631) 765-3502; www.eaglesneck.com. Shelter Island Kayak Tours leads two-hour kayak tours around Coecles Harbor for $45 per person; 71 Cartwright Road, Shelter Island; (631) 749-1990; www.kayaksi.com.

Camping. There are too many campgrounds in the Lake Placid/Northern Adirondacks area to mention each one specifically, but one of the region's best camping options is island camping on Lake George. Some islands have only one campsite, meaning that you'll have an island of your own. For a complete list of New York State Campgrounds visit www.dec.state.ny.us /website/do/reccmpl4.htm, or www.ReserveAmerica.com; or call (518) 474-0456 or (800) 456-2267.

Dogsledding. Crown Point Kennels, located a few miles north of Ticonderoga, offers a variety of rides from a quarter-mile loop to all-day touring. You can also tour the kennels. RR2, 71 Hamilton Road, Crown Point; (518) 597-3850. Cunningham's Ski Barn in North Creek, (518) 251-3215, offers trips in the Lake George region.

Fishing. The Erie County Department of Environment and Planning publishes a *Fishing Guide for Lake Erie and the Niagara River* that includes a list of charter fishing guide services; (716) 858-8390.

Finger Lakes fishing offers lake trout, smallmouth and largemouth bass, pike, pickerel, and more. Charter fishing operations include Eagle Rock

Charters in Cayuga, (315) 889-5925; several in Ithaca, call (800)-284-8422; Watkins Glen Charters, (800) 607-4552; www.fingerlakes.org.

Several charter companies are available to take you fishing on Lake George. Contact the Lake George Chamber of Commerce, (800) 705-0059, (518) 668-5755; www.lgchamber.org.

Hiking. A 265-acre preserve, Tifft Nature Preserve offers a choice of a five-mile nature trail or three boardwalk routes through marshlands. It's an excellent place for bird-watching and a picnic. Tifft Nature Preserve, 1200 Fuhrmann Boulevard, Buffalo; (716) 825-6397.

Highland Forest (see The Best Beaches and Parks section) offers a section of the National Recreational Trail, which passes along the original canal. Old Erie Canal State Park, Dewitt; (315) 687-7821.

Robert H. Treman State Park and Watkins Glen State Park (see The Best Beaches and Parks section on page 310) offer great hiking opportunities. Bear Swamp State Forest near Skaneateles Lake has a 13-mile trail; (607) 753-3095.

Horseback Riding. Deep Hollow Ranch, three miles east of Montauk Village on Long Island, mounts beach and trail rides through thousands of acres. It also offers children's activities, pony rides, and a petting farm; Montauk Highway, Ranch Road, Montauk; (631) 668-2744.

Ice Skating. In downtown Buffalo, there's free ice skating (with inexpensive rentals) on the outdoor Rotary Rink at the Key Center; (716) 856-3150.

Mountain Biking. Ski Plattekill in Roxbury has become a significant Catskills mountain-biking center. It holds 20 miles of downhill single-track (take the ski lift up) and more than 40 miles of cross-country riding. It's open April–November, Saturdays and Sundays 10 a.m.–5 p.m. A rental shop is on-site; call (607) 326-3500. Pearson Park, on Walnut Mountain in Liberty, offers 265 acres of mountain biking trails in wooded and meadows settings; (914) 292-7690.

Rafting. Adirondack Rafting Company offers whitewater rafting through the Hudson River Gorge and Black River Canyon. Choose from tame family-fun floats or high-water adventure; (800) 510-7238, (518) 523-1635; www.raftonline.com.

About a dozen outfitters offer rafting adventures on the Hudson, Indian, Sacandaga, and Schroon rivers. Request a rafting guide from the Warren County Tourism office at (518) 761-6366, ext. 2757.

Skiing. Lake-effect snow yields some excellent skiing within a half-hour's drive of Buffalo. Kissing Bridge Ski Area (with snowtubing), Route 240,

Glenwood; (716) 592-4963; www.sanyips.com/kb. Holiday Valley Ski Area, Ellicottville; (716) 699-2345; www.holidayvalley.com.

Greek Peak Ski Resort is one of the larger alpine areas in the northern part of the state. It has an active snowsports center with 29 trails and 9 lifts. 2000 State Route 392, Cortland, about a half-hour's ride from Ithaca; (800) 955-2754; www.sanyips.com/greekpeak.

The Catskills hold some of New York's better ski areas. Hunter Mountain Ski Bowl in Hunter is the largest (53 trails) and the busiest, offering some of the most advanced terrain in the region; call (518) 263-4223. In Windham, Ski Windham is very family-friendly; call (518) 734-4300. Also good for families is the state-operated Belleayre in Highmount; call (914) 254-5600. Ski Plattekill, operated on weekends and holidays, is one of our favorites for its old-time flavor and friendly ambiance; call (800) 633-3275.

Calendar of Festivals and Events

January

Adirondacks: *Malone Winter Carnival.* Malone comes alive with the stuff that makes Adirondack winters fun; (518) 481-1704.

February

Adirondacks: *Lake George Winter Festival.* Held over multiple February weekends, with events like four-wheel and motorcycle ice-driving races, snowmobile jumping, and the Lake George Polar Bear Club mid-winter swim; (518) 668-5755 or (518) 761-6366.

Buffalo: *Olmstead Winter Carnival.* Delaware Park is the site of winter-sports demos of every sort, plus fireworks, ice dancing, crafts, snow volleyball and baseball, and a chili cook-off.

Syracuse: *Winterfest.* Ten days of indoor and outdoor activities, music, contests, and educational programs; (315) 466-9468; www.syracusewinter fest.com.

May

Finger Lakes: *Marquette Internationale, Corning.* A multicultural festival with music, dance, fine art, food, and more at the Corning Glass Center; (607) 974-8908 or (607) 974-8271.

Hudson Valley: *Telegraph Weekend, Poughkeepsie.* Kids and adults learn the history of the telegraph and can send messages at the Samuel Morse Historic Site; (914) 454-4500.

Catskills: *Irish Festival, East Durham*. Memorial Day weekend is a highlight for this town that's known as the Emerald Isle of the Catskills. Events are held at the Quill Irish Cultural & Sports Centre; (800) 434-3378.

June

Adirondacks: *Festival of the Lakes, Saranac Lake, Lake Placid, and Tupper Lake*. A celebration of the fine and performing arts at three wonderful Adirondack towns set on three beautiful lakes; (888) 701-5977 or (518) 891-1854.

Buffalo: *Juneteenth Festival*. An African-American fest that commemorates the end of slavery; (716) 888-8777; www.juneteenth.com.

Syracuse: *M&T Jazz Fest*. A weeklong celebration with nationally renowned jazz artists playing at Hanover Square; (315) 437-5627; www.syracusejazzfest.com.

Finger Lakes: *Ithaca Festival*. On the first weekend of June, seems like everybody in town participates in this fest; (607) 273-3646.

Waterfront Festival. Watkins Glen celebrates its proximity to the lake with a cardboard regatta and other fun; (607)535-4300.

Hudson Valley: *Great Hudson Valley Balloon Race, Wappingers Falls*. A major balloon fest with aerobatic flying; (914) 463-6000.

Clearwater's Great Hudson River Revival, Poughkeepsie. A longstanding event centered on the 106-foot sloop *Clearwater* to celebrate the improving environmental health of the Hudson River; (800) 677-5667 or (914) 454-7673; www.clearwater.org.

New York City: *Guinness Fleadh*. Some of Ireland's and America's greatest performers on four stages, in a general expression of Irish culture; (212) 307-7171; www.guinnessfleadh.com.

July

Buffalo: *Taste of Buffalo*. One of the country's largest food fests; (716) 831-9376; www.tasteofbuffalo.com.

Rochester Area: *Hill Cumorah Pageant*. Mormons stage *America's Witness for Christ*, an outdoor epic with a cast of 600 for seven days each July; (716) 624-9604; www.hillcumorah.com.

Lilac Festival. This festival kicks off Rochester's traditional hyperactive festival season with lots of flowers and kids' activities; (716) 256-4960; www.roch.com/lilacfestival.

Syracuse: *New York State Rhythm and Blues Festival.* Four days of hot music on 16 stages and also in local clubs; (315) 473-4336; www.nysbluesfest.com.

Finger Lakes: *Oswego Harborfest, Oswego.* Some 200 free performances and attractions, a juried arts and crafts show, fireworks over Lake Ontario, a "battle" of tall ships attacking Fort Ontario, plus a children's parade and park; (315) 343-3733; www.oswego.com/harborfest.

Baseball Hall of Fame Induction Weekend, Cooperstown. The annual ceremony and all its attendant hoopla; (607) 547-0215.

August

Syracuse: *Great New York State Fair;* (800) 475-3247 or (315) 487-7711.

Catskills: *Altamont Fair, Altamont.* The county fair for Albany, Schenectady, and Greene counties; (518) 861-6671.

Hudson Valley: *Sunnyside Storytelling Festival, Tarrytown.* At the home of Washington Irving; (914) 591-8763.

Long Island: *Hampton Classic Horse Show, Bridgehampton.* Reputed to be the country's largest hunter/jumper horse show with more than 1,200 Olympic veterans, world champions, and up-and-coming equine stars coming together; (516) 537-3177; www.thehamptons.com/classic.

September

Rochester: *Clothesline Festival.* The University of Rochester stages one of America's oldest and largest outdoor art shows. Lots of family and kid entertainment; (716) 473-7720; www.rochester.edu/mag/clothes.htm.

Finger Lakes: *Grand Prix Festival, Watkins Glen.* Watkins Glen celebrates its renowned track with music, food, wine tasting, entertainment, and—what else—a sports car rally; (607) 535-4300.

Hudson Valley: *Columbia County Fair, Chatham;* (518) 758-1811.

New York City: *Jim Henson Foundation's International Festival of Puppet Theater.* Eleven days of puppets from around the globe. Free children's performances in playgrounds and public libraries citywide; (212) 794-2400 or (212) 423-3587.

New York City: *San Gennaro Feast & Street Fair.* The city's most renowned street fair; (212) 226-6427.

October

Buffalo/Western NY: *Lucy-Desi Comedy Film Festival, Jamestown.* The Lucy-Desi Museum in Lucille Ball's hometown presents as many as 125 comedic short films; (716) 484-7070; www.lucy-desi.com.

November

Buffalo: *Toy Fest, East Aurora.* Home of the Toy Town Museum and known as Toy Town USA, East Aurora celebrates toys with exhibits, entertainment, and a carnival; (716) 687-5151.

Syracuse: *Lights on the Lake.* From late November through Christmas, Onondaga Lake is lit up for the holidays with the Northeast's largest drive-through light show; (315) 473-7275.

December

Niagara Falls: *A Festival of Lights.* Lights from downtown to the American Falls, including animated displays and laser light shows. Also ice skating, entertainment, and an indoor tropical gardens display. All month long; (716) 285-8484; www.a-festival-of-lights.org.

New York City: *Kwanzaa Fest.* The Jacob Javits Center holds the world's largest celebration of African-American culture and cooperative economics; (718) 671-2811.

Buffalo and Niagara Falls

Buffalo has an undeserved bad reputation for poor weather. Whenever the famous lake-effect snow falls anywhere upstate, meteorologists point to Buffalo. In reality, most of that snow falls beyond the city. The weather in Buffalo isn't really that nasty. In summer, it can be hot, but not too humid, and downright wonderful for water play. Many families take advantage of the watery surroundings with a cruise. The *Miss Buffalo* (call (716) 856-6696 or visit www.missbuffalo.com) sails through the Black Rock Lock and Canal and under the visually striking Peace Bridge to Canada. The *Niagara Clipper* (call (716) 856-6696 or visit www.missbuffalo.com) explores the Niagara River and circumnavigates Grand Island. The summertime weather is also perfect for baseball, and the **Buffalo Bisons** (call (888) 223-6000 or visit www.bisons.com), a AAA Cleveland Indians farm team, play in one of the nicest minor-league stadiums in the country. In winter, the National Hockey League's **Buffalo Sabres** play at **Marine Midland Arena** (call (716) 856-4100 or visit www.sabres.com). **Delaware Park** is Buffalo's equivalent of Central Park. The zoo and the Historical Museum are there, and there's a full realm of recreational activities at the park on Parkside and Elmwood avenues (call (716) 851-5806).

Buffalo is a significant regional theater center, with 14 thriving professional companies. During the school year, the **Theatre of Youth** (call (716) 856-4410 or visit www.artvoice.com/theatre/toy) mounts six productions at the historic **Allendale Theater. Shea's Performing Arts Center** (call (716) 847-1410 or visit www.sheas.org) hosts touring Broadway shows, concerts, recitals, and children's shows. Citywide, you'll find some kind of festival almost weekly from spring through autumn. Locals call their home The 20-Minute City because just about everything can be reached by car within 20 minutes. The Metro Rail, a local trolley/train service, runs from the University of Buffalo to downtown, passing through the heart of the theater district. Downtown, it runs above ground on Main Street and can be ridden for free.

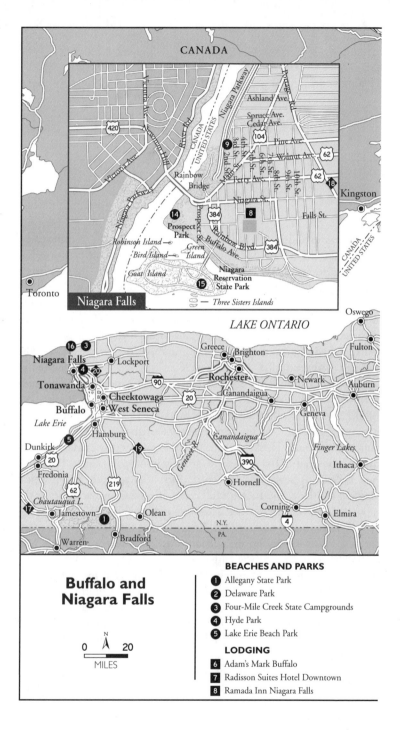

CANADA

Ashland Ave.

Spruce Ave.
Cedar Ave.

9

Pine Ave.

Walnut Ave.

Rainbow
Bridge

62

Niagara St.

18

Kingston

Falls St.

14

Prospect
Park

8

Robinson Island
Bird Island
Green
Island

Goat Island

Niagara
Reservation
State Park

15

CANADA
UNITED STATES

— *Three Sisters Islands*

Niagara Falls

Toronto

LAKE ONTARIO

Oswego

16 **3**

Greece
Brighton

Fulton

Niagara Falls

Lockport

4 **20**

90

Rochester

Newark

Auburn

Tonawanda

Cheektowaga

Canandaigua

20

Buffalo **West Seneca**

Geneva

Lake Erie

Hamburg

Canandaigua L.

Finger Lakes

5

Geneseo R.

Dunkirk

19

390

Ithaca

20

Fredonia

62

219

Hornell

Corning

Elmira

Chautauqua L.

17

Jamestown

Olean

N.Y.
PA.

4

Warren

Bradford

Buffalo and
Niagara Falls

N
0 ⟁ 20
MILES

BEACHES AND PARKS

1 Allegany State Park

2 Delaware Park

3 Four-Mile Creek State Campgrounds

4 Hyde Park

5 Lake Erie Beach Park

LODGING

6 Adam's Mark Buffalo

7 Radisson Suites Hotel Downtown

8 Ramada Inn Niagara Falls

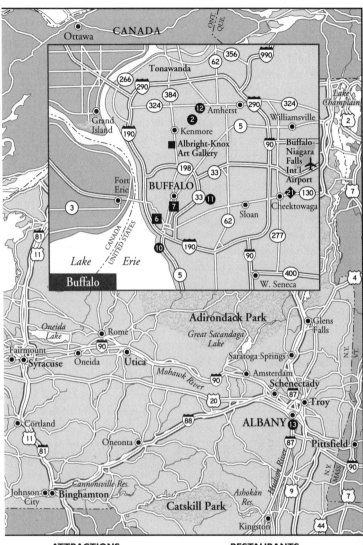

ATTRACTIONS

- **9** Aquarium of Niagara
- **10** Buffalo & Erie County Naval & Military Park
- **11** Buffalo Museum of Science
- **12** Buffalo Zoological Gardens
- **13** Explore & More
- **14** Maid of the Mist
- **15** NY State Park Niagara Reservation
- **16** Old Fort Niagara

RESTAURANTS

- **17** Chautauqua Institution
- **18** Como Restaurant
- **19** Golden Mill Restaurant
- **20** Page's Restaurant
- **21** Polish Villa

Niagara Falls, too, is a 20-minute drive from Buffalo. Although North America holds many waterfalls higher than Niagara, this is the one to which all others are compared. (How often have you heard the phrase "higher than Niagara"?) There are actually two falls—the American Falls and the Horseshoe or Canadian Falls. They stand at 190 and 185 feet tall, respectively, and about 100,000 cubic feet of water rushes over them per second. All the water from Lakes Superior, Michigan, Huron, and Erie travels over the falls on its way into Lake Ontario and, eventually, into the St. Lawrence River.

While thrill-seeking Niagara visitors might consider dropping over the falls in a barrel, better to visit the public library, which contains an excellent archive that includes a history on "stuntsters"—those who actually have gone over the falls or performed other outlandish acts (like crossing the falls on a high wire) for short-term fame. The **Daredevil Museum** (call (716) 282-4046) features stunting memorabilia. For your own adventurous outing, take a speedboat ride through the canyon downriver of the falls. The boat travels among the rapids and into a legendary whirlpool; contact Niagara Jet Boating, 115 S. Water Street, Lewiston; (888) 438-4444; www.whirlpool-jet.com.

Other interesting exhibition spots include the New York Power Authority's **Niagara Power Project Visitors Center** (call (716) 286-6661), set four miles downriver from the falls, where the hands-on exhibits focus on energy, electricity, and history, and the **Schoellkopf Geological Museum** (call (716) 278-1780), where the 12,000-year history of the falls are revealed, as is a stunning gorge view. For a city park in a small city, **Hyde Park** is huge. And it's got it all: picnicking, swimming and wading pools, bocce courts, volleyball courts, baseball fields, indoor ice skating, a play area, hiking/nature trails, tennis, a golf course, an indoor golf center, and fishing. Some activities have fees. It's on Route 62 and Robbins Drive in Niagara Falls (call (716) 286-4956).

Family Lodging

BUFFALO

Adam's Mark Buffalo

Although this 483-room hotel focuses primarily on business travelers, it's an excellent choice for families. It features an indoor pool, a kid-friendly restaurant, and a convenient location near the Naval & Military Park, baseball stadium, and sight-seeing cruises. The hotel offers special Summer Fun packages that combine lodging, breakfast buffet, and tickets to specific attractions, such as a Buffalo Bisons baseball game, a Niagara Falls tour, or entrance to Darien Lake Six Flags Amusement Park.120 Church Street, Buffalo; (716) 845-5100 or (800) 444-2326); fax (716) 845-5100; www.adamsmark.com. Rates $76–125 and up.

Radisson Suites Hotel Downtown

The Radisson is just steps from the theater district and offers easy access to the Metro Rail trolley line, which can take you to the hockey arena, Naval Park, and cruise boats. The Radisson offers 146 suites with refrigerators, in-room coffee makers, dining table, and multiple TVs. No pool is available, however. A continental breakfast is included at an on-site T.G.I. Fridays. 601 Main Street, Buffalo; (716) 854-5500 or (800) 333-3333; fax (716) 854-4836; www.radisson-dt.afterfive.com. Rates $76–125 and up.

NIAGARA FALLS

Ramada Inn

Within walking distance of the falls, this 112-room Ramada offers a heated indoor pool, an on-site restaurant, and a kids-stay-free policy. 219 Fourth Street, Niagara Falls; (800) 333-2557 or (716) 282-1734; fax (716) 282-1881. Rates: $49–169.

Also worth considering are: Quality Inn, 433 Main Street, Niagara Falls, (800) 777-2280 or (716) 284-8801; or Howard Johnson, 454 Main Street, Niagara Falls, (800) 282-5261 or (716) 285-5261.

Attractions

BUFFALO

Buffalo & Erie County Naval & Military Park

One Naval Park Cove, Buffalo; (716) 847-1773;
   www.buffalonavalpark.org

Hours: April–October, daily 10 a.m.–5 p.m.; November, Saturday–Sunday 10 a.m.–5 p.m.

Admission: $6 adults, $3.50 children (6–16) and seniors, free for ages 5 and under; extra charges for Harrier Jet Simulator, $3, and Interactive Helicopter Simulator, $1

Appeal by Age Groups:

Pre-school	Grade School	Teens	Young Adults	Over 30	Seniors
★★★	★★★★	★★★★	★★★★	★★★	★★★★★

Touring Time: Average 3½ hours; minimum 1½ hour

Rainy-Day Touring: Yes

Services and Facilities:

Restaurants Yes; snack bar	Baby stroller rental No
Alcoholic beverages No	Lockers No
Disabled access Yes; to museum and cruiser	Pet kennels No
	Rain check No
Wheelchair rental No	Private tours No

Description and Comments   This is the largest inland park of its kind in the country, and the collection of ships makes it fascinating. Moored here are the guided missile cruiser USS *Little Rock,* the destroyer USS *The Sullivans,* and the submarine USS *Croaker,* all dating from World War II. Start by viewing the ten-minute introductory video and the accompanying tape that gives the submarine's history. The videos, shown three times an hour on the main floor, include some interesting footage from original Movietone News and from the 20th Century Fox film *The Fighting Sullivans.* Then you follow the yellow lines and white arrows to tour the ships and grounds. Everything on and in the ships is well marked and explained, making exploration easy and fun.

Buffalo Museum of Science

1020 Humboldt Parkway, Buffalo; (716) 896-5200; www.sciencebuff.org

Hours: Tuesday–Sunday, 10 a.m.–5 p.m.; Friday evenings until 10 p.m. from September–May

Admission: $5.25 adults, $3.25 children, seniors (62 and older), and students, free for children under 3

Appeal by Age Groups:

Pre-school	Grade School	Teens	Young Adults	Over 30	Seniors
★★	★★★★	★★★	★★★	★★★★	★★★★

Touring Time: Average 2½ hours; minimum 1½ hour

Rainy-Day Touring: Yes

Services and Facilities:

Restaurants No; vending machines available	Lockers No
	Pet kennels No
Alcoholic beverages No	Rain check No
Disabled access Yes	Private tours Yes; call Education
Wheelchair rental No	Department at ext. 338
Baby stroller rental No	

Description and Comments   Attached to a magnet school and housed in a grand old building, this science museum mixes traditional exhibits with the occasional modern interactive display. Of the permanent collection, "Whem

Ankh: The Cycle of Life in Ancient Egypt" stands out. It's a walk-through experience in which you pass through a re-created courtyard and house in the style along the Nile at the time and also through a section of a temple and the house of the dead. Along the way, visitors meet two mummies and a magnificently decorated 2,700-year-old coffin. The Tibetan Mandala on the third floor is the only such sand painting on permanent display in North America. Chant-infused music plays in the background and an accompanying video shows the painting being created. The Summer Science Circus offers daily hands-on activities aimed at 3- to 12-year-olds.

Buffalo Zoological Gardens

300 Parkside Avenue, Buffalo; (716) 837-3900

Hours: June 1–Labor Day, daily 10 a.m.–5 p.m.; after Labor Day–May 31, daily 10 a.m.–4 p.m; closed Thanksgiving and Christmas days.

Admission: $6 adults, $3 children ages 3–14 and seniors (65+), free for ages 2 and under; parking is $3

Appeal by Age Groups:

Pre-school	Grade School	Teens	Young Adults	Over 30	Seniors
★★★★★	★★★★	★★★	★★★	★★★	★★★

Touring Time: Average 4 hours; minimum 3 hours

Rainy-Day Touring: Yes

Services and Facilities:

Restaurants Yes	Lockers No
Alcoholic beverages Yes; wine and beer	Pet kennels No
	Rain check No
Disabled access Yes	Private tours Yes; request one
Wheelchair rental Yes; free	month ahead
Baby stroller rental Yes; free	

Description and Comments   Everybody loves a zoo, and this one is a wonderfully approachable size—great for younger children. It does suffer from some antiquated displays. Docents take up stations throughout the park with "safari carts," wheeled treasure chests that contain hands-on activities and hands-on items that allow kids personal attention and involvement. A band of Conversation Clowns roams the grounds, creating a raucous and fun atmosphere. Puppet shows and live animal shows are staged during summer. The children's zoo has recently been renovated, and the fun walk-through exhibit in the reptile house changes often. Little ones will want to ride the miniature train and the carousel. The zoo is set in Delaware Park, which makes it ideal for a daylong outing of outdoor activities (see The Best Beaches and Parks on page 310).

Explore & More A Children's Museum

430 Main Street, East Aurora; (716) 655-5131

Hours: Wednesday–Saturday 10 a.m.–4 p.m.

Admission: $2 adults, $3 children

Appeal by Age Groups:

Pre-school	Grade School	Teens	Young Adults	Over 30	Seniors
★★★★★	★★★★	★	★	★	★

Touring Time: Average 2½ hours; minimum 1 hour

Rainy-Day Touring: Yes

Services and Facilities:

Restaurants No	Lockers No
Alcoholic beverages No	Pet kennels No
Disabled access Yes	Rain check No
Wheelchair rental No	Private tours No
Baby stroller rental No	

Description and Comments A 20-minute ride south of downtown Buffalo, this site calls itself a museum, but it's more like a play center with an educational theme that changes yearly. Past themes have been "Food" and "Japan." The theme for 2001 is "Games People Play." Explore & More's combination of simplicity (no magical electronics here) and professionally executed activity equipment is charming and terrific. The museum is conceived for children ages 1 to 10, and each room is aimed at certain age groups. Explore & More is located in the basement of an elementary school, but in 2001 it expects to relocate within town to a much larger space that will allow more themes.

A visit to Explore & More can be combined with a field excursion to nearby **Fisher-Price** headquarters, where a large store sells almost anything current in the company's line, and the adjacent **Toy Town Museum** (636 Girard Avenue, East Aurora; (716) 687-5151; www.toytownusa.com). The Toy Town Museum displays Fisher-Price toys dating from 1930, along with other old-time playthings. Augment that with a trip downtown to **Vidler's 5 & 10 Cent Store** (680-694 Main Street, East Aurora; (716) 652-0481). Family-owned since 1930 and set in an 1890s building, Vidler's is a functioning, old-fashioned five-and-dime/general store, right down to the wood plank floors.

NIAGARA FALLS

Aquarium of Niagara

701 Whirlpool Street, Niagara Falls; (800) 500-4609 or (716) 285-3575; www.niagaranet.com/niagara/aquarium

Hours: Memorial Day–Labor Day, daily 9 a.m.–7 p.m.; Labor
   Day–Memorial Day, daily 9 a.m.–5 p.m.

Admission: $6.50 adults, $4.50 seniors and children ages 4–12; free for
   ages 3 and under

Appeal by Age Groups:

Pre- school	Grade School	Teens	Young Adults	Over 30	Seniors
★★★★★	★★★★★	★★★★	★★★★	★★★★	★★★★★

Touring Time: Average 2 hours; minimum 1 hour

Rainy-Day Touring: Yes

Services and Facilities:

Restaurants	No	Lockers	No
Alcoholic beverages	No	Pet kennels	No
Disabled access	Yes	Rain check	No
Wheelchair rental	No	Private tours	No
Baby stroller rental	No		

Description and Comments   This is a small but enjoyable aquarium.
You're greeted by a colony of endangered Peruvian penguins (so fun they
can be watched for hours). Their twice-daily feedings (9:30 a.m. and 2:30
p.m.) are a treat. The sharks get fed once every other day at 11:30 a.m.,
and the harbor seals, located in the outdoor pool, chow down daily at 11
a.m. and 3:45 p.m. At each feeding, the animals' keepers are available to
share information. A troop (or is it a pride?) of California sea lions performs every 90 minutes. Altogether, the aquarium holds 1,500 aquatic
animals in a very kid-friendly environment. Parking is free—a good
thing to know in high season when parking gets tight. From here, you can
cross the pedestrian bridge to board the Viewmobile to access the Niagara
Falls park.

Maid of the Mist

151 Buffalo Avenue, Niagara Falls; (716) 284-8897;
   www.maidofthemist.com

Hours: April–mid-May, weekdays 10 a.m.–5 p.m. and weekends 10
   a.m.–6 p.m.; Victoria Day weekend (late May) 10 a.m.–8 p.m.;
   Memorial Day weekend 9:15 a.m.–8 p.m.; May 30–last weekend in
   June, daily 10 a.m.–6 p.m.; late June–first weekend in August, daily
   9:15 a.m.–8 p.m.; remainder of August–Labor Day, daily 9:15
   a.m.–7:30 p.m.; Labor Day–October closing date, weekdays 10
   a.m.–5 p.m. and weekends 10 a.m.–6 p.m.

Admission: $8.50 adults, $4.80 children ages 6–12, free for ages 5 and
   under; elevator fee, 50¢ extra

Appeal by Age Groups:

Pre-school	Grade School	Teens	Young Adults	Over 30	Seniors
★★★★	★★★★	★★★★★	★★★★★	★★★★★	★★★★★

Touring Time: Average 30 minutes; minimum 30 minutes

Rainy-Day Touring: Yes

Services and Facilities:

Restaurants No	Lockers No
Alcoholic beverages No	Pet kennels No
Disabled access Yes	Rain check No
Wheelchair rental No	Private tours No
Baby stroller rental No	

Description and Comment   Maid of the Mist is a traditional tourist "must" that's been in operation since 1846. The narrated ride aboard a steel double-decker ship takes you to the base of American Falls and into the ring of Horshoe Falls. Rain slickers are provided. It's good for everyone, but preschoolers might be frightened by the noise and force of the water. On the U.S. side, visitors should board at the base of the observation tower at Prospect Point. When boarding from the Canadian side, go to the Maid of the Mist Plaza elevator at the foot of Clifton Hill.

New York State Park Niagara Reservation

Prospect Park, Niagara Falls; Visitor Center, (716) 278-1796; observation tower, (716) 278-1762; Viewmobile, (716) 278-1730; Cave of the Winds, (716) 278-1730; Goat Island, (716) 278-1762; Master Pass Information, (716) 278-1770

Hours: The park is open daily. Viewmobile and Observation Tower operate seasonally; hours vary

Admission: Buy a Master Pass, good for the Cave of the Winds, Viewmobile, Observation Tower, Aquarium, Schoellkopf Geological Museum, and more sites; $21 adults, $16 children under age 12

Appeal by Age Groups:

Pre-school	Grade School	Teens	Young Adults	Over 30	Seniors
★★★★	★★★★★	★★★★★	★★★★★	★★★★★	★★★★★

Touring Time: Average 4 hours; minimum 2 hours

Rainy-Day Touring: Yes

Services and Facilities:

Restaurants Yes	Wheelchair rental No
Alcoholic beverages Yes	Baby stroller rental No
Disabled access Yes	

Baby stroller rental No	Rain check No
Lockers No	Private tours No
Pet kennels No	

Description and Comments This is the oldest state park in the United States, designed by Frederick Law Olmstead (creator of Central Park). You can start at the visitor center, but on crowded summer days, a good approach is to first visit the aquarium and the geological museum, then to walk across the pedestrian bridge and board the Viewmobile for an overview tour of the park. The Viewmobile travels throughout the park, allowing access to scenic viewpoints, the observation tower, the Maid of the Mist boat ride, and Goat Island, the largest of the mid-river islands. Goat Island has a restaurant, snack bar, picnic tables, and access to Cave of the Winds, where you can walk along the base of Bridal Veil Falls. Don't worry—rain gear is provided. Throughout summertime the park features fireworks and laser shows in the evening, as well as festivals and special events. In winter, the lower river is bridged by ice, and the frozen mist sparkles. Some elements—like the Viewmobile, observation tower, and Cave of the Winds—function only in summer.

Old Fort Niagara

Robert Moses Parkway N., Youngstown; (716) 745-7611;
www.oldfortniagara.org

Hours: Daily 9 a.m.–dusk; closed Christmas, Thanksgiving, and New Year's days

Admission: $6.75 adults, $5.50 seniors (62 and older), $4.50 children ages 6–12, free for children under 6

Appeal by Age Groups:

Pre-school	Grade School	Teens	Young Adults	Over 30	Seniors
★★	★★★★	★★★	★★★★	★★★★★	★★★★★

Touring Time: Average 2½ hours; minimum 1½ hour

Rainy-Day Touring: Yes

Services and Facilities:

Restaurants Yes; snack bar	available, free
Alcoholic beverages No	Baby stroller rental No
Disabled access Yes; limited access to upper floors of the historic structures	Lockers No
	Pet kennels No
	Rain check No
Wheelchair rental Yes; one	Private tours No

Description and Comments The fort sits where the Niagara River flows out of Lake Ontario, a strategic military location during colonial days, French/

French Canadian occupation, and throughout the War of 1812. Its history, therefore, bridges a broad range of the North American experience. The introductory 11-minute video gives an excellent overview of just how many historic periods the site has played a role in. The stone fort sitting on the edge of the lake and the many summertime military re-enactments and living history programs highlight any visit. Visitors are often "drafted" into the army to experience life in the 1700s British Army, the Revolutionary American Army, the American Army circa 1812, or the French Army of the French & Indian War during the siege of 1759. Biddle Battle, a combination of cricket and early baseball, is sometimes played, and an ongoing archeological dig operates all summer in the main courtyard.

Family-Friendly Restaurants

BUFFALO

THE BROADWAY MARKET

999 Broadway, Buffalo; (716) 893-2216

Meals served: Breakfast, lunch, and early dinner
Cuisine: A variety
Entree range: A wide range
Children's menu: Not literally
Reservations: No
Payment: Cash at some stands; major credit cards at others

At 100,000 square feet, this is one of the largest indoor markets in the country. It has been around since 1888 and presents a wonderful potpourri of meat and poultry stands, produce counters, bakeries, delis, candy stands, and restaurants. Graze to your heart's content. It's open Monday–Friday 8 a.m.–5 p.m. and Saturday 7 a.m.–5 p.m.; closed Sunday.

GOLDEN MILL RESTAURANT

8348 Boston Colden Road, Colden; (716)941-9357

Meals served: Breakfast, lunch, and dinner
Cuisine: Italian and American
Entree range: $9.95–18.95
Children's menu: Yes
Reservations: Accepted
Payment: All major credit cards

The Golden Mill is set in a feed mill, circa 1830. Its location, while outside Buffalo proper, is convenient to ski areas and to the Explore & More museum. The ambiance is true to the feed mill theme, and the place is filled with early Americana plus some collector's oddities—like a prominently displayed 1925 dentist's chair. In addition to the kids' menu, children can also order from the lighter-fare selections, including choices like an open-face steak sandwich with salad and fries.

POLISH VILLA

2954 Union Street, Cheektowaga; (716) 683-9460

Meals served: Breakfast, lunch, and dinner
Cuisine: Polish
Entree range: $3.65–10.95 (lunch and dinner)
Children's menu: Yes
Reservations: Only for parties of 6 or more
Payment: All major credit cards

Why a Polish restaurant? Because Buffalo is home to a huge Polish population. Here you'll find Polish art and decorations, a casual atmosphere, and a real touch of Poland, about a 20-minute drive east of town on Route 33. Kids will like the pierogi, which are similar to ravioli, while adults may find the kielbasa a savory option. Not to worry—picky eaters can always order steak or seafood.

NIAGARA FALLS

COMO RESTAURANT

220 Pine Avenue, Niagara Falls; (716) 297-7497

Meals served: Lunch and dinner
Cuisine: Italian
Entree range: $3.95–24.95
Children's menu: Yes
Reservations: Yes
Payment: All major credit cards

This landmark eatery has been operating since 1927. It's classic Italian, offering everything from spaghetti to fully gourmet fare such as fillet of sole a la Francesca and clams a la Rocco. Plus, there are an attached deli and, in summer, a custard (soft ice cream) stand. The children's menu is one of the most extensive we've seen, and the staff is super-friendly.

PAGE'S RESTAURANT—HOME OF THE WHISTLE PIG

7001 Packard Road, Niagara Falls; (716) 297-0131

Meals served: Breakfast, lunch, and dinner
Cuisine: American
Entree range: $5–7 (lunch and dinner)
Children's menu: Yes
Reservations: Not normally, but will take them
Payment: V, MC, AE

Just what is a Whistle Pig? It's a cardiovascular-nightmare hot dog, served with bacon and cheese. You don't have to order one, however, as the place offers a full American menu. The soft ice cream, or custard as the locals say, is pretty darned good, too. For summer visitors, there are kiddie rides operating just outside the door.

Side Trip: Chautauqua Institution

The Chautauqua Institution can't be categorized—it's a resort, a learning center, an arts festival, a National Historic Landmark. For nine weeks, beginning in late June and running through August, the place comes alive with performances, workshops, seminars, children's programs, lectures, and all kinds of recreational activities. For kids, in addition to workshops in the arts and sciences, the Children's School functions as an early childhood center for ages three to five. Group One is an all-day program designed for those entering first grade; and Boys' and Girls' Clubs serve kids from second grade through tenth grade, with activities ranging from swimming, music, and arts, to sports and nature study. A Family Entertainment Series takes place on Tuesday evening. The complex inlcudes tennis courts, a golf course, and four public beaches.

Rates: weekly lodging from $85–2,800; hotel rooms, $217–317, American Plan; children's programs $95–115 per week. It's located about 70 miles south of Buffalo in the far southwestern corner of the state. P.O. Box 28, One Ames Avenue, Chautauqua, 14722; (800)-836-2787) or (716) 357-6250; www.ciweb.org.

Rochester

Rochester, like so many upstate New York cities, began as a mill town, using the Genesee River to generate power. By the end of the nineteenth century, men's clothing and horticulture had been added to the city's list of major industries. The twentieth century brought the Eastman Kodak Company, and today the city can thank Kodak's founder, George Eastman, for providing a great range of gardens, parks, and green spaces. Begin at **High Falls** (call (716) 325-2030), located in the heart of the town's historic district. The **Center at High Falls Museum** distributes tourist information and presents a look at the city's history, including fun interactive exhibits. A few shops and restaurants invite exploration. Wander onto the **Pont-de-Rennes Pedestrian Bridge** from which you not only view the falls, but also, in summer, watch the laser light show and fireworks. Nearby, in the heart of downtown, you'll find the **Frederick Douglass Museum & Cultural Center** (call (716) 546-3960), where interactive and historical exhibits depict the great abolitionist's history and other aspects of African-American culture. **Pittsford,** a small town southwest of Rochester, provides excellent access to the Erie Canal and offers a number of outdoor activities, some shopping, and dining. To reach Pittsford take Route 31, an extension of Chestnut Street, or I-590 Exit 2. The **Erie Canal** provides a variety of recreational opportunities, from walking, jogging, and cycling along the banks, to canoeing and taking boat rides on the water. The *Sam Patch Tour Boat* is a re-created canal packet vessel that cruises the upper Genesse River and the Erie Canal; Schoen Place, Pittsford (call (716) 262-5661). The *Fairport Lady* is an open-air, double-decker paddle-wheeler that cruises from Fairport to Pittsford; 10 Liftbridge Lane W., Fairport (call (716) 223-1930). Both boats offer narrated tours highlighting Rochester and Erie Canal history. Lunch and dinner cruises are also offered. Cruise duration and departure times vary seasonally.

Ontario Beach Park offers a swimming beach with a bathhouse, a playground, concessions, a 1905 carousel, basketball and volleyball courts,

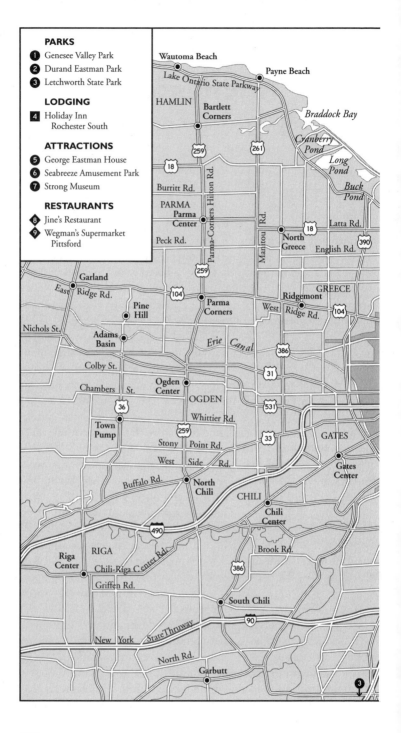

PARKS
1. Genesee Valley Park
2. Durand Eastman Park
3. Letchworth State Park

LODGING
4. Holiday Inn
   Rochester South

ATTRACTIONS
5. George Eastman House
6. Seabreeze Amusement Park
7. Strong Museum

RESTAURANTS
8. Jine's Restaurant
9. Wegman's Supermarket
   Pittsford

Wautoma Beach

Payne Beach

Lake Ontario State Parkway

HAMLIN

Bartlett Corners

Braddock Bay

259

261

Cranberry Pond

18

Long Pond

Burritt Rd.

Buck Pond

PARMA

Parma Center

Latta Rd.

18

Peck Rd.

North Greece

English Rd.

390

259

Garland

GREECE

East Ridge Rd.

104

Parma Corners

Ridgemont

West Ridge Rd.

104

Pine Hill

Nichols St.

Adams Basin

Erie Canal

386

Colby St.

31

Chambers St.

Ogden Center

OGDEN

531

36

Whittier Rd.

GATES

Town Pump

259

Stony Point Rd.

33

Gates Center

West Side Rd.

Buffalo Rd.

North Chili

CHILI

490

Chili Center

RIGA

Brook Rd.

Riga Center

Chili-Riga Center Rd.

386

Griffen Rd.

South Chili

90

New York State Thruway

North Rd.

Garbutt

3

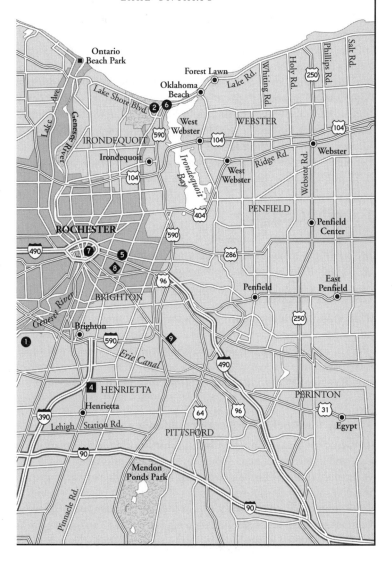

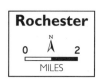
LAKE ONTARIO

Ontario
Beach Park

Forest Lawn

Oklahoma
Beach

Lake Shore Blvd

Lake Rd.

Whiting Rd.

Holy Rd.

Phillips Rd.

Salt Rd.

250

West
Webster

WEBSTER

104

IRONDEQUOIT

590

104

Irondequoit

Genesee River

Lake Ave.

104

West
Webster

Ridge Rd.

Webster Rd.

Webster

Irondequoit Bay

404

PENFIELD

ROCHESTER

590

286

Penfield
Center

490

7

5

8

96

Penfield

East
Penfield

BRIGHTON

Genesee River

250

Brighton

590

1

Erie Canal

9

490

HENRIETTA

PERINTON

4

Henrietta

390

64

96

31

Egypt

Lehigh Station Rd.

PITTSFORD

90

Pinnacle Rd.

Mendon
Ponds Park

90

Wednesday evening concerts in the gazebo, and a pier walkway out to a lighthouse. The **Charlotte-Genesee Lighthouse and Keeper's Residence Museum** in Ontario Beach Park (call (716) 621-6179) can be visited from mid-May to mid-October on Saturday and Sunday afternoons. The **Seneca Park Zoo** (call (716) 467-9453) is set in a beautiful greenspace that sits alongside the river. For a combination of history and nature, drive to Caledonia, about 20 miles west of town, to visit the **Genesee Country Village & Museum** (call (716) 538-6822), a vibrant living history museum. Equidistant from Rochester and Buffalo in Darien Center, about a 45-minute drive, is **Six Flags Darien Lake** (call (716) 599-4641). Six Flags offers a full range of thrill rides, entertainment, and kid stuff, plus a full-service resort hotel, restaurant, and large campground complete with rental RVs. **Durand Eastman Park** on Lakeshore Boulevard (call (716) 342-9810) borders the Lake Ontario shoreline in Rochester. Enjoy easy walking and bicycling along the Erie Canal Heritage Trail's old towpaths and along the Genesee River Trail, where fine city skyline and riverside views are revealed. For public transportation, the Regional Transit System buses (call (888) 288-3777 or (716) 288-1700) reach many attractions in Rochester.

Family Lodging

For comprehensive Rochester-area accommodations with customized package deals involving attractions, amusements, and events, call toll free (877) 386-4676, or visit the website: www.rochgetaway.com.

Crowne Plaza Rochester

This 362-room luxury property lies in the heart of downtown and features an outdoor pool and two on-site restaurants. Rooms come with two telephones, a coffee maker, an iron and full-size ironing board, a clock radio, a large work desk, a hair dryer, and a complimentary *USA Today* newspaper. Rates are $99–155; children age 18 and under stay free. 70 State Street, Rochester; (800) 243-7760 or (716) 546-3450.

Holiday Inn Rochester South/Holidome

This property centers on a large atrium that holds an indoor pool, a game area, and its own restaurant. Rooms are large and comfortable, with in-room coffee makers, ironing boards, and cable TV. Although it's located about ten minutes south of downtown Rochester, it's a pleasant place where kids can roam around safely. Rates are $69–128. Weekender rates are available with coupons redeemable towards breakfast. Children ages 12 and under stay and eat from children's menu for free. 1111 Jefferson Road, Henrietta; (716) 475-1510; fax (716) 427-8673; www.basshotels.com/holiday-inn.

Strathallan Hotel

This all-suite hotel is conveniently located in Rochester's museum, cultural, theatre, and arts district. It holds 156 studio, one-bedroom, and apartment-size suites. Most suites feature microwaves, and some have kitchenettes. An on-site restaurant adds to the convenience. Rates are $125–200. 550 East Avenue, Rochester; (800) 678-7284 or (716) 461-5010.

Attractions

George Eastman House

900 East Avenue, Rochester; (716) 271-3361; www.eastman.org

Hours: Tuesday–Wednesday and Friday–Saturday 10 a.m.–4:30 p.m., Sunday 1–4:30 p.m., Thursday 10 a.m.–8 p.m.; closed Mondays and Thanksgiving, Christmas, and New Year's days; during May, open daily 10 a.m.–4:30 p.m.

Admission: $6.50 adults, $5 seniors (60 and older), $2.50 children, free for children under age 4

Appeal by Age Groups:

Pre-school	Grade School	Teens	Young Adults	Over 30	Seniors
★★★	★★★★	★★★★	★★★★★	★★★★★	★★★★★

Touring Time: Average 3 hours; minimum 1½ hour

Rainy-Day Touring: Yes

Services and Facilities:

Restaurants Yes	Lockers No
Alcoholic beverages No	Pet kennels No
Disabled access No	Rain check No
Wheelchair rental No	Private tours No
Baby stroller rental No	

Description and Comments   George Eastman, in 1881, perfected dry-plate photography, a breakthrough that led to the "Brownie" camera, which allowed photos to be taken by just about anyone. This museum, set in Eastman's house, is dedicated not only to photography and film, but also to the performing arts, film preservation, and to displaying Eastman's magnificent gardens. The kids' highlight is the second-floor Discovery Room, a hands-on science/photo lab place where kids can learn both modern and historic photo techniques. Docents are on hand to help kids make a Thaumatrope (an 1826 invention that moves two pictures together to look like one), a Zoetrope (one of those cylinders with the slots that make pictures move when spun), and several other historical photo and moving-picture devices. There's even a working darkroom and a hologram demo. The museum's historical photograph exhibits and permanent and changing galleries probably will only appeal to older kids and teens, but the technology collection, which contains more than 15,000 pieces of camera equipment including 6,000 still cameras, is arresting.

Tours are offered at 10:30 a.m. and 2 p.m. (2 p.m. only on Sundays). Self-guiding tour materials are available throughout the museum. A Sunday Musicale Series (at 3 p.m.) continues Mr. Eastman's personal tradition of hosting live musical performances. Two movie theaters screen contemporary and classic films six times a week.

Seabreeze Amusement Park & Raging Rivers Water Park

4600 Culver Road, Rochester; (800) 395-2500 or (716) 323-1900

Hours: Amusement park open daily mid-June–Labor Day, Sunday–Thursday noon–10 p.m., Friday–Saturday noon–11 p.m.; open weekends only from mid-May–mid-June. Water park open from mid-May–mid-June daily 11 a.m.–8 p.m., and weekends only from mid-May–mid-June

Admission: $14.50 adult Ride and Slide pass, $10.50 for children under 48 inches tall, $8.95 after 5 p.m., free for ages under 2; $5.95 Admission Plus Pass includes two ride tickets

Appeal by Age Groups:

Pre-school	Grade School	Teens	Young Adults	Over 30	Seniors
★★★★★	★★★★★	★★★★★	★★★★★	★★★★	★★★★

Touring Time: Average 6 hours; minimum 3 hours

Rainy-Day Touring: No

Services and Facilities:

Restaurants Yes	Lockers No
Alcoholic beverages Yes	Pet kennels No
Disabled access Yes	Rain check No
Wheelchair rental No	Private tours No
Baby stroller rental No	

Description and Comments   Seabreeze is an old-fashioned amusement park that's family-friendly in size, but holds enough thrills and pizzazz to amuse everyone. This park opened in 1879 and has been operated by the same family since 1903. It maintains a Victorian feel while offering a modern experience. Roller-coaster junkies will appreciate the 1920 Jack Rabbit wooden coaster as well as the state-of-the-art Quantum Loop. There's a thing called the Screamin' Eagle that whirls you around and turns you upside down 70 feet in the air. There's tamer stuff for little ones and chicken-hearted adults. Live animal shows are a hit with the kids. The water park, too, offers full choices for the tame and for thrill-seekers, from wading pools to big-league slides.

Strong Museum

One Manhattan Square, Rochester; (716) 263-2700, (716) 263-2702, or TDD (716)-423-0746; www.strongmuseum.org

Hours: Monday–Thursday 10 a.m.–5 p.m., Friday 10 a.m.–8 p.m., Saturday 10 a.m.–5 p.m., Sunday noon–5 p.m.; closed Thanksgiving, Christmas, and New Year's days

Admission: $6 adults, $5 seniors and students, $4 children ages 3–17, free for ages 3 and under; 50¢ to ride the carousel

Appeal by Age Groups:

Pre-school	Grade School	Teens	Young Adults	Over 30	Seniors
★★★★★	★★★★★	★★★	★★★	★★★★	★★★★

Touring Time: Average 4 hours; minimum 2 hours

Rainy-Day Touring: Yes

Services and Facilities:

Restaurants Yes	Baby stroller rental Yes; free
Alcoholic beverages Yes; beer and wine	Lockers Yes
	Pet kennels No
Disabled access Yes	Rain check No
Wheelchair rental Yes; free	Private tours No

Description and Comments This may be the mother of all kids' museums. And—especially for younger children—one visit will probably not be enough. Margaret Woodbury Strong was an inveterate collector of, well, just about everything. She amassed one of the world's most comprehensive collections of dolls and dollhouses—and almost anything else you could think of. The museum houses more than 500,000 objects—toys, dollhouses, miniatures, household furnishings, and more. It has also developed into one of the most active, hands-on places anywhere. Pass the ticket booth and you find yourself on Sesame Street, right there on the stoop of old Number 123. Kids can play with the Muppets, and several exhibits allow them to make their own TV show (bring your own video tape or buy one in the gift shop). Other exhibits include a miniaturized supermarket, One History Place, where children experience life a century ago; and Kid-to-Kid, a look at a wide variety of communication tools from tin cans to helicopter radios. Upstairs, the museum aims at an older audience, with Time Lab, a huge warehouse/laboratory filled with objects from different decades of the American twentieth century, plus the doll collection.

Amidst the hurley-burley, small reading nooks can be discovered where kids and adults can take a book time-out. How good is the Strong Museum? We'd go to Rochester just to visit it, even if we did nothing else.

Family-Friendly Restaurants

JINE'S RESTAURANT

658 Park Avenue, Rochester; (716) 461-1280

Meals served: Breakfast, lunch, and dinner
Cuisine: Greek, Italian, American, and specialties
Entree range: $8.45–13.95 (lunch and dinner)
Children's menu: Yes
Reservations: No; but call ahead for parties of six or more
Payment: Major credit cards

Jine's is a local, family-owned restaurant that's been a neighborhood landmark for two generations. There's nothing remarkable about the decor or ambiance, but this is the kind of place where your kids can order grilled cheese and you can get spectacular seafood. It's a neighborhood favorite for breakfast as well.

WEGMANS SUPERMARKET PITTSFORD

3195 Monroe Avenue, Rochester; (716) 586-6680

Meals served: Lunch and dinner
Cuisine: Eclectic
Entree range: $3.95-12.95
Children's menu: No, but plenty of kid-food
Reservations: No
Payment: Major credit cards

Dinner at a supermarket? We can see parents turning green and queasy at the very thought. But this is different. The store is huge, and it has an entire section reserved as a kind of combination cafeteria/cafe. You can order fresh entrees like pepper chicken or Etruscan salmon; nosh on epicurean sandwiches liked grilled Portobello; buy prepared meals microwaved on the spot; or let the kids eat subs, burgers, or pizza. The cafe tables are set on two levels, and the whole experience is fun and rather unlike anything we've ever seen in a supermarket.

Syracuse

Syracuse is a university town, and Syracuse University is its main driving force today. Salt, however, was once its reason for being, and this was the major salt-producing area in the country. To find the city's major visitor attractions, follow the **Syracuse Discovery Trail** road signs posted on major roadways. The trail consists of the **Erie Canal Museum** (call (315) 471-0593), the **Onondaga Historical Association Museum** (call (315) 428-1864), the **Museum of Science & Technology (MOST)** (call (315) 425-0747), the **Everson Museum of Art** (call (315) 474-6064), the **Burnet Park Zoo** (call (315) 435-8511), the **Salt Museum** (call (315) 453-6715), and **Sainte Marie among the Iroquois Living History Museum** (call (315) 453-6767). The Canal Museum (open from May through October) has a unique Weightlock Building, a restored barge weigh station, along with live theatrical representations of the time and an educational gallery. The Everson Museum of Art contains one of the best hands-on kids' galleries we've encountered. The Salt Museum, located in Onondaga Lake Park, reconstructs the old brine (salt water) boiling process. **Onondaga Lake Park** on Roberts Avenue (call (315) 473-4330) closes its four-lane lakeside Parkway to vehicles on summer weekends and welcomes cyclists, in-line skaters, and joggers. Its East Shore Recreation Trail is open year-round. Canoes, in-line skates, and bikes can be rented at the park's west end.

Sports fans should visit the **Carrier Dome,** home to Syracuse University's football and basketball teams; guided tours can be arranged by appointment. **Armory Square** is alive with trendy shops, restaurants, galleries, and a couple of pizza places that are favorites among local teens. The Armory Square area is also the terminus for the **OnTrack** (call (800) 367-8724) train, a line that runs to the University campus and to **Carousel Center,** one of the East's largest shopping malls.

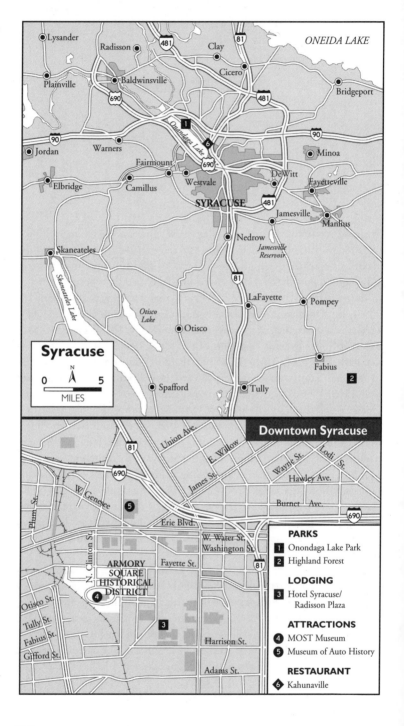

ONEIDA LAKE

Lysander
Radisson
Clay
81
481
Cicero
Plainville
Baldwinsville
Bridgeport
690
Onondaga Lake
1
6
Jordan
Warners
Minoa
Fairmount
90
690
Elbridge
Camillus
Westvale
DeWitt
Fayetteville
SYRACUSE
481
Skaneateles
Nedrow
Jamesville
Manlius
Jamesville
Reservoir
Skaneateles Lake
Otisco
Lake
81
LaFayette
Pompey

Syracuse

0   N   5
MILES

Otisco

Fabius

2

Spafford
Tully

Downtown Syracuse

Union Ave.
81
E. Willow
690
Wayne St.
Lodi St.
James St.
Hawley Ave.
W. Genesee
5
Burnet Ave.
690
Erie Blvd.
W. Water St.
Washington St.
81
ARMORY
SQUARE
HISTORICAL
DISTRICT
Fayette St.
Otisco St.
4
Tully St.
Fabius St.
3
Gifford St.
Harrison St.
Adams St.

PARKS
1 Onondaga Lake Park
2 Highland Forest

LODGING
3 Hotel Syracuse/
Radisson Plaza

ATTRACTIONS
4 MOST Museum
5 Museum of Auto History

RESTAURANT
6 Kahunaville

Family Lodging

Many major chains can be found clustered on Buckley Road at 7th North Street in the Liverpool section, an area about 10 minutes northwest from downtown that's convenient to the huge Carousel Center shopping mall and to Onondaga Lake. Among the options: Econo Lodge Liverpool, 401 7th North Street, (315) 451-6000; Homewood Suites-Liverpool, 275 Elwood Davis Road, (315) 451-3800; and Hampton Inn, 417 7th North Street, (315) 457-9900. The following is recommended for in-town lodging.

Hotel Syracuse/Radisson Plaza

A 420-room hotel in a landmark building in the heart of town within walking distance of Armory Square, OnTrack, and Clinton Square, site of many summer festivals. Indoor pool and two restaurants. Rates range from $89-105; $129 Family Magic price, includes full breakfast for a family of four. 500 S. Warren Street, Syracuse; (315) 422–5121 or (800) 333-3333; fax (315) 422-3440; www.radisson.com.

Attractions

MOST Milton J. Rubenstein Museum of Science & Technology

500 S. Franklin Street, Syracuse; (315) 425-0747; www.most.org

Hours: Monday–Friday 11 a.m.–5 p.m., Saturday–Sunday 9:30 a.m.–
5 p.m.; closed Thanksgiving and Christmas days

Admission: Museum: $4.75 adults, $3.75 children under age 12 and
seniors (62 and older); Omnitheater and Museum Combination:
$9.75 adults, $7.75 children under age 12 and seniors (62 and older);
add $1 for planetarium admission

Appeal by Age Groups:

Pre-school	Grade School	Teens	Young Adults	Over 30	Seniors
★★	★★★★★	★★★★	★★★★	★★★	★★★★★

Touring Time: Average 2 hours (not including Omnitheater); minimum
1 hour

Rainy-Day Touring: Yes

Services and Facilities:

Restaurants No	Lockers No
Alcoholic beverages No	Pet kennels No
Disabled access Yes	Rain check No
Wheelchair rental No	Private tours No
Baby stroller rental No	

Description and Comments   Set in a converted armory, MOST is a wide-open place where kids can do a lot of hands-on science stuff. The IMAX theater is the only domed IMAX in New York state. Among the permanent exhibits: The History of Computation, Computers and Mathematics, The Science Arcade, and The Story of Earth. The planetarium is relatively small—50 seats and a 24-foot dome—but the shows, presented daily at 4 p.m., are worthwhile and include such topics as When Stars Were Alive and Native American Myths and Astronomy. A special star and slide show geared to preschool through second graders plays at 10:30 a.m. on Saturdays and school holidays.

The Museum of Automobile History

321 N. Clinton Street, Syracuse; (315) 478-2277;
www.autolit.com/Museum

Hours: Wednesday–Sunday 10 a.m.–5 p.m.; closed Monday, Tuesday, and major holidays

Admission: $4.75 adults, $3.75 seniors (65 and older), $2.75 children under age 16

Appeal by Age Groups:

Pre-school	Grade School	Teens	Young Adults	Over 30	Seniors
★★	★★★★	★★★★	★★★★	★★★★★	★★★★★

Touring Time: Average 2 hours; minimum 1 hour

Rainy-Day Touring: Yes

Services and Facilities:

Restaurants No	Lockers No; coat rack in winter
Alcoholic beverages No	Pet kennels No
Disabled access No	Rain check No
Wheelchair rental No	Private tours No
Baby stroller rental No	

Description and Comments   This museum bills itself as "the largest museum of its kind in the world." What kind is that? Everything auto—from old cars and memorabilia to classic radio and TV ads and Burma Shave roadside signs. More than 10,000 objects are housed in this cavernous place, including a history of the automobile dating back to the 1770s.

Family-Friendly Restaurants

DANZER'S RESTAURANT

153 Ainsley Drive, Syracuse; (315) 422-0089

Meals served: Lunch and dinner
Cuisine: German and American
Entree range: $9.95-19.95
Children's menu: Yes
Reservations: Yes
Payment: Major credit cards

This German-American restaurant features classics like sauerbraten or Jäger Schnitzel but will allow you to fall back on steaks, honey-dipped fried chicken, roast turkey, and other traditional American fare. Very friendly service and most hospitable to kids, who can eat burgers or dogs if they must.

KAHUNAVILLE

Carousel Center Mall, 9090 Carousel Center, Syracuse; (315) 422-4500

Meals served: Lunch and dinner
Cuisine: American with touches of Caribbean and Asian
Entree range: $6.50-9.99
Children's menu: Yes
Reservations: No
Payment: Major credit cards

A regional chain set in a shopping mall—all the wrong ingredients. But kids will love it. The decor theme is tropical rainforest, and the ambiance is pure overkill. Talking trees, a dancing fountain, a huge arcade, plus all kinds of food children love.

SARATOGA STEAKS AND SEAFOOD

200 Waring Road, DeWitt; (315) 445-1976

Meals served: Lunch and dinner
Cuisine: American
Entree range: $11.95-29.95
Children's menu: Yes
Reservations: Yes
Payment: Major credit cards

You have to love the four-sided stone fireplace in the main dining room. And, if you're a steak-lover, you'll love the steaks. There's also lamb, chicken and seafood, as well as fancier items like Beef Wellington and chicken Cordon Bleu. All the steaks, pork chops, chicken, and prime rib are available in two sizes, with two prices. The desserts are fine as well.

THE FLY BY NIGHT COOKIE COMPANY

14541 Francher Avenue, Fair Haven; (315) 947-5588

This is not a restaurant, but it's worth going well out of your way for. We're talking 65 kinds of homemade cookies—and we do mean homemade—plus pastries and pies guaranteed to make your sweet tooth smile. Coffee, tea, and soft drinks, too. Open from 6 a.m.–10 p.m.

Finger Lakes Region

The Finger Lakes region covers a broad area of west-central New York. There are six lakes in all—Canandaigua, Keuka, Seneca, Cayuga, Owasco, and Skaneateles, listed west to east. According to Iroquois legend, the god Manitou decided to reward the Iroquois Confederacy's courage and devotion by bringing some of the Happy Hunting Ground to earth. His hand slipped, however, impressing six fingers into the earth instead of five. Geologists say that multiple glacier movements scraped out the lakes during the ice ages. Whichever story holds true, the region has gained renown for its beauty— you'll find open water, babbling brooks, raging rivers, farmlands, spectacular gorges, and historical towns—plus its plethora of outdoor activities.

Canandaigua Lake sits about 25 miles southeast of Rochester. **Squaw Island,** at the lake's north end, is one of the few islands in all the Finger Lakes. **Canandaigua,** site of **Sonnenberg Gardens** and the **Finger Lakes Performing Arts Center,** lays at the lake's northern tip. **Naples,** at the south end, is home to an 1800s Main Street, Grape Festival, and several wineries. **Keuka Lake** is Y-shaped and offers fantastic views from a 700-foot bluff between its branches. **Seneca Lake,** the deepest and widest of the Finger Lakes, holds a very steep shoreline at its southern end and some spectacular waterfalls at Hector and Lodi Landing. The lake trout fishing is so fine that the National Lake Trout Derby is staged here over Memorial Day weekend. **Seneca Cruise Company** in Geneva cruises on Seneca Lake (call (315) 789-1822 or (800) 756-7269). **Watkins Glen,** at Seneca Lake's southern tip, is the site of the **Watkins Glen International Raceway** (call (607) 535-2481 or visit www.theglen.com), the famous auto-racing track. It's also home to a beautiful gorge, some 19 waterfalls, and the **Farm Sanctuary** (call (607) 583-2225 or visit www.farmsancturay.org), a home to rescued farm animals.

Cayuga Lake may be best known from the Cornell University alma mater, "Far Above Cayuga's Waters." At Ithaca, the lake connects to the Seneca and Cayuga Canal, which itself connects to the Erie Canal north

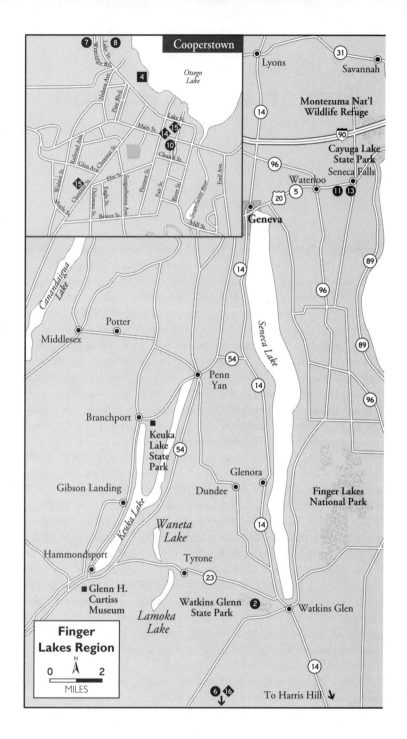

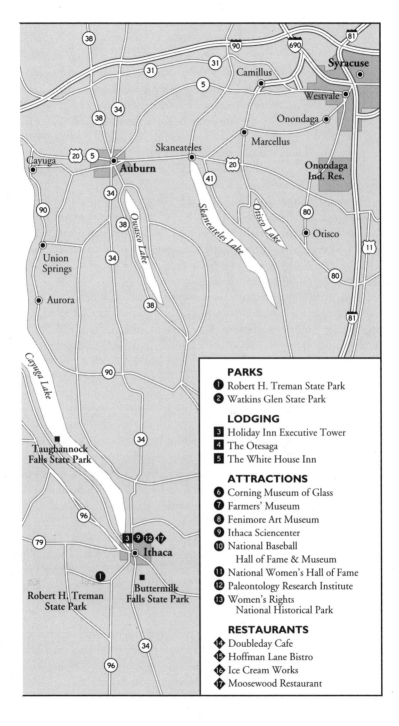

PARKS
1 Robert H. Treman State Park
2 Watkins Glen State Park

LODGING
3 Holiday Inn Executive Tower
4 The Otesaga
5 The White House Inn

ATTRACTIONS
6 Corning Museum of Glass
7 Farmers' Museum
8 Fenimore Art Museum
9 Ithaca Sciencenter
10 National Baseball
   Hall of Fame & Museum
11 National Women's Hall of Fame
12 Paleontology Research Institute
13 Women's Rights
   National Historical Park

RESTAURANTS
14 Doubleday Cafe
15 Hoffman Lane Bistro
16 Ice Cream Works
17 Moosewood Restaurant

of Seneca Falls. The lake is rife with marshlands, extending to the north into the **Montezuma National Wildlife Refuge.** Ithaca sits at the southern end, while **Seneca Falls,** spawning spot for the women's rights movement, is at the north end. **Auburn** anchors the northern end of Owasco Lake. It holds the **Cayuga Museum & Case Research Lab** (call (315) 253-8051), where Theodore Case invented the method for putting sound in films. The water at **Skaneateles Lake** is so pure that it supplies Syracuse and some of its suburbs. **Skaneateles,** its main town, is quaint and rich with historical atmosphere.

Ithaca, a college town that's not only home to Cornell University, but also to Ithaca College, combines the best of small-town America and big college-town sophistication. Downtown is user-friendly, and the plethora of nearby state parks affords much outdoor activity. For scenic cruises on Cayuga Lake at Ithaca, the *M. V. Manhattan* or *Cayuga Breeze* (call (607) 272-4868) give tours and include dinner cruises.

Seneca Falls was used as the prototype town for *It's a Wonderful Life,* the classic Jimmy Stewart movie. But its true claim to fame is its incubating role for the American women's movement, for it was here that the first formal demand for women's rights was made, and the Declaration of Sentiments was presented at Wesleyan Chapel by Elizabeth Cady Stanton, Lucretia Mott, and others. Interestingly, the river was long ago re-routed to accommodate a canal, and the waterfalls that gave the town its name are nowhere to be found. The local historical museum, set in a Fall Street storefront, tells that story very well.

Corning, like many small, upstate New York cities, was shaped by the industrial revolution. In this case, however, it became an international glassmaking center. Who among us has not owned a piece of Corningware or hasn't wanted to own some original Steuben glass? In addition to the Corning Museum of Glass, the town holds a number of glass artists' studios. If it's about glass, Corning's the place.

Cooperstown is between the Finger Lakes and Adirondacks. The town, of course, is famous for being the home of the Baseball Hall of Fame. And that alone commands a visit. For any parent or kid who has ever swung a bat, threw a curve ball, or made a backhand grab, Cooperstown is a must. One of our more memorable family outings was a three-generation, all-male Cooperstown pilgrimage highlighted not by the Hall itself, but by a major whiffle ball game staged on the Hall's back lawn. But, there's more to this village than baseball. There's deep-rooted and well-preserved history here. There's beautiful **Lake Ostego** that can be explored by renting a boat or taking a leisurely cruise with **Lake Ostego Boat Tours** (call (607) 547-5295). There's even, in summertime, the world-class **Glimmerglass Opera**

(call (607) 547-2255) just a few miles up the road. Cooperstown is classic small-town America, and it's as magical as a game-winning home run. For that rainy-day swim, fun workout, or aerobics class, the **Clark Sports Center** (call (607) 547-2800) has facilities and activities for all. Parking in town is very limited. If you're only coming into Cooperstown for the day—or if you're staying out of the downtown area—be sure to take advantage of the **Cooperstown Trolley.** It operates from three parking lots on main routes just outside of town (marked by blue signs), costs only $2 for adults and $1 for children for all-day access, and it stops at all the major attractions.

Family Lodging

Holiday Inn Executive Tower

Set in the heart of Ithaca just a block from the Commons, this hotel features an indoor pool and on-site restaurant, but it's the location that works the most for us. Rates range from $61-85. 222 S. Cayuga Street, Ithaca; (888) 753-8485 or (607) 272-1000.

The Otesaga

The Grand Dame of Cooperstown lodging, the Otesaga hearkens back to an era when only the well-to-do traveled, and they expected the best. It's an imposing brick building—a grand colonnaded entry portico supported by three-story, white columns opens into a grand lobby. Out the back door are a superb golf course and direct lake access. The hotel is open only from late-April through October, and it costs top dollar, but kids under age 18 stay free, paying only for meals and a service fee on the Modified American Plan. Suites and packages including options like golf, boat tours, and museum tickets are available. Rates range from $280 to 415 MAP, plus children's meal ($40 for ages 7–18) and service charge ($11 for ages 7–18; $5 for ages 6 and under). Lake Road, Cooperstown; (800) 348-6222 or (607) 547-9931; fax (607) 547-9675; www.otesaga.com.

The White House Inn

Cooperstown boasts any number of excellent inns and bed-and-breakfasts. The White House stands out as one of the best. The house, listed in the National Historic Registry, was built in 1835. Marjorie and Ed Landers have converted it into a place where anyone from business folks to families can comfortably abide within walking distance to downtown and the Baseball Hall of Fame. The rear carriage house can be rented out as a family suite, and the regular rooms all have private baths. There's off-street parking and a pool with a patio in the back yard. The Landers treat you like family (as good hosts should), and the breakfasts they create are seriously good. Rates range $95–125 for standard rooms and $140–225 for family suites. 46 Chestnut Street, Cooperstown; (607) 547-5054; fax (607) 547-1100; www.cooperstownchamber.org.

Attractions

Corning Museum of Glass

One Museum Way, Corning; (877) 733-2664 or (607) 974-8271; www.cmog.org

Hours: September–June, daily 9 a.m.–5 p.m.; July–August, daily 9 a.m.–8 p.m.; closed Thanksgiving, Christmas Eve, Christmas, and New Year's days

Admission: $10 adults, $5 children (ages 6–17), $9 seniors (60 and older) and college students, $30 families (two adults with dependent children)

Appeal by Age Groups:

Pre-school	Grade School	Teens	Young Adults	Over 30	Seniors
★★	★★★★	★★★★★	★★★★★	★★★★★	★★★★★

Touring Time: Average 2 hours; minimum 1½ hour

Rainy-Day Touring: Yes

Services and Facilities:

Restaurants Yes	Lockers No
Alcoholic beverages Yes	Pet kennels No
Disabled access Yes	Rain check No
Wheelchair rental Yes	Private tours Yes; call ahead, fee
Baby stroller rental No	required

Description and Comments   At this world-famous glass factory and museum, you'll get the whole picture from history to modern-glass sculpture. Start with the "Nature of Glass Theater," an introductory film shown continuously. Don't miss the chance to see glass-making in action at the Steuben Factory, where you get a bird's-eye view of glassmakers at work. You can attend one of the live, narrated demonstrations of glassblowing presented throughout the day. You even get to see the glass baking inside the furnace thanks to overhead monitors. Other cool things: the Glass Innovation Center, which shows how glassmaking inventors changed the Hall of Mirrors; an amazing maze navigated with an instrument used to peer into a patient's stomach; and the Sculpture Gallery.

Farmers' Museum

Lake Road, Cooperstown; (888) 547-1450, (607) 547-1450; www.nysha.org, www.farmersmuseum.org

Hours: April–May, October–November, Tuesday–Sunday 10 a.m.–4
p.m.; June–September, daily 10 a.m.–5 p.m.; closed December–March

Admission: $9 adults, $8 seniors (65 and older), $4 children ages 7–12,
free for ages 6 and under; three-way tickets including the Baseball Hall
of Fame & Museum and the Fenimore Art Museum are available

Appeal by Age Groups:

Pre-school	Grade School	Teens	Young Adults	Over 30	Seniors
★★★	★★★★	★★★	★★★★	★★★★★	★★★★★

Touring Time: Average 3 hours; minimum 1 hour

Rainy-Day Touring: Yes

Services and Facilities:

Restaurants	Yes	Lockers	No
Alcoholic beverages	No	Pet kennels	No
Disabled access	No	Rain check	No
Wheelchair rental	No	Private tours	No
Baby stroller rental	No		

Description and Comments   The museum sits on land that operated as a
working farm dating back to 1813, when it was owned by James Fenimore
Cooper. It functions today as a combination museum and living history
installation. You enter through the Main Barn, which houses exhibits;
move on to the 1845 Village; and then explore Lippit Farmstead, which
still functions as a nineteenth-century farm. Interpretive 20-minute tours
operate daily, and the schedule is peppered with special events, particularly
in summer. Smaller children will love the animals that work on the farm—
the oxen help plow the fields, the chickens and ducks provide eggs for use
in the farmhouse kitchen. Throughout the 23-acre site, demonstrations are
offered in all the old trades and skills, from making wallpaper and weaving
to shoemaking and blacksmithing. The Cardiff Giant tent offers a unique
glimpse into a classic nineteenth-century hoax—alleged to be a petrified
prehistoric man.

Fenimore Art Museum

Lake Road, Cooperstown; (888) 547-1450, (607) 547-1500;
www.nysha.org

Hours: April–May, Tuesday–Sunday 10 a.m.–4 p.m.; June–September,
daily 10 a.m.–5 p.m.; October–December, daily 10 a.m.–4 p.m.;
closed Thanksgiving Day, Christmas Day and January–March

Admission: $9 adults, $8 seniors (65 and older), $4 children (ages 7–12),
free for ages 6 and under; three-way tickets including the Baseball Hall
of Fame & Museum and the Farmer's Museum are available

Appeal by Age Groups:

Pre-school	Grade School	Teens	Young Adults	Over 30	Seniors
★★★	★★★	★★★	★★★★	★★★★★	★★★★★

Touring Time: Average 2 hours; minimum 1 hour

Rainy-Day Touring: Yes

Services and Facilities:

Restaurants Yes	Lockers No
Alcoholic beverages Yes	Pet kennels No
Disabled access Yes	Rain check No
Wheelchair rental No	Private tours No
Baby stroller rental No	

Description and Comments This museum may be a bit staid for many children, but it does contain a terrific collection of New York State-based art. The Bold Experiment exhibit is particularly interesting. It consists of 22 life-mask portrait busts of famous early nineteenth-century Americans. Look, too, for a magnificent collection of Hudson River School paintings. Kids might best like the American Indian Wing, in which more than 750 artifacts are displayed. Outdoors, set way across the expansive rear lawn on the lake's shore, sits an Iroquois bark house, a fun spot that depicts Iroquois life circa 1750.

Ithaca Sciencenter

601 First Street, Ithaca; (607) 272-0600; www.sciencenter.org

Hours: 10 a.m.–5 p.m. Tuesday–Saturday, and Sunday noon–5 p.m.; closed Monday

Admission: $4.50 adults, $4 seniors 64 and older, $3.50 children ages 3–12, free ages 2 and under

Appeal by Age Groups:

Pre-school	Grade School	Teens	Young Adults	Over 30	Seniors
★★★★	★★★★★	★★★	★★★★	★★★★	★★★★

Touring Time: Average 1½ hour; minimum 45 minutes

Rainy-Day Touring: Yes

Services and Facilities:

Restaurants No	Lockers No
Alcoholic beverages No	Pet kennels No
Disabled access No	Rain check No
Wheelchair rental No	Private tours No
Baby stroller rental No	

Description and Comments   This is a small, completely hands-on science museum in a small town that houses a major university—a university that spawned Carl Sagan. You know this place will be fun. There are more hands-on activities packed into this relatively small building than you can shake a stick at, and each one amiably demonstrates a scientific principle. This is the perfect way to defeat rainy-day boredom, but if you visit in nice weather, there's even an outdoor, science-teaching playground, complete with swings that demonstrate, uh, well, something about centrifugal force. Everyone will stand in front of the kinetic ball sculpture for a long time, trying to figure out the routes the balls take as they clunk, bang, ding, and bong their way through this two-story Rube Goldberg–type device. You'll want to check out the walk-in camera and, if you're there at 2 p.m. on a Saturday afternoon, you'll want to catch the free Showtime demonstrations.

National Baseball Hall of Fame & Museum

25 Main Street, Cooperstown; (888) 425-5633, (607) 547-7200; www.baseballhalloffame.org

Hours: May 1–September 30, daily 9 a.m.–9 p.m.; October 1–April 30, daily 9 a.m.–5 p.m.; April, October, November, and December, Fridays and Saturdays 9 a.m.–8 p.m.; closed Thanksgiving, Christmas, and New Year's days

Admission: $9.50 adults, $8 seniors (65 and older), $4 children (ages 7–12), free for ages 6 and under; three-way tickets including the Farmer's Museum and the Fenimore Art Museum are available

Appeal by Age Groups:

Pre-school	Grade School	Teens	Young Adults	Over 30	Seniors
★★★★	★★★★	★★★★★	★★★★★	★★★★★	★★★★★

Touring Time: Average 3½ hours; minimum 1½ hour

Rainy-Day Touring: Yes

Services and Facilities:

Restaurants No	Lockers No
Alcoholic beverages No	Pet kennels No
Disabled access Yes	Rain check No
Wheelchair rental No	Private tours No
Baby stroller rental No	

Description and Comments   An odd thing about this place—to a baseball fan, even a casual one— is that it's forever young. No matter how many times you visit, there's always something fresh about being here, even if it's the rejuvenation that comes from conjuring up beloved memories. Start at the Grandstand Theater with a viewing of the introductory film, a beautifully made depiction of baseball's role in American life. Then, just let your interests take you where they will. We love the old stadia exhibits (because Dad spent so much of his youth watching the Giants and, later, the Mets at the old Polo Grounds in Manhattan). The World Series Room takes you back to mystical moments—even if those are only one year old. The exhibits on African-Americans in Baseball and Women in Baseball illustrate the game's social/historical role. And, of course, there's the Hall of Fame itself, where grandpa just might want to spend an entire afternoon reading plaques. When you're done, walk three blocks over to Doubleday Field, where the Induction Ceremony Game is played annually. It's what a baseball park should be. Your admission is good all day. That's good, because it's not unusual for folks to find themselves wandering back to the Hall after lunch—and then again after dinner.

National Women's Hall of Fame

76 Fall Street, Seneca Falls; (315) 568-8060; www.greatwomen.org

Hours: May–October, daily 9:30 a.m.–5 p.m.; November–April, Wednesday–Saturday 10 a.m.–4 p.m., Sunday noon–4 p.m.; closed on major holidays

Admission: $3 adults, $1.50 seniors 65 and older and students, $7 family groups, free for ages 4 and under

Appeal by Age Groups:

Pre-school	Grade School	Teens	Young Adults	Over 30	Seniors
★	★★	★★★	★★★★	★★★★★	★★★★★

Touring Time: Average 1 hour; minimum 30 minutes

Rainy-Day Touring: Yes

Services and Facilities:

Restaurants No	Lockers No
Alcoholic beverages No	Pet kennels No
Disabled access Yes	Rain check No
Wheelchair rental No	Private tours No
Baby stroller rental No	

Description and Comments   This is a small museum, occupying just a storefront on Seneca Falls' main street. But, beginning with the 10-minute introductory video, it's an inspiring place to visit, and it makes an excellent complementary site to the Women's Rights Park. Among the stories told here: Susan B. Anthony, Abigail Adams, Amelia Earhart, Ella Fitzgerald, Emily Dickinson, and more than four dozen others, both familiar and unfamiliar.

Paleontology Research Institute

1259 Trumansburg Road, Ithaca; (607) 273-6623

Hours: Hours vary seasonally; call ahead

Admission: Free, but donations encouraged; $85 for field trips

Appeal by Age Groups:

Pre-school	Grade School	Teens	Young Adults	Over 30	Seniors
★	★★★	★★	★★★	★★★★	★★★

Touring Time: Average 1 hour plus an hour in the field; minimum 30 minutes

Rainy-Day Touring: Yes

Services and Facilities:

Restaurants No	Baby stroller rental No
Alcoholic beverages No	Lockers No
Disabled access Yes; questionable in the field	Pet kennels No
	Rain check No
Wheelchair rental No	Private tours Yes; for field tours

Description and Comments   PRI functions independently as a nonprofit organization dedicated to education and research. It offers a small museum that displays fossils found in the region and scientific background information on the general geology and paleontology, as well as the area's geological history. Changing exhibits cover a variety of scientific topics. Much that is displayed is aimed at children, including hands-on, interactive exhibits, coloring tables, brain-teaser displays, and touch tables.

But, the real reason to visit PRI is to participate in one of its fossil-hunting field trips. These offer one of the best ways to gain an understanding of how this lake district was formed and to be amazed by the geological and biological changes that are evidenced here. The basic field trips venture only to a scrappy lakeside hill adjacent to a salt mining operation—nothing exotic or beautiful—but seemingly every rock in the endless pile of shale contains a fossil of some sea creature that lived 3.5 million years ago. Trip leaders are dedicated, dynamic, and interested in not only teaching you something, but also in letting you have a good time. By the time you're done, you just may be able to tell a cephalopod or brachiopod fossil from an iron stain.

Women's Rights National Historical Park

136 Fall Street, Seneca Falls; (315) 568-2991; www.nps.gov/wori

Hours: Daily 9 a.m.–5 p.m.; closed Thanksgiving, Christmas, and New Year's days

Admission: $2 adults, free for children under age 17; $1 per adult for tours, free for children under age 17

Appeal by Age Groups:

Pre-school	Grade School	Teens	Young Adults	Over 30	Seniors
★	★★★	★★★★	★★★★	★★★★★	★★★★★

Touring Time: Average 1 hour; minimum 30 minutes

Rainy-Day Touring: Yes

Services and Facilities:

Restaurants No	Lockers No
Alcoholic beverages No	Pet kennels No
Disabled access Yes	Rain check No
Wheelchair rental No	Private tours No
Baby stroller rental No	

Description and Comments   The Park features a small museum with many interactive exhibits that review women's roles through American history. The complete text of the Declaration is inscribed on a marble wall outside. Children should visit to gain insight and appreciation of just how difficult it was for women to gain basic rights, such as property ownership and voting privileges.

Family-Friendly Restaurants

DOUBLEDAY CAFE

93 Main Street, Cooperstown; (607) 547-5468

Meals served: Breakfast, lunch, and dinner
Cuisine: American and Mexican
Entree range: $8–15
Children's menu: Yes
Reservations: No
Payment: Major credit cards

Nothing fancy, but a hometown atmosphere and good homemade food.

HOFFMAN LANE BISTRO

2 Hoffman Lane, Cooperstown; (607) 547-7055

Meals served: Lunch and dinner
Cuisine: Contemporary
Entree range: $4.85 (lunch)–$16.95 (dinner)

Children's menu: Yes
Reservations: Yes
Payment: V, MC, AE

A delightful, modern cafe with outdoor dining in good weather. Gourmet enough for discerning tastes (with dishes like tuna steak au poivre), but the owners have kids and know how to accommodate them.

ICE CREAM WORKS

Baron Steuben "Sweet 7," W. Market Street, Corning; (607) 962-8482

Meals served: Breakfast, lunch, and light dinner (summer); breakfast and lunch (winter)
Cuisine: American
Entree range: $4.50–6.50
Children's menu: No
Reservations: No
Payment: Major credit cards

While the food's not remarkable for ethnicity or originality, the decor makes this a fun place to eat. The furnishings and fixtures hail from the Ellis Ice Cream Parlor of Hornell, New York, circa the early 1880s. Check out the mahogany woodwork: it's hand-carved. The marble soda fountain counter and tabletops are made of stone salvaged from a demolished electric and gas company building in Elmira. The classic American cuisine includes wraps, sandwiches, burgers, and salads. The ice cream and deserts are classic, too.

MOOSEWOOD RESTAURANT

215 N. Cayuga Street, Ithaca; (607) 273-5327

Meals served: Lunch and dinner
Cuisine: Health/natural foods
Entree range: $6–15
Children's menu: No
Reservations: No
Payment: Major credit cards

This place is an international landmark—a throwback to the late 1960s and early 1970s, a recognized force in healthful vegetarian cuisine, and one of the few collectives that have actually stayed intact. The menu changes daily, and there's usually a fish, soup, or salad offering that kids will eat. The bread and desserts are wonderful. Sunday evening is ethnic night. If you're going to be in Ithaca, you really have to eat at Moosewood.

Adirondacks and Lake Placid

Adirondack Park encompasses one-third of the state's total land area. Not all of that is public land, of course, but within its boundaries sit some 3,000 ponds and lakes, 2,000 miles of hiking trails, and 46 high peaks. As might be expected, this region is a camper's delight, holding more than 100 campgrounds, public and private. It's also a scenic delight, offering some of the finest autumnal leaf-peeping vistas in the country. High Peaks Mountain Adventures offers guiding or advice on bicycling, camping, canoeing, hiking, kayaking, mountain biking, rock climbing, and in-line skating in the Adirondacks (call (518) 523-3764 or visit www.hpmac.com).

Perhaps the most visited Adirondack towns are **Lake Placid** and **Lake George.** Lake Placid has twice been the site of the Winter Olympic Games, and it continues to be a major venue for international winter sports competitions. Lake George has been dubbed "the queen of American lakes," which might sound a bit lofty but doesn't detract from the natural beauty. The water is potable—something that can be said about very few heavily used bodies of water these days.

Lake Champlain, half in New York and half in Vermont, runs north from the top of Lake George to **Plattsburgh.** It has been called the sixth Great Lake. Lake Champlain Ferries make regular runs from Vermont to Essex, Plattsburgh, and Port Kent; some ferries operate year-round; (802) 864-9804; www.ferries.com. Just below its south end sits **Whitehall,** birthplace of the U.S. Navy. On the small strip of land between Lakes George and Champlain stands **Ticonderoga,** whose fort proved a key site during the Revolutionary War. Many, many more lakes dot the region. Of those, **Saranac Lake, Raquette Lake, Cranberry Lake, Great Sacandaga Lake, Scroon Lake, and Indian Lake** are the most popular and have abundant vacation facilities.

Although they're technically not in the Adirondacks, we've included in this section **Saratoga,** one of the summer horse-racing capitals of the land, and **Albany,** the state capitol.

Two-time site of the Winter Olympics, **Lake Placid** presents a sports extravaganza. Many Olympic venues are open to the public, and many offer summertime events and/or demonstrations, such as the aerial ski acrobatics demonstrations and competitions at the ski-jumping complex. Oddly, our favorite Lake Placid pastime is not a modern, high-tech activity, but rather an old-fashioned toboggan run on frozen Mirror Lake. (Lake Placid village actually sits on Mirror Lake; Lake Placid lake is just outside of town.) For a few bucks, you can slide for hours. Try it backwards—it's a run you'll never forget. Take a drive to **High Falls Gorge** in nearby Wilmington (call (518) 946-2278), a 700-foot waterfall. In summer, **Lake Placid Marina** (call (518) 523-9704) offers one-hour narrated cruises on Lake Placid in enclosed boats. If you're traveling with little ones, detour over to **Santa's Workshop** in North Pole (call (518) 946-2211 or visit www.north-pole.ny.us). The theme park **Frontier Town** (call (518) 532-7181) in North Hudson features a rodeo, Wild West shows, and horse-powered rides. **Barton's Garnet Mine Tours** (call (518) 251- 2706) reveals the region's mining history and offers gem-cutting demonstrations twice weekly.

Family Lodging

Howard Johnson Resort Inn

Voted the 1999 Howard Johnson Property of the Year, this facility has 92 rooms and an excellent indoor pool complex. Located right on Lake Placid lake, it offers free rowboats, paddleboats, and canoes. Rates range from $78-150. 90 Saranac Avenue, Lake Placid; (800) 858-4656 or (518) 523-9555; www.hojo.com.

Lake Placid Resort/Holiday Inn

Set high on a hill in the center of the village, this hotel offers rooms and suites, with Jacuzzis and fireplaces available in some. All rooms have a coffee maker and refrigerator. Customers can use the indoor pool, game room, private tennis courts, beach, and the resort's 45 holes of championship golf. Laundry facilities are on site. Rates range from $79 to $159. Ski, tour, and golf packages are available. Children under age 19 stay free with parents. 1 Olympic Drive, Lake Placid; (800) 874-1980 or (518) 523-2556; www.lpresort.com.

Trail's End Inn

Built in 1902, this inn transports you to the old-time Adirondack Camp era through touches like wide-board pine floors, brick fireplaces, spacious rooms, sleeping porches, clawfoot bathtubs, and plenty of common areas

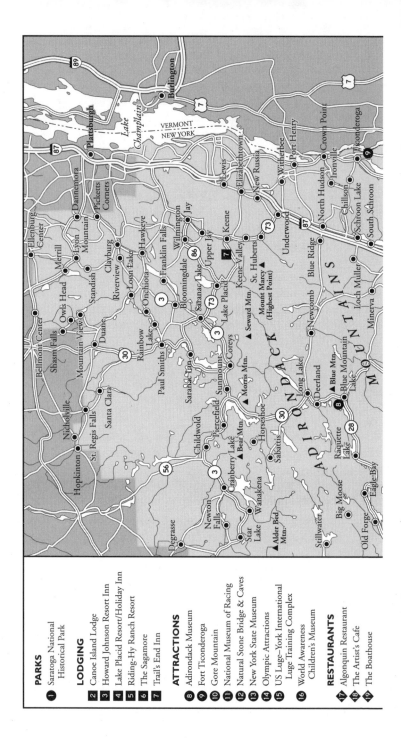

PARKS

1 Saratoga National
Historical Park

LODGING

2 Canoe Island Lodge
3 Howard Johnson Resort Inn
4 Lake Placid Resort/Holiday Inn
5 Riding-Hy Ranch Resort
6 The Sagamore
7 Trail's End Inn

ATTRACTIONS

8 Adirondack Museum
9 Fort Ticonderoga
10 Gore Mountain
11 National Museum of Racing
12 Natural Stone Bridge & Caves
13 New York State Museum
14 Olympic Attractions
15 US Luge–York International
Luge Training Complex
16 World Awareness
Children's Museum

RESTAURANTS

17 Algonquin Restaurant
18 The Artist's Cafe
19 The Boathouse

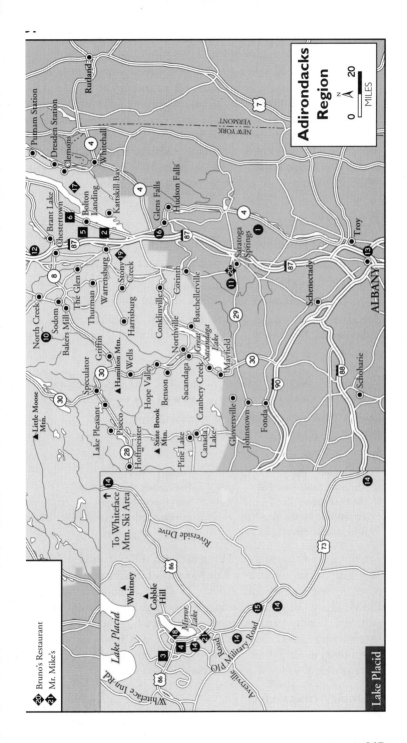

Adirondacks Region

0 · 20
MILES

Lake Placid

Bruno's Restaurant

Mr. Mike's

for guest comfort. Kids love sleeping on a screened Adirondack sleeping porch. Some rooms have shared baths, others have private baths, and there are some two-room suites. The inn also rents two secluded Adirondack cabins, one located five miles away, and another at Tupper Lake. Rates range $72–125 for two people with breakfast; children ages 5–12 are charged $10, children ages 13 and older, $15. Children under age 5 stay free. Cottage rates are $155–175 for up to four people per night. HC1 Box 103, Keene Valley; (800) 281-9860 or (518) 576-9860; fax (518) 576-9235.

Attractions

Adirondack Museum

NY State Routes 28 N. and 30, Blue Mountain Lake; (518) 352-7311; www.adkmuseum.org

Hours: June–mid-October, daily 9:30 a.m.–5:30 p.m.

Admission: $10 adults, $6 children (ages 7–16), $9 seniors, free for children under 7

Appeal by Age Groups:

Pre-school	Grade School	Teens	Young Adults	Over 30	Seniors
★★★	★★★★★	★★★★	★★★★★	★★★★★	★★★★★

Touring Time: Average 3 hours; minimum 2 hours

Rainy-Day Touring: Yes

Services and Facilities:

Restaurants Yes	Lockers No
Alcoholic beverages No	Pet kennels No
Disabled access No	Rain check No
Wheelchair rental Yes; free	Private tours No
Baby stroller rental No	

Description and Comments   This museum is truly a treasure. Sitting on 32 beautiful acres overlooking Blue Mountain Lake, the museum uses two dozen indoor and outdoor exhibits to depict Adirondack history and lifestyle. There are exhibits on logging, mining, boating, overland transportation, hunting, and camping, as well as a huge collection of nineteenth-century landscape paintings and another of freshwater craft. And, there's room to run and let off steam outdoors. Best to pick a nice-weather day, come early, and have lunch in the cafeteria.

Olympic Attractions

Lake Placid; (800) 462-6236, (518) 523-1655; www.lakeplacid.com

Hours: Early June–early October, daily; individual site hours vary

Admission: $16 per person, children 6 and under get in free

Appeal by Age Groups:

Pre-school	Grade School	Teens	Young Adults	Over 30	Seniors
★★★	★★★★★	★★★★★	★★★★★	★★★★★	★★★

Touring Time: Average 4 hours; minimum 2 hours

Rainy-Day Touring: No

Services and Facilities:

Restaurants Yes; at Mt. Hoevenberg	Baby stroller rental No
	Lockers No
Alcoholic beverages Yes	Pet kennels No
Disabled access Yes	Rain check No
Wheelchair rental No	Private tours No

Description and Comments   The $16 Passport gains you summertime entrance to all the Olympic Winter Games venues, including a gondola ride to the summit of Little Whiteface Mountain at Whiteface Ski Area. It also includes the access fee to the Whiteface Mountain Veterans Memorial Highway, the Olympic Museum and Ice Skating Center, the McKenzie Olympic Jumping Complex's Sky Deck via chairlift and elevator, the Olympic Sports Complex at Mt. Van Hoevenberg, and discounts for a summer bobsled ride, biathlon target shooting, and more. When scheduling your sites tour, be aware that special events and weather may affect operations. Among the must-dos are the summer or winter bobsled rides and the trip to the top of the ski jumps. In the four-man bob, two people ride between a driver and a brakeman. You'll be amazed at the speed and the effect of the G-forces on your body as you fly through the turns. As for the ski jumps, well, the view is incredible, and the idea that people actually ski off those things will surely give you pause. Traveling with older kids? Try the biathlon target shooting. Call to check on the hours for the bobsled and target shooting.

US Luge-York International Luge Training Complex

35 Church Street, Lake Placid; (518) 523-2071; www.usaluge.org

Hours: Guided tour Monday–Friday at 2 p.m.

Admission: Free

Appeal by Age Groups:

Pre-school	Grade School	Teens	Young Adults	Over 30	Seniors
★★	★★★★	★★★★★	★★★★★	★★★★★	★★★★★

Touring Time: Average 1 hour; minimum 1 hour

Rainy-Day Touring: Yes

Services and Facilities:

Restaurants No	Lockers No
Alcoholic beverages No	Pet kennels No
Disabled access No	Rain check No
Wheelchair rental No	Private tours No
Baby stroller rental No	

Description and Comments   One of only four indoor luge-training facilities in the world (the others are in Austria, Germany, and Latvia), this one offers a free tour with a video show. Training takes place daily year-round on three iced luge start ramps, so you might just see some top lugers working on their technique.

Family-Friendly Restaurants

THE ARTIST'S CAFE

1 Main Street, Lake Placid; (518) 523-8263

Meals served: Breakfast, lunch, and dinner
Cuisine: American and continental
Entree range: $5.25 (lunch)–$17 (dinner)
Children's menu: Yes
Reservations: Yes
Payment: Major credit cards

An intimate but comfortable place, this cafe displays work from local artists and craftspeople, which livens things up visually. For another visual treat, dine alfresco with a view of the lake.

MR. MIKE'S

332 Main Street, Lake Placid; (518) 523-9770

Meals served: Lunch and dinner
Cuisine: Pizza and Italian
Entree range: $5.50–15.25
Children's menu: No
Reservations: No
Payment: V, MC

Lake Placid houses some pretty fine fine-dining, but for casual fare Mr. Mike's makes a heck of a good pizza. You can order your pizza plain or fancy. Basic parmigiano dishes, too.

Side Trip: Lake George and Vicinity

Despite its ever-growing popularity, **Lake George** remains one of the most pristine large lakes in the Northeast. Perhaps that's because most of its eastern shore is set off as a natural reserve. Whatever the reason, the lake offers a natural paradise with easy access to manmade pleasures.

While **Lake George Village** abounds with souvenir shops, restaurants, and a few spectacular mini-golf courses, the major amusements are found a few miles south in Queensbury. There, **Great Escape and Splashwater Kingdom** amusement park (call (518) 792-3500 or visit www.the-greatescape.com), with its 125-plus rides, is the headliner. Nearby, you'll also find **Skateland Entertainment Center** (call (518) 792-8989), which has go-karts and other action activities, in addition to roller-skating. For younger children, there's **Spanky's Fun Place** (call (518) 761-0449). For those who must shop, this area along Route 9 also holds a bevy of outlet malls. In town, the **House of Frankenstein Wax Museum** (call (518) 668-3377) can fill part of a rainy day in a hokey but fun way.

But the great outdoors is the real reason to come to Lake George. Lake George's water is so clean, it's drinkable. Many resort properties have their own beaches, and public beaches can be found in Lake George Village and many other towns along the shore. To get out on the water, try **Lake George Shoreline Cruises** (call (518) 668-4644 or visit www.lake georgeshoreline.com), who not only offer a variety of lunch, dinner, nighttime, and narrated cruises, but also rent Waverunners, power boats, and snowmobiles, and offer Parasailing adventures. For canoeing and kayaking, guiding service can be obtained from **Beaver Brook Outfitters,** Wevertown, (518) 251-3394; or **Northern Pathfinders,** North Creek, (800) 882-7284 or (518) 327-3378. For those who like to dive, the lake bottom holds wrecks and eye-pleasing zebra mussels. **Northern Lake George Resort,** (518) 543-6528, offers complete diving and resort facilities.

The **Adirondack Mountain Club** offers the most complete information on outdoor adventures, as well as trail maps and many other essentials. Located just off I-87 Exit 21; (518) 668-4447; www.adk.org. A good hike is the trail up Prospect Mountain; it takes about an hour, isn't too steep, and yields great views. The Buck Mountain Trail at Catskill Bay on the lake's east side requires two to three hours of challenging climbing. Check with the Adirondack Mountain Club for trail maps.

FAMILY LODGING

Canoe Island Lodge

North of Lake George Village, this lakeside property features lodging in a carriage house, log cabins, hillside villas, lodges, and waterfront chalets, some with lake views. Sailboats and other craft are available for use, as is water-skiing gear. There are two swimming beaches and a private island used for guest barbecues. A variety of organized activities, a children's program, and theme weekends are offered. For additional recreation, there are tennis courts and adjacent hiking trails. Canoe Island Lodge is family owned and very friendly. Choose the full American Plan (three meals a day) during off-season, or the Modified American Plan (full breakfast and dinner) from July 1–Labor Day. Daily rates: $94–164; children ages 7–12, $51; ages 3–6, $36; ages 6 months–2 years, $18. Weekly rates: $581–1,036; children weekly $321, $219, and $112. P.O. Box 144, Route 9 N., Diamond Point; (518) 668-5592; www.canoeislandlodge.com.

Riding-Hy Ranch Resort

Set on Sherman Lake about a 20-minute drive north of Lake George Village, this is a full-service dude ranch that's dude enough to make you think you've wandered way out West. Open year-round, it offers riding, skiing, and cross-country skiing packages, as well as an indoor pool, a small boating lake, daily organized activities, barbecues, tennis, basketball, a game room, and a full American meal plan. Accommodations are either in the main lodge or individual cabins. Rates: $95–107 per night. Sherman Lake, Warrensburg; (518) 494-2742.

The Sagamore

The granddaddy of all Lake George luxury properties, the Sagamore is on an island, is open year-round, and offers first-class service and amenities. It holds 100 hotel rooms, including 46 suites; 240 rooms at its Lakeside Lodges, including 120 suites with wood-burning fireplaces and terraces; and a selection of new, two-bedroom condominiums. Activities available include Parasailing, mountain biking, rock climbing, ice cream socials, miniature golf, croquet, whitewater rafting, horseback riding, movies, hiking, and arts and crafts. Teepee Club, an organized children's activity program, is offered for ages 4 through 12, and there is a teen club. Rates: hotel rooms and suites, $135–465; lodge rooms and suites, $125–540; condominiums, $285–540. There is an extra charge for children and teen programs and some activities. Special winter ski packages are available. Bolton Landing; (800) 358-3585 or (518) 644-9400.

ATTRACTIONS

Fort Ticonderoga

Fort Road, Ticonderoga; (518) 585-2821; www.fort-ticonderoga.org
Hours: Early May–June and after Labor Day–late October, daily
   9 a.m.–5 p.m.; July and August, daily 9 a.m.–6 p.m.

Admission: $10 adults, $8 seniors, $6 children ages 7–12, free for children under age 7

Appeal by Age Groups:

Pre-school	Grade School	Teens	Young Adults	Over 30	Seniors
★★	★★★★	★★★★	★★★★	★★★★★	★★★★★

Touring Time: Average 2 hours; minimum 1 hour

Rainy-Day Touring: Yes

Services and Facilities:

Restaurants Yes	Lockers No
Alcoholic beverages No	Pet kennels No
Disabled access Yes	Rain check No
Wheelchair rental Yes; free	Private tours No
Baby stroller rental Yes; free	

Description and Comments Fort Ti, as the locals call it, was a key battle site during the Seven Years' War, the French and Indian War, and the American Revolution. Start your visit with the 20-minute guided tour that leaves from the flag bastion, led by uniformed "soldiers." In good weather, it ends with a musket or an artillery demonstration. On the Parade Ground, the knowledgeable staff is available to explain the exhibits, which include eighteenth-century arms, soldiers' personal effects, paintings, and maps, as well as a chronological history of the Ticonderoga peninsula. The fort is said to hold the largest collection of eighteenth-century cannon in the Western Hemisphere. During July and August, the Fort Ticonderoga Fife & Drum Corps performs daily. Kids get to march along. The Corps also re-enacts a historic court martial that took place here. To enjoy a few less violence-oriented moments, stroll The King's Garden, a restored 1920s-era garden.

Gore Mountain

Peaceful Valley Road, North Creek; (800) 342-1234, (518) 251-2411; www.goremountain.com

Hours: Skiing: Early November–April, daily 8 a.m.–4 p.m.; Mountain biking: June 30–Labor Day, Friday–Sunday 10:30 a.m.–5:30 p.m.; post–Labor Day–Columbus Day, Saturday and Sunday 10:30 a.m.–5:30 p.m.

Admission: Skiing: $44 adults (age 20 and older), $39 teens and seniors (ages 13–19 and 65–69), $19 children (ages 7–12), free for children 6 and under and seniors 70 and older. Mountain biking: daily trail access, $9 adult, $4 child; daily lift service and mountain-biking access, $19 adult, $14 child. Scenic gondola ride: $8 adult, $5 children (ages 6–12); free for children 6 and under and seniors 70 and older

Appeal by Age Groups:

Pre-school	Grade School	Teens	Young Adults	Over 30	Seniors
★★★★	★★★★★	★★★★★	★★★★★	★★★★★	★★★★★

Touring Time: Average a full day; minimum 4 hours for the active, 1 hour for gondola riders

Rainy-Day Touring: Yes

Services and Facilities:

Restaurants Yes	Lockers No
Alcoholic beverages Yes	Pet kennels No
Disabled access Yes	Rain check No
Wheelchair rental No	Private tours No
Baby stroller rental No	

Description and Comments   Gore is the largest ski and mountain-bike center in the lower Adirondacks. It is famous for its day care and kids' programs, and it offers full learn-to-ski facilities. In summer, the mountain biking is excellent. If you're not adventurous, take the gondola ride. It yields such incredible views of the high-peaks region that it's a must-do.

Natural Stone Bridge & Caves

535 Stone Bridge Road, Pottersville; (518) 494-2283; www.stonebridge-andcaves.com

Hours: Late May–Labor Day, daily 9 a.m.–7 p.m.; Labor Day–Columbus Day, daily 10 a.m.–6 p.m.

Admission: $8.50 adults, $4.50 children ages 6–12, free for children under 6; adult admission is good all season

Appeal by Age Groups:

Pre-school	Grade School	Teens	Young Adults	Over 30	Seniors
★★★	★★★★★	★★★	★★★★	★★★★	★★★★★

Touring Time: Average 2½ hours; minimum 1½ hour

Rainy-Day Touring: Yes

Services and Facilities:

Restaurants Yes; coffee shop and snack bar	Baby stroller rental No
	Lockers No
Alcoholic beverages No	Pet kennels No
Disabled access No	Rain check No
Wheelchair rental No	Private tours No

Description and Comments   A commercial enterprise, Stone Bridge borders on the hokey, but it's a good place to take little ones, keep them entertained, and expose them to some natural wonders. A descriptive map and well-marked trails lead you through some remarkable natural geology, with waterfalls, a gorge, and several caves. Elementary school-aged kids like the opportunity to sift through flowing water at the gemstone mining installation, and everybody goes home with some kind of found treasure. The trout fishing can be fun, too.

World Awareness Children's Museum

229 Glen Street, Glens Falls; (518) 793-2773; www.worldchildrensmuseum.org

Hours: October–May, Tuesday–Friday 10 a.m.–5 p.m., Saturday 10 a.m.–2 p.m.; June–September, Monday–Friday 11 a.m.–3 p.m.

Admission: $2 per person, free for children under age 2

Appeal by Age Groups:

Pre-school	Grade School	Teens	Young Adults	Over 30	Seniors
★★★	★★★★	★★★★	★★★★★	★★★★★	★★★★★

Touring Time: Average 2 hours; minimum 1 hour

Rainy-Day Touring: Yes

Services and Facilities:

Restaurants No	Lockers No
Alcoholic beverages No	Pet kennels No
Disabled access No	Rain check No
Wheelchair rental No	Private tours Yes; $30 arranged
Baby stroller rental No	in advance

Description and Comments   We can't think of a more noble purpose than a kids' museum for international understanding through art. You'll see some remarkable works in changing, interactive exhibitions. The hands-on exhibits and artifacts allow children to explore and touch, and a variety of workshops and activities allow kids and adults alike to share cultural learning.

FAMILY-FRIENDLY RESTAURANTS

THE BOATHOUSE

Route 9 N., Lake Shore Drive, Lake George; (518) 668-2389

Meals served: Breakfast, lunch, and dinner
Cuisine: American
Entree range: $5 (breakfast)–$22 (dinner)
Children's menu: Yes; $5–7
Reservations: Yes
Payment: MC, V

In a turn-of-the-century boathouse setting, this place is very popular for good, plentiful food and friendly service. Its location right on the lake will make children happy. The cuisine is standard American: seafood, steak, and pasta.

Saratoga Springs and the Albany Area

Saratoga Springs lies just south of the Adirondack Park. Mixing the excitement of thoroughbred racing and world-class performing arts, it's among the region's busiest but most pleasant summertime destinations. The horses have been running at **Saratoga Race Course** (call (888) 285-5961 or (518) 584-6200 or visit www.nyra.com) since 1863, and it's still one of the most beautiful places anywhere to watch these wonderful animals run. Go at dawn to watch them work out, then you can have breakfast, take the tram tour, or watch the paddock show and starting-gate demonstration. The race season runs from late July through Labor Day. Both the New York City Ballet and the Philadelphia Orchestra make their summer home at the **Saratoga Performing Arts Center** (call (518) 587-3330 or visit www.spac.org), and a full spectrum of other performers grace the stage there. Bring a picnic and enjoy the arts in a gracious summertime setting. The Center is located in **Saratoga Spa State Park** (call (518) 584-2000), a 2,200-acre place to play, which also contains the **National Museum of Dance** (call (518) 584-2225), the country's only museum entirely devoted to professional American dance. **Lester Park,** operated by the New York State Museum, is an outdoor geologic exhibit where you can walk across a 490-million-year-old fossil sea floor. Just outside of town, you'll find **Saratoga National Historical Park** (call (518) 664-9821), a pleasant mix of history and nature.

Albany, the state capitol, offers a number of attractions. The **Albany Institute of History & Art** (call (518) 463-4478) covers the Upper Hudson Valley's history, art, and culture. The **Henry Hudson Planetarium** (call (800) 258-3582 or (518) 434-0405) makes an excellent rainy-day destination. Major concerts are staged at **The Egg** (call (518) 473-1061), and tours are also offered of that remarkable egg-shaped entertainment center.

Nearby **Schenectady** (about 10 miles northeast of Albany) offers a boon for history buffs. One of the oldest cities in the country, it was the founding site for Thomas Edison's Edison Machine Works, which evolved into General Electric. The **Hall of History Center** (call (518) 385-1104) documents the electrical industry's history. The more distant past is preserved in the **Historic Stockade** (call (518) 382-7890). Self-guided, recorded, and professionally led tours are available at this historic district. The **Schenectady Museum and Planetarium** (call (518) 382-7890) is devoted to science. Kids especially like the one-third-scale Space Shuttle that allows simulated flight and landing.

Family Lodging

ALBANY

Downtown Albany doesn't offer a great deal of acceptable lodging, but the Wolf Road area—located off Exit 2 of the Northway (I-87, north of the city)—holds a plethora of chain hotels as well as a major shopping mall and many chain and local restaurants. It's definitely an area that can be called a suburban commercial "strip," but it makes the most sense to stay there because from this area it's easy to drive into town (15 minutes) or up to Saratoga (20 minutes) and on into the Adirondacks (45 minutes and more). Among the accommodations: **Albany Marriott Hotel,** 189 Wolf Road, (800) 228-9090 or (518) 458-8444; rates $100–150. **Best Western Albany Airport Inn,** 200 Wolf Road, (800) 458-1016 or (518) 458-1000; rates $80–100. **Days Inn Wolf Road,** 16 Wolf Road, (800) 329-7466 or (518) 459-3600; rates $60–80.

SARATOGA

Holiday Inn Saratoga Springs Hotel and Conference Center

This 168-room hotel with first-class services and amenities is near downtown. It has an on-site restaurant, a heated outdoor pool, free use of the nearby coed YMCA for indoor swimming, and a fitness machine room. In-room HBO and pay movies. Two-room suites are available. Rates are $75–195; special discount packages are available; children under 19 stay for free in parents' room; children under 12 eat for free from the children's menu with a parent who is also dining. 232 Broadway, Saratoga Springs; (518) 584-4550.

Saratoga Downtowner Motel

A family-owned motel with 42 rooms, an indoor pool, and complimentary continental breakfast. It's within walking distance of downtown's restaurants, movies, and shopping. Rates $55–165. 413 Broadway, Saratoga Springs; (888) 480-6160 or (518) 584-6160.

Armory Center

Okay, now this *is* different. A car dealership turned entertainment center. There's an automotive collectibles store, a car wash, a nightclub, a nail salon, and two restaurants. **Bumper's Cafe** (call (518) 436-7747) runs to sandwiches, burgers, and fries as a lunchtime menu, with dinner offerings like chicken teriyaki and blackened swordfish, as well as classics like chicken pot pie; prices range from $6.95–13.95. **Yono's** (call (518) 436-7747) offers fine dining and is less appropriate for small children. 926 Central Avenue, Albany; call (518) 482-0100.

Attractions

National Museum of Racing and Hall of Fame

191 Union Avenue, Saratoga Springs; (518) 584-0400; www.racing museum.org

Hours: September–July, Monday–Saturday 10 a.m.–4:30 p.m., Sunday noon–4:30 p.m.; during racing season (late July–Labor Day), daily 9 a.m.–5 p.m.

Admission: $7 adults, $5 children ages 5–11, students, and seniors 62 and older, free for children under age 5

Appeal by Age Groups:

Pre-school	Grade School	Teens	Young Adults	Over 30	Seniors
★★★	★★★★	★★★★	★★★★★	★★★★★	★★★★★

Touring Time: Average 2 hours; minimum 1 hour

Rainy-Day Touring: Yes

Services and Facilities:

Restaurants No	Lockers No; coat room available
Alcoholic beverages No	Pet kennels No
Disabled access Yes	Rain check No
Wheelchair rental Yes	Private tours No
Baby stroller rental No	

Description and Comments   Thoroughbreds just may be the most beautiful horses of all, and this museum pays homage to them. Some three centuries of racing history and art are covered here. Younger kids will most like the Discovery Paddock, a hands-on activity center where they can dress up in silks, learn to shoe a horse, and practice riding on an "equipony." Everyone will like the Racing Day Gallery and its re-created jockey room. In the Hall of Fame, multimedia kiosks tell each Hall-of-Famer's story, and the film *Race America,* set to Aaron Copeland's music, truly brings these beautiful beasts to life.

New York State Museum

Madison Avenue, Empire State Plaza, Albany; (518) 474-5877; www.nysm.nysed.gov

Hours: Daily 9:30 a.m.–5 p.m.; closed Thanksgiving, Christmas, and New Year's days; Discovery Place hours: after Labor Day–July 4, Monday–Friday 2–4:30 p.m.; July 5–Labor Day and holidays weekends, noon–4:30 p.m.

Admission: Free; suggested donation of $2 per person or $5 per family

Appeal by Age Groups:

Pre-school	Grade School	Teens	Young Adults	Over 30	Seniors
★★★	★★★★	★★★★	★★★★★	★★★★★	★★★★★

Touring Time: Average 2 hours; minimum 1 hour

Rainy-Day Touring: Yes

Services and Facilities:

Restaurants Yes	Lockers Yes; coat room at art exhibits
Alcoholic beverages No	
Disabled access Yes	Pet kennels No
Wheelchair rental Yes	Rain check No
Baby stroller rental Yes	Private tours No

Description and Comments The State Museum covers a wide range of topics and offers a well-presented introduction to New York history, arts, and culture. Younger kids have the most fun at Discovery Place, a hands-on interactive center aimed at preschoolers to eighth graders, where kids play at being entomologists, historians, physicists, and paleontologists. The main exhibition halls feature a Mohawk Iroquois Longhouse, the New York City subway's A-train, and Sesame Street. The museum also presents New York's prehistoric wilderness and an in-depth look at the state's Native Peoples.

Family-Friendly Restaurants

BRUNO'S RESTAURANT

237 Union Avenue, Saratoga Springs; (518) 583-3333

Meals served: Breakfast, lunch, and dinner
Cuisine: American
Entree range: $5.95–22.50
Children's menu: Yes
Reservations: No
Payment: Major credit cards

Bruno's is a lively 1950s theme spot across the street from the racetrack. It's complete with checkerboard tablecloths, a soda fountain, and a jukebox that's a replica of an old Ford Thunderbird. The fare ranges from pizza and burgers to full dinner specials. But the fun's in the decor, the jukebox selections, and the menu covers made from golden-oldie record album jackets.

LILLIAN'S

408 Broadway, Saratoga Springs; (518) 587-7766

Meals served: Lunch and dinner
Cuisine: American
Entree range: $9.95–22.95
Children's menu: Yes
Reservations: Yes
Payment: Major credit cards

One of several worthwhile downtown restaurants, Lillian's is named after Broadway actress Lillian Russell, a summer Saratoga resident. The theater theme has served them well for 26 years. The food runs to steak, seafood, chicken, and a variety of pastas served in an easy-going atmosphere.

Catskills and Hudson Valley

The Catskills and the Hudson Valley cover ground from the northern New York City suburbs to Albany and out to Pennsylvania. The Catskill Mountains are old mountains, and they're an old vacation destination as well. The all-inclusive, destination resort was, if not invented here, certainly perfected here. The area was once known as the Borscht Belt because of all the European-Jewish resorts that flourished here. Today, most of those are gone, but destination resorts still thrive, as do the outdoor lifestyle, the arts, and the scenery. The **Delaware and Ulster Rail Ride** (call (800) 225-4132 or (607) 652-2821) offers short scenic rides from **Arkville.** Another train excursion can be found in **Mt. Trempor** on the **Catskill Mountain Railroad** (call (914) 688-7400). **Livingston Manor** is home to the **Catskill State Fish Hatchery** (call (914) 439-4328) and the **Catskill Fly Fishing Center & Museum** (call (914) 439-4810). **East Durham** is a bastion of Irish culture and home to the **Irish American Heritage Museum** (call (518) 432-6598) and the **Michael J. Quill Irish Cultural and Sports Centre** (call (518) 634-2286), which stages a major festival each summer.

The Hudson Valley is rich in history and scenic beauty. The **Neversink Valley Area Museum** (call (914) 754-8870) in **Cuddebackville** focuses on nineteenth-century life; it's set in the **Delaware & Hudson Canal Park,** where canal tours and a kids' activity center are located. In nearby **High Falls,** the canal life is highlighted at the **Delaware, Hudson Canal Museum** (call (914) 687-9311) complete with a five-locks walk and working model lock. In **Hudson,** the **American Museum of Firefighting** (call (800) 479-7695 or (518) 828-9695 ext. 155), shows off equipment dating to 1725, while Kingston is home to the **Trolley Museum** (call (914) 331-3399). The **Samuel F B Morse Historic Site** (call (914) 454-4500) in **Poughkeepsie** depicts the history of the telegraph. **The Hudson Valley Museum** (call (914) 963-4550) in **Yonkers** features general history, art, science, and Westchester County's only planetarium. The **Hudson Valley Raptor Center** in **Lafayetteville** (call (914) 758-6957) offers sanctuary for and displays on birds of prey. The arts flourish outdoors in **Mountainville** at **Storm King Art Center** (call (914) 534-3115), home to an expansive sculpture garden.

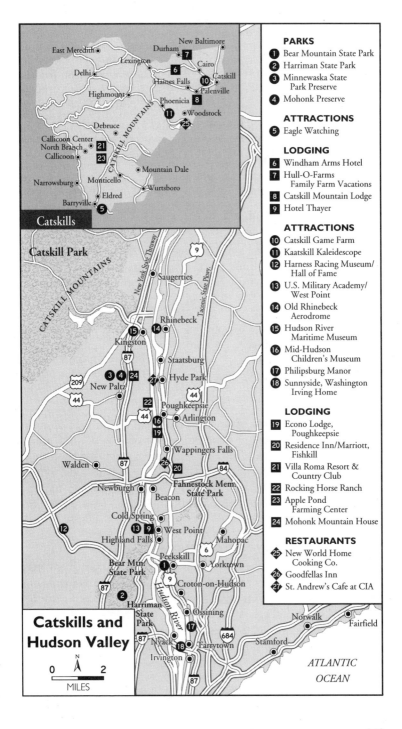

PARKS

1. Bear Mountain State Park
2. Harriman State Park
3. Minnewaska State Park Preserve
4. Mohonk Preserve

ATTRACTIONS

5. Eagle Watching

LODGING

6. Windham Arms Hotel
7. Hull-O-Farms Family Farm Vacations
8. Catskill Mountain Lodge
9. Hotel Thayer

ATTRACTIONS

10. Catskill Game Farm
11. Kaatskill Kaleidescope
12. Harness Racing Museum/ Hall of Fame
13. U.S. Military Academy/ West Point
14. Old Rhinebeck Aerodrome
15. Hudson River Maritime Museum
16. Mid-Hudson Children's Museum
17. Philipsburg Manor
18. Sunnyside, Washington Irving Home

LODGING

19. Econo Lodge, Poughkeepsie
20. Residence Inn/Marriott, Fishkill
21. Villa Roma Resort & Country Club
22. Rocking Horse Ranch
23. Apple Pond Farming Center
24. Mohonk Mountain House

RESTAURANTS

25. New World Home Cooking Co.
26. Goodfellas Inn
27. St. Andrew's Cafe at CIA

Catskills

Catskill Park

Catskills and Hudson Valley

N

0   2
MILES

ATLANTIC OCEAN

383

In **Katonah,** it's classical music all summer at the **Caramoor Center for Music and Arts** (call (914) 232-5035). For something different, the **Diamond Institute** (call (914) 651-1100) in **Florida** demonstrates diamond-cutting techniques. Shoppers will want to stop at **Woodbury Common Mall** (call (914) 928-4000) in **Central Valley,** home to 220 designer stores. And, for an old-time day at the amusement park, people have been flocking to **Playland Park** (call (914) 925-2701) in **Rye** for generations.

Family Lodging

Catskill Mountain Lodge

Thirty-nine rooms, three efficiencies, an outdoor heated pool, a kiddie pool, a playground, and children's movies make this a family-friendly, in-town motel. For adults, it has a microbrew pub, lounge, and restaurant on the premises. Rates $80–85 a night. Route 32A, Palenville; (518) 678-3101.

Econo Lodge

This is a standard 111-room motel, but it's a good value. Kids under age 18 stay free, the motel has a 24-hour restaurant, and a free continental breakfast is offered. Rates are $55–65 a night. 418 South Road (US Route 9) Poughkeepsie; (914) 452-6600.

Hotel Thayer

On-site at the U.S. Military Academy, the Hotel Thayer is listed on the National Register of Historic Places. It recently underwent a $26 million renovation. Although it currently does not have a swimming pool, a new, 132-room wing will soon be added, containing a restaurant and a fitness center with a pool. Rates are $150–180 per night; children stay free. 674 Thayer Road, West Point; (800) 247-5047, (914) 446-4731; www.hotelthayer.com.

Hull-O-Farms Family Farm Vacations

This is a working, 350-acre dairy farm (since 1779) with two guesthouses. Everyone can participate in the farming to whatever extent they wish: milk cows, feed pigs and baby calves, or just ride the tractor. Rates per day: $95 age 15 and older, $60 ages 10–14, $50 ages 5–9, $35 ages 2–4, free for ages under 2. Rates include home-cooked, all-you-can-eat breakfast and dinner. 3739 Route 20, Durham; (518) 239-6950; www.hull-o.com.

Residence Inn by Marriott

Conveniently located for southern Hudson Valley attractions, this is one of Marriott's all-suites properties, with 136 rooms, a pool, complimentary continental breakfast, an exercise room, and easy access to I-84. Rates are $89–229 per night. 2481 Route 9, Fishkill; (914) 896-5210.

Windham Arms Hotel

A full-service, 50-room hotel with rooms and suites, an outdoor pool, tennis, a fitness center, a lounge, its own movie theater, and complimentary shuttle service to area attractions, including skiing and scenic ski-lift rides. Two restaurants are on-site. Rates are $70–330 per night. Route 23, Windham; (518) 734-3000.

FAMILY RESORTS

The Catskills support a long tradition of providing self-contained, full-service family resorts. While the heyday of the "Borscht Belt" and the European-Jewish tradition is long gone, the region still percolates with terrific vacation resorts.

Apple Pond Farming Center

And now for something a little different: a horse-powered, organic farm. Apple Pond has only two guesthouses (one with three bedrooms, the other with one), but its focus is on "small is better" and on the old-fashioned, natural way of doing things. You can help farm, ride or drive horses, work with the sheep and goats, tour the farm, garden and farm organically, make bread and goat cheese, or spin wool. Rates: one-bedroom apartment, $250/weekend and $500/week; three-bedroom apartment, $300/weekend and $600/week. Box 371, Callicoon Center; (914) 482-4764; www.catskill.net/applepon.

Balsam Shade Farm

Open from May through October, this 50-room resort feeds you three meals a day, provides entertainment at night, and offers daytime activities such as swimming in the outdoor pool, playing tennis, working out at the health club, hiking, biking, taking day trips, or playing in the game room. Oh, there are also a climbing wall, high-ropes course, shuffleboard, a softball field, and a playground. Rates are $150 per weekend and $450 per week; 6944 Route 32, Greenville; (518) 966-5315.

Mohonk Mountain House

This expensive but unique place has been a resort since 1869. It stands looking like an elaborate castle before a lake and beneath the surrounding mountains on its own 2,000 acres adjacent to the 5,500-acre Mohonk Preserve. All the amenities anyone could possibly want are offered, from golf and horseback riding to supervised children's activities and hiking or cross-country skiing. There are also on-site concerts, lectures, and films. Rates are $185–475 per night; weekly rates are available. Lake Mohonk; (800) 772-6646.

Rocking Horse Ranch

This is the Big Daddy of the Catskills destination resorts and eastern dude ranches too. Covering 500 acres, Rocking Horse offers nearly anything you can think of, in all seasons, almost all for one price. Consider: indoor heated pool, two outdoor heated pools, adult pool with giant water slide, and children's pool with interactive spray fountain; lake with water-skiing and instruction, big banana watersled ride, paddle boats, and fishing; lit tennis courts, beach volleyball, basketball, handball, bocce, and shuffleboard courts, minigolf, and hay rides. Winter activities are just as extensive, including a small ski hill and a snowtubing run. The supervised children's programs feature day camp for ages 4 to 12. And the list goes on. All-inclusive rates: $160–215 per person; first child (ages 4–15) $80, other children $75 each. Highland; (800) 647-2624, (914) 691-2927; www.rhranch.com.

Villa Roma Resort & Country Club

Villa Roma is a large, 300-room, year-round resort featuring Italian-American cuisine. It was renovated in 1997. Activities and facilities include downhill and cross-country skiing, swimming, tennis courts, indoor racquetball courts, a health club, nightly entertainment, a disco, supervised children's program, and golf. Rates: $211–524 per night for a full American Plan. Callicoon; (800) 727-8455, (914) 887-4880; www.villaroma.com.

Attractions

Catskill Game Farm

400 Game Farm Road, Catskill; (518) 678-9595; www.catskillgame-farm.com

Hours: May 1–October 31, Monday–Friday 9 a.m.–5 p.m., Saturday–Sunday 9 a.m.–6 p.m.

Admission: $14.95 adults, $12.95 seniors 65 and older, $10.95 children ages 4–11, free for ages 3 and under

Appeal by Age Groups:

Pre-school	Grade School	Teens	Young Adults	Over 30	Seniors
★★★★★	★★★★★★	★★★	★★★	★★★	★★★

Eagle Watching

Sullivan County's Mongaup Valley Wildlife Management Area is home to the largest known wintering population of eagles in the northeast. The eagles are drawn by the good fishing in the open waters of the Delaware River and local reservoirs. It has become one of the best places anywhere to sight and appreciate these magnificent birds. The Eagle Institute in Barryville, (914) 557-6162, offers guided eagle watches and interpretive programs during winter weekends. It's a unique opportunity to share something wild and wonderful with your kids. January and February are best.

Touring Time: Average 3 hours; minimum 2 hours

Rainy-Day Touring: Yes

Services and Facilities:

Restaurants Yes	Lockers No
Alcoholic beverages Yes; beer	Pet kennels No
Disabled access No	Rain check No
Wheelchair rental No	Private tours No
Baby stroller rental No	

Description and Comments   Catskill Game Farm has been a mainstay of the region for several generations. It might be a bit tacky, but little kids love it, especially the petting zoo, where they can pet and feed tame animals. In spring, they can bottle-feed baby animals. The park puts on a chimpanzee show on weekends and an elephant show daily during the summer. There's also a playground, and a small water park was recently added.

Harness Racing Museum & Hall of Fame

240 Main Street, Goshen; (914) 294-6330; www.harnessmuseum.com

Hours: Daily 10 a.m.–5 p.m.

Admission: $7.50 adults, $6.50 seniors, $3.50 children ages 12 and under

Appeal by Age Groups:

Pre-school	Grade School	Teens	Young Adults	Over 30	Seniors
★★	★★★★	★★★	★★★★	★★★★	★★★★

Touring Time: Average 1 hour; minimum 40 minutes

Rainy-Day Touring: Yes

Services and Facilities:

Restaurants No	Lockers No
Alcoholic beverages No	Pet kennels No
Disabled access Yes	Rain check No
Wheelchair rental No	Private tours No
Baby stroller rental No	

Description and Comments   This is where harness racing was born, and the museum features exhibits and displays covering the sport, its horses, and its influence on American culture. You'll see champions' sulkies and silks, harness-racing art, and memorabilia. There's also a collection of Currier & Ives trotting prints and other art, including paintings by the nineteenth century's most prominent equine artists. Of most interest to kids are the 3-D simulator that puts you into a race, the talking horse, and the chance to announce a race.

Hudson River Maritime Museum

One Rondout Landing, Kingston; (914) 338-0071;
   www.ulster.net/~hrmm

Hours: Museum: May–October, daily 11 a.m.–5 p.m. Boat tours to lighthouse: July and August, daily at 12:30 p.m., 1:30 p.m., 2:30 p.m. and 3:30 p.m., plus 11:30 a.m. on Saturday and Sunday; in May, June, September, and October, Saturdays, Sundays, and holidays at 12:30 p.m., 1:30 p.m., 2:30 p.m., and 3:30 p.m.

Admission: Museum only: $3 adults, $2 seniors 60 and older, $2 children ages 6–12; free for children 5 and under; museum and lighthouse boat tour: $8 adults, $7 seniors and children ages 6–12, free for children 5 and under

Appeal by Age Groups:

Pre-school	Grade School	Teens	Young Adults	Over 30	Seniors
★★	★★★★	★★★★	★★★★★	★★★★★	★★★★★

Touring Time: Average 2 hours; minimum 1 hour

Rainy-Day Touring: Yes

Services and Facilities:

Restaurants No; plenty nearby	Baby stroller rental No
Alcoholic beverages No	Lockers No
Disabled access Yes; except for boat ride	Pet kennels No
	Rain check Yes; for boat ride
Wheelchair rental No	Private tours No

Description and Comments   Each year, this museum focuses on a different topic in Hudson River history. Displays have included photographs, sunken ships, abandoned boats, brickyards, ice-harvesting equipment, steamboats, and recreation vessels. The former boat shop holds larger artifacts, such as ice yachts, a steam-hoisting engine, and various boats. The Rondout Lighthouse, built in 1913, is the last and largest lighthouse along the Hudson River.

Kaatskill Kaleidescope

5340 Route 28, Mount Trempor; (845) 434-6065; www.catskillcorners.com

Hours: June–October, daily 11 a.m.–7 p.m.; November–May, Wednesday–Sunday 11 a.m.–7 p.m.

Admission: $10 adults, $8 seniors, $8 children under 55 inches tall, $9 families of four or more

Appeal by Age Groups:

Pre-school	Grade School	Teens	Young Adults	Over 30	Seniors
★★★	★★★★★	★★★★	★★★★	★★★★	★★★★

Touring Time: Average 2 hours; minimum 1 hour

Rainy-Day Touring: Yes

Services and Facilities:

Restaurants Yes	Lockers No
Alcoholic beverages Yes	Pet kennels No
Disabled access Yes	Rain check No
Wheelchair rental No	Private tours No
Baby stroller rental No	

Description and Comments   Who thinks these things up? Here, in a renovated dairy barn, we find a collection of giant kaleidoscopes, to peer through, operate, and ride on. There are a series of huge, interactive kaleidoscopes, a gallery of light sculpture, and a thing called the Amazing Don-Doakahedron, which projects images from the Hubble Telescope to create a trip among the stars. The experience starts with a production called "America, The House We Live In," an American-history spectacle with surround-sound stereo. At Christmastime or President's Day, the show becomes "Hexagon Holiday." Seven stores are also on-site, including a kaleidoscope store, a gourmet deli, and a toy store. The Kaatskill Kaleidoscope show is not recommended for kids under age four, but they'll enjoy the other features.

Mid-Hudson Children's Museum

South Hills Mall, 838 South Road, Poughkeepsie; (914) 297-5938; www.mhcm.org

Hours: Tuesday–Sunday 11 a.m.–5 p.m.; closed Mondays (except selected school holidays); closed New Year's Day, Memorial Day, Fourth of July, Labor Day, Thanksgiving, and Christmas

Admission: $3.50 per adult and child; free admission for members and children under 2 years

Appeal by Age Groups:

Pre-school	Grade School	Teens	Young Adults	Over 30	Seniors
★★★★	★★★★★	★★	★★★	★★★	★★★

Touring Time: Average 2 hours; minimum 1 hour

Rainy-Day Touring: Yes

Services and Facilities:

Restaurants No	Lockers No
Alcoholic beverages No	Pet kennels No
Disabled access No	Rain check No
Wheelchair rental No	Private tours No
Baby stroller rental No	

Description and Comments   A vibrant place filled with hands-on stuff to do. Da Vinci Inventions features working models of the artist/inventor's sixteenth-century inventions. Kids will find a 15-foot stegosaurus, a sand table, a fossil dig, puzzles and books, a space shuttle replica, a working construction crane, a telegraph machine, a unique exhibit where they can maneuver a wheelchair obstacle course and read Braille to gain an understanding of persons of all different abilities, and a cool thing called a Gravity Roll, which shows just why a ball stays on a roller-coaster track.

Old Rhinebeck Aerodrome

44 Stone Church Road, Rhinebeck; (914) 758-8610; www.oldrhinebeck.org

Hours: May 15–October 31, daily 10 a.m.–5 p.m.; airshows from mid-June–mid-October, Saturdays and Sundays 2 p.m.

Admission: Monday–Friday $5 adults, $2 children ages 6–10, free for children under 6; Saturday and Sunday airshows, $10 adults, $5 children ages 6–10, free for children under 6

Appeal by Age Groups:

Pre-school	Grade School	Teens	Young Adults	Over 30	Seniors
★★★★	★★★★★	★★★★	★★★★	★★★★★	★★★★★

Touring Time: Average 2 hours; minimum 1½ hour

Rainy-Day Touring: Yes

Services and Facilities:

Restaurants Yes	Lockers No
Alcoholic beverages No	Pet kennels No
Disabled access Yes; but hilly terrain	Rain check Yes
Wheelchair rental No	Private tours Yes; with advanced notice
Baby stroller rental No	

Description and Comments If possible, come when the two-hour airshow is presented. They're wonderfully flown and narrated. The Aerodrome presents antique airplanes from the period of 1900 to 1940. The planes are interesting on display, but they're something special when in the air. If you want to spend the money ($30 per person), they'll take you up for 15 minutes in a 1929 open-cockpit, four-seater biplane, before or after the show.

Philipsburg Manor

Route 9, Sleepy Hollow; (914) 631-3992; www.hudsonvalley.org

Hours: March, Saturday and Sunday 10 a.m.–4 p.m.; April–December, Wednesday–Monday 10 a.m.–4 p.m. Last guided tour at 3 p.m. Closed January and February

Admission: $8 adults, $7 seniors, $4 children ages 5–17, children under five admitted free

Appeal by Age Groups:

Pre-school	Grade School	Teens	Young Adults	Over 30	Seniors
★★★	★★★★	★★★★	★★★★★	★★★★★	★★★★★

Touring Time: Average 2½ hours; minimum 1½ hour

Rainy-Day Touring: Yes

Services and Facilities:

Restaurants Yes	Lockers No
Alcoholic beverages No	Pet kennels No
Disabled access No	Rain check No
Wheelchair rental No	Private tours No
Baby stroller rental No	

Description and Comments You can tour this working, eighteenth-century farm on your own or with an interpreter in period costume. The main buildings include a stone manor house with seventeenth- and eighteenth-century furnishings, a working, water-powered grist mill (always a kid favorite), and a period barn. Around the grounds you'll find cattle, oxen, sheep, and chickens. Special events are staged regularly.

Note: If you're coming from Manhattan or northern New Jersey, an entertaining and interesting way to reach Philipsburg Manor and Sunnyside (see below) is to take a New York Waterway narrated boat trip. Call (800) 533-3779 for information.

Sunnyside, Washington Irving Home

West Sunnyside Lane, Tarrytown; (914) 631-8200; www.hudsonvalley.org

Hours: March, Saturday and Sunday 10 a.m.–5 p.m.; April–December, Wednesday–Monday 10 a.m.–5 p.m. (last tour at 4 p.m.)

Admission: $8 adults, $7 seniors, $4 children ages 5–17, children under five admitted free

Appeal by Age Groups:

Pre-school	Grade School	Teens	Young Adults	Over 30	Seniors
★	★★★★	★★★	★★★★	★★★★★	★★★★★

Touring Time: Average 2½ hours; minimum 1½ hour

Rainy-Day Touring: Yes

Services and Facilities:

Restaurants Yes	Lockers No
Alcoholic beverages No	Pet kennels No
Disabled access Partial	Rain check No
Wheelchair rental Yes; free	Private tours No
Baby stroller rental No	

Description and Comments   This is the restored home of writer Washington Irving, America's first successful and internationally known author, best remembered for penning *The Legend of Sleepy Hollow* and *Rip Van Winkle*. It's on a beautiful setting on the Hudson River. Interpreters in mid-Victorian period costumes lead tours. Sunnyside is best visited when a special event is taking place, particularly around Halloween when everybody can scare themselves silly with tales of the Headless Horseman.

U.S. Military Academy at West Point

Visitors Center, West Point; (914) 938-2638; www.usma.edu

Hours: Visitors Center open daily 9 a.m.–4:45 p.m.; West Point Museum open daily 10:30 a.m.–4:15 p.m.; both are closed Thanksgiving, Christmas, and New Year's days

Admission: Free

Appeal by Age Groups:

Pre-school	Grade School	Teens	Young Adults	Over 30	Seniors
★★	★★★★	★★★★	★★★★	★★★★★	★★★★★

Touring Time: Average 2 hours; minimum 1 hour

Rainy-Day Touring: Yes

Services and Facilities:

Restaurants Yes; in Hotel Thayer	Baby stroller rental No
Alcoholic beverages Yes; in Hotel Thayer	Lockers No
	Pet kennels No
Disabled access Yes	Rain check No
Wheelchair rental Yes; in museum only	Private tours No

Description and Comments   Believe it or not, the U.S. Military Academy ranks among the state's top-three tourist attractions. You can take a guided bus tour (see West Point Tours, below), or you can follow the self-guiding driving or walking tours. Start at the Visitors Center, where a video on cadet life and West Point history is shown every half-hour. The West Point Museum holds collections representing all major military categories, and every American armed conflict is represented. The Large Weapons Gallery displays artillery pieces, a World War I tank, an atomic bomb like the one dropped on Nagasaki, and the cannon that fired the first American shot of World War I. Fort Putnam was built in 1778, and from it most of West Point and the surrounding Hudson River Valley can be seen. Trophy Point offers spectacular views and holds links from the Great Chain that was stretched across the Hudson River during the Revolutionary War to prevent British ships from sailing upriver.

West Point Tours

425 Main Street, Highland Falls; (914) 446-4724; www.westpointtours.com

One-Hour Tours: April–October, $6 adults, $3 children; depart the Visitors Center Monday–Saturday at 10 a.m., 10:30 a.m., 11 a.m., 11:45 a.m., 12:45 p.m., 1:30 p.m., 2 p.m., 2:40 p.m., 3:15 p.m., and 3:30 p.m.; Sunday tours at 11 a.m. November–April, daily at 11:30 a.m. and 1:30 p.m.

Two-Hour Tours: May–October, $8 adults, $5 children; depart Monday–Saturday at 11:15 a.m. and 1:15 p.m.; Sunday tours at 1:15 p.m.

This is a way in which to tour the Academy by bus. The company utilizes full-sized tour buses and experienced guides, with stops at the Cadet Chapel and Trophy Point. The chapel is built in the form of a cross and contains what is claimed to be the largest church organ in the world. Trophy Point offers spectacular river views, plus some War Relics, and is, in effect, an outside museum. We recommend these guided tours for families with older children or for those who simply do not want to walk.

Hudson River Cruises

Departing from a dock adjacent to the Hudson River Maritime Museum, this company offers two-hour sightseeing cruises on Tuesdays through Sundays, departing at 11:30 a.m. and 2 p.m. Specialty and theme cruises are also offered. Basic cruise prices: $13 adult, $12 seniors 60 and older, $6 children ages 4-11, and free for children under 4. The Hudson is a Nationally Designated Heritage River, and the scenery is magnificent. The boat passes a variety of magnificent estates, under several bridges, past an antique lighthouse, and by various islands, all accompanied by historical and anecdotal narration. Rondout Landing, Kingston; (800) 843-7473, (914) 255-6618; www.hudsonrivercruises.com.

Family-Friendly Restaurants

ST. ANDREW'S CAFE OR APPLE PIE BAKERY CAFE

1946 Campus Drive, Hyde Park; (845) 471-6608 (restaurant reservations), (845) 452-9600 (general information)

Meals served: Lunch and dinner
Cuisine: Continental and pizza
Entree range: $6.75–15 (St. Andrew's Cafe); $5.25 (Apple Pie Bakery)
Children's menu: No
Reservations: Not required for St. Andrew's or Apple Pie Bakery
Payment: Major credit cards

Everyone should visit and eat at Culinary Institute of America (CIA) sometime. It's the world's only residential college devoted entirely to culinary education. The property was once a Jesuit seminary, built in the late 1800s, and it has some marvelous stained-glass windows to prove it. The campus' views of the Hudson are magnificent. All meals are created and served by advanced students, which translates into superb food and service. CIA has two other restaurants, but they're quite formal and will probably make your kids fidget. For instance, in the American Cafe, men are asked to wear jackets. The

Apple Pie Bakery Cafe features gourmet sandwiches, soups, salads, pizza, and heavenly pastries.

GOODFELLAS INN

1954 Route 52 Hopewell Junction; (914) 226-6003

Meals served: Lunch and dinner
Cuisine: American and pasta
Entree range: $9.99–20
Children's menu: Yes ($4.25)
Reservations: No
Payment: Major credit cards

This is a local neighborhood restaurant/tavern with a friendly flair and an outdoor dining deck. It also has a lighted volleyball court and horseshoe court. Goodfellas does things like offer 20¢ wings during Mets, Yankees, Knicks, or Rangers games. Parents should try the Steak & Beer Special with onion rings for $9.99. You can build a burger, create a chicken sandwich, or choose pizza or pasta.

NEW WORLD HOME COOKING CO.

Route 212, Woodstock; (914) 246-0900; www.newworldhomecooking.com

Meals served: Lunch and dinner
Cuisine: Eclectic, with an emphasis on Latin and Caribbean
Entree range: $13.95–21.05 (dinner)
Children's menu: Yes
Reservations: Yes
Payment: Major credit cards

OK, we all know that Woodstock didn't take place in Woodstock. But this place is a carryover, where international music plays, and the culinary eye is on the organic and interesting. It's "an interpretation of the American melting pot," as chef Ric Orlando puts it. Kids will be fascinated by the open kitchen; they can actually watch the chefs at work. On the menu, you'll find items like Northwind Farms free-range turkey medallions with adobo (a Latin marinade), roasted-corn salsa, black beans, brown rice, and seared greens; Ropa Vieja, a Cuban pot roast; and The Divine Trilogy of Macaroni. On the kids' menu? Pasta with butter and cheese or chunky red sauce, free-range beef burger with cheese, free-range turkey drumstick, and more.

New York City

Although most visitors limit their stays to Manhattan, New York City is actually made up of five boroughs: **Manhattan, The Bronx** (to Manhattan's north), **Queens** (to the east), **Brooklyn** (to the southeast), and **Staten Island** (to the southwest). Within most of Manhattan, the streets are laid out in a logical grid: numbered streets run east-west, the farther north the street, the higher the number; numbered avenues run north-south, the higher the number the farther west it is; almost all streets support one-way traffic, with Broadway being the most notable exception. Downtown, south of First Street, however, in the areas where Manhattan was settled, the streets are not laid out with any logic. Down there, even seasoned New Yorkers need a map.

Manhattan is loosely divided into a number of neighborhoods. Midtown, running roughly from 34th Street north to Central Park at 59th street, is the heart of things. From 59th Street to 96th Street west of Central Park lies the Upper West Side; east of the park it's the Upper East Side. South of 34th Street on the west is Chelsea. Working south, you'll find Greenwich Village, east and west, then arts-rich SoHo and Tribeca, as well as Little Italy, followed by Chinatown, and Wall Street and the Financial District. Uptown north of 110th Street lies Harlem. East of Harlem is Spanish Harlem. And, finally, up north are the residential neighborhoods Washington Heights, Fort George, and Inwood.

Start your visit at the New York City Convention & Visitors Bureau's **Times Square Visitor Information Center** (call (800) 692-8474 or (212) 397-8222) at 810 7th Avenue at 53rd Street to pick up printed guides and maps and to get advice. Their *Ticket Axis* system provides touch-screen, up-to-date information on attractions and events. The kiosks sell general-admission tickets to top attractions and the *CityPass,* which is good for discounted admission to New York Skyride, Top of the World Trade Center, Intrepid Sea-Air-Space Museum, Circle Line, Museum of the City of New

York, New York Hall of Science, New York Botanical Gardens, Museum of Financial History, and Brooklyn Museum of Art.

Manhattan contains a lifetime's worth of attractions. The **New Museum of Contemporary Art** (call (212) 219-1222; 583 Broadway) in SoHo offers art for and by teens. **El Museo del Barrio** (call (212) 831-7272; 1230 Fifth Avenue at 104th Street) is the country's only art museum devoted to Puerto Rican and Latin American artists. Kids love the corkscrew gallery ramps at the **Guggenheim Museum** (call (212) 423-3500; 1071 5th Avenue at 89th Street) and some of the unusual art and design holdings at the **Museum of Modern Art** (call (212) 708-9490; 11 W. 53rd Street). The **Forbes Magazine Galleries** (call (212) 206-5548; 62 5th Avenue at 12th Street) contain an incredible collection of Faberge eggs and toy boats. For a look at nineteenth-century immigrant life, the **Lower East Side Tenement Museum** (call (212) 431-0233; 90 Orchard Street at Broome Street) is a real eye-opener.

On the more modern front, **MTV Studios** at Times Square is always a happening place. The **Sony IMAX Theater** (call (212) 833-8100, 1998 Broadway at 68th Street) plays IMAX/3-D films. **Chelsea Piers** (call (212) 336-6666; 23rd Street at Hudson Street) is a 30-acre riverside sports complex that offers everything from golf and skateboarding to ice skating and bowling. At **Rockefeller Center/Radio City Music Hall** (call (212) 632-4041; 49th Street at 6th Avenue) you can tour the buildings, the NBC Studios, see the Rockettes perform, or ice skate at Christmastime under the famous tree. For the price of subway fare, you can ride the **Roosevelt Island Aerial Tram** over the East River. Don't miss **Central Park** (call (212) 794-6564; see The Best Beaches and Parks on page 310). Running from 59th Street to 100th Street and encompassing 840 acres, Central Park is smack in the middle of everything. For other outdoor options, **Flushing Meadows Corona Park,** on the site of the 1939 and 1964 Worlds Fairs, is the home of the National Tennis Center (which is open to the public), Shea Stadium, a zoo, museums, and hundreds of acres of open space (call (718) 760-6565). **Prospect Park** is the heart of recreation in Brooklyn. Within its 520 acres are myriad ball fields, a wildlife center, a children's zoo, and a 1776 Dutch Colonial village (call (718) 399-7339).

Beyond Manhattan, the **Staten Island Children's Museum** (call (718) 273-2060) and the **Brooklyn Children's Museum** (call (718) 735-4400) both contain excellent hands-on exhibits and activities. The **Brooklyn Museum of Art** (call (718) 638-5000) is actually the city's second largest art museum. **Coney Island** (call (718) 266-1234) remains a vibrant amusement park and beach with a boardwalk, a place where the famous Nathans' hot dogs still reign. In Queens, the **American Museum of Moving Image**

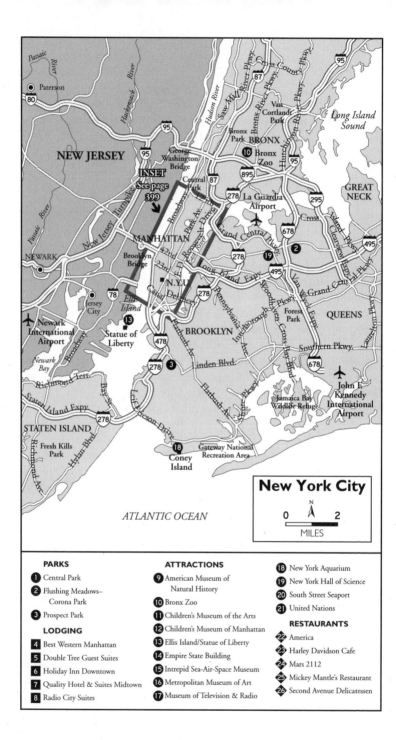

New York City

0 — 2 MILES
N

PARKS
1. Central Park
2. Flushing Meadows–Corona Park
3. Prospect Park

LODGING
4. Best Western Manhattan
5. Double Tree Guest Suites
6. Holiday Inn Downtown
7. Quality Hotel & Suites Midtown
8. Radio City Suites

ATTRACTIONS
9. American Museum of Natural History
10. Bronx Zoo
11. Children's Museum of the Arts
12. Children's Museum of Manhattan
13. Ellis Island/Statue of Liberty
14. Empire State Building
15. Intrepid Sea-Air-Space Museum
16. Metropolitan Museum of Art
17. Museum of Television & Radio
18. New York Aquarium
19. New York Hall of Science
20. South Street Seaport
21. United Nations

RESTAURANTS
22. America
23. Harley Davidson Cafe
24. Mars 2112
25. Mickey Mantle's Restaurant
26. Second Avenue Delicatessen

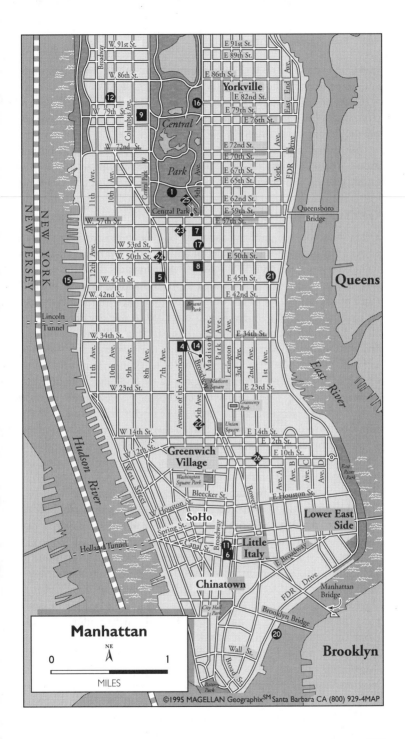

Manhattan

0   NE   1

MILES

©1995 MAGELLAN Geographix^SM Santa Barbara CA (800) 929-4MAP

(call (718) 784-0077) is housed in a former silent-movie production studio and, more recently, shooting studio for *The Bill Cosby Show*.

Upon arrival in the city, pick up copies of *New York, WHERE,* and *Time Out New York* magazines; they contain all the current listings for events, shows, and exhibitions.

You neither need nor want your car in Manhattan. If you are driving, expect to park the car for the duration of your stay, preferably in your hotel's garages, and expect it to cost anywhere from $15–30 per day.

GETTING AROUND

Here's the scoop: use public transportation. Pick up bus and subway maps at the Time Square Visitors Center or any major subway station. The system looks confusing, but since most of Manhattan is laid out in a grid, it can be deciphered without too much effort. Bus and subway fare is $1.50; you'll need exact change on the bus and to buy a token for the subway. Better to purchase the Unlimited Ride MetroCard. A one-day version, called a Fun Pass, costs $4, the seven-day card costs $17, a 30-day version costs $63, and unlimited rides are allowed during those time periods. Contrary to myth, the subways are not dangerous; for maximum safety, stand in the middle of the platform when waiting for trains, and ride the middle cars.

Taxis are expensive but can be the quickest and easiest way to get from point to point. Fares start at $2 and increase by 30¢ for every one-fifth of a mile or 90 seconds standing time; you'll also incur a 50¢ night surcharge for rides between 8 p.m. and 6 a.m. Yellow medallion cabs, as opposed to private car services, or so-called "gypsy" cabs, are the only ones authorized to pick up passengers on the city streets.

To get to and from the airports (see Getting There on page 305), New York Airport Service Express, (call (718) 706-9658), provides bus service from JFK to the Port Authority Bus Terminal (42nd Street and 8th Avenue) daily at 30-minute intervals for $13. Gray Line Air Shuttle, (call (800) 451-0455 or (212) 315-3006), offers on-demand, shared minibus service for $14. Super Shuttle Manhattan, (call (800) 258-3826), offers on-demand, shared door-to door service for $14. Taxis to Manhattan from JFK must charge the city's prescribed flat fare of $30 to the first Manhattan destination. The return fare from Manhattan to JFK is the meter reading, plus tolls. From La Guardia Airport, New York Airport Service Express Bus charges $10 to travel to the Port Authority Bus Terminal. Gray Line Air Shuttle's shared mini-bus costs $13, and taxi fare can range from $16–26 plus tolls. Newark Airport is located about 16 miles southwest of Manhattan in New Jersey. New Jersey Transit, (201) 762-5100, runs buses 24 hours a day to and from the Port Authority Bus Terminal. Olympia Airport Express, (212) 964-6233 or (908) 354-3330, runs buses to the Port Authority Bus Terminal every 20 minutes, or to Grand Central Terminal (120 East 41st Street at Park Avenue) for $10, with connecting service available to many hotels for an additional $5. Gray Line Air Shuttle offers shared minibus service to Port Authority for $10, or to anywhere between Battery Park and 125th Street for $14. Taxi fare runs between $30–34, plus tolls.

Family Lodging

Face it: lodging in Manhattan is not cheap. You can easily pay $400 or more a night in high season. But a city with more than 65,000 hotel rooms can offer more affordable alternatives, many of which are family-friendly. We recommend staying in Midtown Manhattan. It may cost a bit more, but it will put you right in the heart of things near shopping, museums, theaters, and subway lines. A central location will ease a lot of logistical pain. In addition to the handful of choices noted here, the New York Convention & Visitors Bureau produces a fairly comprehensive list of lodging options. NYCVB also offers a Peak Season Hotel Hotline at (800) 846-7666.

Best Western Manhattan

Conveniently located near the Empire State Building, Macy's, and Madison Square Garden, the Best Western has 176 guest rooms, 35 of which are suites. Continental breakfast is included, as are in-room coffee makers, irons, ironing boards, and hair dryers. A fitness center is on-site, and two restaurants are adjacent, one Asian, the other Italian. Rates: $179–199 for rooms, $239–269 for suites. 17 W. 32nd Street; (800) 567-7720 or (212) 790-2705.

Double Tree Guest Suites

This is an all-suites hotel in the heart of the theater district. All rooms are equipped with kitchenettes. Rates: $210–750. 1568 Broadway (at 47th Street); (800) 325-9033 or (212) 719-1600.

Holiday Inn Downtown

With a setting near Canal Street, this hotel offers a good location for visitors who want to frequent SoHo, Chinatown, Little Italy, and Greenwich Village. The 227 rooms have in-room coffee makers, irons and ironing boards, and movies. Rates: $170–269. 138 Lafayette Street; (212) 966-8898.

Quality Hotel & Suites Midtown

Within walking distance of Rockefeller Center, Radio City Music Hall, 5th Avenue, and many museums, this 192-room hotel holds 20 suites. Rooms have in-room coffee makers and a complimentary continental breakfast is included. Rates: $179–209. 59 W. 56th Street; (800) 567-7720 or (212) 719-2300.

Radio City Suites

When traveling with kids, why not stay in an apartment? With 113 one- and two-bedroom units set in the heart of Midtown/Rockefeller Center, this is a relatively affordable place to stay that still provides hotel-like features such as a concierge, on-site laundry facilities, and 24-hour front desk and security. A coffee shop is next door. Rates: $155–195. 142 W. 49th Street; (877) 921-9321 or (212) 730-0728.

Attractions

American Museum of Natural History/ Rose Center for Earth & Space

Central Park West & 79th Street; (212) 769-5100; advance tickets (212) 769-5200; www.amnh.org

Hours: Sunday–Thursday 10 a.m.–5:45 p.m., Friday and Saturday 10 a.m.–8:45 p.m. Space show runs continually Sunday–Thursday 10:30 a.m.–5 p.m., Friday and Saturday 10:30 a.m.–8 p.m.

Admission: Museum and Rose Center: $10 adults, $7.50 seniors and students, $6 children.; including space show: $19 adults, $14 seniors and students, $11.50 children

Appeal by Age Groups:

Pre-school	Grade School	Teens	Young Adults	Over 30	Seniors
★★★★	★★★★★	★★★★	★★★★	★★★★★	★★★★★

Touring Time: Average 4 hours; minimum 2 hours

Rainy-Day Touring: Yes

Services and Facilities:

Restaurants Yes	Lockers No; cloak room
Alcoholic beverages Yes	Pet kennels No
Disabled access Yes	Rain check No
Wheelchair rental Yes; free	Private tours No
Baby stroller rental No	

Description and Comments The Rose Center, an investment of $210 million, has made this among the world's best science museums. The architecture alone—a four-million-pound aluminum sphere sitting inside a huge glass cube—is worth the visit. All ages will find it a marvelous place in which to marvel at the universe. The new Space Theater actually makes you feel like a space traveler, and the interactive displays are, needless to say, state-of-the-art. Still, no matter how great the new Rose Center may be, the Museum of Natural History remains a world-class place in itself.

From its famous dinosaur skeletons to its fossil collection and its IMAX theater, it remains a must-see. Museum guided tours are offered; call for schedule information.

Bronx Zoo

Pelham Parkway at Fordham Road, Bronx; (718) 367-1010; www.bronxzoo.com

Hours: April–October, Monday–Friday 10 a.m.–5 p.m., Saturday, Sunday, and holidays 10 a.m.–5:30 p.m.; November–March, daily 10 a.m.–4:30 p.m. Special Holiday Lights display: day after Thanksgiving–January 2, daily 5:30 p.m.–9 p.m. Children's Zoo and rides closed during winter

Admission: Thursday–Tuesday: $9 adults, $5 seniors 65 and older and children ages 2–12. November 2–January 3: $6 adults, $3 seniors and children. January 3–March 31: $4 adults, $2 children and seniors; children under age 2 always get in free; extra charges for Children's Zoo and special rides (see description below)

Appeal by Age Groups:

Pre-school	Grade School	Teens	Young Adults	Over 30	Seniors
★★★★★	★★★★★	★★★★	★★★★★	★★★★★	★★★★★

Touring Time: Average 5–6 hours; minimum 4 hours

Rainy-Day Touring: Yes

Services and Facilities:

Restaurants Yes	Baby stroller rental No
Alcoholic beverages Yes	Lockers No
Disabled access Yes	Pet kennels No
Wheelchair rental Yes; to reserve call (718) 220-5188	Rain check No
	Private tours Yes

Description and Comments The Bronx Zoo is the largest urban zoo in the country, and it's a delightful place to spend a day. More than 6,000 animals live here. To avoid confusion and exhaustion, check the zoo map on the website and try to plan ahead for your visit. The highlight exhibits are Jungle-World, an indoor rain forest; Himalayan Highlands, home to snow leopards and red pandas, among others; the Bengali Express, a monorail ride through Asia; and the Children's Zoo, a place about which our near-adult children still talk enthusiastically, especially the spider's web and crawl-through prairie dog tunnel. There's much more, of course, and some attractions cost extra, like the Bengali Express ($2), the Children's Zoo ($2), camel rides ($3), Skyfari gondola ride ($2), and the Zoo Shuttle train ($2). Be aware that the

Children's Zoo and the Bengali Express are closed in winter. Free zoo walking tours, led by volunteer docents, can be arranged by calling (718) 220-5141 a few weeks ahead of your visit. While the zoo provides plenty of snack bars and restaurant facilities, food costs can add up. You might consider bringing a picnic and giving the kids a snack allowance for the day.

You can reach the zoo from Manhattan by subway on the IRT #2 or #5 trains, or by several buses. Allow at least an hour to get there. If you drive, parking costs $6. On the same trip, you can also visit the nearby Bronx Botanical Garden at 200th Street & Kazimiroff Boulevard, Bronx; (718) 817-8700.

Children's Museum of the Arts

182 Lafayette Street (between Broome and Grand Streets); (212) 941-9198; www.ny.com/museums/children.museum.of.the.arts.html

Hours: Wednesday noon–7 p.m., Thursday–Sunday noon–5 p.m.

Admission: $5 per person; pay as you wish on Wednesdays 5–7 p.m.; children under 12 months and adults over 65 get in free

Appeal by Age Groups:

Pre-school	Grade School	Teens	Young Adults	Over 30	Seniors
★★★★★	★★★★★★ ★		★★★	★★★★	★★★★

Touring Time: Average 2 hours; minimum 1 hour

Rainy-Day Touring: Yes

Services and Facilities:

Restaurants No	Lockers No
Alcoholic beverages No	Pet kennels No
Disabled access Yes	Rain check No
Wheelchair rental No	Private tours No
Baby stroller rental No	

Description and Comments An arts museum in the country's arts capital, but this one is designed especially for little ones. Aimed at 2–10-year-olds, the museum includes a Creative Play Area, designed for children ages 5 and under; the Artist's Studio, where children over age 5 can work on daily art projects that encourage problem solving (and, on any given day, they may find themselves working with a professional artist from the community); the Actor's Studio, for imaginative playacting; the Ball Pond, a kinesthetic and motor skills experience; Magnetic Masterpieces, reproductions of famous artworks cut into magnetic puzzle pieces; and more.

Children's Museum of Manhattan

212 W. 83rd Street; (212) 721-1234; www.cmom.org

Hours: Wednesday–Sunday 10 a.m.–5 p.m.; closed Monday and Tuesday but open on school holidays

Admission: $6 adults and children, $3 seniors 65 and older, free for children under age 1

Appeal by Age Groups:

Pre-school	Grade School	Teens	Young Adults	Over 30	Seniors
★★★★★	★★★★★	★★★	★★★★	★★★★★	★★★★★

Touring Time: Average 2½ hours; minimum 1½ hour

Rainy-Day Touring: Yes

Services and Facilities:

Restaurants No	Lockers No; coat check room
Alcoholic beverages No	Pet kennels No
Disabled access No	Rain check No
Wheelchair rental No	Private tours No
Baby stroller rental No	

Description and Comments   This children's museum offers five floors of great stuff. Maybe the best exhibit is Body Odyssey, where kids crawl through a blood tunnel, head through the digestive tract, or hang out in the lungs. Exhibits are aimed at specific age groups up to age 12, including infants. The schedule is peppered with special events and performances as well.

Ellis Island Immigration Museum/ Statue of Liberty National Monument

Ellis Island; (212) 363-3200; www.nps.gov/stli; ferry ticket/schedule information: (212) 269-5755

Hours: Daily 9:30 a.m.–5 p.m.; closed Christmas Day. Ferries leave approximately every 45 minutes, 9 a.m.–5 p.m.

Admission: Sites are free. Ferry fare, $7 adults, $3 children ages 3–17, free for children under age 3

Appeal by Age Groups:

Pre-school	Grade School	Teens	Young Adults	Over 30	Seniors
★★★	★★★★★	★★★★★	★★★★★	★★★★	★★★★★

Touring Time: Average 6 hours; minimum 4 hours

Rainy-Day Touring: Yes

Services and Facilities:

Restaurants Yes	Lockers No
Alcoholic beverages No	Pet kennels No
Disabled access Yes	Rain check No
Wheelchair rental Yes; free	Private tours No
Baby stroller rental No	

Description and Comments   Everybody loves the Statue of Liberty, but Ellis Island, where 12 million immigrants first came ashore in America, is something really special. The Immigration Museum tells their story. The introductory film is poignant, a must-see. The live performance, *Ellis Island Stories,* is quite worthwhile. Even if your relatives didn't pass through Ellis Island, you'll be moved by a visit here, and the kids will learn something important about how this country was populated.

The Statue of Liberty draws large crowds. The number of people permitted to walk the 354 steps to the crown is limited each day; if you want to take the challenge, be on the morning's first ferry. Otherwise, you can ride the elevator to the top of the pedestal to see magnificent Manhattan harbor views.

This trip, even when done to its minimum, requires a half-day. To do it justice, prepare to devote most of the day. The Circle Line Statue of Liberty Ferry leaves from Battery Park in Lower Manhattan; ferries also leave from Liberty State Park in Jersey City, New Jersey. As you wait on the ferry line in Battery Park, you'll be entertained by a variety of street performers, some of whom are actually pretty good. National Park Service rangers conduct 45-minute tours of Ellis Island, and a more extensive tape-recorded tour can be rented for $4.

Empire State Building Observatories/New York Skyride

350 5th Avenue; (212) 736-3100; www.esbny.com; Skyride information: (888) 759-7433 or (212) 279-9777; www.skyride.com

Hours: Observatories open daily 9:30 a.m.–midnight; Skyride open daily 10 a.m.–10 p.m.

Admission: Observatories only: $6 adults, $3 seniors, children, and military; observatories and Skyride combination: $14 adults, $9 children

Appeal by Age Groups:

Pre-school	Grade School	Teens	Young Adults	Over 30	Seniors
★★★★	★★★★★	★★★★	★★★★★	★★★★★	★★★★★

Touring Time: Average 1½ hour; minimum 1 hour

Rainy-Day Touring: Yes

Services and Facilities:

Restaurants No	Lockers No
Alcoholic beverages No	Pet kennels No
Disabled access Yes	Rain check No
Wheelchair rental No	Private tours No
Baby stroller rental No	

Description and Comments   For the grand view of New York City, we prefer the Empire State Building over the World Trade Center because of the Skyride. The Skyride is a motion-simulation ride that evokes an aerial view of the city, plus some surprises that include underwater and subterranean adventures. Kids love it. Pick up a printed brochure before going to the top of the building; it provides an excellent description of what you'll be seeing. As you would imagine, it's best to go up there on a clear day or night.

Intrepid Sea-Air-Space Museum

Pier 86, 12th Avenue at W. 46th Street; (212) 245-0072; www.intrepidmuseum.org

Hours: Monday–Friday 10 a.m.–5 p.m., Saturday and Sunday 10 a.m.– 6 p.m.

Admission: $12 adults, $9 veterans and U.S. Reservists, $9 seniors, college students, and students ages 12–17, $6 children ages 6–11, $2 children ages 2–5, free for children under age 2; wheelchair patrons pay half price; active-duty U.S. military get in free. Flight simulator: $5 per person

Appeal by Age Groups:

Pre-school	Grade School	Teens	Young Adults	Over 30	Seniors
★★★	★★★★★	★★★★★	★★★★★	★★★★★	★★★★★

Touring Time: Average 3 hours; minimum 2 hours

Rainy-Day Touring: Yes

Services and Facilities:

Restaurants Yes	Lockers No
Alcoholic beverages No	Pet kennels No
Disabled access Yes; partial	Rain check No
Wheelchair rental Yes; loan	Private tours Yes
Baby stroller rental No	

Description and Comments   The mainstay of this popular museum is the circa 1943, 40,000-ton, 900-foot aircraft carrier USS *Intrepid,* docked in the Hudson River. Other vessels include the USS *Edson,* a 4,000-ton destroyer, and the USS *Growler,* a 3,000-ton, guided missile submarine, circa 1958. In addition to all the interactive and video displays and the opportunity to clamber around on the ships, you get to see close-up views of some pretty remarkable aircraft parked on the flight deck. They range from World War II war birds to the Lockheed A-12 Blackbird, the world's fastest aircraft and ultimate spy plane (it flies up to three-and-a-half times the speed of sound). If you like hardware, military or otherwise, you'll love this. Kids (and parents, too) can also fly a jet mission on the Flight Simulator. The museum stages many special events, but its Military Salute Week, held annually during the week of July Fourth, attracts vessels from all over the world that are showcased to the public.

Note: The *Intrepid* sits on the far west side at Midtown, eight blocks north of the New York Waterways Pier and four blocks from the Circle Line. If you're taking one of these boat tours, you should consider visiting the *Intrepid* on the same day.

Metropolitan Museum of Art

5th Avenue and 82nd Street; (212) 535-7710; www.metmuseum.org

Hours: Thursday–Sunday 9:30 a.m.–5:30 p.m., Friday and Saturday
    9:30 a.m.–9 p.m.; closed Monday and Thanksgiving, Christmas
    and New Year's days

Admission: Pay what you will; suggested prices: $10 adults, $5 seniors
    and students, free for children under age 12

Appeal by Age Groups:

Pre-school	Grade School	Teens	Young Adults	Over 30	Seniors
★★★★	★★★★	★★★★	★★★★★	★★★★★	★★★★★

Touring Time: Average 3 hours; minimum 2 hours

Rainy-Day Touring: Yes

Services and Facilities:

Restaurants Yes	Lockers Yes; coat check room
Alcoholic beverages Yes	Pet kennels No
Disabled access Yes	Rain check No
Wheelchair rental Yes; free	Private tours No
Baby stroller rental No; baby backpack carriers available	

Description and Comments Don't come to the Met expecting to see it all. Rather, pick areas of interest and concentrate on them. The ancient Egypt and medieval armor exhibits are always popular with children. Pick up a museum map/guide at the information desk. Volunteers lead daily one-hour guided walking tours, some covering the overall collection and others focusing on specific departments or themes. With older kids or teens, you can opt for the Key to the Met Audio Guide ($5), which interprets artworks in the permanent collection and special exhibitions. At 1 p.m. on weekends, the Museum stages "Hello, Met!" for families with kids ages 5 to 12. It's an hour of discussion and sketching that introduces you to the museum's resident masterpieces.

Museum of Television & Radio

25 W. 52nd Street; (212) 621-6600; daily activity information, (212) 621-6800; www.mtr.org

Hours: Tuesday, Wednesday, and Friday–Sunday noon–6 p.m.; Thursday noon–8 p.m.; theaters open until 9 p.m. on Friday; closed Monday and on New Year's, Independence, Thanksgiving, and Christmas days

Admission: $6 adults, $4 seniors and students, $3 for children ages 13 and under

Appeal by Age Groups:

Pre-school	Grade School	Teens	Young Adults	Over 30	Seniors
★★★	★★★★	★★★★★	★★★★★	★★★★★	★★★★★

Touring Time: Average 2½ hours; minimum 1½ hour

Rainy-Day Touring: Yes

Services and Facilities:

Restaurants No	Lockers No
Alcoholic beverages No	Pet kennels No
Disabled access Yes	Rain check No
Wheelchair rental No	Private tours No
Baby stroller rental No	

Description and Comments   Here's a museum dedicated to broadcasting. The old TV shows create the biggest lure for kids, but the old-time radio elements can be fascinating to older children. On Saturdays, "Re-creating Radio" workshops are offered for families with children age 9 and older. On Saturdays and Sundays, the museum mounts screenings specifically for children. Don't miss the Children's Festival in November. Museum tours are offered daily, as are screenings and radio shows from the museum's huge collection. The daily schedule, which can include live radio broadcasts, is available at the front desk.

New York Aquarium

Surf Avenue and W. 8th Street, Coney Island, Brooklyn; (718) 265-3474; www.nyaquarium.com

Hours: Daily 10 a.m.–5 p.m.

Admission: $9.75 adults, $6 seniors 65 and older and children ages 2–12, free for children under age 2

Appeal by Age Groups:

Pre- school	Grade School	Teens	Young Adults	Over 30	Seniors
★★★★★	★★★★★	★★★★★	★★★★★	★★★★★	★★★★★

Touring Time: Average 3 hours; minimum 2 hours

Rainy-Day Touring: Yes

Services and Facilities:

Restaurants Yes	Lockers No; coat check room
Alcoholic beverages Yes; beer	Pet kennels No
Disabled access Yes	Rain check No
Wheelchair rental Yes; free	Private tours No
Baby stroller rental No	

Description and Comments   Although Brooklyn's Coney Island can seem far away, the aquarium is worth the trip. It has all the requisite attractions for a major facility of this type, including the Discovery Cove touch tank; "Fish that Go Zap!" about electric eels and others; many more hands-on exhibits and video displays; a chance to see Beluga whales very much up-close; and dolphin shows. You can get there on the IND subway, D or F trains, and can combine the trip with a day at the beach or playing on the classic Coney Island amusements.

New York Hall of Science

47-01 111th Street, Flushing Meadows Corona Park; (718) 699-0005; www.nyhallsci.org

Hours: July 1–August 31, Monday 9:30 a.m.–2 p.m., Tuesday–Sunday 9:30 a.m.–5 p.m.; September 1–June 30, Monday–Wednesday 9:30 a.m.–2 p.m. and Thursday–Sunday 9:30 a.m.–5 p.m.; closed Labor Day, Thanksgiving Day, Christmas Eve, Christmas Day, and New Year's Day

Admission: $7.50 adults, $5 seniors 62 and older and children ages 4–17; science playground: $2 per person. From September 1–June 30, free on Thursday and Friday 2–5 p.m.

Appeal by Age Groups:

Pre-school	Grade School	Teens	Young Adults	Over 30	Seniors
★★★★★	★★★★★	★★★★★	★★★★★	★★★★★	★★★★★

Touring Time: Average 3 hours; minimum 2 hours

Rainy-Day Touring: Yes

Services and Facilities:

Restaurants No	Lockers No; coat check room
Alcoholic beverages No	Pet kennels No
Disabled access Yes	Rain check No
Wheelchair rental Yes; free	Private tours No
Baby stroller rental No	

Description and Comments   Another terrific science museum, the New York Hall of Science has more than 185 exhibits. Kids absolutely love the Science Playground, an outdoor 30,000-square-foot exhibit to climb over, around, under, and through (open only to kids ages 6 and older). Other eye-openers include Marvelous Molecules, where a 35-foot glucose molecule hangs above you, and where kids can build their own molecule model. The Technology Gallery is all about cyberspace, including the chance to go online. At Window on the Universe, you can link online to astronomy databases around the world and see images from online observatories. There's plenty more, from microbes to machines.

You can reach the museum from Manhattan by subway on the IRT #7 train. It's near Shea Stadium; if you're planning to attend a Mets game, you could make a day of it. Plus, it's in Flushing Meadows/Corona Park, if you'd care to throw in a picnic.

South Street Seaport Museum/ South Street Seaport Marketplace

207 Fulton Street; museum, (212) 748-8600; marketplace, (212) 732-7678; museum, www.southstseaport.org; marketplace, www.southstreetseaport.com

Hours: Museum: April 1–September 30, daily 10 a.m.–6 p.m., Thursday 10 a.m.–8 p.m.; October 1–March 31, daily 10 a.m.– 5 p.m.; closed Tuesday

Admission: Museum: $6 adults, $5 seniors, $4 students, $3 children, free to museum members

Appeal by Age Groups:

Pre-school	Grade School	Teens	Young Adults	Over 30	Seniors
★★★★	★★★★★	★★★★★	★★★★	★★★★★	★★★★★

Touring Time: Average 4 hours (including marketplace); minimum 2 hours

Rainy-Day Touring: Yes

Services and Facilities:

Restaurants Yes	Lockers No; coat check room
Alcoholic beverages Yes	Pet kennels No
Disabled access Yes	Rain check No
Wheelchair rental Yes; free	Private tours No
Baby stroller rental No	

Description and Comments Set in what was once the country's leading port, this 11-square-block, cobblestone-paved historic district in lower Manhattan is a pedestrian-only zone. South Street is rich with eighteenth- and nineteenth-century buildings, and the nation's largest wholesale fish market still operates here. The South Street Seaport Museum tracks the Port of New York's history, including its commercial and cultural impact on the city, state, and nation. The museum comprises galleries and exhibits, living history programs, special events, and educational programs. It holds the largest privately owned collection of historic vessels (in tonnage) in the United States, and it is those ships that are no doubt the main draw for children. On weekends at 1 p.m. kids can join the crew of the *Peking* and help raise sails or toss lines. At the Maritime Crafts Center you can watch a professional woodcarver at work.

The marketplace holds more than 100 shops and 35 restaurants, including national chains, local merchants, and ethnic and fast-food restaurants. Special events are staged throughout the year, especially in summertime. You can climb aboard New York Waterway's Lower Harbor Cruise (see the Guided Tours section on page 416) from here.

United Nations

First Avenue and 46th Street; (212) 963-8687; www.un.org

Hours: March–December, tours daily 9:30 a.m.–4:45 p.m.; January–February, Monday–Friday 9:30 a.m.–4:45 p.m.; tour schedule may be limited during the general debate (end of September to mid-October); closed Thanksgiving, Christmas, and New Year's days

Admission: $7.50 adults, $6 seniors, $5 high school and college students, $4 students grades 1–8; children under age 5 not permitted on tour

Appeal by Age Groups:

Pre-school	Grade School	Teens	Young Adults	Over 30	Seniors
N/A	★★★	★★★★	★★★★★	★★★★★	★★★★★

Touring Time: Average 1½ hour; minimum 1 hour

Rainy-Day Touring: Yes

Services and Facilities:

Restaurants Yes	Lockers No; coat check room
Alcoholic beverages Yes	Pet kennels No
Disabled access Yes	Rain check No
Wheelchair rental No	Private tours No
Baby stroller rental No	

Description and Comments   The older your children, the more they will appreciate this tour, but it's really a special place that deserves to be visited. Be aware that preschoolers are not permitted on the tour. The tour covers the UN's work and the functions of its related organizations. You'll see the main Council Chambers, the General Assembly Hall, and some art and other donated objects that usually come with fascinating stories. We love the Marc Chagall stained-glass window and the Norman Rockwell mosaic.

Family-Friendly Restaurants

Where to eat? You'll have only 17,000 eateries to choose from. In addition to the kid-friendly sites noted here, think ethnic: Italian in Little Italy, Chinese in Chinatown, Indian on East 6th Street, Ukranian in the East Village . . . the list goes on. To save money, don't be afraid to stop into a neighborhood deli or small grocery store, or even to indulge in a classic street vendor hot dog.

AMERICA

9 E. 18th Street; (212) 505-2110

Meals served: Lunch and dinner
Cuisine: American
Entree range: $9.95–19.95
Children's menu: No
Reservations: No
Payment: Major credit cards

A huge place, always noisy and crowded, but they serve things like Fluffernutter sandwiches and macaroni and cheese for kids.

HARLEY DAVIDSON CAFE

1370 6th Avenue (at 56th Street); (212) 399-6000

Meals served: Lunch and dinner
Cuisine: American, with a touch of Mexican
Entree range: $9.95–19.95
Children's menu: No
Reservations: Yes
Payment: Major credit cards

The food may not be remarkable (from dogs, burgers, and meat loaf to fajitas, barbecue, and chicken pot pie), but the ambiance will blow the kids away. This is a Harley circus, with hands-on stuff to touch and play with and lots of motorcycle memorabilia. A fun spot.

MARS 2112

1633 Broadway (at 51st Street); (212) 582-2112

Meals served: Lunch and dinner
Cuisine: American
Entree range: $11.55–24.95
Children's menu: Yes ($8.95)
Reservations: No
Payment: Major credit cards

This isn't about the food. This is about an intergalactic experience that begins with an entrance through a time-travel spaceship ride and continues with a high-tech dining experience that simulates somebody's idea of life on Mars in the year 2112. Who thinks these things up? We don't know, but as theme restaurants go, this one's going to be memorable.

MICKEY MANTLE'S RESTAURANT

42 Central Park South at 6th Avenue; (212) 688-7777

Meals served: Lunch and dinner
Cuisine: American
Entree range: $11.95–19.95
Children's menu: Yes
Reservations: Yes
Payment: Major credit cards

Good food in an upscale sports-themed atmosphere. Plenty of Yankee memories and a gift shop, too.

SECOND AVENUE DELICATESSEN & RESTAURANT

156 2nd Avenue at 10th Street; (212) 677-0606

Meals served: Lunch and dinner
Cuisine: Jewish kosher deli
Entree range: $14–24
Children's menu: No
Reservations: No
Payment: Major credit cards

OK, there are a lot of delis in New York, and some may be more famous than this one, but it's our favorite. Unpretentious, set in the funky East Village, and often a madhouse, it has been lauded for having the best pastrami sandwich in the city and as serving the best chopped liver and corned beef on earth. If you're gonna go to New York, you've gotta eat in a deli. Good choice, this one.

Tickets, Tickets, Tickets

New York is the country's theater capital, and no visit is complete without attending a play. But there's a lot more going on than plays. Dance, music, and TV shows in particular. How to get tickets? For theater tickets at retail, call Tele-charge, (212) 239-6200, or from outside New York, (800) 432-7250; Ticketmaster, (212) 307-4100 or from outside the New York metro area (800) 755-4000; or Broadway Line, (888) 276-2392 or (212) 302-4111. For reduced-price seats, two TKTS booths, one at Times Square (47th Street at Broadway) and the other at the World Trade Center, sell same-day tickets for popular Broadway and Off-Broadway plays, (212) 768-1818. You have to stand in line and pay cash, but the 50% discount makes it worthwhile. Other sources of reduced-price tickets include Playbill On-Line (www.playbill.com) and Theatre Development Fund, (212) 221-0885 or www.tdf.org.

As for TV-show tickets, they're always free. The Montel Williams Show, David Letterman, Rosie, Saturday Night Live, and Emeril are among the shows taped here. Visit www.NewYorkShow.com; for a fee, they'll help you get tickets.

THE BEST THINGS IN LIFE ARE FREE

Sure, the cost of living in New York is high. But it's incredible how much you can do here for *nuttin!* The best ride in the city is the free **Staten Island Ferry.** Just hop on, ride out to Staten Island, stay on the boat, and ride back for fantastic views of downtown and the Statue of Liberty. The

Tourneau Time Machine (call (212) 758-7300) at 57th and Madison Avenue features watchmakers in action, plus interactive and historical exhibits about timepieces. Free concerts of all kinds take place throughout the summer, including midday pop, jazz, rock, and country music at the **World Trade Center;** the **Metropolitan Opera** performing in the parks in each borough; and the **New York Philharmonic Orchestra** and ongoing **Summertime Festival** performing on Central Park's Great Lawn.

The **Sony Wonder Technology Lab** (call (212) 833-8100) at 550 Madison Avenue reveals the wonders of modern electronics, and the **NBC Studio Tour** (call (212) 664-7174) at Rockefeller Center takes you behind the scenes at the TV station. Free entertainment at **Citicorp Center** (call (212) 559-6758) at 153 E. 53rd Street. Tours of **Grand Central Terminal** (call (212) 340-2345) are led on Wednesdays at 12:30 p.m., and self-guiding tours of the **New York Stock Exchange** (call (212) 656-5267) are available daily at 9 a.m. Tour **St. Patrick's Cathedral,** 5th Avenue at 50th Street, to see Gothic architecture at its finest. The **World Financial Center** (call (212) 945-0505), near the World Trade Center, also stages frequent free concerts and events. Also downtown, the **National Museum of American Indian** (call (212) 514-3700), part of the Smithsonian Institution, charges no admission.

GUIDED TOURS

There's a tour for every taste and interest, on any type of conveyance— foot, bus, boat, even helicopter. With kids, we recommend an around-the-island boat tour, or a get-on-and-off bus tour as second choice.

Big Apple Greeter. This is one of our favorites. Knowledgeable volunteers accompany visitors on two- to four-hour journeys in any of the five boroughs. It's free. Make reservations at least a week in advance; (212) 669-8159 or www.bigapplegreeter.org.

Boat Tours. NY Waterway, (800) 533-3779, and Circle Line Sightseeing Yachts, (212) 563-3200, offer harbor and around-Manhattan cruises from Hudson River Pier 78 (38th street) and Pier 83 (42nd Street), respectively. Both also offer tours from South Street Seaport.

Bus Tours. Open-air, double-decker buses are used on many tours operated by Gray Line, (212) 397-2620. Get-on/off "Total New York" tour tickets ($59 adults, $39 children ages 5-11) are good for two days and one evening and include admission to the Statue of Liberty/Ellis Island, Top Of The

World Trade Center Observatories, and the Empire State Building.

Special Tours. Joyce Gold History Tours, (212) 242-5762; Just Brooklyn Tours, (718) 968-0352; Big Onion Walking Tours, (212) 439-1090, led by Columbia University historians. Citywalks Walking Tours, (212) 989-2456; Harlem Your Way Tours Unlimited, (800) 382-9363); Backstage on Broadway, (800) 445-7074.

PROFESSIONAL SPORTS

New York counts itself among the few cities to field a team in every major sport, plus more than one in some. While baseball tickets are usually readily obtainable, basketball, hockey, and football tickets can be hard to get, unless you buy them well in advance.

Baseball. The Yankees play at Yankee Stadium, (718) 579-4531, at 161st Street and River Avenue in the Bronx. Reach the stadium by the IRT #4 train, or the IND B and D trains. The Mets play at Shea Stadium, (718) 507-8499, on Grand Central Parkway in Queens. The IRT #7 train takes you there.

Basketball and Hockey. The Knicks and the Rangers play at Madison Square Garden, (212) 465-6744, at 7th Avenue and 31st Street, which is served by 6th or 8th Avenue IND trains (A, D, E, and F).

Football. Guess what? The Giants and Jets play in New Jersey. Home games are at Giants Stadium in East Rutherford, (201) 935-8222, at the Meadowlands Sports Complex. To get there, take special buses from the Port Authority Bus Station.

Soccer. The NY/NJ MetroStars play at Giants Stadium, (888) 463-8767. *U.S. Open Tennis Championships.* The USTA National Tennis Center, (718) 760-6200, in Flushing Meadow is the site of the country's premier tennis tournament each September. Go to the early rounds, and you can stand courtside to see some superb players up close.

Long Island

Long Island stretches 125 miles east from New York City, paralleling the southern Connecticut coast and revealing a surprisingly rich and varied environment. The inner/western reaches of the island, where potato and other farms once flourished, have now been developed into dense suburbs (this is, after all, the site of Levittown, birthplace of the modern suburb). But all along the shoreline, you'll find beaches to play on and a surprising amount of preserved open space in state and county parks. Think of the island in five zones: on the western end, the North and South Shore; in the middle, central Suffolk County; and to the east, the North and South Fork.

On the **North Shore,** in **Cold Spring Harbor** (near the fish hatchery and aquarium) the **Cold Spring Harbor Whaling Museum** (call (516) 367-3418) covers the history of whaling. **Kings Point** is home to the Merchant Marine Academy, where the **American Merchant Marine Museum,** (call (516) 773-5515) holds model ships and World War II artifacts. **Sagamore Hill National Historic Site** (call (516) 922-4788), Teddy Roosevelt's home, and the **Theodore Roosevelt Sanctuary** (call (516) 922-3200), a nature center and history museum, make an interesting day in **Oyster Bay.** In **Southold,** regional history is the subject of the **Southold Historical Museums** (call (516) 765-5500), while the **Horton Point Lighthouse/Nautical Museum** (call (516) 765-5500) focuses on things maritime.

Along the **South Shore,** in addition to holding **Hecksher State Park** (see The Best Beaches and Parks, page 310), **East Islip** is home to the antique, hand-carved **Empire State Carousel** (call (516) 277-6168).

In the mid-island, **Central Suffolk,** everyone should stop by the **Big Duck** (call (516) 852-8292) in **Flanders,** a duck-shaped building with gift shop specializing in "duck-a-bilia." Flanders is also the place for waterplay at **Splish Splash Water Park** (call (515) 727-3600). The **Hallockville Museum Farm** (call (516) 298-5292) in **Riverhead** offers living history circa 1765, while **Atlantis Marine World** (call (516) 208-9200), opened in June 2000, is the state's newest aquarium. The **Animal Farm Petting Zoo** (call (516) 878-1785) and the **Island Game Farm** (call (516) 878-6670) in **Manorville** are popular with small children.

At the island's east end, the **North Fork** is home to sea and railroad museums, the **East End Seaport Museum** (call (516) 477-2100, and the **Railroad Museum of Long Island** (call (516) 447-0439) in **Greenport**. The **South Fork** offers the **Sag Harbor Whaling & Historical Museum** (call (516) 725-0770) in **Sag Harbor,** the **Montauk Point Lighthouse** (call (516) 668-2544) in **Montauk,** and living history at **Bridgehampton Historical Society Museum** (call (516) 537-1088) in **Bridgehampton.** Indeed, the **Hamptons** (East, South, and West) have long been a favorite upscale vacation destination.

To get on the water, **South Bay Paddlewheel Cruises** offers lunch and dinner cruises on an old-time paddlewheeler in Great South Bay for $40–55 per person; Brightwater (call (631) 321-9005 or visit www.lauren-kristy.com). **Okeanos Ocean Research Foundation** sets sail daily for whale-watching from Montauk (call (516) 728-4522). From May-October, **Discovery Wetland Cruises** utilizes a 35-passenger pontoon boat to sail from Stony Brook Harbor into the surrounding wetlands with a naturalist aboard to explain ecology, geology, and history (call (631) 751-2244 or visit www.wardmelvilleheritage.org).

Several ferries operate between southern Connecticut and Long Island. Docks are found in Port Jefferson, Orient Point, and Montauk, with service to New London and Bridgeport. Cars cost approximately $30–35 each way, plus a per-passenger fee. Call (516) 473-0286, (516) 323-2525, or for foot passenger-only service, (800) 666-8285.

Family Lodging

Best Western Bar Harbour

Best Western Bar Harbour is a 51-room, comfortable motel that's on a main thoroughfare in the south shore section. It offers good access to Jones Beach, Fire Island, Bethpage State Park, and the Sunrise Mall. Kids will like the pool, and restaurants are nearby. Rates: $78–110; kids stay free. 5080 Sunrise Highway, Massapequa Park; (516) 541-2000.

Ocean Beach Resort

A full resort property in the South Fork, Ocean Beach Resort has 80 rooms. It's open mid-March through November. The resort has the whole, high-end beach experience, with private beach frontage, an indoor/outdoor pool, and efficiency apartments. It's within walking distance of

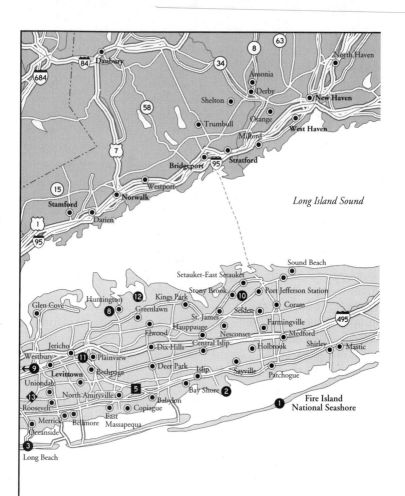

Setauket-East Setauket
Sound Beach
Stony Brook
Port Jefferson Station
Kings Park
Coram
Glen Cove
Huntington
Greenlawn
Selden
St. James
Farmingville
Hauppauge
Nesconset
Medford
Elwood
Central Islip
Holbrook
Shirley
Jericho
Dix-Hills
Mastic
Westbury
Plainview
Deer Park
Levittown
Bethpage
Islip
Sayville
Patchogue
Uniondale
North-Amityville
Bay Shore
Roosevelt
Babylon
Copiague
Merrick
Bellmore
East
Massapequa
Oceanside

Long Island Sound

Fire Island
National Seashore

Long Beach

Danbury
North Haven
Ansonia
Derby
New Haven
Shelton
Orange
West Haven
Trumbull
Milford
Stratford
Bridgeport
Westport
Norwalk
Stamford
Darien

BEACHES AND PARKS

1 Fire Island National Seashore

2 Hecksher State Park

3 Long Beach Island Resort

4 Westhampton Beach

LODGING

5 Best Western Bar Harbour

6 Ocean Beach Resort

7 Townsend Manor Inn

Long Island

0   N   1.5

MILES

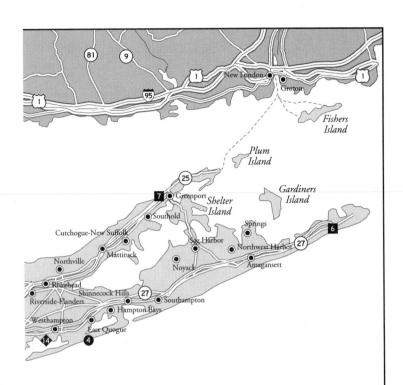

ATTRACTIONS

- **8** Cold Spring Harbor Aquarium
- **9** Long Island Children's Museum
- **10** Museums at Stony Brook
- **11** Old Bethpage Village Restoration
- **12** Vanderbilt Museum/Planetarium

RESTAURANTS

- **13** B.K. Sweeney's American Grill
- **14** Dora's

Montauk village. Rates: $80–255. South Emerson Avenue, Montauk; (631) 668-4000.

Townsend Manor Inn

This small, year-round hotel in the North Fork section has a restaurant, a pool, some efficiencies among its 23 units, and a waterfront setting. Rates: $60–185. 714 Main Street, Greenport; (631) 477-2000.

Attractions

Cold Spring Harbor Fish Hatchery & Aquarium

Route 25 A, Cold Spring Harbor; (516) 692-6768; www.cshfha.org

Hours: Daily 10 a.m.–5 p.m.; closed Easter, Thanksgiving, and Christmas days

Admission: $3.50 adults, $1.75 children ages 5–17, free for seniors age 65 and older and children under age 5

Appeal by Age Groups:

Pre-school	Grade School	Teens	Young Adults	Over 30	Seniors
★★★★	★★★★★	★★★★	★★★★★	★★★★★	★★★★★

Touring Time: Average 2 hours; minimum 1 hour

Rainy-Day Touring: Yes

Services and Facilities:

Restaurants No	Lockers No
Alcoholic beverages No	Pet kennels No
Disabled access Yes	Rain check No
Wheelchair rental No	Private tours No
Baby stroller rental No	

Description and Comments   "Daddy, where do fish come from?" Well, some come from the hatchery, and this is one of the finer facilities for demonstrating how they're raised. You'll find brook, brown, and rainbow trout. The in-house aquarium displays species of freshwater fish, aquatic reptiles, and amphibians native to New York. Facilities include outdoor ponds, habitat exhibits, a hatch house, an aquarium, and a main exhibit building.

Long Island Children's Museum

550 Stewart Avenue, Garden City; (516) 222-0218; www.licm.org

Hours: Tuesday–Friday 10 a.m.–4 p.m., Saturday 10 a.m.–5 p.m.; Sunday hours: May–October noon–5 p.m. November–April 10 a.m.–5 p.m.; closed Monday

Admission: $5 per person

Appeal by Age Groups:

Pre-school	Grade School	Teens	Young Adults	Over 30	Seniors
★★★★★	★★★★★	★	★	★★★★	★★★★

Touring Time: Average 2 hours; minimum 1 hour

Rainy-Day Touring: Yes

Services and Facilities:

Restaurants No	Lockers No
Alcoholic beverages No	Pet kennels No
Disabled access Yes	Rain check No
Wheelchair rental No	Private tours No
Baby stroller rental No	

Description and Comments This is a small but nicely executed museum aimed at 2–12-year-olds. In 2001, the museum will expand when it moves into an airplane hangar at the former Mitchell Field in Garden City.

Museums at Stony Brook

1208 Route 25A, Stony Brook; (631) 751-0066; www.museumsatstony brook.org

Hours: September–November and January–June, Wednesday–Saturday and Monday holidays 10 a.m.–5 p.m., Sunday noon–5 p.m.; July, August, and December, Monday–Saturday 10 a.m.–5 p.m., Sundays noon–5 p.m. Closed Thanksgiving, Christmas Eve, Christmas, and New Year's days.

Admission: $4 adults, $3 seniors 60 and older, $2 children ages 6–17 and college students, free for children under age 6; $1 on certain holidays

Appeal by Age Groups:

Pre-school	Grade School	Teens	Young Adults	Over 30	Seniors
★★★	★★★★	★★★★	★★★★	★★★★★	★★★★★

Touring Time: Average 2 hours; minimum 1 hour

Rainy-Day Touring: Yes

Services and Facilities:

Restaurants No	Lockers No
Alcoholic beverages No	Pet kennels No
Disabled access Yes	Rain check No
Wheelchair rental No	Private tours No
Baby stroller rental No	

Description and Comments Three main museums make up this multi-building property. Kids like the Carriage House, home to one of the best horseless carriage collections in the United States, with more than 100 on display at any given time, plus other artifacts from the carriage era. Also of interest to children is the History Museum, where one gallery holds miniature rooms and a collection of hand-carved, antique duck decoys.

Old Bethpage Village Restoration

Round Swamp Road, Old Bethpage; (516) 572-8400;
  www.liglobal.com/c_g/towns/oldbethpage

Hours: March–October, Wednesday–Sunday 10 a.m.–5 p.m.;
  November–December, Wednesday–Sunday 10 a.m.–4 p.m.;
  closed January and February

Admission: $6 adults, $4 seniors and children ages 6–12, free for children
  under age 5

Appeal by Age Groups:

Pre-school	Grade School	Teens	Young Adults	Over 30	Seniors
★★	★★★★	★★★	★★★★	★★★★★	★★★★★

Touring Time: Average 2 hours; minimum 1 hour
Rainy-Day Touring: Yes

Services and Facilities:

Restaurants	Yes	Lockers	No
Alcoholic beverages	No	Pet kennels	No
Disabled access	Partial	Rain check	No
Wheelchair rental	Yes; free	Private tours	No
Baby stroller rental	Yes; free		

Description and Comments   The Old Bethpage Restoration is a 200-acre living history museum focused on nineteenth-century life on Long Island. Exhibits manned by costumed interpreters and farm animals.

Vanderbilt Museum-Historic Mansion and Planetarium

180 Little Neck Road, Centerport; (631) 854-5579; www.vanderbiltmuseum.org

Hours: Tuesday–Saturday 10 a.m.–4 p.m., Sunday and holidays noon–5 p.m.; closed Monday; Planetarium open Labor Day–June, Friday–Sunday; call for expanded summer schedule

Admission: General: $5 adults, $1 children. For either mansion tour or planetarium show: $8 adults, $6 seniors and students, $4 children ages 12 and under. Both mansion tour and planetarium: $11 for adults, $9 for seniors and students, $7 children ages 12 and under

Appeal by Age Groups:

Pre-school	Grade School	Teens	Young Adults	Over 30	Seniors
★★★	★★★★	★★★	★★★★	★★★★★	★★★★★

Touring Time: Average 1½ hour; minimum 1 hour
Rainy-Day Touring: Yes
Services and Facilities:

Restaurants No	Baby stroller rental No
Alcoholic beverages No	Lockers No
Disabled access Yes, planetarium;	Pet kennels No
No, mansion	Rain check No
Wheelchair rental No	Private tours No

Description and Comments This Spanish-Moroccan mansion overlooks Northport Harbor. Of most interest to kids is the vast collection of marine and wildlife species, including some outlandishly beautiful and rare shells. Kids also love the planetarium, where the feature sky show is augmented by a Saturday morning show designed for children under age seven and a family show at 1 p.m.

Family-Friendly Restaurants

B.K. SWEENEY'S AMERICAN GRILL

479 Sunrise Highway, Lynbrook; (516) 887-8384

Meals served: Lunch and dinner
Cuisine: American
Entree range: $7.95–22.95
Children's menu: Yes
Reservations: No
Payment: Major credit cards

They call themselves a pub, but they'll gladly feed your child a PB&J. Porterhouse steak is the specialty, but there are plenty of other standard American choices. This is a warm and friendly place.

DORA'S

105 Montauk Highway (Oak Street), Westhampton Beach; (516) 288-9723

Meals served: Lunch and dinner
Cuisine: American
Entree range: $9.95–21.95
Children's menu: Yes
Reservations: No
Payment: Major credit cards

A locals' favorite with down-home cooking and a very casual atmosphere.

Index

434 Index